The Letters of Gertrude Bell

By

Gertrude Bell

(Volume I)
1927

The Echo Library 2006

Published by

The Echo Library

Echo Library
131 High St.
Teddington
Middlesex TW11 8HH

www.echo-library.com

Please report serious faults in the text to complaints@echo-library.com

ISBN 1-40680-052-X

PREFATORY NOTE

IN the letters contained in this book there will be found many Eastern names, both of people and places, difficult to handle for those, like myself, not conversant with Arabic. The Arabic alphabet has characters for which we have no satisfactory equivalents and the Arab language has sounds which we find it difficult to reproduce. We have therefore in dealing with them to content ourselves with transliterations, some of which in words more or less frequently used in English have become translations, such as 'Koran,' 'kavass,' etc. But even these words (there are many others, but I take these two as an example) which have almost become a part of the English language are now spelt differently by experts, and at first sight it is difficult to recognise them in 'Quran' and 'qawas'—which latter form is I believe in accordance with the standardised spelling now being officially introduced in Bagdad. Gertrude herself in her letters used often to spell the same word in different ways, sometimes because she was trying experiments in transliteration, sometimes deliberately adopting a new way, sometimes because the same word is differently pronounced in Arabic or in Turkish. These variations in spelling have added a good deal to the difficulty of editing her letters especially as reference to expert opinion has occasionally shown that experts themselves do not always agree as to which form of transliteration is the best.

I have therefore adopted the plan of spelling the names as they are found when they occur in the letters for the first time, and keeping to it. Thus Gertrude used to write at first 'Kaimmakam,' in her later letters 'Qaimmaqam.' I have spelt it uniformly with a K for the convenience of the reader; and so with other words in which the Q has now supplemented the K.

The word 'Bagdad' which used to be regarded as the English name of the town, a translation and not a transliteration, was spelt as I have given it in Gertrude's first letters long ago. It is now everywhere, even when regarded as a translation, spelt 'Baghdad' and it ought to have been so spelt in this book. The same applies to the name 'Teheran' which is now always spelt 'Tehran' but of which I have preserved the former spelling.

Dr. D. G. Hogatth has been good enough to read the preceding pages of this Prefatory Note, and to give them his sanction. He adds the following paragraph:

"A more difficult question still in reproducing proper names has been raised by the vowel signs in Arabic, including that for the ain and by the diacritical points and marks which convey either nothing or a false meaning to uninstructed Western eyes."

I have therefore omitted the vowel signs altogether.

My own interpolations, inserted where required as links or elucidations, are indicated by being enclosed in square brackets and by being "indented," i.e., printed in a shorter line than the text of the letters.

The formulae beginning and ending the letters have been mostly omitted, to save space and to avoid repetition. The heading H. B. at the top of a letter means that it is addressed to Gertrude's father, and the heading F. B. means that it is addressed to me.

I am most grateful to the people who have given me counsel and help in compiling this book: Sir Valentine Chirol, Mrs. W. L. Courtney, H. E. Sir Henry Dobbs, Dr. D. G. Hogarth, Elizabeth Robins, and Major General Sir Percy Cox, who has had the kindness to read and correct many of the Proofs.

I am also much indebted to the following for placing at my disposal maps or photographs, letters or portions of letters from Gertrude in their possession, or accounts of her written by themselves: Captain J. P. Farrar, Vice-Admiral Sir Reginald Hall, Mrs. Marguerite Harrison, Hon. Mrs. Anthony Henley, The Dowager Countess of Jersey, Mary Countess of Lovelace, Hon. Mildred Lowther, Mr. Horace Marshall, Hon. Mrs. Harold Nicolson, Sir William Ramsay, Mr. E. A. Reeves, Miss Flora Russell, Lady Sheffield, Mr. Lionel Smith, Mr. Sydney Spencer, Lady Spring Rice, Colonel E. L. Strutt. Also for clerical help given me by Mrs. D. M. Chapman and my secretary Miss Phyllis S. Owen.
FLORENCE BELL
Mount Grace Priory,
August 1927.

CONTENTS

I	1874-1892 Childhood, Oxford, London	01
II	1892-1896 Persia, Italy, London	13
III	1897 Berlin	23
IV	1897-1899 Round The World, Dauphina, Etc.	27
V1	1899-1900 Jerusalem And The First Desert Journeys	33
VI1	1900 Desert Excursions From Jerusalem	51
VII	1901-1902 Switzerland, Syria, England	76
VIII	1902-1903 Round The World For The Second Time	96
IX	1903-1909 England, Switzerland, Paris	107
X	1905 Syria, Asia Minor	112
XI	1905-1909 London, Asia Minor, London	145
XII	1910-1911 Italy, Across The Syrian Desert	168
XIII	1913-1914 The Journey To Hayil	198
XIV	1914-15-16 War Work At Boulogne, London And CAIRO	228
XV	1916-1917 Delhi And Basrah	236

INTRODUCTION

TO THE LETTERS OF GERTRUDE BELL

Gertrude Bell, happily for her family and friends, was one of the people whose lives can be reconstructed from correspondence.

Through all her wanderings, whether far or near, she kept in the closest touch with her home, always anxious to share her experiences and impressions with her family, to chronicle for their benefit all that happened to her, important or unimportant: whether a stirring tale of adventure or an account of a dinner party. Those letters, varied, witty, enthralling, were a constant joy through the years to all those who read them. It was fortunate for the recipients that the act of writing, the actual driving of the pen, seemed to be no more of an effort to Gertrude than to remember and record all that the pen set down. She was able at the close of a day of exciting travel to toss a complete account of it on to paper for her family, often covering several closely written quarto pages. And for many years she kept a diary as well. Then the time came when she ceased to write a diary. From 1919 onwards the confidential detailed letters of many pages, often written day by day, took its place. These were usually addressed to her father and dispatched to her family by every mail and by every extra opportunity. Besides these home letters, she found time for a large =and varied correspondence with friends outside her home circle both male and female, among the former being some of the most distinguished men of her time. But the letters to her family have provided such abundant material for the reconstruction of her story that it has not been found necessary to ask for any others. Short extracts from a few outside letters to some of her intimate friends, however, have been included. The earlier of these letters, written when she was at home and therefore sending no letters to her family, show what her home life and outlook were at the time of her girlhood, when she was living an ordinary life—in so far as her life could ever be called ordinary. They foreshadow the pictures given in her subsequent family letters of her gradual development on all sides through the years, garnering as she went the almost incredible variety of experiences which culminated and ended in Bagdad. Letters written when she was twenty show that after her triumphant return from Oxford with one of the most brilliant Firsts of her year she threw herself with the greatest zest into all the amusements of her age, sharing in everything, enjoying everything, dancing, skating, fencing, going to London parties; making ardent girl friendships, drawing in to her circle intimates of all kinds. She also loved her country life, in which her occupations included an absorbing amount of gardening, fox hunting—she was a bold rider to hounds—interesting herself in the people at her father's ironworks, and in her country village, making friends in every direction. And when she was wandering far afield (her wanderings began very early—she went to Roumania when she was twentytwo and to Persia when she was twentythree) she was always ready to take up her urban or country life at home on her return with the same zest as before, carrying with her, wherever she was, her ardent zest for knowledge, turning the flashlight of her eagerness on to one field of the mind after another and making it her own, reading, assimilating, discussing until the years found her ranged on equal terms beside some of the foremost scholars of her time.

To most people outside her own circle Gertrude was chiefly known by her achievements in the East, and it is probably the story of these that they will look for in this book. But the letters here published, from the time she was twenty until the end of her life, show such an amazing range of many sided ability that they may seem to those who read them to present a picture worth recording at every stage.

Scholar, poet, historian, archaeologist, art critic, mountaineer, explorer, gardener, naturalist, distinguished servant of the State, Gertrude was all of these, and was recognised by experts as an expert in them all.

On the other hand, in some of the letters addressed to her family are references to subjects or events that may seem trivial or unimportant. But Gertrude's keen interest in every detail concerning her home was so delightful, and present her in such a new light to many who knew her only in public that these passages have been included.

Her love for her family, for her parents, for her brothers and sisters, her joy in her home life, has always seemed to those who shared that life to be so beautiful that it is worth dwelling on by the side of more exceptional experiences, and by the side of the world-famous achievements of one whose later life especially might well have separated her in mind and sympathy as well as in person from her belongings. But her letters show how unbreakable to the last was the bond between her and her home, and above all between her and her father. The abiding influence in Gertrude's life from the time she was a little child was her relation to her father. Her devotion to him, her whole-hearted admiration, the close and satisfying companionship between them, their deep mutual affection—these were to both the very foundation of existence until the day she died.

CHAPTER I
1874-1892

CHILDHOOD-OXFORD-LONDON

[THIS is the earliest letter extant from Gertrude, dated when she was six years old. It is addressed to me, at a time when she was not yet my little daughter but my "affectionate little friend." Mopsa, about whom she writes, was a large grey Persian cat, who played a very prominent part in the household.]

REDBARNS, COATHAM, REDCAR, Sept., 25th, 1874.
MY DEAR FLORENCE,
Mopsa has been very naughty this morning. She has been scampering all over the diningroom Cilla says. I had a great Chase all over the hall and dining room to catch her and bring her to Papa. She bit and made one little red mark on my hand. During breakfast she hissed at Kitty Scott. Auntie Ada had her on her knee and Kitty was at one side. As Auntie Ada let Mopsa go down she hissed at Kitty and hunted her round to my side of the table. Please Papa says will you ask Auntie Florence if she will order us some honey like her own. I gave Mopsa your message and she sends her love. I forgot to say Kitty was very frightened. I send you my love and to Granmama and Auntie Florence. Your affectionate little friend
GERTRUDE BELL.

At the time that the above letter was written, the two children were living with their father at Redcar on the Yorkshire coast. His unmarried sister, Ada Bell, was then living with them.

Gertrude was eight when her father and I were married. She was a child of spirit and initiative, as may be imagined. Full of daring, she used to lead her little brother, whose tender years were ill equipped for so much enterprise, into the most perilous adventures, such as commanding him, to his terror, to follow her example in jumping from the top of a garden wall nine feet high to the ground. She used to alight on her feet, he very seldom did. Or she would lead a climbing expedition on to the top of the greenhouse, where Maurice was certain to go through the panes while Gertrude clambered down outside them in safety to the bottom.

They both of them rode from a very early age, and their ponies, of which they had a succession, were a constant joy.

From her early years Gertrude was devoted to flowers and to the garden. I have found a diary of hers when she was eleven. It was an imposing looking quarto volume bound in leather, apparently given her for a Christmas present in 1878 but only kept for a few pages, alas. I have left her own spelling.]

Jan. 11. 1879 Sunday—we played in liberry morning.
Feb. 11. Read Green till 9. Lessons went off rather lazily. We went into the

gardin. I looked at flowers. Stilted.

Feb. 14. 1879—St. Valentines Day. I got 12 valentines. The lessons went very badly. The lessons themselves were good. Each got twopence . . . we caught a pigion we put it into a basket.

15 Feb. The pigion was brought into our room it drank some milk Maurice spilt a lot on my bed. So we went into the cuboard. Breakfast. I read all the morning. Dinner. I read all the afternoon. Tea. I played with Hugo. Mother read to us. Taught Maurice geography and read. Went to bed tired, had a little talk not fun and went to sleep.

Feb, 16 . . . . We now have out some yellow crocus and primroses snodrops and primroses. Primroses and snodrops in my garden. Crocus in Papas.

[The only remaining entry in the diary is an account of her birthday, the day she was eleven, Monday, 14th of July. The record, the celebrations, and all the presents seem amusingly childish for a little girl who was reading Green's history before breakfast, and devouring every book she could find.]

When I woke up I went to see the time. It was a quarter to seven. I woke Maurice. Then I hid my face and he got out his presents. He gave me scales a fireplace with pans kitchen furniture. Then I found under my pillow a book from nurse then we got up. When we were ready we went into Mother's room and there I found a hopping toad from Auntie Bessie dinner set from Mother, watering can from Papa. Then we went downstairs to breakfast Mother and Maurice and I cooked a dinner because it was wet. We had soup fish mince crockets Puding, cheese and butter and desert.

[Gertrude never entirely mastered the art of spelling, and all her life long there were certain words in her letters that were always spelt wrong. She always wrote 'siezed,' 'ekcercise,' 'exhorbitant.' Sometimes she wrote 'priviledge.'

The cooking lessons referred to in the diary and sometimes in the early letters did not have much praftical result. She never excelled in this art.

The two or three Years following the time described in the diaries were spent happily at Redcar with Maurice—years of playing about, and studying under a German governess, and having pet animals, of which there were always one or two on hand. There were periodical onslaughts Of grief when one of these died, grief modified by the imposing funeral procession always organised for them and burial in a special cemetery in the garden.

Gertrude's and Maurice's earliest and favourite companion from babyhood onwards, was Horace Marshall their first cousin and son of their mother's sister Mrs Thomas Marshall. Then after their father's second marriage the two Lascelles boys came into the circle as intimates and cousins, the sons of my sister Mary spoken of in the letters as Auntie Mary, wife of Sir Frank Lascelles.

Florence Lascelles, my sister's only daughter, is constantly mentioned in the letters. She was a good deal younger than her two brothers and Gertrude, but as she grew up she was always one of Gertrude's chosen friends and companions. She married Cecil Spring Rice in 1904.

When Gertrude was fifteen and Maurice had gone to school, she went, first as a day scholar and afterwards as a boarder, to Queen's College in Harley Street, where a friend of her mother's, Camilla Croudace, had just been made Lady Resident. Gertrude lived at first at 95 Sloane Street with my mother Lady Olliffe, who took her and Maurice to her heart as if they had been grandchildren of her own.

The History Lecturer at Queens College at that time was Mr. Cramb, a distinguished and inspiring teacher. Gertrude's intelligence and aptitude for history impressed him keenly, and he strongly urged us to let her go to Oxford and go in for the History School. The time had not yet come when it was a usual part of a girl's education to go to a University, and it was with some qualms that we consented. But the result justified our decision. Gertrude went to Lady Margaret Hall, in 1886 just before she was eighteen, she left it in June 1888 just before she was twenty, and wound up, after those two years, by taking a brilliant First Class in Modern History.

One of her contemporaries at Lady Margaret was Janet Hogarth, now Mrs. W. L. Courtney, who, in a delightful article contributed to the North American Review, entitled "Gertrude Bell, a personal study" and also in her interesting book "Recollected in Tranquillity," has described Gertrude as she was when she first arrived at Lady Margaret Hall I quote both from the article and the book.

". . . . . Gertrude Lowthian Bell, the most brilliant student we ever had at Lady Margaret Hall, or indeed I think at any of the women's colleges. Her journeys in Arabia and her achievements in Iraq have passed into history. I need only recall the bright promise of her college days, when the vivid, rather untidy, auburnhaired girl of seventeen first came amongst us and took our hearts by storm with her brilliant talk and her youthful confidence in her self and her belongings. She had a most engaging way of saying 'Well you know, my father says so and so' as a final opinion on every question under discussion-[and indeed to the end of her life Gertrude, with the same absolute confidence would have been capable of still quoting the same authority as final].

"She threw herself with untiring energy into every phase of college life, she swam, she rowed, she played tennis, and hockey, she danced, she spoke in debates; she kept up with modern literature, and told us tales of modern authors, most of whom were her childhood's friends. Yet all the time she put in seven hours of work, and at the end of two years she won as brilliant a First Class in the School of Modern History as has ever been won at Oxford."

And Many years later Mrs. Courtney who had herself taken a first class (in Moral Philosophy) the same year as Gertrude, writes as follows in the 'Brown Book', which is the organ of Lady Margaret Hall:

"I never lost touch with her for well nigh forty years after we parted in the First Class, as she said the day I went round to Sloane Street to wish her joy when the History List appeared"

The untidiness in Gertrude's appearance referred to by Mrs. Courtney gradually gave place to an increasing taste for dress, and she is remembered by more than one person who saw her during the finals of the History School appearing in different clothes every day. The parents of the candidates were admitted to the 'viva voce' part of the examination, and I have a vivid picture in my memory of Gertrude, showing no trace of nervousness sitting very upright at a table, beneath which her slender feet in neat brown shoes were crossed. She was, I have since been told, one of the first young women at Oxford to wear brown shoes, of which she set the fashion among her contemporaries.

Mr. Arthur Hassall of Christchurch, Oxford, who knew her well, records the following incident of Gertrude's 'viva voce.' I quote from his letter: "S. R. Gardiner, the famous historian of the times of James I and Charles I, began to 'viva voce' Miss Bell. She replied to his first question 'I am afraid I must differ from your estimate of Charles I.' This so horrified Professor Gardiner that he at once asked the examiner who sat next to him (I think it was Mr. H. O. Wakeman) to continue the 'viva voce.'"

The result of the whole examination however did her so much credit that she may perhaps be forgiven this lapse into unparalleled audacity.

Mrs. Arthur Hassall also writes: "Gertrude went to the four balls given at Commemoration that week, of which the last was the night before her 'viva voce,' and danced all the evening looking brilliantly happy." She also writes: "she was the only girl I have ever known who took her work for the schools and her examination in a gay way."

After the happy culmination of her two years at oxford she rejoined her family in London and then at Redcar. My sister-Sir Frank Lascelles being at that time Minister—at Bucharest—begged me to send Gertrude to stay with them for the winter, after the return from Oxford, opining that frequenting foreign diplomatic Society might be a help for Gertrude "to get rid of her Oxfordy manner." My sister was very fond of Gertrude, whom she called her niece and treated like a daughter: they were the greatest friends. The effect however on Gertrude's "Oxfordy manner" of the society of foreign diplomats was not all that Lady Lascelles had hoped, for it is recorded that on one occasion when a distinguished foreign Statesman was discussing some of the international problems of Central Europe, Gertrude said to him, to the stupefaction of her listeners and the dismay of her hostess: "Il me semble, Monsieur, que vous n'avez pas saisi l'esprit du peuple allemand."

There is no doubt that according to the ordinary canons of demeanour it was a mistake for Gertrude to proffer, as we have been shown on more occasions than one, her opinions, let alone her criticisms, to her superiors in age and experience.

But it was all part of her entire honesty and independence of judgment: and the time was to come when many a distinguished foreign statesman not only listened to the opinions she proffered but accepted them and acted on them.

Gertrude hardly ever dated her letters except by the day of the week, sometimes not even that, so that where the envelope has not been preserved I have had to guess the year by the context. By some mischance none of her letters from Bucharest seems to have been preserved, but we know that she was extremely happy there, and keenly interested in her new surroundings. From Bucharest she returned to London, from London she Went to Redcar, enjoying herself everywhere. At Redcar she shouldered the housekeeping and also various activities among the women at the ironworks, Clarence, Often mentioned, being Bell Bros. ironworks on the north bank of the Tees.

Her letters of this time give a picture of her relation to the Younger children her step-brother and her two Step-sisters, Hugo, Elsa and Molly. Hugo was ten years Younger than Gertrude, Elsa eleven years younger, Molly thirteen years. Her letters often recount what she was doing with her two little sisters who adored her. Hugo by this time had gone to school. Some letters are here given that she wrote between 1889 and 1892 during the time spent in England in one of our two homes either in London in the house shared with my mother or at Redcar, where we lived until 1904. These letters are mostly about every day happenings, always lifted into something new and exciting by Gertrude's youthful zest. Some of these early letters are to her parents, others of which fragmentary extracts are given, are to Flora Russell who remained her intimate friend all her life. Flora was the elder daughter of Lord and Lady Arthur Russell, who lived in Audley Square. The Audley Square circle, the house, the hosts, the people who used to assemble there, formed for Gertrude, as for many others, a cherished and congenial surrounding.]

To H.B.
LONDON, 1889.
. . . . The little girls spent all day with Hunt [their nurse] at her brother-in-laws. They came home at eight, radiant. Molly says he was a very kind man, he gave them strawberries and cream and lots of flowers but to their surprise he had no servants though he has a conservatory! We suppose he must be a market gardener. . . .

To F.B.
RED BARNS, 1889.
I think the reason the books were so high was because of the dinner party it was before I began to keep house wasn't it, so I am not responsible, though I feel as if I were.

I paid everything but the butcher with what you sent, and had over 1 pound balance which I have kept for next time.

I went to Clarence today and arranged about the nursing lecture tomorrow, there were a lot of things to prepare for it. Then I paid some visits and came home with Papa at 4:35. Molly and I have since been picking cowslips in the fields. It is so heavenly here with all the things coming out and the grass growing long. I am glad I'm here.

To F.B.
LONDON 1889.
I must tell you an absurd story. Minnie Hope was sitting with an Oxford man. Presently he grabbed her hand and said "do you see that young lady in a blue jacket?" "yes" said Minnie lying low. "Well," said he in an awestruck voice, "she took a first in history!!"

TO F-B.
LONDON, Friday, 14th February, 1889.
.... In the afternoon Sophie [my younger sister, now Mrs. H. J. Kitcat] and I walked across the Green Park to the London Library where I had a delicious rummage with a very amiable sub-librarian who routed out all the editions of Sir Th. Browne and Ph. Sidney for me to see I took down the names and dates and armed with these I felt prepared to face Bain himself.

To F.B.
LONDON, July 5th, 1889.
Billy [Lascelles] and I sat in the garden and had a long talk so long that he only left himself a quarter of an hour to catch his train. I expect he missed it. He wanted to take me with him to Paddington and send me back in a hansom, don't be afraid, I didn't go What would have happened if I had, it was ten o'clock!

Yesterday morning I went to the French Literature class at Caroline's [Hon. Mrs Norman Grosvenor] house, I came back here, dressed, and went to Queen Street for a seven o'clock dinner we were going to the Spanish exhibition after it.

We drove in hansoms to the exhibition and Captain —— brought me home, I hope that doesn't shock you; I discussed religious beliefs all the way there and very metaphysical conceptions of truth all the way back that sounds rather steep doesn't it—I love talking to people when they really will talk sensibly and about things which one wants to discuss. I am rather inclined to think however that it is a dangerous Amusement, for one is so ready to make oneself believe that the things one says and the theories one makes are really guiding principles of one's life whereas a matter of fact they are not at all. One suddenly finds that one had formulated some view from which it is very difficult to back out not because of one's interlocutor but because the mere fact of fitting it with words engraves it upon one's mind. Then one is reduced to the disagreeable necessity of trying even involuntarily to make the facts of one's real life fit into it thereby involving oneself in a mist of half-truths and half-falsehoods which cling about one's mind do what one will to shake them off.

It's so hot this morning, I went into the gardens to be cool, but presently came the babies who announced that they were barons and that they intended to rob me. I was rather surprised at their taking this view of the functions of the aristocracy, till I found that they had just been learning the reign of Stephen. Molly informed me in the pride of newly acquired knowledge that there were at least 11,000 castles in his time! So we all played at jumping over a string, not a very cooling occupation, till fortunately Miss Thomson came and called them in. Did we tell you how Molly puzzled and shocked her dreadfully the other day by asking her suddenly what was the French for "this horse has the staggers"! ....

To F.B.
RED BARNS, October 30, 1889.
The ladies of Clarence were friendly, and oh, unexpected joy!—their

accounts came right. . . .

The children and I played the race game in the nursery. They have a great plan but unfortunately they have not hit upon any way of carrying it out, of all catching the measles and being laid up together indefinitely. It seemed to me a gruesome form of conversation and I left them discussing it and their supper very happily. They have expressed no regrets as to your absence. . . .

To F.B.
RED BARNS, November 25th, 1889

My gown came from Kerswell this morning-charming I am so glad I did not have a black one. I had a delightful dancing lesson, learnt two more parts of the sword dance, began the minuet. It is lovely, you must learn it the first dancing lesson you are here. It was so fine this afternoon, a rough sea almost up to the esplanade. I walked a long time and then came in and did history for tomorrow.

[i.e. to prepare the children's lesson for the next day. She was then teaching them history.]

To F.B.
RED BARNS, December 1, 1889

. . . . The little girls and I went out before lunch. They came up into my room and I made them some Turkish coffee After lunch, they then disappeared. I expect to see them again shortly. They had supper with me last night by which they were much amused. . . .

I have read Swinburne's Jonson which I will keep for you, it is quite excellent. I should very much like for a Christmas present Jonson's works edited by Gifford in 3 vols. not big ones I think. There are some of his masques I want to read. I don't think they are to be found anywhere else. . . .

The little girls think it is a great pity you are coming back so soon, because we are so comfortable. We shall be delighted to have you though, one's own society palls after a time.

We had a capital cooking lesson yesterday, made scones and gingerbread and boiled potatoes . . . ..

To F.B.
LONDON, 1889.

About the little girls frocks Hunt would like to have one for Molly made of cambric matching the pattern of Elsa, 16d a yard 40 in. wide: the other two one for each little girl of nainsook which is a shade finer and will she says wash better, 13d. and 38 in. wide. There are two insertions, one at 6d. not very pretty, one at 10d. very pretty indeed.

Would you like to have Molly's cambric frock trimmed with the 6d. insertion and the two nainsook frocks with the 10d or would you prefer them to be all trimmed with the cheaper insertion? The cheap insertion is not at all bad and I think it would not look otherwise than well but there is no doubt that the other is nicer. However it is also 4d a yd. dearer. . . .

Mr. Grimston says that he cannot supply us with mutton for 9d a pound, it is so dear now. I have asked the other butchers and find they are all selling it at 10d or 10+ a pound so I think it would be best to pay him 10d for legs and loins what say you? . . . .

To F.B.
LONDON, February 12, 1890.
. . . .Met Lord —— in Piccadilly who stopped and said Oh, how do you do? and then of course had nothing more to say. So I told him I was going to the Russells' where he said we should probably meet and then we went our ways, It is so foolish to stop and talk in the street one only does it out of surprise.

. . . . Miss Croudace gave me tickets for a soirée at the Old Water Colours this evening, but I have no one to take me so I can't go. . . .

To F.B.
RED BARNS, April 2nd, 1890.
I have just returned from Clarence where I found only a few mothers but some very agreeable ladies amongst them. I walked back with a very friendly lady I wonder who she was. She lives in the New Cottages and only comes up to the other end of Clarence for the Mothers' Meeting and for confinements!

. . . . Elsa's cambric frock is quite charming. It fits her perfectly and is most becoming. I never saw her look so bewitching and so grown up too.

To F.B.
RED BARNS, April 17th, 1890.
. . . . I should like to go to the first drawing room if You could because I shall want some evening gowns and shall have none till I can use my court gown.

To F.B.
RED BARNS, April 18th, 1890.
I like the pattern you sent us very much, it is charming. I certainly think a green velvet train would be nicer than a black don't you? I am just going to Clarence so goodbye.

To F.B.
RED BARNS, Nov. 26, 1890.
. . . . The little girls and I had a peaceful evening together. They appeared about half past six and I read them selections from Stanley's letters by which they were much interested.

We looked out his route in the map. Molly was so enthusiastic that she carried the atlas and the Times up to the nurses and expounded it all to Lizzie. Elsa had great difficulty with her knitting. The stitches kept dropping in the most unaccountable way and had to be picked up from the very bottom of the cuff. 3 guinea pigs have been sold! the little girls have realised 2/6 by the transaction.

[Lizzie, first our nursery maid, then lady's maid, was Hunt's daughter. She was with us 38 years and is still in touch with us all.]

To F.B.
RED BARNS, 1890.

The children rode on donkeys this afternoon but it was not very successful for we refused the assistance of the donkey boy and consequently could not get the donkeys to move! We passed a ridiculous hour and finally left our beasts standing peacefully on the esplanade and came home. I don't think judging by their former activity that there was any fear of their escaping.

To F.B.
London, 1890.

This is just a little line to tell you how I am getting on. I had a very nice morning. Lizzie and I went out together and did some delightful shopping in Sloane Street and then walked up Piccadilly and up Bond Street and went on myself in a hansom to the National Gallery where I spent a peaceful hour.

To F.B.
LONDON, Feb. 8th, 1892.

All the sales are over I'm afraid. I went to Woollands this afternoon for the sashes, they had nothing approaching the colour, but I will find it somewhere. I am much interested about your gown, though as you rightly supposed a little sorry its black!. . . .

Today Flora and I called on Sarah Lyttelton [now Hon. Mrs. John Bailey] and had a delightful long talk with her. I like her so much. . . I want some sashes which are either in a cardboard box or on the high shelf outside my bedroom door. If there are any ribbons I should like them too. . . .

I went to Audley Square where Henry James appeared.

To F.B.
LONDON, Feb. 14, 1892.

Horace came here about three on Saturday and we walked to Kensington Square, where I took him to call on Mrs. [J. R.] Green. It was pleasant and amusing. . . . Mrs. Green told me that Mr. York Powell had said to her this is not a becoming story, and suited for the ears of one's immediate family only that I was the only girl he had ever examined who knew how to use books or had read things outside the prescribed course and that he thought I had got into the heart of my subject. What a little daring it takes to deceive his misguided sex!

To F.B.
LONDON, Feb. 16th, 1892.

. . . . I ordered the buttons today at Woollands. I hope they will prove satisfactory.

I regret to announce to you the death of my trumpeter, under which painful circumstances I'm bound to tell you that Lady Edward [Cavendish] has been very complimentary about me to Auntie Mary. She is pleased to approve of me. We all dined at Devonshire House on Thursday.

The Lyttelton have invited me to a dance of theirs on the 25 th. I shall go if Lady Arthur will take me. I suppose I can ask her.

Feb. 18th.
This afternoon I called on the Lushingtons.
[She was at this time staying in London with Lady Lascelles.]

To F.B.
LONDON, Feb. 20, 1892.
We dined at Devonshire House. There were there Lady Edward, William Egerton, Alfred Lyttelton and Victor Cavendish [now Duke of Devonshire] who came in from the House announcing that he must be back in 30 minutes but finally stayed till ten. Victor C. is tremendously interested in his politics, talks of nothing else; it is very nice to see, as genuine enthusiasm always is.

To F.B.
LONDON, Feb. 22nd, 1892.
. . . . Yesterday such an absurd thing happened. Auntie Mary had gone out; Florence and I were walking together; the boys alone here, hear a ring and a voice asking for Lady Lascelles, then for me, then angrily, "Well, it's a very odd thing for I was told particularly to come here this afternoon." Presently we came in and found Lord Stanley's card-now this was very odd for Lord Stanley does not know Aunt Mary—We wondered what could be the explanation until tea time when Auntie Maisie came she said "I hear Henry is giving you Persian lessons!" Then it appeared that Grisel Ogilvie to whom I had related my attempts to find a teacher of Persian had sent him—he is a good Persian scholar. Auntie Maisie had met him at Dover Street at lunch and he had told her he was coming here to teach me—and had asked if he Would be likely to find us in. She had said "no" but he had come all the same. . . .

I had another offer of lessons on Saturday afternoon at Miss Green's from Mr. Strong. I feel I shall end by receiving special instruction from the Shah in person. . .

To F.B.
London, Feb. 26th, 1892.
I have been paying a visit to Maclagan this morning. Which I think was wise as I have been feeling tired and unenergetic lately. He gave me a tonic and told me to take care of myself and not do too much. . . .

It was pleasant at Mansfield Street. Mr. William Peel, Horace, Diana, Harold, Grisel, Mildred Hugh Smith. [Horace Marshall, Diana Russell, Harold Russell, Lady Grisel Ogilvie and Mildred Hugh Smith, now Countess Buxton, G.B.E.]

Uncle Lyulph presently went to sleep; Harold, Mildred and I had a long and amusing talk together which lasted all the evening. She is such a nice girl.

On Thursday I walked in the afternoon with Flora and went back with her to tea. . . .

The Stanley dance was extraordinarily successful. There were about 20 little girls and ten big ones and a few young men. We danced wildly with the children and the young men. At eight a kind of elaborate tea was provided for the children and for us a small dinner of soup and cutlets and so on. Uncle Lyulph was quite taken aback by the splendor of his party, "I knew we should have something to eat," he said, "but this gloat I certainly did not expect." He was so much pleased by the success of the evening that Auntie Maisie thinks he will let her give a real grown up ball. . . .

["Uncle Lyulph," then Lord Stanley of Alderley, afterwards Lord Sheffield. "Auntie Maisie," now Lady Sheffield.]

[During this year, there are very few letters to her family. I have inserted a few extracts from her letters to Flora Russell, recording some of her doings.]

To Flora Russell
REDCAR, Jan. 4, 1892

My DEAREST FLORA, * * * *I had a long and delightful letter from Clara the other night, she is a person who charms and interests me immensely [Clara Grant Duff, now Mrs. Huth Jackson].

To the same.
RED BARNS, Jan. 10, 1892.

Lady Arthur's approval is very well worth having, and I am grateful to you for telling me of it. . . .

To the same.
RED BARNS, Jan. 23, 1892.

We have spent a racketing fortnight dancing and acting; I am just beginning to fall back into my usual peaceful frame of mind which is rather difficult to regain. I feel to have got rather behindhand with the whole world during the course of it and that I must hurry along very fast to catch it up again. But it's the old world I really want to catch up. I have just got to an inviting stage in my Latin when I feel there is really no reason I shouldn't read anything-and as a matter of fact I can read nothing without dictionaries and great labour. The slough of despond is nothing to it. But I mean to wade on diligently for the next fortnight and stumble as best I may over the horrid catching briars of prepositions and conjunctive moods. . . .

To the same.
RED BARNS, August 13, 1892.

We spent a madly amusing five days at Canterbury, of which nothing remains to tell except that we danced every night, saw a good deal of cricket and talked a little. . . .

Do you remember discussing what other girls do with their days? Well! I have found out what one particular class does they spend the entire time in rushing from house to house for cricket weeks, which means cricket all day and dancing all night; your party consists of an eleven and enough girls to pair off with you discuss byes and wides and Kemp at the wicket and Hearne's batting and any other topic Of a similar nature that may occur to you. It seems to me to be rather a restless sort of summer. . . .

To the same.
RED BARNS, July 22, 1892.

The Lascelles are moved to Teheran which is rather thrilling. They are coming back to England now and my uncle goes to Persia in October, my aunt later, I don't know when. I should like her to take me out with her, Persia is the place I have always longed to see, but I don't know if she will.

I expect my aunt will be rather annoyed for she will hate being so far away, but it is a great promotion. As for me if only I go there this winter everything will have turned out for the best.

I wear a blue green velvet in my hair which is becoming.

To the same.
RED BARNS, Dec. 23, 1892.

I have been reading Latin with great energy. It's a language of which I know very little but whose difficulties must be mastered somehow for I constantly find myself brought up against a blank wall by my ignorance of it. It is very interesting to learn but I could wish it were a little easier. . . .

To the same.
RED BARNS, 1892.

This is for the private eye: Bentley wishes to publish my Persian things, but wants more of them, so after much hesitation I have decided to let him and I am writing him another six chapters. It's rather a bore and what's more I would vastly prefer them to remain unpublished. I wrote them you see to amuse myself and I have got all the fun out of them I ever expect to have, for modesty apart they are extraordinarily feeble. Moreover I do so loathe people who rush into print and fill the world with their cheap and nasty work and now I am going to be one of them. At first I refused, then my mother thought me mistaken and my father was disappointed and as they are generally right I have given way. But in my heart I hold very firmly to my first opinion. Don't speak of this. I wish them not to be read.

To the same.
RED BARNS, Jan. 28, 1892.

I read a certain amount of history with the children's lessons, for exercise, and the works of Balzac for amusement. Dante for edification. It's an agreeable and a varied programme.

CHAPTER II
1892-1896

PERSIA, ITALY, LONDON

[GERTRUDE went to Teheran, to her great joy, in the spring of 1892. Her letters from Persia, of which there were a good many, are like those from Roumania unfortunately not to be found. The only one we have is addressed to her cousin Horace Marshall, written from Gula Hek, the exquisite summer resort of the British Legation.]

To Horace Marshall
GULAHEK, June 18, 1892.

DEAR COUSIN MINE, Are we the same people I wonder when all our surroundings, associations, and acquaintances are changed? Here that which is me, which womanlike is an empty jar that the passer by fills at pleasure, is filled with such wine as in England I had never heard of, now the wine is more important than the jar when one is thirsty, therefore I conclude, cousin mine, that it is not the person who danced with you at Mansfield St. that writes to you today from Persia-Yet there are dregs, English sediments at the bottom of my sherbet, and perhaps they flavour it more than I think. Anyhow I remember you as a dear person in a former existence, whom I should like to drag into this one and to guide whose spiritual coming I will draw paths in ink. And others there are whom I remember yet not with regret but as one might remember people one knew when one was an inhabitant of Mars 20 centuries ago. How big the world is, how big and how wonderful. It comes to me as ridiculously presumptuous that I should dare to carry my little personality half across it and boldly attempt to measure with it things for which it has no table of measurements that can possibly apply. So under protest I write to you of Persia: I am not me, that is my only excuse. I am merely pouring out for you some of what I have received during the last two months.

Well in this country the men wear flowing robes of green and white and brown, the women lift the veil of a Raphael Madonna to look at you as you pass; wherever there is water a luxuriant vegetation springs up and where there is not there is nothing but stone and desert. Oh the desert round Teheran! miles and miles of it with nothing, nothing; ringed in with bleak bare mountains snow crowned and furrowed with the deep courses of torrents. I never knew what desert was till I came here; it is a very wonderful thing to see; and suddenly in the middle of it all, out of nothing, out of a little cold water, springs up a garden. Such a garden! trees, fountains, tanks, roses and a house in it, the houses which we heard of in fairy tales when we were little: inlaid with tiny slabs of looking glass in lovely patterns, blue tiled, carpeted, echoing with the sound of running water and fountains. Here sits the enchanted prince, solemn, dignified, clothed in long robes. He comes down to meet you as you enter, his house is yours, his garden is yours, better still his tea and fruit are yours, so are his kalyans (but I think kalyans are a horrid form of smoke, they taste to me of charcoal and paint and nothing else.) By the grace of God your slave hopes that the health of your nobility is well? It is very well out of his great kindness. Will your magnificence carry itself on to this cushion? Your magnificence sits down and spends ten minutes in bandying florid compliments through an interpreter while ices are served and coffee, after which you ride home refreshed, charmed, and with many blessings on your fortunate head. And all the time your host was probably a perfect stranger into whose privacy you had forced yourself in this unblushing way. Ah, we have no hospitality in the west and no manners. I felt ashamed almost before the beggars in the street they wear their rags with a better grace than I my most becoming habit, and the veils of the commonest women (now the veil is the touchstone on which to try a woman's toilette) are far better put on than mine. A veil should fall from the top of your head to the soles of your feet, of that I feel convinced, and it should not be transparent.

Say, is it not rather refreshing to the spirit to lie in a hammock strung between the plane trees of a Persian garden and read the poems of Hafiz-in the original mark you! out of a book curiously bound in stamped leather which you have bought in the bazaars. That is how I spend my mornings here; a stream murmurs past me which Zoroastrian gardeners guide with long handled spades into tiny sluices leading into the flower beds all around. The dictionary which is also in my hammock is not perhaps so poetic as the other attributes let us hide it under our muslin petticoats.

This also is pleasant: to come in at 7 o'clock in the morning after a two hours' ride, hot and dusty, and find one's cold bath waiting for one scented with delicious rose water, and after it an excellent and longed for breakfast spread in a tent in the garden.

What else can I give you but fleeting impressions caught and hardened out of all knowing? I can tell you of a Persian merchant in whose garden, stretching all up the mountain side, we spent a long day, from dawn to sunset, breakfasting, lunching, teaing on nothing but Persian foods. He is noted for his hospitality every evening parties of friends arrive unexpectedly "he goes out, entertains them" said the Persian who told me about it, "spreads a banquet before them and relates to them stories half through the night. Then cushions are brought and carpeted mattresses and they lie down in one of the guest houses in the garden and sleep till dawn when they rise and repair to the bath in the village." Isn't it charmingly like the Arabian Nights! but that is the charm Of it all and it has none of it changed; every day I meet our aged kalendars and ladies who I am sure have suits of Swans feathers laid up in a chest at home., and some time when I open a new jar of rose water I know that instead of a sweet smell, the great smoke of one of Suleiman's afreets will come out of its neck.

In the garden there are big deep tanks where in the evenings between tennis and dinner I often swim in the coldest of cold water. Before we left Teheran when it was too hot to sleep, I used to go out at dawn and swim under the shadow of the willows. We were very glad to leave Teheran though we liked the house there. It began to be very stuffy and airless; here, though we are only 6 miles away, there is always air, except perhaps between two and four in the afternoon when one generally sleeps. We are much higher up and much nearer the hills and all round us are watered fields where the corn is almost ripe for cutting The joy of this climate! I do think an English summer will be very nice after it.

I learn Persian, not with great energy, one does nothing with energy here. My teacher is a delightful old person bright eyes and a white turban who knows so little French (French is our medium) that he can neither translate poets to me nor explain any grammatical difficulties. But we get on admirably nevertheless and spend much of our time in long philosophic discussions carried on by me in French an by him in Persian. His point of view is very much that of an oriental Gibbon, though with this truly oriental distinction, that he would never dream of acknowledging in words or acts his scepticism to one of his own countrymen. It would be tacitly understood between them and their intercourse would be continued on the basis of perfect agreement. Now this is a great simplification and promotes, I should imagine, the best of good manners. . . .

Goodbye, write to me and tell me how the world goes with you.

[This letter, bearing the impress of her youth, shows the first effect on Gertrude's mind of the impact of the East. It practically summarises her impressions. We have further records of them in a book she wrote the year after her return, published by Bentley in 1894, entitled "safar Nameh " i.e., "Persian Pictures," in which the life of the town and of the bazaars, the desolate places so strangely near them, the dwellers in the tents, the divine Persian gardens and many other aspects of her surroundings, are described with the glowing eagerness of a first experience. The little book attracted attention and was favourably reviewed.. I have dwelt on it here, for the interest of comparing it in one's mind with the books of Eastern travel Gertrude was to publish many years later, when she was no longer a spectator only, but a sharer to the full in the Eastern life that she described.

She had, as we have seen in many of the letters, a special and very valuable gift, that of forming extremely vivid impressions, whether of places or of human beings. She would dive beneath the surface, estimating, judging, characterising in a few words that were not often mistaken. She would ride through a countryside and report on its conditions, human, agricultural, economic, and her report would be adopted. When she came into contact with human beings, whether chiefs of the desert or men and women of her own Western world, she would label them, after her first meeting with them, in a sentence.

I am not pretending that her judgments were always infallible. But on the whole they were correct often enough to enable her to thread her way successfully through the labyrinth of her experiences.

It was characteristic of Gertrude, and it was an inestimable advantage to her, that she insisted on learning Persian before going to Teheran. She arrived there knowing as it is commonly called, the language, i.e., able to understand what she heard and what she read. But she had not yet reached the stage in which the learner of a language finds with rapture that a new knowledge has been acquired, the illuminating stage when not the literal meaning only of words is being understood, but their values and differences can be critically appreciated. It was not long before Gertrude was reading Persian Poetry by this light and with the added understanding brought to her by her knowledge of Western literature.

She was wont when she was at home and someone asked her a question about history to reply with a laugh " Oh! that is not my period," although it must be confessed that an answer to the question was generally forthcoming. But in literature it would be hard to say offhand what was her " period."

She published a translation of the Divan of Hafiz in 1897. The book includes a life of Hafiz, which is practically a history of his times as well as a critical study of his work. These, and the notes on his poems at the end of the book, show how wide was her field of comparison. She draws a parallel between Hafiz and his contemporary Dante: she notes the similarity of a passage with Goethe: she compares Hafiz with Villon, on every side gathering fructifying examples which link together the inspiration of the West and of the East.

The book on its publication was extremely well received.

I quote here from two of the translations.]

TO HAFIZ OF SHIRAZ

    (Two first stanzas)
    Thus said the Poet: " When Death comes to YOU,
    All ye whose life-sand through the hour-glass slips,
    He lays two fingers on your ears, and two
    Upon your eyes he lays, one on your lips,
    Whispering: Silence. "Although deaf thine ear,
    Thine eye, my Hafiz, suffer Time's eclipse,
    The songs thou sangest still all men may hear.
    Songs of dead laughter, songs of love once hot,
    Songs of a cup once flushed rose red with wine,
    Songs of a rose whose beauty is forgot,
    A nightingale that piped hushed lays divine:
    And still a graver music runs beneath
    The tender love notes of those songs of thine,
    Oh, Seeker of the keys of Life and Death!"

DIVAN OF HAFIZ xlv

    (From poem on the death of his son)
    The nightingale with drops of his heart's blood
    Had nourished the red rose, then came a wind,
    And catching at the boughs in envious mood,
    A hundred thorns about his heart entwined,
    Like to the parrot crunching sugar, good
    Seemed the world to me who could not stay
    The wind of Death that swept my hopes away.
    Light of mine eyes and harvest of my heart,

> And mine at least in changeless memory!
> Ah! when he found it easy to depart,
> He left the harder pilgrimage to me!
> Oh Camel driver, though the cordage start,
> For God's sake help me lift my fallen load,
> And Pity be my comrade of the road!
> He sought a lodging in the grave—too soon!
> I had not castled, and the time is gone.
> What shall I play? Upon the chequered floor
> Of Night and Day, Death won the game—forlorn
> And careless now, Hafiz can lose no more.

Gertrude, who was an ardent lover of poetry all her life long, and who kept abreast of the work of the moderns as well as of their predecessors, seemed, strangely enough, after the book of Hafiz had appeared, to consider her own gift of verse as a secondary pursuit, and to our surprise abandoned it altogether. But that gift has always seemed to me to underlie all she has written. The spirit of poetry coloured all her prose descriptions, all the pictures that she herself saw and succeeded in making others see.

It was a strangely interesting ingredient in a character capable on occasion of verydefinite hardness and of a deliberate disregard of sentiment: and also in a mental equipment which included great practical ability and statesmanlike grasp of public affairs.

But in truth the real basis of Gertrude's nature Was her capacity for deep emotion. Great joys came into her life, and also great sorrows. How could it be otherwise with a temperament so avid of experience? Her ardent and magnetic personality drew the lives of others into hers as she passed along.

She returned to England from Teheran in December of 1892. In January 1893 we find her starting for Switzerland and northern Italy with Mary Talbot, a beloved friend who had been with her at Lady Margaret Hall. Mary Talbot married the Rev. W. O. Burrows, now Bishop of Chichester, in 18 96. She died, to Gertrude's great sorrow, in 1897.

In April she went to Algiers with her father to stay with some of his relations, afterwards going back to Switzerland, and then joining Maurice, who was established in a German family at Weimar that he might learn the language. Needless to say that as soon as Gertrude arrived at Weimar she arranged to have German lessons, and went three times a week to talk with " a delightful old lady living in whose house do you think?—Frau von Stein's!" Her letters all through these travels from the beginning of the year are as usual amusing and full of observation, whether describing the flamboyant setting of the foreign residents at Algiers or the trim traditional life of the ladies of Weimar. But it is not worth while to take up space by accounts of routes already well- trodden, or places and social surroundings well known.

Gertrude came back to England from Germany in the early summer of 1893 and does not seem to have gone abroad again until the spring of 1896. There are no letters of the two intervening years. and unfortunately no records. In the spring of 1896 Gertrude travelled in the north of Italy, first in the company of Mrs. Norman Grosvenor and then of Mrs. J. R. Green, both of whom were her dear friends. Her father was with her part of the time.

They stayed in Venice, they stayed in Florence. As might be expected, on her arrival in Italy, Gertrude at once arranged to have Italian lessons. She writes from Venice "At 3 I had my parlatrice until 4. "

The Talbots (now General the Hon. Sir Reginald and Lady Talbot) were staying in Florence, which was a great added enjoyment. Lady Talbot was Mrs. Grosvenor's sister.

After Gertrude's return from Italy she was at home until the end of the year.]

To F.B.
LONDON, 1896.

One line to say we had a most amusing party at the Portsmouths yesterday. I made the acquaintance of Miss Haldane, whom I have long wished to know, and I am going to tea with her tomorrow. Haldane was most complimentary about my book—which I think he hasn't read by the way. A delightful review in the Athenaeum.

E. and I dined with the Stracheys first—very pleasant, we four, St. Loe had just finished reviewing my book!

Flora lunched today and we went out together afterwards. Tomorrow I have a Buddhist Committee lunch.

I wrote my review of Lafcadio this morning, the sort of blissful morning when one suddenly realises at the end of a few hours that one has been quite unconscious of the passing Of time. I'm just going to finish it now.

Moll looked charming last night.

To F.B.
LONDON, Feb. 12th, 1896.

I Studied my grammar this morning and went to the London Library where I looked through volumes and volumes of Asiatic Societies . . . and found little to my purpose.

To F. B.
LONDON, Thursday, Feb. 14th, 1896.

I had a very nice evening with the Ritchies—Pinkie Was there and she played the piano, and we talked (not wile she played) and it was very merry. They are looking very well. I think they are coming to you for Easter.

I came away rather early for I had a lesson at 5. My Pundit was extremely pleased with me, he kept congratulating Me on my proficiency in the Arabic tongue! I think his other pupils must be awful duffers. It is quite extraordinarily interesting to read the Koran with him and it is such a magnificent book! He has given me some Arabian Nights for the next time and I have given him some Hafiz poems to read, so we shall see what we shall see. He is extremely keen about the Hafiz book. . . .

To F.B.
LONDON, Feb. 17, 1896.

This morning I stayed in and read some most illuminating articles on Sufyism. There's a lot to know but I guess I'll know some of it before I've done. I expect I shall get my reading ticket tomorrow.

To F.B.
LONDON, Feb. 24, 1896.

My Pundit brought back my poems yesterday he is really pleased with them. I asked him if he thought they were worth doing and he replied that indeed he did. He is full of offers of assistance and wants to read all that I have done, which from a busy man is, I think, the best proof that he likes what he has seen. Arabic flies along I shall soon be able to read the Arabian Nights for fun.

To F.B.
LONDON, 1896.

My domino is going to be so nice and it will cost me very little for it is all made of a beautiful piece of white stuff Papa gave me in Algiers. Lizzie is making it. . . .

Give my love to Lisa. [Elizabeth Robins, the dear friend of us all, and the constant guest—then as now.] I wish I could come and have a long talk with her tonight over the fire.

To H. B.
PALAZZO GRITTI (VENICE), Saturday, April 14th, 1896.

Mrs. Green went in the morning to see Lady Layard, who offered us her gondola to go out and see the arrival of the Emperor. Meanwhile I went and called upon the Wards who are at the Hôtel de l'Europe and found them all and combined many meetings. Dorothy and Arnold walked me home.

At 2 Mrs. Green and I started out in a splendid gondola and went nearly to the Lido amidst a crowd of boats. It was very gorgeous for the Municipio appeared in splendid gondolas hung with streamers and emblems and rowed by 8 gondoliers in fancy dresses of different colours. About 3 the Hohenzollern steamed in through the Lido port, a magnificent great white ship with all the sailors dressed in white and standing in lines upon the deck. The guns fired, the ships in the harbour saluted and all the people cheered. The Hohenzollern anchored nearly opposite the Piazzetta and we saw the King and Queen and a crowd of splendid officers Come up in a steam launch all hung with blue. They went on board the Hohenzollern and presently we saw them all go away again with the Emperor and his two little boys. We were much amused, and for magnificence there never was anything like a festa with the Ducal Palace for background. It was a very imperial way of arriving to steam up in your gorgeous white ship. I only wished it had not been that Particular emperor we were welcoming.

To H. B.
VENICE, PALAZZO GRITTI, Thurrsday, April, 1896.
Mrs. Green and I went out in a gondola and saw the sun set behind the Euganean Hills. . . . she is a great dear. . . .
To H. B. FLORENCE, Sunday, April, 1896.
Caroline [Grosvenor] is a delightful companion we are particularly happy.

To F.B.
LONDON, May 7th, 1896.
I had a real busy morning and settled all my summer clothes and ordered a gown at Mrs. Widdicombe's. I hope it will be ready before you come as I should like you to pronounce upon it. Tomorrow I intend to spend an hour or two over my Hafiz things and get them all straight.

To F.B.
LONDON, Saturday, May 13th, 1896.
I went to the British Museum on my bicycle this morning. It adds a great joy to my studies and I feel all the brisker for it. The children have had a tennis court marked in the square. I am just going out to see! them play. They are looking blooming and are such angels! However we will try not to be too foolish about our family.

To F.B.
LONDON, Sat., May, 1896.
. . . I was invited to Lady Lockwood's dance but I really couldn't be bothered to hunt up a chaperon and go to it. . . .

To F.B.
LONDON, Monday, May 11th, 1896.
. . . About the children's flower gowns—we finally decided that the cheapest and best thing we could do was to trim the gowns with field flowers (artificial of course), buttercups) daisies and forget me-nots. We have cut a sort of ruche of tulle round the bottom of the skirt with little bunches of flowers tucked into it, and hung flowers from the neck and from the waist in little streams—on the whole I think this plan has made as much show as possible for as little money and the dresses look quite charming . . . I hope I've done right about it. The children were extremely anxious to have their gowns very flowery. Elsa was inclined to think that they didn't look flowery enough as it was, but we all assured her they were very very nice, and I really think 15/- is enough to have spent on this absurd amusement. . . .

To F. B.
LONDON, 1896.
We had a very merry dinner and started out about ten, along the

embankment, the Strand and through the City to the Tower Bridge, then home by Holborn Viaduct and oxford Street. The Strand was pretty full but the City quite empty, all brilliantly lighted and the asphalt pavement excellent good going. It was a delicious night with a little moon and I enjoyed it extremely. We went back to supper with the Tyrrells and I was not in till 1:30. However I went Off after breakfast to the Museum where I asked for a book they' hadn't got! It is rather funny that I should have exhausted the whole British Museum in a fortnight, but it's also a bore, for I wanted a nice French translation and now I shall have to fall back on the original Persian which they have. . . .

I have told Lizzie about the bonnet and cloak so you will find them ready.

To F.B.
LONDON, May 15th, 1896.

Our party last night was a great success, the babies looked charming. I was much complimented upon their appearance. It was most amusing being a chaperon. I sat on a bench and watched them dancing round and knew just what you felt like at Oxford. . . .

To F.B.
LONDON, Thursday, May, 1896.

Went up to the Museum this morning and read a Persian life of Hafiz with a Latin crib. I think I got at the meaning of it with the help of a Persian dictionary, but a Latin translation is not so clear to me as it might be. . . . I didn't go to Lady Pollock's on Tuesday, because I had Promised to go to a party at Audley Square and I couldn't combine the two unchaperoned. Audley Square was amusing . . .. I am going down to Caroline (in Kent) for Whitsuntide. I want to bicycle down on Saturday if I can get an escort, it's only 17 miles, and send my luggage by train. London is beginning to feel very Whitsuntidy. Beatrice Clementi came to see me this afternoon just before I went out. She is to be married in November. . . [to Sir Douglas Brownrigg, Bt., now Rear Admiral, retired.]

To H.B.
LONDON, June, 1896.

It is very close here and has been raining a good deal think of ordering a tasteful costume for Ascot consisting of a short skirt, a waterproof and a large umbrella. Florence and I arranged the flowers at 95 and did the dinner table at 90 most elegantly—I dine there tonight. The rest of the party are Lady Edward John Cavendish and Mr. Chirol. Then I had a long talk with Auntie Mary, who seems very brisk and well.

I took Florence with me to try on my gown and we walked together in the Square until a storm of rain came on and drove us in.

Auntie Maisie asks me to dine with her Friday and go to a ball, and Maurice is to come to dinner if she can possibly find a place for him, and at any rate to come in directly after dinner and go to the ball too.

To F.B.

LONDON, Thursday, June, 1896.

... We have had a most delightful day. We started about 10:30, Gerald, Florence, Uncle Frank and I, got to Ascot half an hour before the first race, which we saw from the top of the Royal Enclosure Stand; then we lunched in the Bachelors' tent, Billy being our host, and I sat next Colonel Talbot and was much amused. He had a Carpenter niece with him. Then we went back and saw all the races over the railing of the Royal enclosure, which is just opposite the winning post. The family had small bets on, mostly unsuccessful (I didn't bet, I need not say). . . .

At the end of all we had tea in the Guards' tent and came home very comfortably, getting in about 7:30. I am going again tomorrow. . . .

My gown was a dream and was much admired. I am going this evening with Auntie Mary and Florence and the Johnsons to sit out of doors in the Imperial Institute and listen to the band rather nice as it is very hot.

Florence and I did amuse ourselves so much! What a dear Lord Granville is. . . .

To F. B.
LONDON, July 14th, 1896.

Thank you very much for your letter and will you thank the little girls for me, I have no time to write to them today. Hugo came up in great form and we started off to Lord's together, but on the way discovered that he had lost the blue tassel on his umbrella, which saddened us dreadfully! So we tried in many shops to get one, and failed alas! However we were Comforted at Lord's when we saw that many many Eton boys had no tassel! We had the most excellent places, we carried our lunch with us and supplemented it with green-gages, after eating which we both made fervent wishes as they were the first we had eaten this year. I asked Hugo what he had wished, to which he replied, "Why I wished Eton might win—what in the world is there to wish for besides? He was such a darling!

To F. B.
LONDON, 1896.

I saw Heinemann this morning. He was extremely pleasant. I told him a lot about the book and he expressed a desire to see it. So at any rate it will have a reading. I shall send him the poems and preface from Berlin, Mr. Strong cannot come to town and has not yet finished the preface. . . .

CHAPTER III
1897

BERLIN

[IN January 1897 we find her starting for the British Embassy at Berlin. Her first letter is sent from the station at York.]

To F.B.
YORK, Jan. 6th, 1897.

I can't conceive what I am doing in this station, nor why I am going away. It's too silly. I wish I were stopping quietly at home.

All sorts of smart people on this platform! One begins to realise what the world is like when one gets to York, doesn't one. Never mind, I'll be smart too presently!

To F.B.
BERLIN, Saturday, Jan. 1897.

The reason why I had not sent the poems to H. was because Mr. Strong has not yet sent me back the preface. . . . I hope I may get it by the next bag. Meantime I have sent the 30 poems with their notes to H. and explained to him why the preface is not with them and apologised for the delay.

To her sister.
BERLIN, Jan. 22nd, 1897.

DEAREST ELSA, I made my bow to the 'Kaiser Paar' on Wednesday. It was a very fine show. We drove to the Schloss in the glass coach and were saluted by the guard when we arrived. We felt very swell! Then we waited for a long time with all the other dips. in a room next to the throne room and at about 8 the doors were thrown open. We all hastily arranged one another's trains and marched in procession while the band played the march out of Lohengrin. The Emperor and Empress were standing on a dais at the end of the room and we walked through a sort of passage made by rows and rows of pages dressed in pink. The 'Allerbôchst' looked extremely well in a red uniform—I couldn't look at the Empress much as I was so busy avoiding Aunt Mary's train. She introduced me and then stood aside while I made two curtseys. Then I wondered what the dickens I should do next, but Aunt Mary made me a little sign to go out behind her, so I 'enjambéd' her train and fled!

To F.B.
BERLIN, Jan. 24th, 1897.

. . . . The Princess Frederic Leopold's ladies asked when I was going to be introduced to her . . . . we arranged that I should be presented during the first polka of the first Court ball. . . .

To F.B.
BERLIN, Monday Jan. 25th, 1897.

. . . We have been skating all the afternoon with surprising energy, A very ridiculous thing happened-I had retired into a secluded corner and put my muff down to make a centre round which to skate a figure, when suddenly I was aware of a short fat German gentleman arriving into the middle of my figure on his back. He picked up my muff and himself and handed them both to me, so to speak, with a low bow. . . . We propose if the frost lasts making a big party, sledging down to Potsdam and skating there. I hope it will come off, it Would be very amusing. . . .

To F.B.
BERLIN, Thursday, Jan. 28th, 1897.

On Thursday afternoon I went with Aunt Mary to see Florence perform the gavotte. A great 'Probe' at the Kaiserhof to which all the people who were going to dance at the Court Ball came . . . . After the lesson was over there were a couple of waltzes, so I offed with my coat and danced too. There is a rather nice sort of variant of the 'pas de quatre' which they call the 'pas de patineur' which I quickly learnt. . . .

To F.B.
BERLIN, Tuesday, 1897.

. . . .F. and I went to see Henry IV last night, the Emperor having invited all the Embassy to come to the royal box. Uncle F. and Aunt M. were dining with the Frederic Leopolds so they were obliged to decline the box for themselves but the Emperor said that he hoped we should go as we should be chaperoned by Countess Keller, one of the ladies-in-waiting. Accordingly we went off by ourselves and sat very comfortably with Countess Keller in the second row of chairs-no one might sit in the front row even when the royalties were not in the box. All the Embassy and a lot of the Court people were with us, the Emperor and Empress were in a little box at the side. The play was very well done. The Falstaff excellent and the whole thing beautifully staged. There was no pause till the end of the second act when there was a long entr'acte. Countess Keller bustled away and presently came hurrying back and whispered something to Knesebeck and Egloffstein, two of the Court people, and they came and told F. and me that we were sent for. So off we went rather trembling, under the escort of Countess K. and Egloffstein who conducted us into a little tiny room behind the Emperor's box where we found the 'Kaiser Paar' sitting and having tea. We made deep curtseys and kissed the Empress's hand, and then we all sat down, F. next to the Emperor and I next to the Empress and they gave us tea and cakes. It was rather formidable though they were extremely kind. The Emperor talked nearly all the time; he tells us that no plays of Shakespeare were ever acted in London and that we must have heard tell that it was only the Germans who had really studied or really understood Shakespeare. One couldn't contradict an Emperor, so we said we had always been told so. Egloffstein's chair broke in the middle of the party and he came flat on to the ground which created a pleasing diversion I was so glad it wasn't mine! Countess K. was a dear and started a new subject whenever the conversation languished. After about 20 minutes the Empress got up, we Curtseyed to her, shook hands with the Emperor. Florence thanked him very prettily for sending for us and we bowed ourselves out. Wasn't it amusing! Florence said she felt shy but she looked perfectly self possessed and had the prettiest little air in the world as she sat talking to the Emperor. I felt rather frightened, but I did not mind much as I knew I need do nothing but follow Florence's lead. The Empress sits very upright and is rather alarming. He flashes round from one person to the other and talks as fast as possible and is not alarming at all. . . . We go again tonight to the second part . . . but we shall not be sent for as Uncle Frank and Aunt Mary will be there.

To F. B.
BERLIN, Feb. 5th, 1897.
. . . .The Court Ball on Wednesday was a fine show. We were asked for eight o'clock and at a quarter past we formed up for waiting. The ambassadresses sat on a line of chairs to the left of the throne in the Weiser Saal, and we stood meekly behind them. After about half an hour someone tapped tapped on the floor with a wand and in came a long procession of pages followed by the 'Kaiser Paar' and all the 'Furstliche Personen.' The whole room bobbed down in deep curtseys as they came in . . . . In to supper . . . . back to the ball room. The room was almost empty and the few people that were there were dancing the 'trois temps'—one is only allowed to dance the 'deux temps' when the Empress is there. It was a very delicious half hour for the floor is peerless and all these officers dance so well. Then followed the gavotte which Florence danced very prettily.

To H. B.
BERLIN, Feb. 8th, 1897
I wish you many many happy returns of your birthday and may your children become less and less tiresome with every succeeding year!. . . .
The house is all upside down for the ball. Wherever one goes one finds lines and lines of waiters arranging tables. We can seat 340 people at supper. There are to be tables in all the ball rooms, the Chancery ante-room and even the big bedroom. We all intend to bring our partners up to the big bedroom which makes a delightful supper-room. Florence and I went into the kitchen this morning and inspected the food. I never saw so many eatables together. . . .

To F.B.
BERLIN, Feb. 10th, 1897.
* * * *It was a great success and very splendid. Florence and I were of course (as it was in our own house) covered with bows and loaded with flowers. There were supper tables in all the drawing rooms—it looked extremely nice. . . .
I went to tea with Marie von Bunsen and stayed till past 7. She is most

interesting. . . .

To F.B.
BERLIN, Feb. 12th, 1897.

The Court Ball on Wednesday was much nicer than the first one. . . . The Emperor wore a gorgeous Austrian uniform in honour of an Austrian Archduke who was there—the brother of the man who is heir to the throne. He will be Emperor himself someday as the heir is sickly and unmarried. The Emperor William is disappointing when one sees him close; he looks puffy and ill and I never saw anyone so jumpy. He is never still a second while he is talking. . . .

Uncle Frank is in a great jig about Crete. He thinks there is going to be red war and an intervention of the Powers and all sorts of fine things. I wonder.

To F.B.
BERLIN, Feb. 14th, 1897.

. . . . Florence and I spent the most heavenly morning at the 'Haupt Probe'. . . Since then we have been bicycling round the house for exercise as it is raining and we could not go out. . . .

On Friday Mr. Acton, Mr. Spring Rice and Lord Granville dined with us. After dinner we played hide and seek till we were so hot we could play no longer and finished up the evening with pool and baccarat . . . . I went to the National Gallery to see the modern pictures . . . .I had been reading about modern German painters and knew what I wanted to look at. . . . Should like to go out but I mayn't go by myself. So I suppose I can't!

To F.B.
BERLIN, Feb. 17th, 1897.

[The play referred to in this letter is the second part of Henry IV.]

We had a most exciting evening at the play yesterday. We were all sent for in the entr'acte. We had a very agreeable tea with the Emperor and Empress and her sister. . . . It was like an act out of another historical drama—but a modern one. A sheaf of telegrams were handed to the Emperor as we sat at tea. He and Uncle fell into an excited conversation in low voices; we talked on to the Empress trying to pretend we heard nothing but catching scraps of the Emperor's remarks, " Crete . . . . Bulgaria . . . . Serbia . . . . mobilizing," and so forth. The Empress kept looking up at him anxiously; she is terribly perturbed about it all and no wonder for he is persuaded that we are all on the brink of war. . . .

CHAPTER IV
1897-1899

ROUND THE WORLD, DAUPHINIE, ETC.

[GERTRUDE came back to England at the beginning of March. My sister Mary Lascelles died on April 3rd, after three days' illness. Her death made a terrible gap in Gertrude's life.]

To F.B.
REDCAR, April 7th, 1897.

I have been to Clarence today it was no use sitting and moping so I thought I had better make myself useful if I could. . . .

[In August of that year we all went to the Dauphiné, staying at La Grave under the shadow of the Meije, objective of all Dauphin climbers, This holiday makes an epoch, as it was the beginning of Gertrude's climbing experiences, although this year she did nothing very adventurous.

She went over the Brèche with two guides, slept at the refuge, came down over the Col des Cavales and proudly strode back into the village next morning between her guides, well pleased with herself.

She was at home with us all the rest of the year.

On the 29th December 1897 Gertrude and her brother Maurice left home for Southampton, to embark on a voyage round the world.

Gertrude kept a diary letter on the voyage. She posts from Jamaica, Guatemala, San Francisco—wherever she had an opportunity. It is not worth while reproducing all that she and Maurice saw on this well-known route, which has so often been described. They enjoyed it all, taking part in the unpretentious diversions of a voyage. They asked the Captain's permission to mark out a golf course on board, which had a great success.]

"There are a lot of children on board, with whom I have made friends," she writes.

"Eight of us are playing a piquet tournament: I am first favourite at present."

(Then there was a ball on board.]

"We took a great deal of trouble to make it go, Maurice was the life and soul of it."

[Then we are told of]

"a partial eclipse of the moon, seated in the stalls, so to speak, our deck chairs. It was most luxuriously arranged by nature."

"I won the piquet tournament to the great joy of the other members of the party."

[She and Maurice returned to London in June.

In September, after a delightful two months in the West of Scotland—we had taken the Manse at Spean Bridge for the summer—Gertrude is at Redcar again, enchanted to return to her books.]

To F.B.
REDCAR, September 2nd, 1898.
. . . .Hugo has been playing golf and we are now going to have a game of racquets before settling down to our work. Oh, how I wish I were going to have a month of this. The bliss of being really at work is past words.

Herbert Pease stands for Darlington, I see in the evening papers . . . ..

To H. B.
Saturday 22nd September, 1898.
. . .I'm going to Rounton on Sunday . . . . having finished a great batch of Arabic and Persian for Mr. Ross. [Now Sir Denison Ross.]

To F.B.
REDCAR, Autumn 1898.
I have been at the Infirmary all the afternoon. I've got another engagement—to lecture at the High School. I've been arranging about my lantern slides. . . .

By the way, confided to Lisa that she felt quite anxious about Elsa because she thought we were all so beautiful and so clever that we couldn't all go on living. Elsa won't mind being the 'offer' to the jealous gods, I hope!

To F.B.
LONDON 1898.
. . . . That angel of a Mr. Vaughan Williams has found me a real Persian at least he is an Afghan and his name is Satdar and he speaks beautiful Persian. I have written to him today. Isn't it interesting. . . .

[Gertrude begins the year 1899 at Redcar, she and Hugo are left together for a few days at Red Barns.]

To F.B.
REDCAR, January 6th, 1899.
. . . . Hugo and I have made an excellent 'ménage'—we get on admirably and I have come to know him much better, chiefly because he has told me all his views as to his future. They are rather a blow to me, I admit. He is one of the most lovable and livable with people I have ever come across.

To her sister Elsa.
LONDON, Jan. 1899.
. . . . I thought the braid a little too braidy. A modification of it would be lovely. I should have no braid on the coat just the seams strapped. 'Tis very smart so. I went to Prince's this morning and skated . . . . with Flora and a lot of people. . . . Next time I'm in London I shall have a few lessons there. It's silly not to be able to skate well when everybody does.

My new clothes are very dreamy. You will scream with delight when you see

me in them!
To F. B.
LONDON, Jan. 1899.

I have sent off the purple dress and a grey one which is nine guineas and very nice indeed. It has a dark coat and everything suitable to Elsa. My only doubt is whether the black trimming is not too black. There is another most elegant elephant grey costume strapped with grey, but the coat is quite tight fitting so that it might not be so becoming to Elsa. . . . .

To F.B.
LONDON, Thursday, Mar. 17th, 1899.

. . . I write from a sofa. This morning at Prince's I fell violently on my knees and when I shortly after took my skates off, I found I couldn't walk. . . . Maclagan, however, says I must lie up for a few days. Isn't it boring? I'm writing to all the amusing people to come and see me, having dressed the part well in a Japanese tea gown. . . .

I shall beguile the time with my pundits while I'm invalided. I've told them all to come.

It is so provoking because I was getting to skate really well.

[In the spring of the year 18 99 Gertrude went abroad again to Northern Italy, by herself, then to Greece, with her father and her uncle Thomas Marshall, a classical Scholar and translator of Aristotle, deeply interested at going to Greece for the fifth time. A most successful tour altogether. In Athens they find Dr. Hogarth and go the Museum, " where Mr. Hogarth showed us his recent finds-pots Of 4000 B.C. from Melos. Doesn't that Make one's brain reel?" Another distinguished archaeologist, Professor Dôrpfeld is there also. They listen with breathless interest to his lecture on the Acropolis: "he took us from stone to stone and built up a Wonderful chain of evidence with extraordinary ingenuity until we saw the Athens of 600 B.c. I never saw anything better done."

She also writes from Athens Papa has bought him a grey felt hat, in which he looks a dream of beauty and some yellow leather gaiters to ride in the Peloponnesus. He will look smart, bless him . . . . . .

Then to Constantinople, and back again to England in May.

In August she started with Hugo for Bayreuth, joining on the way Sir Frank Lascelles and his daughter Florence, and Mr. Chirol (now Sir Valentine Chirol). They go to Nuremberg and Rothenburg on the way, enjoying themselves ecstatically everywhere. She writes] " this is really too charming. You never met a more delightful travelling party. Florence is in the seventh heaven all the time. His Ex. a perfect angel, Mr. Chirol, and in fact all of us, endlessly cheerful and delighted with everything." [They hear Parsifal and The Ring at Bayreuth. Gertrude, "tief gerührt", as she tells us, sends home long, vivid descriptions of the performances. These letters on a subject now almost hackneyed are too long to insert here. She was not, and did not pretend to be, an expert on music) but she cared for it very much.

Hugo, who was an admirable musician, was conservative in his tastes and was at first prepared to be on the defensive with regard to Wagner. Gertrude also records some personal social experiences.]

To F.B.
BAYREUTH.

Frau Cosima has asked us all to a party on Friday evening. Great Larks! . . . . The restaurant was crowded when the door opened and in came the whole Wagner family in procession, Frau Cosima first on Siegfried's arm. There was a great clapping as she passed down the room to her table.

To F.B.
BAYREUTH, Wed. Aug. 16th, 1899.

This morning about half past 8 came a message from the Grand Duke [of Hesse] asking us whether we could be at the theatre at 9 as he would show us the stage. We bustled up and arrived only a few minutes late. It was most entertaining; we were taken into every corner, above and below. We descended through trap doors and mounted into Valhalla. We saw all the properties, and all the mechanism of the Rhine maidens; we explored the dressing rooms, sat in the orchestra and rang the Parsifal bells! The Grand Duke was extremely cheerful and agreeable—he's quite young—and of course everyone was hats off and anxious to show us all we wanted to see. It's a very extraordinary place, the stage; the third scene of Siegfried was set. We shall feel quite at home when we see it tonight. Hugo is delighted with it all. He was much impressed by the Walküre though he says it will take a great deal to make him a Wagnerian.

[After Bayreuth the party breaks up, all of them except Gertrude returning to England.]

I'm awfully sorry to have parted with Hugo. He really is one of the most delightful people in the world. The Harrachs, you will be glad to hear, thought him very beautiful . . . when I told you that they were people of discernment!

[After this Gertrude went back through Switzerland to the Dauphiné and fulfilled her year old purpose of ascending the Meije.)

To H.B.
LA GRAVE, Monday, 28th August, 1899 .

I sent you a telegram this morning [" Meije traversée") for, I thought you would gather from my last that I meant to have a shot at the Meije and would be glad to hear that I had descended in the approved, and in no other manner. Well, I'll tell you—it's awful! I think if I had known exactly what was before me I should not have faced it, but fortunately did not, and I look back on it with unmixed satisfaction—and forward to other things with no further apprehension. . . .

We left here on Friday at 2:30, Mathon, Marius and I, and walked up to the Refuge de l'Alpe in two hours. Two German men turned up at the Refuge. . . . Madame Castillan gave us a very good supper and I went at once to bed. I got off at 4:30 and got to the top of the clot at 8:10. In the afternoon, there arrived a young Englishman called Turner with Rodier as guide and a porter. I went out to watch the beautiful red light fading from the snows and rocks. The Meije looked dreadfully forbidding in the dusk. When I came in I found that Mathon had put my rug in a corner of the shelf which was the bed of us all and what with the straw and my cloak for a pillow I made myself very comfortable. We were packed as tight as herrings, Mr. Turner next to me, then the two Germans and Rodier. Mathon and the porters lay on the ground beneath us. Our night lasted from 8 till 12, but I didn't sleep at all. Marius lighted a match and looked at his watch. It was ten o'clock. " Ah, c'est encore trop matin," said Rodier. It seemed an odd view of 10 p.m. We all got up soon after 12 and I went down to the river and washed a little. It was a perfect night, clear stars and the moon not yet over the hills. . . . We left half an hour later, 1 a.m., just as the moon shone into the valley. Mathon carried a lantern till we got on to the snow when it was light enough with only the moon. . . .

At 1:30 we reached the glacier and all put on our ropes. . . . It wasn't really cold, though there was an icy little breath of wind down from the Brèche. This was the first time I had put on the rope . . . . we went over the glacier for another hour . . . . we got into the Promontoir, a long crest of rock and rested there ten minutes . . . . we left there at 2:40. . . . We had about three hours up very nice rock, a long chimney first and then most pleasant climbing. Then we rested again for a few minutes. . . . I had been in high feather for it was so easy, but ere long my hopes were dashed! We had about two hours and a half of awfully difficult rock, very solid fortunately, but perfectly fearful. There were two places which Mathon and Marius literally pulled me up like a parcel. I didn't a bit mind where it was steep up, but round corners where the rope couldn't help me! . . . . And it was absolutely sheer down. The first half-hour I gave myself up for lost. it didn't seem possible that I could get up all that wall without ever making a slip. You see, I had practically never been on a rock before. However, I didn't let on and presently it began to seem quite natural to be hanging by my eyelids over an abyss. . . . just before reaching the top we passed over the Pas du Chat, the difficulty of which is much exaggerated. . . . It was not till I was over it that Mathon told me that it was the dreaded place. We were now at the foot of the Pyramide Duhamel and we went on till we came in sight of the Glacier Catré, where we sat down on a cornice, 7:45. . . . The Germans got up a quarter of an hour later having climbed up the rock a different way. . . . At 8:45 we got to the top between the Pic du Glacier carré and the Grand Pic de la Meije and saw over the other side for the first time. We left at 9 and reached the summit at 10:10, the rock being quite easy except one place called the Cheval Rouge. It is a red flat stone, almost perpendicular, some 15 feet high, up which you swarm as best you may with your feet against the Meije, and you sit astride, facing the Meije, on a very pointed crest. I sat there while Marius and Mathon went on and then followed them up an overhanging rock of 20 feet or more. The rope came in most handy—! We stayed on the summit until 11. It was gorgeous, quite cloudless. . . . I went to sleep for half-an-hour. It's a very long way up but it's a longer way down-unless you take the way Mathon's axe took.

The cord by which it was tied to his wrist broke on the Cheval Rouge and it disappeared into space. There's a baddish place going down the Grand Pic. The guides fastened a double rope to an iron bolt and let Mr. Turner and me down on to a tiny ledge on which we sat and surveyed the Aiguille d'Arve with La Grave in the foreground. Then was a very nasty bit without the double rope ow anyone gets down those places I can't imagine. However, they do. Then we crossed the Brèche and found ourselves at the foot of the first dent. Here comes the worst place on the whole Meije. I sat on the Brèche and looked down on to the Châtelleret on one side and La Grave on the other. . . . Then Mathon vanished, carrying a very long rope, and I waited. . . . Presently I felt a little tug on the rope. " Allez, Mademoiselle," Said Marius from behind and off I went. There were two little humps to hold on to on an overhanging rock and there La Grave beneath and there was me in midair and Mathon round the corner holding the rope tight, but the rope was sideways of course that's my general impression of those ten minutes. Added to which I thought at the time how very well I was climbing and how odd it was that I should not be afraid. The worst was over then, and the most tedious part was all to come. It took us three hours to get from the Grand Pic to the Pic Central up and down over endless dents. We followed the crest all the way, quite precipitous rock below us on the Châtelleret side and a steep slope on the other. There was no difficulty, but there was also no moment when you had not to pay the strictest attention. . . . I felt rather done when we got to the Pic Central. . . . There was an hour of ice and rock till at last we found ourselves on the Glacier du Tabuchet and with thankfulness I put on my skirt again. It was then 3 and we got in at 6:30. The glacier was at first good then much crevassed. We skirted for nearly an hour the arête leading up to the Pic de Momme and it was 5:30 before we unroped. . . . When I got in I found everyone in the Hotel on the doorstep waiting for me and M. Juge let off crackers, to my great surprise. . . .

I went to bed and knew no more till 6 this morning, when I had five cups of tea and read all your letters and then went to sleep again until ten. I'm really not tired but my shoulders and neck and arms feel rather sore and stiff and my knees are awfully bruised.

[After the Meije there is one more letter, too long to insert here, from La Grave, in which she relates her successful ascent of the Ecrins. She comes back to England in the middle of September, well pleased, as shown by her letters, with her progress in climbing.]

CHAPTER V
1899-1900

JERUSALEM: FIRST DESERT JOURNEYS

IN November 1899 she starts for Jerusalem, with many hopes and plans, including learning more Arabic. Dr. Fritz Rosen was then German Consul at Jerusalem. He had married Nina Roche, whom we had known since she was a child, the daughter of Mr. Roche of the Garden House, Cadogan Place. Charlotte Roche was Nina's sister. They made everything easy for Gertrude.

On the way she writes a long letter from Smyrna, where everyone was most kind and hospitable. She describes the "Mediterranean race " to which the inhabitants of Smyrna belong].

It speaks no language though it will chatter with you in Half a dozen, it has no native land though it is related by marriage to all Europe, and with the citizens of each country it will talk to its compatriots and itself as " we "; it centres round no capital and is loyal to no government though it obeys many. Cheerful, careless, contented, hospitable to a fault, it may well be all, for it is divested of all natural responsibilities, it has little to guard and little to offer but a most liberal share in its own inconceivably hugger mugger existence. Kindness is its distinctive quality, as faras I have sampled it, and I hope I may have many opportunities of sampling it further.

[From Beyrout she writes]

We settled that when I come riding down from Damascus in the spring . . .

[The last part of the voyage is made on a Russian boat] all the stewards speak Russian and we communicate by signs, my fellow passengers are an American Catholic Priest and a Russian engineer and 400 Russian peasants who are making a pilgrimage to Jerusalem.

To F.B.
S.S. RUSSIA, Sunday 10th Dec., 1899.

The pilgrims are camped out all over the deck. They bring their own bedding and their own food and their passage from Odessa costs them some 12 roubles. They undergo incredible hardships: one woman walked from Tobolsk, she started in March.

To H.B.
HOTEL JERUSALEM, 13th December, 1899.

Here I am most comfortably installed. I am two minutes' walk from the German Consulate. My apartment consists of a very nice bedroom and a big sitting room, both opening on to a small vestibule which in its turn leads out on to the verandah which runs all along the first story of the hotel courtyard with a little garden in it. I pay 7 francs a day including breakfast, which is not excessive. My housemaid is an obliging gentleman in a fez who brings me my hot bath in the morning and is ready at all times to fly round in my service. I spent the morning unpacking and turning out the bed and things out of my sitting room; it is now most cosy two armchairs, a big writing table, a square table for my books, an enormous Kiefert map of Palestine lent me by Uncle Tom and photographs of my family on the walls. The floor is of tiles but they have laid down a piece of carpet on it. There is a little stove in one corner and the wood fire in it is most acceptable. I propose buying a horse! for which I shall pay about 18 pounds and sell him at the end for no less, I hope. The keep is very little, Dr. Rosen says, and you see the alternative would be to use theirs. Now they have only 3 for their 3 selves and I already have all my meals except breakfast with them, so don't think I can infringe further on their hospitality.

We got in soon after 8, and the kind Rosens came on board with a kavass and carried me off to a very nice hotel where we breakfasted. The garden was full of parrots and monkeys which breakfasted also when I had finished. It was a delicious sunny day. We drove round about Jaffa, caught the only train at 1:20 to Jerusalem. It was 5 before we arrived, Charlotte met us. The Consulate is small but very comfy, all the rooms open on to a long central living room which is full of beautiful Persian things. The two boys were much excited by my arrival and greeted me with enthusiasm. They are perfect dears, these people. I feel as if I should love them very much indeed. And so charming about all arrangements, hospitality and kindness itself.

Today Dr. R. and I went for a long walk, I left a card and a letter of introduction on Mrs. Dickson at the English consulate. One's first impression of Jerusalem is extremely interesting, but certainly not pleasing. The walls are splendid (Saracenic on Jewish foundations), but all the holy places are terribly marred by being built over with hideous churches of all the different sects.

[Gertrude's interest in the holy places was that of the archaeologist only and not that of the believer.

There is no space to insert in extenso her long and interesting letters from Jerusalem, where she was entirely happy learning Arabic, exploring her surroundings, and being admitted into the delightful intimacy of the Rosens. But some extracts from the letters are given here.]

To F.B.

This morning I went out with Charlotte and the children (I have not Yet got my teacher). The two boys rode on a donkey and looked angels. They are delicious children. I saw a charming little horse, a bay, very well bred with lovely movements rather showy, but light and strong and delightful in every way We have embarked on negotiations for him which promise to take some time as they now ask 40 pounds and my price is 18 to 20! He comes of a well known stock so that I should run no risk of losing on him when I sell him. Charlotte, Dr. R'. and I rode this afternoon, I on a pony belonging to the hotel keeper, very bad, much too small and slow, he wouldn't do at all. My saddle had to be wrapped round him!

This morning I had my first lesson. My teacher's name is Khalil Dughan and he is exactly what I want. I learnt more about pronunciation this morning than I have ever known. In the afternoon, Nina, Dr. R. and I rode out.

To F.B.
December 13th, 1899

My days are extremely full and most agreeable. I either have a lesson or work alone every morning for 4 hours-the lesson only lasts one and a half hours. I have 3 morning and 3 afternoon lessons a week. I am just beginning to understand a little of what I hear and to say simple things to the servants, but I find it awfully difficult. The pronunciation is past words, no western throat being constructed to form these extraordinary gutturals. Still it's really interesting. We lunch at 12:30 and go out about 2, generally riding till 5. Then I come home to my work till 7 when I dress and go in to dinner. I aim at being back by 10 to get another hour's work but this doesn't always happen, especially now when Nina is very busy preparing a Xmas tree and we spend our evenings tying up presents and gilding walnuts, Dr. R. reading to us, the while, all his travel letters from Persia—extremely interesting.

My horse is much admired. My teacher, also, is a success. He has the most charming fund of beautiful oriental stories and I make him tell them to me by the hour as I want to get used to the sound of words. He is a Christian and his family claims to have been Crusaders.

He has given me a lecture of his, written out in English on the customs of the Arabs. It begins "The Arabs are the oldest race on earth; they date from the Flood!!" Comes my housemaid, "The hot water is ready for the Presence," says he. "Enter and light the candle," say I. "On my head," he has replied—it sounds ambiguous in English! That means it's dressing time.

To her sister Elsa.
JERUSALEm, December 20th, 1899.

The days fly here so that I scarcely know how to catch at them for a moment's time to write to you. It is now 11 p.m. and I must go to bed quickly so as to be up early and prepare my lesson before my Arab comes. (I may say in passing that I don't think I shall ever talk Arabic, but I go on struggling with it in the hope of mortifying Providence by my persistence. I now stammer a few words to my housemaid—him of the fez—and he is much delighted.) With Charlotte, who is a most spirited companion, I explored a great part of the inner town. We are quite the family party and I love them all. The boys are angels. Now to bed.

The first night of rain I was awakened by a rushing sound of water and found that it was falling in sheets on to my pillow! I took up my bed and walked and spent the rest of the night in peace.

To F.B.
JERUSALEM, Thursday, Dec. 28, 1899.

It has rained quite persistently for 5 days. You may imagine how I say 'Heil dir, Sonne!' this morning when I woke and saw the sun. Yesterday the Rosens had a Xmas tree for all the German children. It was most successful and the children were dears. I am beginning to feel very desperate about Arabic and I am now going to try a new plan. A Syrian girl is to come and spend an hour with me 3 Or 4 times a week and talk to me. I shall take her out walks sometimes, if she is satisfactory, and converse with her. It is an awful language.

To F.B.
JERUSALEM, Jan. 1st, 1900.

Will You order Heath to send me out a wide gray felt sun hat (not double, but it must be a regular Terai shape and broad brimmed) to ride in, and to put a black velvet ribbon round it With Straight bows. My Syrian girl is charming and talks very Prettily but with a strong local accent. It adds enormously to one's difficulties that one has to learn a patois and a purer Arabic at the same time. I took her out for a long walk on Friday afternoon and went photographing about Jerusalem. She was much entertained, though she was no good as a guide, for she had never been in the Jewish quarter though she has lived all her life here! That's typical of them. I knew my way, however, as every Englishwoman would it's as simple as possible.

She came with us on the following day on a most delightful expedition. We started at 9 in the morning it was Sunday and therefore a legitimate holiday-and rode down the Valley of Hinnon and all along the brook Kedron (which is dry at this season) through a deep valley full of immensely old olive trees and rock tombs scarcely older. Then up a long hill and down on the other side into a shallow naked valley, where there were many encampments of the black Bedouin tents, and so into an extraordinary gorge called the Valley of Fire. The rock lies in natural terraces and is full of caves; the Brook Kedron (it had rejoined us in a roundabout way) has cut the steepest, deepest cleft for its bed and on either side rise these horizontal layers of stone. They have been a regular city of anchorites, each living in his cave and drawing his ladder up behind him when he went in. Half a mile or so further on lies the citadel of this cave town, the Monastery of Mar Saba, itself half cave and half building, its long walls and towers creeping up the steep rock, the dome of its chapel jutting out from it, and the irregular galleries and rows of cells hanging out over a precipice. The rock itself is full of little square windows and these are the cave cells and probably about as old as St. Saba who lived in the 6th century.

To F.B.
JERUSALEM, Jan. 5th, 1900.

What a terrible time it is. I feel such a beast to be writing to you about my pleasant doings in the midst of all this, still I can do no good to you all by being very anxious. On Wednesday we rode down to the Dead Sea, over a long stretch of country on which grew thorny plants, then through a curious belt of hard mud heaps, then along the Jordan valley and finally across a bit of absolute desert, white with salt and plantless. It was a glorious day, bright and hot.

To Her Sister.
JERUSALIM, Jan. 11th, 1900.

My DEAREST ELSA, It is sad about Berlin and all your beautiful clothes. I was thrilled by your account of your coat it sounds too beautiful. But dear, dear! that you should not be going to shine in it in imperial circles! I am extremely happy and much amused, and I am very busy with Arabic. Whenever I can I get Ferideh to come and spend the afternoon with me, but as she teaches in a school, I can usually only get her on a Saturday. She comes to tea with me, however, two other days a week and we converse for an hour. I often go walking alone of an afternoon and explore the surrounding country And nearly always find some exciting flower among the rocks. The earliest flower place is the Valley of Hinnon. I went there yesterday afternoon for starch hyacinths and cyclamen and had a tremendous scramble. As I came back along the Road I met an Arab who greeted me avffably and told me he had seen me climbing on the rocks. So we walked home together We had a long talk—my conversations are limited to rather simple subjects. The first thing they always say is, "We have heard that there is a great deal of water in your country." then I expatiate on the greenness of it and the distance and the cold and so forth. It's awful fun.

To H.B.
JERUSALEM, Jan. 11th, 1900.

I am just beginning to feel my feet after a fearful struggle. The first fortnight was perfectly desperate—I thought I should never be able to put two words together. Added to the fact that the language is very difficult there are at least three sounds almost impossible to the European throat. The worst I think is a very much aspirated H. I can only say it by holding down my tongue with one finger, but then you Can't carry on a conversation with your finger down your throat can you? My little girl Ferideh Yamseh is a great success. She talks the dialect, but that is all the better as I want to understand the people of hereabouts. I went to visit her and her family after dinner yesterday—they are quite close. It was most amusing. I found the mother a pretty charming woman who has had ten children and looks ridiculously young (they marry at 13). Two sisters and presently a brother came in. The mother talks nothing but Arabic so the visit was conducted in that language with great success Ferideh interpreting from time to time. I was regaled on cocoa, a very sweet Arab pastry and pistachios which I love and shown all the photographs of all their relations down to the last cousin twice removed. . . .

My Sheikh has just told me that Ladysmith is relieved I do hope it is true and that this is the beginning of good news. I am sending you a little packet of seeds. They are more interesting for associations sake than for the beauty of the plant—it is the famous and fabulous mandrake. By the way the root of the mandrake grow to a length of 2 yards, so I should think somebody shrieks when it is dug up if not the mandrake, then the digger.

I took Ferideh for a drive and a walk yesterday and talked Arabic extremely badly and felt desponding about it. However there is nothing to be done but to struggle on with it. I should like to mention that there are five words for a wall and 36 ways of forming the plural. And the rest is like unto it.

To H.B.
JERUSALEM, Jan. 11th-14th, 1900.

Sunday 14. This goes tomorrow. It ought to reach you in a week as it goes by a good post via Egypt. The posts are arranged thus: Sunday and Monday outgoing posts and the rest of the week nothing. Dr. R. Nina and I rode this afternoon, heavenly weather. We went an exploring expedition through a lovely valley under a place called Malba. The path of course awful. In one place we had to get off, pull down a wall and lead our horses over it. There are no decent paths at all, only the hard high road. I so often wish for you—always when I'm making a nice expedition. Next spring let us come here together. Anyhow let us have a nice travel together soon.

To F. B.
JERICHO, January 17th, 1900.

I rode down here yesterday afternoon with Isa, one of the kavasses. We started at 1:30 and got here at 5, which was pretty good going. It was a most pleasant day for riding, cool and not sunny, today is brilliantly sunny, I came down the last hill in company with a band of Turkish soldiers, ragged, footsore, weary, poor dears ! but cheerful. We held a long conversation. The Russian Pilgrim House we visited last night and found it packed with pilgrims as tight as herrings sleeping in rows on the floor. Even the courtyard was quite full of them and on a tree an eikon round which a crowd of them were praying, Charlotte and I rode off with Isa about 11 and went down to the Jordan, taking our lunch with us. There ,*we found an enormous crowd assembled. Bedouin and fellaheen, kavasses in embroidered clothes. Turkish soldiers, Greek priests and Russian peasants, some in furs and top boots and some in their white shrouds, which were to serve as bathing dresses in the holy stream and then to be carried home and treasured up till their owner's death. We lunched and wandered about for some time, I photographing some of these strange groups—long haired Russian priests in their shrouds standing praying in the hot sun by the river bank, among the tamarisk bushes and the reeds, every one, men and women, had chains of beads and crucifixes hung round their necks. The sun was very hot and we waited and waited while those who were going to be baptised signed their names and paid a small fee. We found ourselves ensconced on willow boughs just opposite to the place where the priests were coming down to bless the water. We waited for about half an hour, then the crowd opened and a long procession of priests came to the water's edge with lighted candles. The shrouded people clambered down the mud banks and stood waist deep In the stream until the moment when the priest laid the cross three times upon the water, then suddenly, with a great firing off of guns, everyone proceeded to baptise himself by dipping and rolling over in the water. It was the strangest sight. Some of them had hired monks at a small fee to baptise them and they certainly got their money's worth of baptism, for the monks took an infinite pleasure in throwing them over backwards into the muddy stream and holding them under until they were quite saturated. We then rowed back, returned to our horses and got back about 5.

To F.B.
JERUSALEM, Feb. 18th, 1900.

There is a regular commerce apart from all others here to supply the Russian pilgrims with relics, souvenirs and the necessities of Russian peasant life. I bless the typewriter. it is such a joy to open an envelope of yours and find long sheets from the typewriter. It is rather terrible to think that Maurice is off; I hoped he wouldn't leave till the end of the month, Anyhow you will telegraph to me on his arrival, won't you, and all items of news you receive from him which can be conveyed by telegram. He writes in great spirits and it may be that it will be good for him, the out-of-door life there. My last letter I have sent home to be forwarded to him. Do you know the way when something disagreeable happens, that one looks back and tries to imagine what it would have been like if it hadn't happened? That's how I feel about his going.

[Maurice had gone out to the Boer War in command of the Volunteer Service Company, Yorkshire Regiment. He and Gertrude were bound together by the closest affection and her constant anxiety and solicitude about him is shown in her letters.]

Do you know these wet afternoons I have been reading the story of Aladdin to myself for pleasure, without a dictionary! It is not very difficult, I must confess, still it's ordinary good Arabic, not for beginners, and I find it too charming for words. Moreover I see that I really have learnt a good deal since I came for I couldn't read just for fun to save my life. It is satisfactory, isn't it? I look forward to a time when I shall just read Arabic like that! and then for my histories! I really think that these months here will permanently add to the pleasure and interest of the rest of my days! Honest Injun. Still there is a lot and a lot more to be done first—SO to work!

To F.B.
JERUSALEM, Feb. 28, 1900.

Sunday, was too many for me. I did not go out at all but sat It home and read Aladdin and looked at the streaming rain. Monday was a little better. Charlotte and I put on short skirts and thick boots and went for a long walk to a lovely spring she knew of. We walked down a deep valley which s long as we have known it has been as dry as a bone and where to our surprise we found a deep swift stream, Ain Tulma, our object, was on the other side and as there are no bridges in this country, (there being no rivers as a rule) there was nothing for it but to take off our shoes and stockings and wade. The water came above our knees. The other side was too lovely—the banks of the river were carpeted with red anemones, a sheet of them, and to walk by the side of a rushing stream is an unrivalled experience in this country. When we got to Ain Tulma we found the whole place covered with cyclamen and orchis and a white sort of garlic, very pretty, and the rocks out of which the water comes were draped in maidenhair. There were a lot of small boys, most amiable young gentlemen, who helped us to pick cyclamen, and when I explained that I had no money they said it was a bakshish to me—the flowers. We had a very scrambly walk back, waded the stream again and when we got to a little village at the foot of the hill, we hired some small boys to carry our flowers home for us. (In this village I lost my way and we found ourselves wandering over the flat roofs and Jumping across the streets below!) I hurried on (as it was 5 and I had a lesson at 5:30) with 5 little beggar boys in my train. They were great fun. We had long conversations all the way home. It's such an amusement to be able to understand. The differences of pronunciation are a little puzzling at first to the foreigner. There are two k's in Arabic—the town people drop the hard k altogether and replace it by a guttural for which we have no equivalent; the country people pronounce the hard k soft and the soft k ch, but they say their gutturals beautifully and use a lot of words which belong to the more classical Arabic. The Bedouins speak the best; they pronounce all their letters and get all the subtlest shades of meaning out of the words. I must tell you this is a great day—a German post office has been opened, and we expect marvels from it. There is parcel post and all complete and I advise you to put German Post Office on to your letters to me. One of our kavasses has gone to be Post Office kavass and as I passed down the Jaffa Street he rushed out open armed to greet me and begged me to come in. So in I went and retired behind the counter and shook hands warmly with the two post masters (they dined with us a few nights ago) and bought 6 stamps to celebrate the occasion—which I didn't pay for, as I had no money—the kavass saying all the time—"Al! ketear 'al!" which means "It is extremely high," and is the superlative of admiration in Arabic. The tourists who were sending off telegrams were rather surprised to see someone seemingly like themselves come in hand in hand with an old Arab and fall into the arms of the officials behind the counter! It was extremely high!

Friday 2. Today came the joyful news of the relief of Ladysmith. My horse is extremely well. We are going for a long ride tomorrow. The R's and I have been planning expeditions. We mean to go for 10 days into Moab about the 18th. It will be lovely. We shall take tents, Dr. R. Nina and I. Our great travel is not till the end of April, but I shall go to Hebron some time early in April. Goodbye.

To F.B,
JERUSALEM, March 6th, 1900.

By the way, I hope Elsa clung to the Monthly Cousin article and did not allow it to be published elsewhere. The style of it was only suited to that journal, but I'm glad it pleased. It's a gorgeous day. I'm going riding in my new hat!

[The Monthly Cousin was a typewritten and handwritten periodical edited by Elsa and Molly, of which the contributors were the wide family circle of the Bells and of their cousins. It appeared regularly from 1897 to 1907, and has been preserved as a precious family record. Gertrude revelled in it, and on occasion contributed to it.]

To H.B.
AYAN MUSA, Tuesday, March 20, 1900.
From my tent.

I left Jerusalem yesterday soon after 9, having seen my cook at 7 and arranged that he should go off as soon as he could get the mules ready. (His name is Hanna—sounds familiar doesn't it! but that H is such as you have never heard.) I rode down to Jerusalem alone—the road was full of tourists, caravans of donkeys carrying tents for cook and Bedouin escorts. I made friends as I went along and rode with first one Bedouin and then another, all of them exaggerating the dangers I was about to run with the hope of being taken with me into Moab. Half way down I met my guide from Salt, east of Jordan, coming up to meet me. His name is Tarif, he is a servant of the clergyman in Salt and a Christian therefore, and a perfect dear. We rode along together, sometime, but he was on a tired horse, so I left him to come on slowly and hurried down into Jericho where I arrived with a Bedouin at 1—famished. I went to the Jordan hotel. We then proceeded to the Mudir's for I wanted to find out the truth of the tales I had been told about Moab, but he was out. By this time Tarif and Hanna had arrived and reported the tents to be one and a half hours behind, which seemed to make camping at the Jordan impossible that night. . . I determined to pass that night in Jericho and make an early start.

This morning I got up at 5 and at 6 was all ready, having sent on my mules and Hanna to the Jordan bridge. I knocked up the Mudir and he said he would send a guide to Madeba to make the necessary arrangements for me. The river valley is wider on the other side and was full of tamarisks in full white flower and willows in the newest of leaf, there were almost no slime pits and when we reached the level of the Ghor (that is the Jordan plain) behold, the wilderness had blossomed like the rose. It was the most unforgettable sight—sheets and sheets of varied and exquisite colour—purple, white, yellow, and the brightest blue (this was a bristly sort of Plant which I don't know) and fields of scarlet ranunculus. Nine tenths of them I didn't know, but there was the yellow daisy, the sweet scented mauve wild stock, a great splendid sort of dark purple onion, the white garlic and purple mallow, and higher up a tiny blue iris and red anemones and a dawning pink thing like a linum. We were now joined by a cheerful couple, from Bethlehem, a portly fair man in white with a yellow keffiyeh (that's the thing they wear round their heads bound by ropes of camel hair and falling over the shoulders) and a fair beard, riding a very small donkey, and a thinner and darker man walking. The first one looked like a portly burgher. He asked me if I were a Christian and said he was, praise be to God! I replied piously that it was from God. So we all journeyed on together through the wilderness of flowers and every now and then the silent but amiable Ismael got off to pick me a new variety of plant, while the others enlivened the way by stalking wood pigeons, but the pigeons were far too wily and they let off their breech loaders in vain and stood waist deep in flowers watching the birds flying cheerfully away—with a "May their house be destroyed!" from my Christian friend. A little higher up we came to great patches of corn sown by the Adwan

Bedouins, Arabs' we call them east of Jordan, they being the Arabs par excellence, just as we call their black tents 'houses,' there being no others. Then goodbye to the flowers! Now we saw a group of black tents far away on a little hill covered with white tombs—Tell Kufrein it is called—and here the barley was in ear and, in the midst of the great stretches of it, little watch towers of branches had been built and a man stood on each to drive away birds and people. One was playing a pipe as we passed—it was much more Arcadian than Arcadia. We had now reached the bottom of the foothills, and leaving the Ghor behind us, we began to mount. We crossed a stream flowing down the Wady Hisban (which is Heshbon of the fish pools in the Song of Songs) at a place called Akweh. It was so wet here that we rode on to a place where there were a few thorn trees peopled by immense crowds of resting birds they seize on any little bush for there are so few and the Arabs come and burn the bush and catch and cook the birds all in one! On the top of the first shoulder we came to spreading cornfields. The plan is this—the "Arabs" sow one place this year and go and live somewhere else lest their animals should eat the growing corn. Next year this lies fallow and the fallow of the year before is sown. Over the second shoulder we got on to a stretch of rolling hills and we descended the valley to Ayan Musa, a collection of beautiful springs with in Arab camp pitched above them. I found the loveliest iris I have yet seen—big and sweet-scented and so dark purple that the hanging down petals are almost black. It decorates my tent now. Half an hour later my camp was pitched a little lower down on a lovely grassy plateau. We were soon surrounded by Arabs who sold us a hen and some excellent sour milk, 'laban' it is called. While we bargained the women and children wandered round and ate grass, just like goats. The women are unveiled. They wear a blue cotton gown 6 yards long which is gathered up and bound round their heads and their waists and falls to their feet. Their faces, from the mouth downwards, are tattooed with indigo and their hair hangs down in two long plaits on either side. Our horses and mules were hobbled and groomed. Hanna brought me an excellent cup of tea and at 6 a good dinner consisting of soup made of rice and olive oil (very good!) an Irish stew and raisins from Salt, an offering from Tarif. My camp lies just under Pisgah. Isn't it a joke being able to talk Arabic! We saw a great flock of storks today (the Father of Luck, Tarif calls them) and an eagle. I am now amongst the Bilka Arabs but these particular people are the Ghanimat, which Hanna explains as Father of Flocks.

Wed. 21. Well, I can now show you the reverse side of camping. I woke this morning at dawn to find a strong wind blowing up clouds from the east. At 7 it began to rain but I nevertheless started off for the top of Siagheh, which is Pisgah, sending the others straight to Madeba. I could see from it two of the places from which Balaam is supposed to have attempted the cursing of Israel and behind me lay the third, Nebonaba in Arabic. The Moses legend is a very touching one. I stood on the top of Pisgah and looked out over the wonderful Jordan valley and the blue sea and the barren hills, veiled and beautified by cloud and thought it was one of the most pathetic stories that have ever been told. I then rode to Nebo, the clouds sweeping down behind me and swallowing up the whole Ghor. As I left Nebo it began to stream. Arrived at Madeba about 11:30, wet through. As I rode through the squalid muddy little streets, to my surprise I was greeted in American by a man in a waterproof. He is a photographer, semiprofessional, and his name is Baker and he is very cheerful and nice. He is travelling with a dragoman. I selected my camping ground on the lee-side of the village and Mr. Baker took me to the Latin monastery where he is lodging to keep out of the wet while my camp was being put up. I sent up to Government House, so to speak, to find out what my Mudir's letter had done for me in the matter of to-morrow's escort. The answer came that this Mudir was away but that the Effendi was coming to see me. He appeared, a tall middle-aged Turk; I invited him into my tent with all politeness and offered him cigarettes (you see a bad habit may have its merits!) while Hanna brought him a cup of coffee. But—the soldier was not to be had! There weren't enough. I determined to wait till the coffee and cigarettes had begun to work and turned the conversation to other matters-with as many polite phrases as I could remember. Fortunately I fell upon photography and found that his great desire was to be photographed with his soldiers. I jumped at this and offered to do him and send him copies and so forth and the upshot of it was that for me he would send a soldier tomorrow at dawn. I think it's rather a triumph to have conducted so successful a piece of diplomacy in Arabic, don't you? The wind has dropped and the sky is clear, but it's cold and dampish. I had the brilliant idea of sending into the town for a brazier which was brought me full of charcoal and put into my tent. I have been drying my habit over it. From my camp I look over great rolling plains of cornfields stretching eastwards.

Thursday 22. This has been a most wonderful day. Hanna woke me at 5:30. By 6:30 I had breakfasted and was ready to start. I sent up to know if my soldier was coming. He arrived in a few minutes, a big handsome cheerful Circassian mounted on a strong white horse, and a little before seven we started off. In a dip we came suddenly upon a great encampment of Christians from Madeba and stopped to photograph them and their sheep. They were milking them, the sheep being tied head to head in a serried line of perhaps forty at a time. We went on and on, the ground rising and falling and always the same beautiful grass-no road, we went straight across country. Another big encampment of Christians. The people were most friendly and one man insisted on mounting his little mare and coming with us, just for love. So we all cantered off together, through many flocks and past companies of dignified storks walking about and eating the locusts, till we came to the road, the pilgrim road to Mecca. Road of course it is not: it is about one-eighth of a mile wide and consists of hundreds of parallel tracks trodden out by the immense caravan which passes over it twice a year. We next came to some camps and flocks of the Beni Sakhr, the most redoubted of all the Arab tribes and the last who submitted to the Sultan's rule—"Very much not pleasant" said Tarif—and now we were almost at the foot of the low hills and before us stood the ruins of Mashetta. It is a Persian palace, begun and never finished by Chosroes 1, who overran the country in 611 of our era and planned to have a splendid hunting box in there. Grassy plains which abound in game. The beauty of it all was quite past words. It's a thing One will never forget as long as one lives. At last most reluctantly, we turned back on our four hours' ride home. We hadn't gone more than a few yards before three of the Beni Sakhr came riding towards us, armed to the teeth, black browed and most menacing. When they saw our soldier they threw us the salaam with some disgust, and after a short exchange of politenesses, proceeded on their way—we felt that the interview might have turned differently if we had been unescorted. We rode on straight across the plains putting up several foxes and a little grey wolf. Unfortunately we did not see the white gazelles of which there are said to be many, also jackals and hyenas. Just as we came to the edge of the corn fields, again two of the Beni Sakhr sprang up seemingly out of the ground and came riding towards us. Exactly the same interview took place as before and they retired in disgust. We got in at 5, quite delighted with our day. Don't think I have ever spent such a wonderful day.

Friday 23. Hanna woke me at 6:30 just in time to see a lovely sunrise across the Madeba plains. At 7:30 I went up to the Sarai to see if the Effendi wanted to be photographed but I found him so busy that he had not had time to get into his swell clothes, so we arranged that it was to be for when I came back. The Effendi insisted on sending a soldier with me to Kerak. It is quite unnecessary, but this is the penalty of my distinguished social position and also, I think, of my nationality for the Turks are much afraid of us and he probably thinks I have some project of annexation in my mind! The Circassian—for he is again a Circassian, is good looking and pleasant. They are an agreeable race. I was off at eight. We were on the Roman road all the day-paved on the flat, hewn out of the rock in the gorges. Oh, my camp is too lovely to-night! I am in a great field of yellow daisies by the edge of a rushing stream full of fish and edged with oleanders which are just coming out. (I have a bunch of them in my tent.) On either side rise the great walls of the valley and protect me from every breath of wind. I have just been having a swim in the river under the oleander bushes and Tarif has shot me a partridge for dinner . . . . There is a very pretty white broom flowering. Mashallah! Oh, the nice sound of water and frogs and a little screaming owl!

Saturday 24. Gaisse aus Kerak! Do you know where to find it on the map? it's quite a big place I assure you. . . .

I half climbed up on a little plateau near the river—a Roman guard house. The place was remarkable for possessing two trees—terebinths; they are the only trees I have seen for four days. A little hill called Shikan which I can see from my windows in Jerusalem. Ruins of a Moabite town, supposed to be the capital of King Sihon and therefore very very old. I could see the terraced lines of the old vineyards . . . and the Roman road straight as an arrow, paved and edged with a low double wall, one stone high. There were lots and lots of ruins, villages and towns—what a country it must have been! At 11:30 we reached a place that had been a land mark. Quite suddenly, there opened below us an enormous valley, splitting in the middle to make place for a steep hill almost as high as the plateau on which we were standing, and the top of the hill was set round with great Crusader forts with acres of mud roofs between-it was Kerak. We went down and down and up and up and at 5 o'clock passed under the northern fort and entered the town. . . . to see the English doctor, Johnson is his name, to whom I had letters. . . . After tea Dr. Johnson took me down to my camp where we found an . . . official who had come to find out who I was and whither going. My camp is pitched in the north-west angle of the town. The steep valley goes straight down below me; I am just under the great north-west fort and beyond it I look right down the valley across the Dead Sea to the hills of Judea—and Jerusalem. . . .

Sunday 2 5. I'm going on to Petra! What with giving out that I'm a German (for they are desperately afraid of the English), I have got permission and a soldier from the Governor and this is always difficult and often impossible, and I can't but think that the finger of Providence points southwards! I would telegraph to ask your permission, but there's no telegraph nearer than Jericho! I think a missionary and his wife, Mr. and Mrs. Harding, are coming with me; they are nice people and I shall like to have them. He has gone to see about mules, etc., now, and we are off at dawn. I have Spent a pleasant day here. . . . I photographed and came back to my tent determined to penetrate into the southwest fort which is now used as barracks for the Turkish soldiers. Dr. Johnson had told me I could not possibly get permission, so I asked for none, but took Hanna and walked calmly in, in an affable way, greeted all the soldiers politely and was shown all over! As I was walking about I came to the edge of a deep Pit and Whom should I see at the bottom of it but my poor Madeba friends! It was the prison, there were underground chambers on either side of the pit, but they were all sitting outside to enjoy the sun that struggles down at midday. We greeted each other affectionately. I then went down a long outer stair to a lower floor, so to speak, of the forts, and here again was shown great vaulted rooms cut out of the rock. These are all inhabited by soldiers and mules. I felt I had done a good morning's sight-seeing and came back to my tent where I was presently fetched by a little Turkish girl, the daughter of an Effendi, who told me her mother was sitting down in the shadow of the wall a little below my camp and invited me to come and drink coffee. We went down hand in hand and I found a lot of Turkish women sitting on the ground under a fig tree, so I sat down too and was given coffee and as they all but one talked Arabic, we had a cheerful conversation. We had a glorious view down the valley and across the Dead Sea—It is supposed to be the tomb of Noah and honoured as such. It's a glorious hot night. We bought a lamb to-day for a medijeh, . . . which seems cheap. He was a perfect love and his fate cut me to the heart. I felt if I looked at him any longer I should be like Byron and the goose, so I parted from him hastily—and there were delicious lamb cutlets for supper.

My soldier is again a Circassian-his name is Ayoub—job. He appears to possess the complacent disposition of his namesake, but he has little of the Arabic, his native tongue being of course Turkish. We have a beautiful flowery place for our camp and I have been bathing in the stream. The men have shot partridges, and caught fish in a most ingenious way. They put a basin weighted with some stones in the stream with a little bread in it and cover it with a cloth in which there are a few holes. The fish swim in to eat the bread and can't get out. They are very small. My servants are admirable. My own camp goes like clockwork with never a hitch. Hanna is the prop and stay of it all. The two muleteers are also extremely good servants and we have vowed always to travel together....

We heard that we were still 6 hours from Wady Musa. One of the great difficulties of this journey is that no one knows the distances even approximately and there is no map worth a farthing. Another is that the population is so scant we can't get food! This is starvation camp tonight, we have nothing but rice and bread, a little potted meat. No charcoal and no barley for our horses.

We have been on the Roman road all day. The men are all in good spirits and we are extremely cheerful. It is a good joke, you know....

Thursday 29. Wady Musa—at length we have arrived and it is worth all the long long way. We descended to the village of Wady Musa where we hoped to get provisions, but devil a hen there was, so we despatched a man post haste to the nearest Bedouin camp for a lamb, and as yet—7 p.m.—none has appeared! However, we have got laban and barley and butter so we can support life with our own rice and bread. What the people in Wady Musa live on I can't imagine. They hadn't so much as milk. These things settled, we rode on and soon got into the entrance of the defile which leads to Petra. The Bab es Sik is a passage about half a mile long and in places not more than 8 ft. wide; the rocks rise on either side straight up 100 ft. or so, they are sandstone Of the most exquisite red and sometimes almost arch overhead. The stream runs between, filling all the path, though it used to flow through conduits, and the road was paved; oleanders grew along the stream and here and there a sheaf of ivy hung down over the red rock. We went on in ecstasies until suddenly between the narrow opening of the rocks, we saw the most beautiful sight I have ever seen. Imagine a temple cut out of the solid rock, the charming facade supported on great Corinthian columns standing clear., soaring upwards to the very top of the cliff in the most exquisite proportions and carved with groups Of figures almost as fresh as when the chisel left them all this in the rose red rock., with the sun just touching it and making it look almost transparent. As we went on the gorge widened, on either side the cliffs were cut out into rock tombs of every shape and adorned in every manner, some standing, columned, in the rock, some clear with a pointed roof, some elaborate, some simple, some capped with pointed pyramids, many adorned with a curious form of stair high up over the doorway..... The gorge opened and brought us out into a kind of square between the cliffs with a rude cut theatre in it and tombs on every side. We went on and got into a great open place the cliffs widening out far on every side and leaving this kind of amphitheatre strewn over with mounds of ruins. And here we camped under a row of the most elaborate tombs, three stories of pillars and cornices and the whole topped by a great funeral urn. They are extremely rococo, just like the kind of thing you see in a Venetian church above a seventeenth century Doge leaning on his elbow, but time has worn them and weather has stained the rock with exquisite colours—and, in short, I never liked Bernini so well!. . . . It is like a fairy tale city, all pink and wonderful. The great paved roads stretch up to a ruined arch and vanish; a solid wall springs up some 6ft. 'A rose red city half as old as Time'—I wish the lamb had come!

Friday, 30. I have had a busy day. An hour before dawn Ayoub and I started off riding, with a shepherd to guide us, to the top of Mount Hot—you realise that no daughter of yours could be content to sit quietly at the bottom of a mountain when there was one handy!—we rode up nearly to the top and then dismounted and climbed to the highest summit on which stands, whose tomb do you think! Aaron's! I have never seen anything like these gorges; the cliffs rise for 1000 ft. on either side, broken into the most incredible shapes and coloured!—red, yellow, blue, white, great patterns over them more lovely than any mosaic. I came back to my tents and found we had bought fifty eggs, some figs and a sheep! but unfortunately the sheep has grown rather old in his long journey to us.

Saturday 31—We left Petra at 7 this morning with great regret. It was looking too exquisite and I longed for another day, but the Hardings were bound to be back. I certainly underestimated the length of the entrance gorge.

Saturday, April 1. We were Off at 7 this morning and rode two and a half hours along our former road across the wide stretching uplands. The monotony was broken by keeping a watch for the Roman milestones. We were going very slowly so as to keep in touch with the mules and we passed one every quarter of an hour the whole way. The paved road was often very well preserved. It was blazing hot. We lunched at the opening of the usual broad shallow valley where there was a very dirty pool at which the mules watered, and one tiny thorn bush under the shade of which we tried to sit, but as it was 1 ft.there was not much shade to be had. In all this country there is practically no water, there are a few cisterns scattered over the hills and, I should think, emptied before the middle of the summer, and where we are camping a couple of wells, and that's absolutely all! I nearly went to sleep on my horse this morning, but was wakened up by hearing Ayoub relating to me tales of Ibn Rashid. One gets so accustomed to it all that one ceases to be bored. We set off again at 12 and Ayoub sighted some Arabs on a hill top so he and I and Hanna and Tarif left the others and rode up and over the hill and found a lot of Arabs watering their flocks at a 'bit' (that's a cistern). It was a very pretty sight. They brought the water up in skins and poured it into the stone troughs all round and the sheep and goats drank thirstily. We followed the Roman road, which runs straight over the tops of the hills. . . . our camping place down in the valley at 2:30. It is called Towaneh and was once a big town, the ruins of it stretch up on either side of the valley, but there is nothing now but a cluster of black tents a few hundred yards below us. I paid a call on some Arab ladies and watched them making a sort of sour cream cheese in a cauldron over their fire. They gave me some when it was done, we all ate it, with our fingers, and then they made me coffee, and we drank it out of the same cup, and it was quite good. It was very difficult to understand them for their vocabulary is perfectly different from mine; however, we got along by keeping to simple subjects! These people are gipsies, some of them have just been dancing for me, round my camp fire. It was quite dark, with a tiny new moon, the fire of dry thorns flickered upfaded and flickered again and showed the circle of men crouching on the ground, their black and white cloaks wrapped round them and the woman in the middle dancing. She looked as though she had stepped out of an Egyptian fresco. She wore a long red gown bound round her waist with a dark blue cloth, and falling open in front to show a redder petticoat below. Round her forehead was another dark blue cloth bound tightly and falling in long ends down her back, her chin was covered by a white cloth drawn up round her ears and falling in folds to her waist and her lower lips tattooed with indigo! Her feet, in red leather shoes, scarcely moved but all her body danced and she swept a red handkerchief she held in one hand, round her head, and clasped her hands together in front of her impassive face. The men played a drum and a discordant fife and sang a monotonous song and clapped their hands and gradually she came nearer and nearer to me, twisting her slender body till she dropped down on the heap of brushwood at my feet, and kneeling, her body still danced and her arms swayed and twisted round the mask like face. She got up, and retreated again slowly, with downcast eyes, invoking blessings upon me at intervals, till at last I called her and gave her a couple of besklihs. Near Damascus is their home, and they are going back there from Mecca where they have been near the Prophet (thanks be to God!) and they have seen the holy city (God made it!) and they hope to reach Damascus in safety (if God please!). They talked Arabic to me, but to each other the gipsy tongue which sounded more like Turkish than anything else.

Monday 2. We left this morning at 7. It was very hot, a strong baking wind from the south and a heavy hot mist, most unpleasant. Through this we rode for two hours or more straight on up the side of the valley. The morning's amusement was again the milestones which are wonderfully well preserved, many of them still standing upright in groups of three or four. I have counted as many as eight in one place—I don't know why this is, unless every succeeding emperor who mended the road put up a few milestones of his own. The inscriptions are always visible, but would generally be very difficult to decipher, the letters being much worn. Besides which a mass of Arab tribe marks have been cut on top of them. Many of them, however, have been read by the learned. We went to a tiny village called Aineh where there is a lovely spring and a watermill. We were still six hours from Kerak and Ali black in the face from the heat, so that I thought he was going to have a sunstroke. The Hardings were obliged to go on, but I decided to stay here. They have been very nice. My camp is pitched half way up the hill, with the head of the spring at my door and in front, deep corn fields where the barley is standing in the ear and the storks walking solemnly up to their necks in green. There has been an immense flock of them flying and settling on the hillside, and when I took a stroll I soon found what was engaging the attention of the Father of Luck. The ground was hopping with locusts; on some of the slopes they have eaten every leaf and they are making their way down to the corn. I have just been watching my people make bread. Flour was fortunately to be got from the mill below us; they set two logs alight and when they had got enough ashes they made an immense cake, 2 ft. across and half an inch thick, of flour and water and covered it over with hot ashes. After a quarter of an hour it had to be turned and recovered and the result is most delicious eaten hot; it becomes rather wooden when it is cold. The flour is very coarse, almost like oatmeal. These are the Moments when my camp is at its best—half a dozen ragged onlookers were sitting round in the circle of flickering light and a tiny moon overhead. . . .

One of my muleteers, Muhammad, is a Druze. If all his sect are like him, they must be a charming race. He is a great big handsome creature, gentle and quiet and extremely abstemious. He eats nothing but rice `and bread and figs. it makes me the more keen to go to the Hauran which is the chief centre of then, and I want very much to take these two muleteers with me: they are very capable and obliging, and Muhammad would be interesting to have in a Druze country. One mayn't know or see anything of their religious observances, but he has been telling me a great deal about their life and customs. He says nearly all the people in the Lebanon are Druzes. He himself comes from Beyrout, where he lives next door to Ali. They both talk with the pretty, soft, sing-song accent of the Lebanon. I have a good variety of accents with me for Tarif has the Bedouin and Hanna the real cockney of Jerusalem. They appeal to me sometimes to know which is right. I never was so sunburnt in my life; I'm a rich red brown, not at all becoming! in spite of the Quangle Wangle hat you sent me.

Friday 6. (Jericho again). Madeba, in proportion to its size, must have the largest number of mosquitoes and fleas of any inhabited spot on the globe. Chiefly owing to the mosquitoes, my night was rather a restless one, it also rained a great deal and rain makes an unconscionable noise on a tent, besides the fact is I was troubled to think of my poor people outside. There was still a little rain when I got up at 5, but the clouds lifted and we had no more. I broke up my camp here, and rode myself into Jericho with Hanna. We came down the same road that we had come up-but-the Ghor had withered. In one little fortnight the sun had eaten up everything but the tall dry daisy stalks. It was almost impossible to believe that it had been so lovely so short a time ago. Jericho doesn't look at all nice, all burnt up and withered.

Our plans are these: the Rosens and I start off on Monday fortnight, the 23rd, and go up together to the Hauran. It will take us about a fortnight. They come home and I go straight up to Damascus, a couple of days or so, and so perhaps across to Palmyra, and the rest as before, reaching Jerusalem again about the end of May.

To her sister.
JERUSALEM, April 9th, 1900.

DEAREST ELSA, It is so amusing to have a letter with photographs in it. I quite understand your impressions of Florence and Venice. To this day I feel more inside Florence, myself, but I went to Venice knowing the East and knowing a good deal of Italy and for those reasons I think I found it easier to become a part of it. Also, I was there a month, nearly, you must remember. But it is very strange—'unheirnlich', some silly German said and it's not as silly as it sounds at first. It's a heavenly feeling when suddenly the thing jumps at you and you know you understand. I daresay you don't, but it doesn't matter, the feeling is there. I don't think you get it out of books a bit, though books help to strengthen it, but you certainly get it out of seeing more and more, even of quite different things. The more you see, the more everything falls into a kind of rough an ready perspective, and when you come to a new thing, you haven't so much difficulty in placing it and fitting it into the rest. I'm awfully glad you love the beginnings of things—so do I, most thoroughly, and unless one does, I don't believe one can get as much pleasure out of the ends. The early Florentines are too wonderful—there's such a feeling for beauty even in the woodenest of them, and they are so earnest, bless them, that they carry one with them—well, very nearly up into Paradise and down into Hell! Now, rejoice with me! my travel photographs are all right. I've only seen the negatives, but they are lovely and you shall have a Monthly Cousin article, illustrated, on Petra. I was dreadfully nervous about them, for when it was so hot that the chocolate melted in the canteen, I thought the gelatine might have melted in the camera. I have gone into summer clothes, which always feels very festive, don't you think? Tell the ditty Moll, talking of clothes, that I've got a little present for her. It's a complete Bethlehem costume, with the high hat and the veil and everything. She can wear it at the next fancy dress ball if she likes. It was made for her by a dear little Bethlehem woman who comes to the Consulate to do the washing.

CHAPTER VI
1900

DESERT EXCURSIONS FROM JERUSALEM

To H.B.
JERUSALEM, April 13th, 1900.

To-morrow the Rosens and I are going off after lunch to Neby Musa, where we are to camp for 2 nights. I think it will be immensely amusing. Oh, Father dearest, don't I have a fine time! I'm only overcome by the sense of how much better it is than I deserve! . . .

To H.B.
JERUSALEM, Sunday, 22nd April, 1900.

* * *but perhaps you haven't had time to read it yet! I have had the most madly rushing days since I wrote last. My acquaintance here now comprises a set of the ruggedest, wildest looking Dervishes! but in spite of their appearance they are quite human and eager to stop and have a chat when we meet in the bazaar. I went to call on my teacher in the afternoon and found his pretty wife and four charming children all expecting me. They gave me odd (and nasty) things to eat and a narghileh to smoke, which I hated, but to my relief found that with the best of good will I couldn't keep it alight, so that I didn't have much of it. Saturday was the great day here, the day of the annual miracle of the Holy Fire. Charlotte and I went off to the Russian Consulate, for we were to go to the Russian balcony to see the ceremony in the Church of the Holy Sepulchre. The church was packed, every soul having bunches of candles in his hand to receive the Holy Fire. There was a moment of breathless interest—you know the murmur of a great crowd which is waiting for something to happen; it was intoxicating, I never felt so excited in my life. Suddenly the sound of the crowd rose into a deafening roar and I saw a man running from the corner of the sepulchre with a blazing torch held high over his head. The crowd parted before him, the flying figure and the flaming light disappeared into the dark recesses of the church-he had been the first to receive the heaven-sent fire. Then followed a most extraordinary scene. On either side of the sepulchre the people fought like wild beasts to get to the fires for there were two issuing from the two windows of the sepulchre, one for the Greeks and one for the Armenians. In an instant the fire leapt to the very roof; it was as though one flame had breathed over the whole mass of men and women. Every soul was bearing a light, torch or candle or bunch of tapers—behind us in the Greek church, which is almost dark, there was nothing but a blaze of lights from floor to dome, and the people were washing their faces in the fire. How they are not burnt to death is a real miracle. . . . Then came a man from the sepulchre with a whip, bursting through the crowd, and behind him the Patriarch in his mitre holding two great torches over his head and two priests holding up his arms, and they ran, like men carrying some great tidings, through the narrow Passage which had been cleared for them and which closed up behind them like water, and passed below us and up the Greek church to light the candles on the High Altar. I have a vision of looking up into the huge dome and seeing high high up, an open window with men standing in it, and their torches flaming between the bright sun and the dense smoke. Well, I can scarcely tell you about it sensibly, for as I write about it, I am overcome by the horrible thrill of it.

Monday, April 30th. DERAA. 1900. This morning we none of us had a very long way before us so I didn't get up till 6:30, which was most pleasant. When i looked out of my tent door, there was Mount Hermon gleaming all Its snows, right in front of me. It was so beautiful I had the greatest difficulty in not turning my face northwards and rushing straight for it, but the Druze mountains were standing mistily on the eastern horizon and I must try for them first. We breakfasted, as usual, in front of the Rosens' tent, with Hermon occupying the fourth place at our table, and at 8:30 we very sadly parted and I went east and they west. I have two muleteers, Muhammad and Yakoub, and Hanna. I rode for three hours over the great Hauran plain, through streets of corn. There were villages scattered about and the people looked prosperous. There were also tracts of country ploughed and lying fallow for next year's crops. They practically never manure, so that they can't grow barley two years running. The maps mark this country as belonging to the Anazeh, a great tribe which stretches to the Euphrates, but they appear to have withdrawn their black tents further eastward, probably because of the encroaching Turkish government. After three hours' ride we came to a mud and stone built village standing upon a little hill, with a mosque on top. (By the way, it was very curious yesterday returning to the Arab villages after the neat Circassian streets and courtyards.) The people were very busy cutting grass and bringing it home on the backs of camels, laden string after string of them. In these villages they use nothing but camels, with a little donkey to lead the string. There was a strong, cool west wind, but the sun was blazing hot, so hot that one had to put on a coat to keep it out. I wear a big white keffieh bound over my hat and wound round me so that only my eyes show, and they are partly hidden by a blue veil; but the chief comfort of this journey is my masculine saddle, both to me and to my horse. Never, never again will I travel on anything else; I haven't known real ease in riding till now. Till I speak the people always think I'm a man and address me as Effendim! You mustn't think I haven't got a most elegant and decent divided skirt, however, but as all men wear skirts of sorts too, that doesn't serve to distinguish me. Mount Hermon was a great joy all along the road; it looked now like a white cloud hanging in mid air. About two we entered Deraa, built of black volcanic stone it is, all bare and dusty, with a black ruined tower. The mules were behind; Hanna and I rode down to the well at the east of the town and sat there waiting for half an hour in the dust and the sun, watching the countless string of camels bringing in the corn which is ripe here. They don't reap it, but pluck it up by the roots. At last we rode back to see what the mules were doing and found that they had arrived, and that my tents were pitched on a hill by some ruined Roman baths, in sight of Hermon and the Jebel Druze. You wouldn't believe how soon the most unpromising spot changes into a comfy, home-like place as soon as one's tents are up and one's horses tethered. I rested and had tea, and then made an attempt to see an extraordinary underground town there is here, and which is supposed to belong to the times of Og the king of Bashan. But I could not get any one who knew the way, and after grubbing about under the earth for an hour, amongst the remains of hyenas' meals, I came away disgusted.

BOSRAH, Wednesday, May 2nd. I am deep in intrigues ! I will tell you all from the beginning. We set off with a soldier for guide across the corn-covered plains; here and there a black village stood out from the green and the ground was covered with black porous stone. The volcanic peaks of the Jebel Druze lay ahead of us eastwards all day. At 11 I got to the first really interesting village, jizeh, and here I saw the building of this country. You must understand that the peculiarities of it depend on the faft that there was (and is) no wood at all, and when the Romans made a great colony here in the first century, about, they built entirely with stone—the rafters are long bits of stone stretched across from arch to arch over the rooms, the doors are solid blocks of stone with charming patterns carved on them; the windows even are stone perforated with holes and carved between the holes. All this in black basalt; it is curious to see. There was one perfect house in jizeh, small and four-square, with a cornice running round near the top On the outside, but it had no window at all. There was another, the beautiful walls of which were standing, and the stone roof, but the original door and windows were gone. It was turned into a mosque. Bosrah stood up, black and imposing, before us for miles before we arrived, a mass of columns and triumphal arches with the castle dominating the whole. I went up the square tower of the minaret and looked out over the town-columns and black square towers over every ruined church and mosque, and the big castle and the countless masses of fallen stone. I had been joined by a cheerful, handsome person, the Mamur (the Sultan's land agent) who climbed with me in and out of the churches and the fallen walls and the ruined houses. Such a spectacle of past magnificence and present squalor it would be difficult to conceive. There were inscriptions everywhere, Latin, Greek, Cufic and Arabic, built into the walls of the Fellahin houses, topsy turvy, together with the perforated slabs that were once windows, and bits of columns and capitals of pillars. After two hours of this I began to feel light-headed with fatigue and hunger. At last he took me to the top of the castle to see the view of the town and introduced me to the head of the soldiers, who produced chairs and coffee on his roof-top, and subsequently glasses of arrack and water in his room below. The Mamur is a Beyrouti and talks Arabic, but the other is a pure Turk, and our common tongue is French—most inadequate on his side. At length I induced them to let me go, and retired to my tents below the castle. I found the Mudir (Governor of the town) waiting for me, a handsome, dignified Arab, much looked down on by the whipper-snapper Turkish officials. We exchanged polite greetings and I retired to my dinner and my bed. This morning the Mamur appeared at eight to take me to a ruined village to the north. I went first to see the Mudir, whom I found sitting in his arched and shaded courtyard. He gave me coffee and negotiations began. "Where was I going?" "To Damascus." "God has made it! there is a fine road to the west with such and such places in it, very beautiful ruins." "Please God I shall see them! but I wish first to look upon Salkhad." (This is in the heart of the Druze country, where they don't want me to go) "Salkhad! there is nothing there at all, and the road is very dangerous. It cannot happen." "There has come a telegram from Damascus to say the Mutussarif fears for the safety of your presence." (This isn't true) "English women are never afraid." (This also isn't true!) "I wish to look upon the ruins." And so on and so off, till finally I told him I was going nowhere to-day and he said he would come and see me later. We parted, he saying "You have honoured me!" and I "God forbid!!" and I rode off with the Mamur to a village Khutbet, crossing many beautiful Roman bridges on the Way.-There was nothing of interest there) and we turned east to Jemurrin, where there are some very beautiful ruined houses. They used no mortar, but the walls are built in a most wonderful way, the stones being often notched out and fitted into one another. We got back about 11. I lunched, After which my two Turkish friends came to call, but fortunately did not stay long. While they were with me, a Druze Sheikh was hanging round my tent, but I could not speak to him under the eyes of the officials. A Bedouin has also been to ask if I want to go east, but I prefer to put myself under the protection of the Druzes. It's awfully amusing, and my servants fully enter into the fun of the thing. If only I Could put myself into communication with the Druzes, all Would be Well. If not, I shall try starting very early to-morrow, And making a dash for them; once into their country I'll move quickly and it will be difficult for the Turks to catch me, for they are horribly afraid of the Druzes. I may fail—God is He who knows! I gather that the two Turks would put nothing In my Way to stop me out of jealousy of the Mudir, who is the local authority. But one can't never tell how much they Say is true, and I keep my own counsel as far as possible. & yet I haven't let on that the places I want really to go to are not Salkhad at all but some ruined towns further north, but they know. There are no Druzes living in Bosrah. I took a walk by myself this afternoon. Walking about Bosrah Is like trying to walk about a room on the furniture only. The game is never to get off the house-tops and one generally succeeds. After tea the Mamur came to fetch me and took me up to the military gentleman's room in the castle. They both had their eyes nicely blacked with kohl, but otherwise their toilette was incomplete. The Rais el Askar was being shaved while I sat and drank coffee. We then took a walk about the town which I lengthened out till sunset, because I wanted to miss the Mudir's visit; but he did not come, and I hope this may mean that he doesn't want to know my movements officially. I hope so. Meantime, we all feel like conspirators.

JEBEL DRUZE,
Thursday, May 3rd.

I've slipped through their fingers, and as yet I can scarcely believe in my good fortune. The story begins last night; you must hear it all. I dined early and as I was sitting reading in my tent, I heard the voice of the Mudir. I blew out my light and when Hanna came to tell me of his coming, I sent him a message that I was very tired and had gone to bed. I heard this conversation: Hanna "The lady has been awake since the rising of the sun—all day she has walked and ridden, now she sleeps." Mudir. "Does she march to-morrow?" Hanna. "I couldn't possibly say, Effendim." Mudir, "Tell her she must let me know before she goes anywhere." Hanna. "At your pleasure, Effendim." And he left, but not without having assured me that he meant to stop me. I hastily re-arranged my plans. He knew I was going to Salkhad and when he found that I had flown, he would send after me along that road as far as he dared; I decided, therefore, to strike for a place further north, Areh, where I saw in Murray that a powerful Druze sheikh lived. Moreover the road lay past jemurrin, which I knew, and whither I could find my way. Providence watched over me, as you will see, in this resolution. I told my servants. Muhammad tried to dissuade me, saying that if I told the Mudir I was going to Suweidah, north of Areh, he would raise no difficulties as there were Turkish soldiers there; but I knew better, and besides, what was the good of being passed from the hands of one Turkish official to another? I afterwards found out that Muhammad, poor dear! was terrified out of his life and was trying all he knew to prevent my going. I went to bed, but what with excitement and dogs, I didn't sleep much. At two Hanna called me and I got up into the shivering night. By three I was ready, and the packing up began under the stars. It was bitter cold—one felt it after the heat of the days and in our thin summer clothes. I walked backwards and forwards and prayed Heaven that no soldier would look over the castle wall, see our lantern, and come to enquire what was happening. Fortunately the Mudir lived inside the town. The stars began to pale and that darkest moment of the night, when the east whitens, set in. At 4 we were off. It was a ticklish business finding our way in the dark round the walls to the east, I didn't know this bit of the road, having only seen the beginning and the end of it. The houses seemed to finger out towards us, and suddenly we would find ourselves heading inwards and were obliged to retrace our steps. It took us near an hour, but at last we were past the N.E. corner and I hit on the jemurrin road. We had met only two men driving out their cows. By this time the little band of cloud in the east had turned pink; half an hour later it was gold and we saw the black ruins of jemurrin in front of us. The sun rose just as we had passed them. Now we had to find our way by my excellent map; it was not difficult for we had the Roman road for our guide, but oh! it seemed long to the first Druze village. Muhammad was trembling lest he should see either a Druze or a soldier. I feared the latter only, but much. I was borne up by the extraordinary beauty of Hermon, with the dawn touching its snows. The road rose gradually; we could see nothing ahead but the top Of the west slope of corn, and a black village where I hoped we should find Druzes, but which turned out to be only a ruin—Deir Zubier was its disappointing name. There was a man among the corn, however, with the white turban and black keffiyeh of the Druze and I greeted him thus (it is the right form) "Peace be upon you! oh, son of my uncle!" He put us into the path, which we had missed. At length we came to the top of the last slope and saw in front of us a rolling fertile, watered country, scattered over with little volcanic hills, and behind it, higher hills and the pointed peak of the Kulieb rising over all-the Little Heart, the highest of the Jebel Druze. In front of us, not half a mile away was the tiny village of Miyemir. I hurried on. At the foot of the hill on which it lay was a pool and fig trees near by. The women were filling their earthenware jars at the water, Druze women in long blue and red robes and white muslin veils drawn over their heads and round their faces, and by the water stood the most beautiful boy of 19 or 20. I dismounted to water my horse; the boy (his name is Saif ed Din, the Sword of the Faith) came up to me, took my hands and kissed me on both cheeks, rather to my surprise. Several other men and boys came up and shook hands with me; they were all more or less beautiful, and so are the women, when you can see their faces. Their eyes look enormous, blacked with kohl, men and women alike; they are dark, straight browed, straight shouldered, with an alert and gentle air of intelligence which is extraordinarily attractive. I asked Saif ed Din if he would show us the way to Areh, but he said he was busy and it was only half an hour off, so we rode on. But we hadn't gone a quarter of a mile before he repented and came running after us to offer his services, touching his heart and his forehead in token of obedience, So we went on through meadows, cornfields and vineyards in this pleasant country of little hills, and the muleteers began to sing and the kindly white turbaned people working in the vineyards stopped to salute as we passed, and I laughed for joy all the way at the thought of the Mudir and the Turks. And so about 8:30 we reached Areh. Some persons of apparent importance were standing by their house doors at the bottom of the hill, so I rode up and gave them the salaam. They took me by both hands and begged me to alight and drink coffee with them. This was just what I wanted, for I needed information. We walked hand in hand, Druze fashion, with our little fingers clasped, not our hands, to the nearest houses. As I entered they said "Are you German?" and when I told them I was English they nearly fell on my neck—you need no other introduction here. With many Mashallahs! they piled all their cushions on to a raised seat for me, brought a stool for my feet and water for me to wash my hands, and then sat round in a circle on the clean matted floor making coffee for me. The nicest of them all, Hamma Hamid, sat by me and laid his hand on my shoulder when he talked to me. I told them all my tale and how I escaped from the government and come to them, interrupted by many interjections of welcome and assurance that there was no government here (Turks, that means), and that I was safe with them and might go where I pleased. The sense of comfort and safety and confidence and of being with straight speaking people, was more delightful than I can tell you. They asked about the war and knew the names of all the towns and generals and were very sympathetic about Maurice—were cultivated, civilised human beings. The coffee finished (very good it was) I asked if I could see the Sheikh. "Sheikh!" said they, "Yahya Beg is the head of all the Druzes in the land, of course you must visit him." So we went off to the top of the little hill on which stands the Beg's verandahed house, Hammad and I finger in finger, and as we went he told me that the Beg had been five years in prison in Damascus and had just been let out, three weeks ago, and warned me that I must treat him with great respect. I said my Arabic and not my feelings would be at fault, and indeed I would defy any one not to treat Yahya Beg with respect. He is the most perfect type of the Grand Seigneur, a great big man (40 to 50, I suppose) very handsome and with the most exquisite manners. We walked straight into his reception room, where he was sitting on a carpet with six or eight others eating out of a big plate. He beckoned me into the circle, and I ate too, using the thin slabs of bread for spoon and fork. The food was laban, and an excellent mixture of beans and meat. I should have liked to have eaten much more of it, but the Beg had finished and I was afraid it wouldn't be polite. The plate was removed and he piled up his cushions for me on the floor and I waited till he sat down, very politely, for he's a king, you understand, and a very good kink too, though his kingdom doesn't happen to be a large one. Then I had to tell my tale over again and the Beg shut his big eyes and bowed his handsome head from time to time, murmuring "Daghy, daghy"—it is true—as I spoke. I told him all I wanted to see and that I didn't want to see Suweidah because of the Turks in it—there's a telegraph too, greatest danger of all—and he was most sympathetic and arranged all my travels for me and told me to take Saif ed Din with me and to count on his protection wherever I went. So we drank coffee and then someone suggested I should photograph the Beg (to my great delight) and I posed him in his verandah and very splendid he looked. So we parted, and I walked down to a delicious water meadow where I found my horses and mules grazing and set off with Saif ed Din and another gentleman called Aly, whose functions I don't rightly know, but who seems an agreeable travelling companion. Saif ed Din, walking along briskly while I rode, his embroidered skirts neatly buttoned up over a white petticoat. On the way we met a troop of shining ones, all in their best, carrying guns and lances. They were going to congratulate the Beg on his safe return. They stopped to greet me and bid me every kind of welcome—it's a pleasant change after being with people whose one idea is to tell you not to go anywhere! We went gradually upwards towards the second ridge of hills, Saif ed Din showing me the plain where the great battle was fought, four years ago; they say 500 Druzes fell and 1400 Turks. At first we went through corn and meadows, then up a stony ground with grass between the stones. The country is thinly peopled, but there are Bedouins scattered about, who come in with their flocks for the pasturage and pay rent in money and camels. The Druzes use them as servants. The ruined sites are countless. On the southernmost corner of the ridge, finely situated, is the village of Habran, where I now am. My camp is pitched by a big pond, in a meadow, with evergreen oaks growing about in it and the black village behind. Kulieb stands over me to the north—dear Little Heart! I did not dare to think last night that I should ever be so near it. We got into camp at 12:30. I washed and lunched and slept, and at four went off with Saif ed Din to explore. The village is full of the old stone houses, more or less ruined and built up again. The best house I saw, with its arches inside and stone rafters and corbels supporting them, is now used as the Druze church—Khelweh, they call it. The village is beautifully clean, full of fruit trees, and hay drying on the flat roofs. The women were coming down to the various ponds on all sides with their jars for water on their heads. The Sheikh of the village took me to his house, spread some carpets and cushions outside and made me coffee—a lengthy process, as you begin from the beginning, roast and pound it. I didn't mind, however, as I lay on my cushions talking to all the pleasant friendly people and watching the light fade on Kuleib. since dinner I have been swimming in the pond—it's almost a lake and quite deep. The women are very shy; they don't unveil even to me, but they let me photograph them. They appear to spend most of their leisure time mending their mud roofs, but the men treat them with great respect and affection even when they are muddy up to their elbows. Isn't this all too wonderful? I'm so delighted with it! But I began my day at 2, so good night. The Sheikh of the village invited me to dinner, but I refused on the plea of fatigue. To-day when I was having my first coffee party in Areh, Hammad asked me to tell them something out of the Bible. I translated for them "Love thy neighbour as thyself," which seemed a good all round maxim, and they were much pleased with it.

Friday, 4th. After breakfast this morning, I found the good Sheikh had been waiting round my tents since dawn to take me to his house. I went first to a Mazar close to my tent—a Mazar is generally the tomb of a saint or a sheikh. It was a very well Preserved example of the old type of house building—stone doors and rafters, etc. Nusr ed Din (this is his name, by the Way, not Saif ed Din, as Hanna told me) kissed the threshold and the door posts and all the arches and the corners of the tomb Most devoutly. I then went up to the Sheikh's house and was given a most excellent breakfast—I wished I hadn't eaten before as I should have liked to have breakfasted on it. It consisted of 10 or 12 leaves of their delicious thin bread, a bowl of milk with sugar and a little brown meal in it, and a bowl of laban. Coffee began and ended the meal. It was eight before I was off. Its name was Ayun. I went there and was well rewarded, for in the first place it was a ruined Roman village, which had apparently never been re-inhabited, and one could therefore trace the exact shape and style of the houses; and in the second, there was a Mazar in it and a troop of women and children from a neighbouring village were visiting it, all dressed in their best and the boys carrying branches of briar and long stalks of flowering hemlock. Their religion is most mysterious. They seem to think all saints are equally worshipable except Muhammad, who they say is no saint at all. They have prayers every night, but especially on Friday night. They are divided into two kinds, Initiated and the Uninitiated, but the only difference between them seems to be that the Initiated don't smoke—it would seem an odd religious distinction! They have sacred books which are only read by the appointed elders. From Ayun we rode over a little rise which brought us out face to face with Salkhad. A most wonderful place. A great castle built in, and rising out of, the cone of a volcano. The outside is almost perfect, old foundations (of dateless antiquity they say; it's one of the places that is mentioned as belonging to Og, King of Bashan), then probably Roman work, and all worked over by Saracens. The Castle of Salkhad is the last outpost of the hills which here drop away into a few volcanic tells—

and then the desert till the Euphrates. There are one or two inhabited villages at the foot of the hills and a few ruins on the tells, and after that no one knows anything about it and it's white on the map. But from my feet, almost, and running in a straight line south east as far as the eye could see was the track of a Roman road—and the other end of it is at Bagdad. I wished the Mudir could have seen me! The Arabs were pasturing enormous flocks of camels. I found my camp pitched and surrounded by some hundred people, amongst whom two little sons of the Sheikh—he is a nephew of Yahya Beg's, who welcomed me with the most exquisite politeness. After I had had tea and washed—by dint of shutting my tent door—I came out to find two little daughters of the Sheikh waiting for me and we Went off hand in hand to their house, with all the population of the town following me. The Sheikh was not there, but a lot of women and children received me and we sat in an open verandah till I couldn't stand the crowd any longer, when one of the boys took me into an inner room and I sat and drank coffee. The Sheikh's children, boys and girls, are most beautiful creatures, and there were some lovely girls amongst the coffee party. I asked them if they ever unveiled. They said never, not even when they are alone or when they go to bed! There came a lot of Christians to see me; there are many in this country; they come to escape from the oppression of the Turks.

Saturday, 5th. A Christian lady sent me a delicious dish for breakfast— some flat thin bread with cream rolled up in it, slightly salted.

. . . . There is a Mazar outside the town. I went in and found a charming room with a row of columns supporting the dome roof and lots of little children, sitting on the floor, to whom the schoolmaster was teaching reading. The Mazar itself Was an inner domed chamber with a tomb in it. I was off at 7:30 with Nusr ed Din. The barley was most beautiful, but alas! lots of locusts eating it. He begged me to come a little out of the route to Sehweh and honour his mother by drinking coffee with her. It was a charming village, new, but built with old materials brought from El Kafr on the usual volcanic tell. Corn, figs, vines and such a look of prosperity. I sat under a Mulberry tree with Nusr ed Din's family, nice handsome People, and ate fried eggs and bread and drank coffee and milk the whole village crowding round. When one expostulates they say: "We wish to gaze upon you, because you have honoured us." The Sheikh is Nusr ed Din's uncle. I visited him and his wife and tried to please, apparently with success.

I also bought from the wife of Nusr ed Din's cousin a Druze woman's robe, which I intend to present to Elsa. It is very pretty and extremely interesting, for the costume has died out in all places but these hills. An hour's ride up a hill side, prettily wooded with stunted oak and hawthorn in full flower, brought us to El Kafr, where I found my tent pitched. I am just at the foot of Kuleib, but, contrary to my custom, I have not gone up it, because it is Sirocco which makes one feel as if one were made of blotting paper and also spreads a thick, hot mist over the world. Directly I arrived, the Sheikh's son and some other persons of importance came to see me. They were a group of the most beautiful people you would wish to see. Their average height was about 6 ft. 1 in. and their average looks were as though you mixed up Hugo and you, Father.

At 4 I sallied out with Ali, whose native town it is. I don't need him really—it's an absurd luxury to have two guides, but when I tell him to go he replies that he is my brother and must accompany me everywhere—not without recompense, of course! I returned the call of the Sheikh's son and while I was drinking coffee the old Sheikh arrived. He had been to see Yahya Beg, and half expected me because the Beg had asked after me in the following terms: "Have you seen a queen travelling, a consuless?" They offered me a sheep, but I refused it. I hope I did right; one never knows and I'm terribly afraid of committing solecisms. I feel it would be too silly, under these exceptional conditions, not to see all I can in a country which so few people have seen. It's extraordinarily enjoyable too. They took me to see the Khelweh, which was bigger and better than any I have yet seen. It was divided into two parts by a thin black curtain, one being the Harem for the women. The straw objects are for putting the holy books on. . . . There came a gentleman with a poem in Arabic which he had composed in my honour. I said I didn't know the custom in his country, but in mine, if anyone wrote a poem about me, I should certainly give him a shilling. He said "Yes, it would happen." I gave him a quarter of a medjideh, and he presented me with a copy of the poem, so we were both pleased. . . . I have told them all that I am going to bring you, Father, here next year, and they are much delighted and bid you "relationship and ease."

Sunday, 6th. I sent my mules straight to Busan this morning, with my brother Ali, and rode with Hanna and Nusr ed Din S.E. to a place called Salah. We passed under the foot of Kuleib, where there were delicious pastures, after which we got out on to a very desolate country, stony and quite uncultivated. There is however, water and plenty of grass, and the Arabs pasture their camels here. It seems to extend down all this E. watershed to the desert. Last night was so warm after the Sirocco east wind, that I slept with no blankets; to-day the wind has changed to the W. and is blowing strong and cold. It brought up a lot of cloud with it; Kuleib was wrapped in mists when I got up and there has been light cloud all day and cold all day. I am now wrapped in all my cloaks; it's most odd to be cold

Monday, 7th. When you are travelling in hot countries, the primary rule is always to bring your winter clothes. I have had reason too-day to be glad that I had learnt it. I meant to camp another night in the hills, go up Kuleib and be on the spot for the Druze gathering to-morrow, but when I woke I found the west wind colder than ever and the hills wrapped in cloud. I therefore decided to come straight across the ridge and sleep at Kanawat, much to my servants' delight, for a town is a better camping place in rainy weather than a mountain side. Before I left I explored Busan, which is an interesting place because the old houses are better preserved than usual. Most Of them are not lived in: they have big dark stables beneath and roofless rooms, many windowed, above. Some staircases were standing and I saw one house with a little bath room, the stone conduit for the water being still visible. I got a photograph between the blowing mists. We were off at 8:30 across the hills. My faith! it was cold. I thought the bare Plateau on the top of the ridge would never end. I was truly glad when Nusr ed Din said "Mashallah! Kanawat!" and I saw its ruined temples standing up on a spur of the hills. It is splendidly placed; one looks all down across the great Hauran plain and I got in at 12 and it began to rain in sharp showers. We rode up to the temples, at the top of the town, and I lunched in a Mazar, a little room leading out of a temple and was very grateful to Saint Whatever his name may be, for his roof. I have pitched my camp hard by, with two temples to the right and one to the left, and there's another further down to the west. From my tent door I look out on to great Corinthian columns and a doorway most elaborately carved. The work here is much better than any I have seen to the S. and E. The rain held up more or less till 3, and I had time to explore the town- alone, for a wonder. The streets are paved with the red paving; there is a splendid house in the middle with steps leading up to it. Inside it a big court with a stair, the steps of which were built into the wall on one side and standing free on the other, but so massive that few of them have broken away. They led up to a balcony, made in the same manner, with the stones just standing out from the wall, but all broken. This ran round two sides of the court, and the windows and doors of the rooms opened on to it. On the north side of the town is a deep rocky valley with a stream at the bottom and willows growing in it. There is a tiny theatre among the willows and a charming little building which the books say was a bath, and above a ruined castle and a round tower. I am much tempted to pay a flying visit to Suweidah, but I think perhaps it would be rather silly. I should look such an idiot if I were caught by the Turks and my further progress stopped! You will be pleased to hear that the prophet job is buried at Busan. I visited his Mazar. It is evidently much honoured for the door and some broken columns in front of it were all red with blood. (N.B. This is not true! The prophet job is buried here. I don't know who the much honoured saint at Busan was.) s

Tuesday, 8th. Dawned fine and I was in high spirits. But the clouds blew over after an hour and all the hills were wrapt in the mists, and I spent the day visiting Kenath and her daughters—you know Kanawat is Kenath? I took Nusr ed Din and we rode on to the hills to a place called Sia, once a great suburb of Kanawat and now a heap of stones. From thence we rode over a charming hill through a thicket of stunted oak full of a purple flowering vetch and other pretty things, and when we came to the edge of it there was Suweidah not two miles from us. I was very keen to go to it, but Nusr ed Din shook with fear and said it was inhabited by the Osmanli, the accursed, and why did I want to go? So I turned reluctantly away. I don't see what they could do to me, but I might get some of my kind hosts into trouble.

Wednesday, 9th. Before leaving this morning I went to the house of my friend, Ali el Kady, to drink a cup of tea—these were the terms of his invitation. He was very vague about the tea making, consulting me as to whether he ought to boil the water and the milk together. I said that wasn't the way we did it usually. He gave me an extraordinary variety of foods, a pudding, some very good fried cakes dipped in honey and almonds and raisins, both of them swimming in a sweet syrup—the almonds were excellent, It is fortunate that my digestion is ostrich-like, for I seem to eat very odd things at the oddest hours. I parted here with Nusr ed Din. I am sorry to leave the little hills. Though they are so small, they have quite the air of a mountain district and also the climate. The hot, fine weather has come back to-day. We went on, skirting the hills, north by east. Mount Hermon was a shining glory across the plain to the west and beyond him, northwards, stretched the long line of the Anti-Lebanus, also snow-topped. The Jebel Druize end in tiny volcanoes the beginning of the purely volcanic Lejah. It all looks black and uncanny—cunheimlich.

It is 2n extraordinary bit of country, but I decided after taking thought, not to go through it. It is very bad for the beasts., So rocky. I must come back here from Damascus some year and explore it all thoroughly. We rode all day with the Lejah on the left and Mount Hermon in front of us, flanked by the Lebanus. The corn is ripe here and they are plucking it out by the roots, which is their form of reaping. It was excellent going and we made very good time. A little Past 4 we reached the last village at the N.E. corner of the Lejah, and here I camped, it being only a seven or eight hours' ride to Damascus. It is also the last Druze village, alas! The Sheikb and all the swells came to call and took me into the village to look round. Dear, nice people! I am sorry to leave them. I haven't left them yet, however, for the Sheikh, Ibrahim, is still in my tent door as I write. He makes well, I must say, being singularly beautiful. It is a hot, hot night.

Friday, 11th. Damascus, but a long, long day to get to it. We were off at 6, and after an hour's riding we got to Burak and passed the first Turkish garrison without remark. Then came an endless five hours; we never seemed to gain on the scenery. We went on to the River Awaj, where we watered man and beast under the poplars and willows, a charming spot. Here I rode on alone up the Black Mountains a low range of hills separating the Awaj valley from the Abana, and at the top I saw far away in a green plain and ringed round with gardens, Damascus. This is the way to arrive at a great eastern city. I journeyed along with the trains of camels carrying the merchandise of Damascus to and fro, and the Arabs on their pretty mares, and the donkey boys bringing in grass and all the varied population of an oriental road. But the way was very long. It was 4 before I got into the town. I dawdled up through the bazaars and stopped to eat ices made of milk an snow and lemonade from a china bowl half full of snow and half of lemon juice and water-nothing was ever so good. At 5 I reached my hotel, saw that my horse was properly looked after—and went off to the German Consulate to get the box of clothes I had sent from Jerusalem. There I also, to my joy, found letters from you all. A very civil Oriental secretary has been giving me advice about Palmyra, whither I shall go, if your telegram is satisfactory, on Wednesday, returning here In about a fortnight. Dearest Father! you are a perfect angel to let me do all this! I don't see that the Palmyra journey ought to be much more expensive than all the others. It seems I don't have to take more than three soldiers at the outside. I've got so many things to say to you, Mother, that I should have to make my letter as long again if I began saying them. it is at times a very odd sensation to be out in the world quite by myself, but mostly I take it as a matter of course now that I'm beginning to be used to it. I don't think I ever feel lonely, though the one person I often wish for is Papa. I think he really would enjoy it. I keep wanting to compare notes with him. You, I want to talk to, but not in a tent: with earwigs and black beetles around and muddy water to drink! I don't think you would be your true self under such conditions. . . . Of course Arabic makes just all the difference. It would be small fun without.

To her family.

DAMASCUS, May 14th, 1900.

Beloved Family.-

To-day came your telegram which it was a great relief to receive.

I'm Off to-morrow with an escort Of 3 soldiers and all promises well. I expect to be back in a fortnight. I shall meet Charlotte here, spend another couple of days, and then with her, Over the hills to Baalbec and the Cedars. Beyrout (a week or so), from whence by boat to Jerusalem.

KUREIFEH,

May 15th. I got Off this morning at 9. After the usual difficulties attending the first day's start, an hour's vigorous activity found us all In the saddle. You never can get off the first day, so what's the good Of bothering? I have three soldiers, Ali, Musa and Muhammad. Following Lattiche's excellent advice, I have arranged to give then half a medjideh a day each, and they keep themselves which is a great simplification for us. They seem pleased, and as I believe they levy food and barley on the inhabitants as they go along, it pays them amply! We left the town by the north east gate, and rode for three hours through gardens, orchards, vineyards, the road bordered by big shady walnuts and running water everywhere. We stopped once by a little stream where a gentleman was making coffee on a mud stove and some others were smoking narghilehs under a clump of poplars. We watered our horses and drank little cups of coffee and rested for a quarter of an hour and then rode on to a khan, where I lunched under the trees by the edge of the clearest water. From here the country began to change. An hour or so of corn fields and vineyards, and barrenness and waterlessness began. All the great rivers which flow down from the snows of Hermon seem to die off when they see the bare volcanic hills of the Saffa across the plain. In the map they just end. I don't know what becomes of them. . . . At the top of the pass there was a well of rain water, very good, said Ali, and I made Hanna fetch me a cupful. It was, however, full of little red animals swimming cheerfully about, and one must draw the line somewhere, so I did not partake. I heard the story of Shibly Beg's capture from Lüttiche. . . . There's a cuckoo here; let me quickly write and tell the Spectator.

Wednesday, 16th. We were off at 5, Ali and I going ahead to see about camels for the desert. To jarad at about 7:30. We went to the house of one Sheikh Ahmed and Ali went off to see about camels to carry our water for the night, while I lay on his cushions and ate white mulberries and drank coffee. They pressed a narghileh on me, but I firmly refused. Never again; it's too nasty.

A boring delay now occurred, for we waited for the mules and they went straight on without calling for us and waited in Nasariyeh. The time was filled in by the good Sheikh's giving us an excellent meal, bread and olives, and dibbis and butter, laban and eggs. The worthies of the village came and talked to me, and very pleasant people they were. Lüttiche says the Arabs settled hereabout are the best people in all Syria, being descended straight from the original invaders. At 9:30 we went on again, muleless, depending on getting our corn for the night in Nasariyeh. We passed through a little village and then on through a desert plain.

At 11:50 we reached Nasariyeh—may God destroy its houses! there was no corn in them. The camels had not come up and anyhow there was nothing to be done but to send back to the village, and accordingly Hanna and Jacoub rode off together. I lunched under a white umbrella, for there was no shade. Nasariyeh is a new place, the property of the Sultan. It lies in the middle of the wide, flat valley between bare hills that we have been following all day, and beyond it there is no water for twelve hours. There was an enormous caravan of camels grazing near their piled up saddles and a little tent in which were seated some merchants from Bagdad, the owners of the caravan. They had been two months on the way, said one of them, who came down to our canal to get water; he walked as slowly as a camel and was about as communicative, answering me in a sort of dazed way as if the desert had got into his brain, and turning slowly, heavily away with his water-skin. Hanna and I, after taking counsel together, had bought eight skins and four leather bottles in Damascus, which was lucky, for we found none here. When they came to fill them, however, they found that one had a big hole in it and came despairingly to tell me. For once I was equal to the occasion. Do you remember, Father, the Greek boy we met as we went over the hills from Sparta, whose skin of oil broke? I had seen him mend it cunningly with a stone and a bit of string and I mended mine with much skill in the same way. It has held, too. The sun was so hot it burnt one through one's boots. I have gone into linen and khaki. The latter consists Of a man's ready-made coat, so big that there is room in it for every wind that blows, and most comfy; great deep pockets. The shopkeeper was very anxious that I should buy the trousers too but I haven't come to that yet. We got Oft at 1:30; having sent the three camels on, and rode till 5, When we just pitched down anywhere, in the desert it's all the same. The road was enlivened by Ali and Muhammad the soldiers, who are both extremely intelligent and who related to me many interesting tales. The soldiers are delighted that I can talk Arabic; they say it's so dull when they can't talk to the gentry.They talk Kurdish together, being of Kurdish parentage, but born in Damascus. Their Arabic is very good. Mine is really getting quite presentable. I think I talk Arabic as well as I talk German (which isn't saying much perhaps!), but I don't understand so well. It's so confoundingly—in the Bible sense!—rich in words. This is my first night in the desert—the first of I wonder how many dozens, scores—Heaven knows! There was a great stretch of shining salt to our right as we passed Nasariyeh, and while we rode I saw immense plaques of water on the horizon—always on the horizon, the farther we rode the further they went. We passed a ruined khan half an hour from here—I believe they occur at regular intervals all the way to Palmyra. I meant to be a couple of hours farther on, but the delays prevented it, and start under the moon to-morrow. The smooth, hard ground makes a beautiful floor to my tent. Shall I tell you my chief impression—the silence. It is like the silence of mountain tops, but more intense, for there you know the sound of wind and far away water and falling ice and stones; there is a sort of echo of sound there, you know it, Father. But here nothing.

KARYATEIN,

Thursday, 17th. I got up at 1:30 this morning and dressed quickly, but the packing up always takes rather longer by night, and we were not Off till 3:45. Such a night, with a bright moon and the vague, wide desert between the low hills! It was bitter cold; I should think there must be 50 difference between the night and the day. (This is not excessive. Dr. R. has registered up to 70 degrees difference.) My hands and feet were quite numb before the sun rose and for half an hour after. By 8 it was broiling and at mid-day my off foot was burnt through my boot. It was a pretty dull ride. The chief distraction was the catching of a jerboa. He was a darling, but I let him go again and he hopped off on his long hind legs in a futile manner. I am going to travel by night from here. I have two days of from 10 to 12 hours each, waterless both of them, and it's too hard on the beasts to go in the hot sun. It's also hard on me, though I read when I travel by day which I can't do at night.

I can all but sleep in the saddle, however, which passes the time wonderfully. Yesterday I fell off. I was still sitting sideways in my saddle with a map in one hand and a parasol in the other when suddenly my horse began to trot. I hadn't even got the reins in my hands, so I jumped off, much to the amusement of my soldiers. They are a good lot, my soldiers, quite the best I have yet had. This journey is being made much more amusing than I expected. I thought it would be rather tame after my recent experiences, but I'm enjoying it very much. This sort of life grows upon one. The tedious things become less tedious and the amusing more amusing, especially as Arabic grows. It's a cloudy night, hot consequently, and I'm going to bed.

Friday, 18th. And to sleep for nine hours, as it proved. I have made for myself an enormous muslin bag in which I sleep and which protects me from all biting animals down to sand flies. I'm very proud of this contrivance, but if we have a ghazu of Arabs I shall certainly be the last to fly, and my flight will be As one Who runs a sack race.

Sunday, 2 0th, Palmyra, for I've got here at last, though after such a ride! We left Karyatein on Friday evening at 5:30. At dusk we found ourselves in the desert region. The night closed in very dark, the west being thick with cloud. My rolling stone which gathers moss all the way had picked up another companion, One Ahmed, white robed and perched up on the top of a camel. The Agha had provided him as a guide. I was not on the ordinary road I must tell you, having decided to make a détour to the south in Order to avoid going and coming by the same route. No tourist ever goes this way. It leads to a spring called Ain el

Wu'ul, the Spring of the Deer, in the S. hills, which is half way between Karyatein and Palmyra. This we had to make as soon as possible after sunrise for the sake of the beasts for whom we had no water. It was very strange pacing on in the silent dark behind my white robed guide, the three soldiers, black shadows, beside me and the mules tinkling behind. For the first few hours there was a sort of path which one could see white and clear through the scrubby desert plants; when it left off Ahmed turned off resolutely into the broken ground under the hills, guiding himself by the stars in the clear east and by a black hill which stood out in front of us, and from which, he said, the Spring was seven hours away. The ground was very rocky; the horses' hoofs rung out on the rough slabs of stone. We went on and on and I talked first with one of my men and then with another, and at intervals I half fell asleep and woke up to see Ahmed's swaying figure like a kind of beckoning Fate leading us into a grim waterless world. Across the range of hills there is a country that no one ever travels over-right away to Nejd there is not a spring—not a well; 44 waterless days, said Ahmed. He imparted me scraps of information at intervals; he knew the name of every hill and every bare furrow—I was surprised to find that they had names, but it seems they have. This was the sort of conversation. "Where is the Lady;?" "Here, oh, Ahmed." "Oh, Lady, this is the Valley of the Wild Boar." There didn't seem anything to say about it except that it was a horrid sandy little place, so I replied that God had made it. Ahmed accepted this doubtful statement with a "God the Exalted is merciful!" on which Ali, the five times hadgi, would break in with "Praise be to God who is Great! may he prolong the life of the Sultan!" Soon after 3, Ahmed said "Oh, Lady! the light rises." I looked and the east was beginning to pale. I felt as if I had been sitting in my saddle for a lifetime an my horse felt so too. He was so hungry that he began to snatch at the camel's food as he passed—now the names of these plants I know, but only in Arabic, so I think it best not to tell. I was also hungry, and I had a light refection of chocolate and an orange, and then I got off and walked for near an hour, Ahmed walking too to keep me company. The light came quickly across the stony ground in the furrows. We mounted and rode on till 5, when the sun was behind some clouds. We were now coasting along the foot of the hills and Ahmed began to look about and wonder where the spring was. He had only been there once in his life before. The hills consisted of a long range of little stony peaks with a valley running up between them every quarter of a mile or so; in one of these valleys, high up, was the spring; the question was which. Ahmed wasn't sure, so he left me with the camel and set off running into the hills to explore. The others came up, and I made Hanna give me a bit of bread and a cup of milk which had turned into butter and whey (but awfully good) and I fell asleep almost while I was eating it. I had been riding for 12 hours. Half an hour later I heard my men say that Ahmed was beckoning to us. We had gone a good bit too far. We rode back half an hour, entered one of the valleys and climbed up it nearly to the top, and there on a tiny platform between rocks, we found the spring. it was only a very small cup, 6 or 8 feet across, More perhaps, and about 10 feet deep of water the cup being barely half full. The water was clear and cold but covered with masses of weed and full of swimming things of all kinds. The soldiers and the beasts didn't seem to mind, however, and I shut my eyes and drank too. It was past 7 when we got to it. I had something to eat, climbed up to a shady cave, and slept till 1, indifferent to the fact that my bed was thistles and my bed fellows stinging flies. If we had missed this one spring hidden in the hills we should have been hard put to it. The good Hanna gave me an excellent lunch of fried croquettes and a partridge that he had killed, and tea. I had told him to cook nothing but his conscience was too much for him, and he had made a charcoal fire between some stones, and Prepared these masterpieces, bless him! At 3 we were off again. and down into the plain, and then straight east at the foot of the hills. It had never been really hot all day, fortunately; the sun set without a cloud and it began to be very cold. We rode till 7 and then stopped for the animals to eat and for us to eat too. I put on gaiters, a second pair of knickerbockers and a covert coat under my thick winter coat, rolled myself up in a blanket and a cape and went to sleep all the men following my example, rolled up in their long cloaks. The cold and the bright moon woke me at midnight and I roused all my people (with some difficulty!) and at one we were off. Again, you see, we had to reach our water as soon as possible after the sun, so that the animals might not suffer too much from thirst. We went on and on; the dawn came and the sun rose—the evening and the morning of the second day, but I seemed to have been riding since the beginning of time. At sunrise, far away in the distance, on top of one of a group of low hills, I saw the castle of Palmyra. We were still five hours away. They were long hours. Except Petra, Palmyra is the loveliest thing I have seen in this country, but five hours away. They were long hours. The wide plain gradually narrowed and we approached the W. belt of hills, rocky, broken and waterless. It's a fine approach, the hills forming a kind of gigantic avenue with a low range at the end behind which Palmyra stands, and the flat desert, very sandy here, running up to them. My horse was very tired and I was half dazed with sleep. As we drew near Palmyra, the hills were covered with the strangest buildings, great stone towers, four stories high, some more ruined and some less, standing together in groups or bordering the road. They are the famous Palmyrene tower tombs. At length we stood on the end of the col and looked over Palmyra. I wonder if the wide world presents a more singular landscape. It is a mass of columns, ranged into long avenues, grouped into temples, lying broken on the sand or pointing one long solitary finger to Heaven. Beyond them is the immense Temple of Baal; the modern town is built inside it and its rows of columns rise out of a mass of mud roofs. And beyond all is the desert, sand and white stretches of salt and sand again, with the dust clouds whirling over it and the Euphrates five days away. It looks like the white skeleton of a town, standing knee deep in the blown sand. We rode down to one of the two springs to which it owes its existence, a plentiful supply of the clearest water, but so much impregnated with sulphur that the whole world round it smells of sulphur. The horses drank eagerly, however, and we went on down a line of columns to the second spring which is much purer, though it, too, tastes strongly of sulphur. If you let it stand for 12 hours the taste almost goes away, but it remains flat and disagreeable, and I add some lemon juice to it before I drink it. It's very clean, which is a blessing. We pitched our tents by a charming temple in the very middle of the ruins—it was 10:30 before the mules came up, we having got in at 10. I was too sleepy to be very hungry, but someone brought a big bowl of milk and I ate sour bread and dibbis, while the brother of the Sheikh talked to me and the howling wind scattered the sand over us. There seems to be always a wind here; it was such a hurricane in the afternoon and evening that I thought my tent would go, but it held firm. What with one thing and another, it was 11:30 before I could retire and wash and go to bed, but I then slept most blissfully for a couple of hours; after which I had tea and received all the worthies of the town-the Mudir is an old Turk, who talks much less Arabic than I do—and when I had sent them away happy I walked Out and down the street of columns into the Temple of the Sun—the town, I should say, for it is nearly all included within its enormous outer walls. The stone used here is a beautiful white limestone that looks like marble and weathers a golden yellow, like the Acropolis.

Monday, 21st. I got up feeling extremely brisk, and spent the whole morning exploring Palmyra. Except Petra, Palmyra is the loveliest thing I have seen in this country. but Petra is hard to beat.

Wednesday, 23rd. We were off at 5, just as the sun rose. As I rode over the hill, Palmyra looked like a beautiful ghost in the pale stormy light. I am returning by the ordinary tourist route, The old high road across the desert. Last night there arrived from the East a big caravan Of camels belonging to the Agail Arabs, who are going to sell them in Damascus. The chief man of them is one Sheikh Muhammad. I had met him yesterday in Palmyra, and he told me that 'Please God, who is great,' he meant to travel with me. He comes from Nejd, and talks the beautiful Nejd Arabic; there are one or two Bagdadis with him, and the rest of the party are the wildest, unkemptest Agail camel drivers. The interesting part of it is that the Agail are some of the Rashid's people, and I'm going to lay plans with Sheikh Muhammad as to getting into Nejd next year. I found them breakfasting on dates,-camels' milk and the bitter black coffee of the Arabs—a peerless drink. I also made a supplementary breakfast with them and then we all started off together. The reason Sheikh Muhammad wants to travel with me is that he is anxious to have the extra protection of my three soldiers—he has two of his own—fearing a raid of Arabs on his camels on the way to Karyatein. I think it's great sport; I'm not sorry to be able to do a good turn to an Agail, and he and his Bagdadis are very interesting to talk to, with their dragoman on the box and their mules following behind the crowds of tents. We had a very agreeable chat and they gave me some gingerbread biscuits, for which I blessed them and we made plans for meeting in Damascus. I wouldn't really have changed places with them, and I prefer a Sheikh from Nejd to a dragoman from Jerusalem as a travelling companion. We got to our camping place, Ain el Baida, about 11:30—It's a short march, but there's no water beyond. It was again blazing hot. I was glad to get under the shadow of my tent and to lunch and sleep. Since then I've been watching the troops of camels come slowly in, their masters carrying a club or an enormous lance 12 feet long, and all the process of drawing water from the deep well and emptying it into basins hastily scooped out in the ground for the camels to drink. The Agail have pitched a black tent not far from me, and stuck a lance into the ground beside it, and they are now making bread for their supper.

Thursday, 24th. I wish I could manage to travel on the approved lines, but the fates are against me. I had laid all my plans for coming back from Palmyra like a lady, but no! it was not to be. We got off rather late this morning 5:30, it was before I left Ain El Baida, and then the mules were not ready. I started without them—a fatal step, as you will see. The Agail were off half an hour before, the good Sheikh Muhammad having put two water skins for me on his camel. Ahmed, my guide, put another two on his camel and I told the muleteers to bring the other four, so that we should have enough water for our beasts and could sleep comfortably in the desert. There is no water between Ain el Baida and Karyatein, three hours on. I caught up the Agail who had stopped to breakfast and were making coffee and baking bread—they eat nothing in the morning before they start. We stopped, too, and had some coffee and dates and my soldiers ate bread new baked—very good, I tasted it—and drank camels' milk. They eat surprisingly little, these Arabs, when they are travelling. Nothing but bread and dates and milk and coffee, and little enough of that. Often the bread runs short, and only dates and milk remain. It was a wild looking party that was gathered round the coffee pot. There's lots of negro blood in them, owing, I think, to their having negro slaves, one of whom was with them. They intermarry a great deal with these slaves and the son of a slave woman is as good as another. Sheikh Muhammad went to and fro, superintending the cooking and bringing food for us all. I had intended to go on another two hours and camp, leaving a short day's march into Karyatein next morning, but at Kast el Khair we found that the two water skins on Sheikh Muhammad's camel had leaked and were quite empty, and Hanna told me that Yacoub, the muleteer, had refused, after I left, to carry his two skins and had poured the water out on the ground. So here we were with two skins and a couple of leather bottles for ten animals and seven people. There was nothing to be done but to make a dash for Karyatein, The Agail were rather distressed at this, being still terrified for their camels, but what was I to do. They had no water, camels needing none and after I had watered my beasts at Kars el Khair, I had none—I couldn't keep my camp 24 hours waterless. we were only seven hours from Karyatein., and we had done barely seven that morning, in fact our horses were so brisk that Ali, Muhammad the soldier, Ahmed the guide and I got into Karyatein in five hours-but we rode for it! I came in the last hour or two on Ahmed's camel—it's the greatest relief after you have been riding a horse for 8 or 9 hours to feel the long comfy swing and the wide soft saddle of a camel beneath you. We got in at 6 and went to the house of one Abdullah the priest. He took us into a big vineyard of his and brought me a carpet and some cushions to lie on, and bread and dibbis to eat. Hanna and my third soldier, Musa, arrived at seven, but my mules didn't get in till 9:30, having done a 16 hours' day. I rolled myself up in a rug and my carpet and made a pretence of going to sleep under the stars, but it was pretty cold and the attempt wasn't very successful. I was glad to get into my tent again and to bed about 11, feeling as if I had had enough of travelling for one day.

Friday. I found my camp pitched in Mahin near the water, and hundreds of camels drinking near it. A big company of the Hasineh Arabs had just arrived, moving from their winter quarters and their black tents were pitched not far from me. Their Sheikh, Muhammad, came to call on me, a boy of 20 or younger, handsome, rather thick lipped, solemn, his hair hanging in thick plaits from under his kefflyeh. He carried an enormous sword, the sheath inlaid with silver. After he had gone, his sister and some other women appeared in all the trailing dirt of their dark blue cotton robes. Sheikh Muhammad is a great swell. He owns 500 tents and a house in Damascus, and Heaven knows how many horses and camels. After tea, I returned his call and sat on carpets and cushions in the big Sheikh's tent, the Hasineh making a circle round me while I drank coffee. The Sheikh's mother also appeared and was treated with great honour, Muhammad getting up and giving her his place on the carpet and his camel saddle to lean on. After a bit, one of the black browed, white robed Arabs took a rubaba, a single stringed instrument played with a bow, and sang to it long melancholy songs, monotonous, each line of the verse being set to the same time and ending with a drop of the voice which was almost a groan. The murmur of the rubaba ran through it all—weird and sad and beautiful in its way. All the silent people sat round looking at me, unkempt, half-naked, their keffiyehs drawn up over their faces, nothing alive in them but their eyes, and across the smouldering fire of camels' dung, the singer bent his head over the rubaba or looked up at me as he sent the wailing line of his song out into the dark. Sometimes one would come in to the open tent (the front is never closed) and standing on the edge of the circle, he greeted the Sheikh with a "Ya Muhammad!" his hand lifted to his forehead and the company with "Peace be upon you," to which we all -answered "And upon you peace!" Then the circle spread out a little wider to make room for the new comer.

At last I got up and said good-bye, I hadn't gone more than a few steps than my soldiers told me I had committed a fearful solecism. They had killed a sheep for me and were preparing a dinner, of which I ought to have partaken, and further, said Ali "Muhammad is a great Sheikh and you ought to give him a present." I went back to my tent rather perturbed, what could I give? Finally, after thinking things over, I sent one of my soldiers with Ali's pistol wrapped up in a pocket handkerchief (you can give nothing to an Arab but arms or horses) and a message that I hadn't known he had meant to do me such honour and would he accept this present (net value 2 pounds). He returned answer that he was grateful, that he was doing nothing but his duty and would I honour them? So back I went with Athos, Porthos and What's-his-name, and we all sat down again on the cushions and carpets and waited. We waited till 9:30! I wasn't bored (though I was hungry!). One by one, the Arabs dropped in till the circle stretched all round the big tent; at intervals the talk went round—the politics of the desert: who had sold horses, who owned camels, who had been killed in a raid, how much the blood money would be or where the next battle. It was very difficult to understand, but I followed it more or less. Besides the bitter black coffee, we were handed cups of what they called "white coffee"—hot water, much sweetened and flavoured with almonds. At length came a black slave with a long spouted water jar in his hand, to me first and then to all the company. We held out our hands and he poured a little water over them. And at last dinner—four or five men bearing in an enormous dish heaped up with rice and the meat of a whole sheep. This was put down on the ground before me, and I and some ten others sat round it and ate with our fingers, a black slave standing behind us with a glass which he filled with water as each guest required it. The food was pretty nasty, saltless and very tough—but it was 9:30! They eat extraordinarily little, and I was still hungry when the first circle got up to make place for the second. More hand-washing, with soap this time, and I bowed myself out and retired to biscuits and bed. It was rather an expensive dinner, but the experience was worth the pistol.

Sunday, 27th. It was interesting this morning to see the Hasineh on the move. Sheikh Muhammad had only twenty or thirty of his five hundred tents with him, yet the camels filled the plain like the regiments of an army, each household marching with its own detachment of camels....

Monday, 28th. Sending my mules by a desert road, I took two of my musketeers and Hanna, and rode to an exquisite place called Mualula. It is interesting as being one of three places—the other two are close by—where the old Syrian language is spoken, the language in which Christ spoke. Most of the inhabitants are Christians—their Christianity dates from the first century—and there are two big convents, Catholic and Greek. I spent a charming hour in the Greek convent, where the monks and nuns were delightful people. The Prior is a Greek, pleasant, intelligent and cultured....

Tuesday, 29th. I had a very beautiful ride into Damascus. The air was sweet with the smell of figs and vines and chestnuts, the pomegranates were in the most flaming blossom, the valley was full of mills and mill races bordered by long regiments of poplars—lovely, it must be at all times, but when one comes to it out of the desert it seems a paradise. I got to Damascus soon after two and rode through the bazaars, eating apricots, with which all Damascus is full. Now he who has not eaten the apricots of Damascus has not eaten apricots. To my joy I found Charlotte here when I arrived and letters. Telegrams from you and the war news excellent.... 95 [Sloane St.] will be splendid I Tell my sisters I love their letters and fly to them as soon as I get my post.... I do fervently hope to be in London about the 21st. I should like a week there because I am somewhat ragged, as you may well imagine. I wish I were as well stocked with clothes as Elsa, tell her! As for my travelling clothes-'nein!!' Oh, my dear family! I do long to be with you again. I want to have the most fearful long talk about nothing with my sisters and about things with my father and about everything taken together with my mother. By the way, did I mention that Damascus is a singularly beautiful place? I found a delightful letter from Caroline here. Much love to her.

[Gertrude's letters until her return to England are very vaguely dated, but it is clear that she remained with the Rosens, making more or less distant excursions with them at intervals. In one of her letters I find:

Nina and Dr. Rosen are perfectly delightful travelling Companions, we have just been agreeing that for a dwelling anything but a tent is merely a kind of makeshift.

[She writes delightful descriptions of the country she passes through, of its wealth of flowers, of its smiling Prosperity alternated with desert wilderness. She describes Baalbek and the Lebanon Range. She and her companions ride to the place where the great cedars flourish.]

To H.B.
ARAK EL EMIR, Wednesday, 30th May, 1900.

From my Camp. (Arabia, suggests Dr. R., in case you shouldn't know where the above important place is). Well, we left yesterday after lunch, after a tremendous getting off, such a packing and saying Goodbye! I never had my hand kissed so often! it was blazing hot, but a furious wind got up as we rode down to Jericho. It made us a little cooler but raised such storms of dust as I have never seen. We could neither speak nor hear nor see, and when we arrived in Jericho we looked as if we had just been dug up from an untimely grave. We spent a very comfortable night and got off at 5 this morning. The wind had gone and had taken with it the heat, and the flies, so that we had a most pleasant ride across the Ghor. We crossed the Jordan by the bridge and then turned away a little further northwards than my former road, getting into the foothills about 8. From thence we rode up a long winding grassy valley, very pretty, with plenty of corn in it and all the fields full of lovely pink hollyhock and flowering caper, which is like St. John's wort, but with pink stamen and white petals. This valley led us up on to a little col from whence we looked down into the beautiful Wady Sir with Arak el Emir lying in the bottom of it. Heights thinly covered with oak behind. Now this place is very interesting. It was a palace built by an enterprising gentleman called Hyrcamus about 200 years before Christ, and Josephus describes it so accurately that one can to this day trace the lines of the moats and tanks and gardens. Of the palace little remains except a great 'pan de mur' built of enormous stones, the upper ones carved with lions. You can trace a long road leading up to some cliffs about a quarter of a mile behind (from these the place takes its name, Arak meaning cliff) in which are cut a regular town of caves, one of them being an enormous stable with mangers for 100 horses cut in its walls. We got here at 1, very hungry and instantly lunched by the stream which is bordered by thickets of oleander. At our feet was a beautiful little blue lake, Yamonneh, with a great spring flowing out of the rocks high up above it and a silvery water flower growing over it in patches. It was such an odd combination to see a mountain lake looking quite civilised, and camels beside it! Both the lake and the spring dry up in summer—there is awfully little water on this side of the hills. We then rode W. up the cleft, a deep valley full of corn and scrubby trees which had expended most of their energy in growing along the ground, and got into our camp at 6. I was glad to see it for had been rather a poor thing all day and hadn't expected nearly such a long ride. The result was that I was dead beat and slept very badly and felt extremely miserable this morning.

Tuesday, 5th June. However, we had a very interesting and a short day before us. We rode up to the crest of Lebanon, and then all along the ridge to the highest point, Jebel Mahmal. It was gorgeous, the sea on one side and the desert on the other, Hermon to the south and Horns to the north. We rode to within an hour of the top and might have ridden all the way, except that it was rather a Pull for the horses. There were no rocks, only Slopes Of gravel, more or less steep, with occasional patches Of snow and a good deal of mud where the snow had just melted—We were 10,000 feet up. There is no glaciation, but they say a little snow lies the summer through. Below us lay the cedar clumps protected by an amphitheatre of hills, and the great gulf of the Wady Kadisha running down to Tripoli with villages scattered along its brink. We sleep in one of them to-morrow. There were some exciting clumpy Alpine things growing—one a very dwarf broom covered with yellow flowers, the others, pink and white and purple, I didn't know. There was also a charming tiny tulip, Purple outside, and white within, with a yellow centre, and a lovely pale blue scilla. We got down to the cedars at 1:30, after a very rough descent; and found our tents pitched under the trees. After having been told so Often that they are ragged and ugly, I am agreeably disappointed in them. There are about 400 of them. Some very fine old trees, grass and flowers growing under them—a heavenly camping ground. At this moment it is too delicious! a low Sun. birds singing in the great branches and the pale brown, snow-sprinkled hills gleaming behind. We are extremely happy.

Wednesday, 6th. There is such an exquisite village in front of me that I can scarcely take my eyes off it to write to you. Its name is Hasrun and it stands perched up on cliffs over the deep valley Kadisha' the stream being 1,000 feet or more below it, and the mountains rise above it, and the whole is a red gold at this moment, for the sun is busy sinking into the sea out Tripoli way. We spent a delicious lazy morning at the cedars, breakfasted and lunched under the big trees and photographed and drew and listened to the birds. The ground is covered with tiny cedars, but they never grow up under the shadow of their parents (how different from the Belgian Hare!) but wither off when they have reached the height of about 2 inches-which is small for a tree. There were, however, outside the big trees a few saplings which had sprung up of themselves and were growing extraordinarily slowly; they were five years old, said the guardian of the wood, but they were not more than 18 inches high. I have brought a lot of cones away with me. Shall we try and make them grow at Rounton? It would be rather fun to have a real Cedar of Lebanon—only I believe they don't grow more than about 20 feet high in 100 years, so we at least shall not be able to bask much under their shadow. We tore ourselves away at 1, the guardian of the woods making us low salaams as we rode off. He was a beautiful creature tall and straight and dressed in a red and gold cotton coat and a white felt scull cap on his curly head. There were pale periwinkles growing on the edge of the wood and a sweet-scented pink daphne inside—well, well, we were sorry to go. . . .

[Gertrude brought the cones home, and distributed them to her family and friends—and so there is a real Cedar of Lebanon growing on the lawn at Rounton now. It is about 16 ft. high. Another stands on Sir George Trevelyan's lawn at Wallington.]

Thursday, 7th, We started off at 6:30 this morning. There is very lovely broom in this country with flowers much larger than ours. On the very highest col, from which the snow had just melted, the ground was blue with sweet violets. From this highest col we saw our ultimate destination far away and behind it a great hog's back called Jebel Sunnin, white with snow. Below us was a place called Akurah, to which we descended by an awful road, and lunched, it being then 1. We lay under some mulberry trees and all the population sat round on walls and looked at us—stalls full, dress circle full., upper boxes full!

We reached Aflea, which is one of the wonders of the Lebanon. The river Adonis—for this is the site of the Venus and Adonis legend—springs out of a great cave high up in the cliff and round the cave are several other springs, starting straight out of the rock and foaming down into the valley, falling in 3 or 4 cascades into deep blue pools and hurrying away under planes and walnut trees. The water is ice-cold; I have just been bathing in it. It's a very hot close night. We are going to dine outside my tent. There is such a roar of water! The moon is shining on the great cliffs and the steep steep banks of the valleys and mountain sides, up which climb black companies of cypresses, and there are little twinkling lights on all the hills. . . . .

Friday, 8th There came one from the village this morning to tell me about the road. I said You will come with us, oh my uncle?" He replied, "Upon my head and eyes, oh my sister." So I returned to my breakfast well pleased. But when it came to getting on my horse, Hanna told me that the Metawaileh (he belonged to that peculiar Muhammadan sect—please note that in the plural the accent is on the second syllable—Metawaileh; this puzzled me a good deal at first!) had retired, saying that he had business, an excuse so palpably absurd that it was almost rude Of him not to find a better. Well, we had to start Off over the hills alone, leaving our guide of yesterday, Martin, to take the mules straight to Reifun. The result was we went a long 'giro,' an hour or more out Of Our road, Charlotte, Hanna and I, and then we found a charming gentleman called Masa, pasturing his flocks on the hill-side, and he mounted his mare and came with us—a Christian he was, as all the people are in this country, the Metawaileh being merely servants here. At last, after an appalling road, we came into a great amphitheatre of hills and saw the Roda Bridge, our object, in front of us, and all our path, and here Masa left us, after stoutly refusing to be tipped. We got to the natural bridge at 12 and lunched there, and very wonderful it was, with a rushing torrent flowing under it. We set off again at 1 and rode over hill and down valley by road, perfectly indescribable. I have been on worse, but never for so long. The rhododendron was flowering and masses of yellow broom, and the hills were terraced for mulberry and vine right up to the summit. After we had gone about 2 hours I saw that my horse was lame and, on examination, found that he had lost a shoe. Fortunately we were near a village, so that we could stop and put things right-all the horses needed looking to, and no wonder. I talked to the village people while we waited-charming people they all were, Maronites, most intelligent. Lots of them emigrate to America.

Saturday, 10th. And so to-day. We set off about 7-it was already fearfully hot, we walked 3 hours leading our horses, over the devilish road. Then we got on to the carriage road to Beyrout and followed it all along the coast arriving at 3 about. We shall go to Jaffa to-morrow, as there is a boat and I am anxious to get home. But you know, dearest Father, I shall be back here before long! One doesn't keep away from the East when one has got into it this far.

CHAPTER VII
1901-1902

SWITZERLAND-SYRIA-ENGLAND

TO F.B.
REDCAR, March 5th, 1901.
[She had been on the golf links.]

It was a regular March day with a bitter wind. The pools of water on the links were as blue as the cracks in a glacier and the wind shivered them into steely lines. They reminded me of a simile in an Arab war song—"the folds of their coats of mail were like the surface of a pool which is struck by the pressing wind. . . ."

[Gertrude does not seem to have left England again until the late summer of 1901 when she returns to Switzerland for some more climbing.]

To H. B.
GRINDELWALD, Sunday, 1901.

. . . . I'm enjoying myself madly—I had a very interesting day on the Schreckhorn yesterday. We went up from here on Friday to the Schwartzegg Hut and lunched on the way at a little place called the Baregg. After we had been at the nice comfy hut about an hour (during which time I had seen a friendly marmot—he sat for some time on a rock looking at me and then hopped thoughtfully away) there arrived two young men Gerard and Eric Collier with their guides . . . .. We had a most cheerful evening and retired to bed on our shelf at 8:30 BY 11:30 we were off. " Schreckhorn !", said one of the Colliers' guides like an omnibus conductor, and we walked off into the night. Till 4 we climbed up a series of snow couloirs and small arêtes, a little steep cutting, but all quite easy; then we got on to the rocks and sat down to breakfast till the dawn came. It was bitter cold. We then had 2 hours of arête, one or two nice traverses at the top, but the rock very rotten and requiring great care. The Colliers did it in excellent style. At 6 we got out into sunshine on a snow saddle and saw down the other side. I was beginning to think that the Schreckhorn had an absurd reputation, but the hour of arête from the saddle to the top made me alter my opinion. It's a capital bit of rock climbing, a razor edge going quite steep down, snow on one side and rock on the other, not quite solid so that you have to take the greatest care, and with a couple of very fine bits of climbing in it. It raises the Schreckhorn into the first class among mountains, though it's rather low down in its class. After 5 minutes of wondering what was going to happen next, I found my head and my feet and had a thoroughly enjoyable hour. We got to the top at 7 and the Colliers about a quarter of an hour later. . . . We parted at the Schrund, they going over Grimsel way. I took the snow couloir, which was rather imprudent; we glissaded down as hard as ever we could go and good luck was with us, for not one stone fell while we were in it. We got down to the hut at 12. Here rather a comic incident occurred. We had left provisions and wood for our return and imagine our feelings at finding 3 Frenchmen burning our wood and making our tea! I said very politely that I was delighted to entertain them, but that I hoped they would let us have some of the tea, since it was really ours. They looked rather black, but made no apologies, nor did they thank me and I went away to change my things outside. When I came back they had gone, but they left the following entry in the visitors' book, "Nous sommes montés au refuge sans guides. Vue splendide! mais quelle faim! Heureusement nous avons trouvé du thé." I completed the entry by adding, "NB. It was my tea! " and signing my name. . . . . But for the moment all our thoughts are turned to the virgin arête on the Fingeraarhorn and we are going up to the Schwartzegg to have a shot at it. It has been tried unsuccessfully 3 times; I don't suppose we shall manage it, but we shall have an amusing time over it. We keep it a deadly secret!. . . .

To F.B.
KURHAUS, ROSENLAUI, BERNER OBERLAND, August, 1901.

I am established for a day or two in this enchanting spot, having been driven out of the higher mountains by a heavy snowfall on Monday, which renders the big things impossible for a day or two. Here, there is a fascinating little rock range, which can be done in almost any weather. So I walked over on Tuesday by the Great Scheidegg and was at once received into the bosom of the Collier family. . . . We spent Tuesday afternoon playing cricket, the whole family and I, with fir tree branches for stumps, and large butterfly nets handy to fish out the balls when they went into the river! Yesterday my guides and I were up at 4 and clambered up on to the Engelhorn range to take a good look round and see what was to be done. It was the greatest fun, very difficult rock work, but all quite short. We hammered in nails and slung ropes and cut rock steps- mountaineering in miniature. Finally we made a small peak that had not been done before, built a cairn on it and solemnly christened it. Then we explored some very difficult rock couloirs, found the way up another peak which we are going to do one of these days. . . . I shall probably stay here till Sunday morning which will give the snow time to get right. Then I shall return to my great schemes. . . .

To H.B.
ROSENLAUI, Sunday, 8th September, 1901.

I am now going to give you a history of my adventures. Friday: we set out before dawn, the mists lying low everywhere on the sporting chance of finding fine weather above them. We walked up the hour and a half of steep wood which is the Preface to every climb here, and got to our familiar scene of action, a rocky valley called the Ochsenthal. Our problem was to find a pass over a precipitous wall of rock at he S. end of it. Now this rock wall had been pronounced impossible by the two experts of these parts and by their Guide,. We cast round and finally decided on a place where the rock wall was extremely smooth, but worn by a number of tiny water channels, sometimes as much as 3 inches deep by 4 across. These gave one a sort of handhold and foothold. just as we started up it began to snow a little. The first 100 feet were very difficult and took us three quarters of an hour. The rock was excessively smooth and in one place there was a wall some 6 feet high where Ulrich had to stand on Heinrich's shoulder. Above this 100 feet it went comparatively easily and in an hour we found ourselves in a delightful cave, so deep that it sheltered us from the rain and sleet which was not falling thick. Here we breakfasted, gloomily enough. After breakfast things looked a little better and we decided to go on though it was still raining. The next bit was easy, rocks and grass and little ridges, but presently we found ourselves on the wrong side of a smooth arête which gave us no hold at all. We came down a bit, found a possible traverse and got over with some difficulty. A rotten couloir and a still more rotten chimney and we were on the top of the pass, rh. 2000. from the cave. We were pleased with ourselves! It was a fine place; about 2000 feet of arête, less perhaps, between the great peak of the Engelhorn on the right and a lower peak on the left, which is the final peak of that arête of 4 peaks we did the other day. We called this 5th peak of our arête the Klein Engelhorn. . . . The whole place up there is marked with chamois paths, no one, I expect, having ever been there before to disturb them. There is, however, an old old cairn on the low slopes of the Engelhorn, made by some party who, having come over the Engelhorn, tried to traverse down the N. side and turned back at this place. We know that neither the N. nor the S. side of the Gemse Sattel, as we have called it, has ever been done. Indeed the S. side may be impossible, but I don't think it is. They say it is, but we know that the experts may be mistaken. It was snowing so hard that we decided we could do no more that day and returned by the way we had come. . . . We got down the smooth rocks with the help of the extra rope. It was most unpleasant, for the water was streaming down the couloirs in torrents and we had to share the same couloirs with it. It ran down one's neck and up one's sleeves and into ones boots— disgusting! However, we got down and ran home through the woods. In the afternoon it cleared and at dawn on Saturday we were off again. We went again to the top of the Gemse Sattel; it was a beautiful day and we knew our way and did the rocks in an hour and ten minutes less than we had taken the day before. Here we breakfasted and at 10 we started off to make a small peak on the right of the saddle which we had christened beforehand the Klein Engelhorn. We clambered up an easy little buttress peak which we called the Gemse Spitz and the Klein Engelhorn came into full view. It looked most unencouraging; the lower third was composed of quite smooth perpendicular rocks, the next piece of a very steep rock wall with an ill-defined couloir or two, the top of great upright slabs with deep gaps between them. It turned out to be quite as difficult as it looked. We got down the Gemse Spitz on to a small saddle, did a very difficult traverse forwards and upwards above the smooth precipitous rocks, scrabbled up a very shallow crack and halted at the bottom of a smooth bit of overhanging rock. The great difficulty of it all was that it was so exposed, you couldn't ever get Yourself comfortably wedged into a chimney, there was nothing but the face of the rock and up you had to go. For this reason I think it more difficult than the Simili Stock. Well, here we were on an awfully steep place under the overhanging place. Ulrich tried it on Heinrich's shoulder and could not reach any hold. I then clambered up on to Heinrich, Ulrich stood on me and fingered up the rock as high as he could. It wasn't high enough. I lifted myself a little higher—always with Ulrich on me, mind!—and he began to raise himself by his hands. As his foot left my shoulder I put up a hand straightened out my arm and made a ledge for him. He called out, "I don't feel at all safe—if you move we are all killed." I said, "All right, I can stand here for a week," and up he went by my shoulder and my hand. It was just high enough. Once up he got into a fine safe place and it was now my turn. I was on Heinrich's shoulder with one foot and with one on the rock. Ulrich could not help me because he hadn't got my rope-I had been the last on the rope, you see, and I was going up second, so that all I had was the rope between the two guides to hold on to. It was pretty hard work, but I got up. Now we had to get Heinrich up. He had a rope round his waist and my rope to hold, but no shoulder, but he could not manage it. The fact was, I think, that he lost his nerve, anyhow, he declared that he could not get up, not with 50 ropes, and there was nothing to do but to leave him. He unroped himself from the big rope and we let down the thin rope to him, with which he tied himself, while we fastened our end firmly onto a rock. There we left him like a second Prometheus—fortunately there were no vultures about! So Ulrich and I went on alone and got as far as the top of the first great slab which was a sort of gendarme.

[I must add as a footnote to this letter that when Gertrude came home to us and related the thrilling ascent, still more exciting naturally in the telling, she told us that after it was over Ulrich had said to her, "If, when I was standing on your shoulders and asked you if you felt safe, you had said you did not, I should have fallen and we should all have gone over." And Gertrude replied to him, "I thought I was falling when I spoke.")

Here Ulrich shouted down to me, "It won't go!" My heart sank—after all this trouble to be turned back so near the top! Ulrich came down with a very determined face and announced that we must try lower down. We were now on the opposite side of the mountain from that on which we had left Heinrich. We went down a few feet and made a difficult traverse downwards above a precipice till we came to a chimney. I leant into the crack, Ulrich climbed on to my shoulder and got to the top. It was done! a few steps more brought us to the very top of all and we built a cairn and felt very proud. There was a difficult moment coming down the first chimney. We had left our thin rope with Heinrich, SO we had to sling the thick rope round a rock for Ulrich to come down on. But it was still wet from the day before and when we got to the bottom the rope stuck. He went up and altered its position and came down and it stuck again. Again he went up, and this time he detached it and threw it down to me and came down without a rope at all. I gave him a shoulder and a knee at the last drop. So we got back and rescued Heinrich and after a great deal of complicated rope work we reached the Gemse Sattel again after 4 hours of as hard rock climbing as it would be possible to find. Lunch was most agreeable.

Our next business was to get up the Engelhorn by the arête up which I told you we saw the chamois climb the other day. This proved quite easy-it has not been done before, however-and at 3:30 we were on the top of the Engelhorn. Now we had to come down the other side—this is the way the Engelhorn is generally ascended. It's a long climb, not difficult, but needing care, especially at the end of a hard day when you have no finger tips left. . . . It was 7 o'clock before we reached the foot of the rocks. It Was too late and too dark to think of getting down into the valley so we decided that we would sleep at the Engen Alp at a shepherd's hut. We wandered over Alps and Alps—not the ghost of a hut was to be found. It was an exquisite starry night and I had almost resigned myself to the prospect of spending the whole night on the mountain side, when suddenly our lantern showed us that we had struck a path. At 9:30 we hove up against a chalet nestled in to the mountain side and looking exactly like a big rock. We went in and found a tiny light burning. in a minute 3 tall shepherds, with pipes in their Mouths, joined us and slowly questioned us as to Where we had come from and whither we were going. We said we were going no further and would like to eat and sleep. One of the shepherds lighted a blazing wood fire and cooked a quantity of milk in a 3-legged cauldron and we fell to on bowls of the most delicious bread and milk I ever tasted. The chalet was divided into two parts by a wooden partition. The first Part was Occupied by some enormous pigs, there was also a ladder in it leading up to a bit of wooden floor under the roof where the fresh hay was kept. Here I slept. The other room had a long berth all down one side of it and a shelf along another filled with rows of great milk tins. The floors were just the hard earth and there was a wooden bench on which we ate and a low seat by it. I retired to my hayloft, wrapped myself in a new blanket and covered myself over with hay and slept soundly for 8 hours when my neighbours, the pigs, woke me by grunting loudly to be let out. The shepherd gave us an excellent breakfast of milk and coffee—we had our own bread and jam. It was so enchanting waking up in that funny little place high up on the mountain side with noisy torrents all round it, The goats came flocking home before we left: they had spent a night out on the mountains, having been caught somewhere in the dark and they bleated loud complaints as they crowded round the hut, licking the shepherd's hand. It was about 7:30 before Ulrich and I set off down the exquisite Urbach Thal; Heinrich had gone on before. We walked down for a couple of hours discussing ways up the Engelhorn and the Communal System! then we turned into the valley of the Aar and dropped down on to Innertkirchen in the green plain below. This is Ulrich's native place. We went to his home and found his old father, a nice old man Of 70, who welcomed us with effusion. It was an enchanting house, an old wooden chalet dated 1749, with low rooms and long rows of windows, with muslin curtains, and geranium pots in them. All spotlessly clean. They gave me a large—well, lunch, it was 11:30, of eggs and tea and bread and cheese and bilberry jam, after which Ulrich and I walked up through the woods here and arrived at 2 in the afternoon. I don't think I have ever had two more delightful alpine days. Tomorrow I go over to Grindelwald; the weather looks quite settled. Wednesday up to the hut, from whence on Wednesday night we try the Finsteraarhorn arête. If we do it we sleep at another hut On Thursday night, and at the Grimsel on Friday and Saturday. Sunday night we bivouac under the Lauteraarhorn and Monday try the arête to the Schreckhorn. Probably I should leave for England on Tuesday. . . .

I am very sorry to leave this nice place. What do you think is our fortnight's bag? Two old peaks. Seven new peaks—one of them first-class and four others very good. One new saddle, also first-class.

The traverse of the Engelhorn, also new and first-class.

That's not bad going, is it! . . . .

To F. B.
GRINDELWALD, September 12th, 1901.

Our tale is a sad one. We went up to a hut for the new Finsteraarhorn arête yesterday morning, in very shaky weather. it shook down, rained all the afternoon, and at 6 a.m. this morning began to snow. By 8, when we left, there were 3 inches of new snow, so we raced back to Grindelwald. . . . It is very provoking, when one feels one might do really good climbs! We hope to do a new Engelhorn peak, and we have not yet quite abandoned all hopes of one of the high arêtes. I would like to have one of them to my name! It is a silly ambition, isn't it! Still one does like to have the credit one really deserves.

To F. B.
November 27, 1901.

Of course I will take the Mothers' Meeting on Wednesday. I will find out about sending out the invitations. Will you tell me what you want read—any of the Health Book?—and if so, where is it? I can look out some story. . . .

To F.B.
RED BARNS, Thursday, December 18, 1901.

All has gone off quite well. We had over 200 people. Your telegram arrived and I read it out to them in the middle of my speech! The magic lantern slides are lovely, it was most exciting seeing them. . . .

Tell Father I've written to Maurice by every mail all about him! He mustn't get to think there's nothing else to write about! Hugo says Prout's an old fogey—that's what he says! I say Hugo is a great darling!

To F.B.
RED BARNS, December 29, 1901.

I have spent the afternoon in Clarence and Middlesbrough and made all the arrangements for the teas. My slides are announced, so all is well. . . .

Hugo sends seasonable wishes. He has retired into Cicero.

[1902. Gertrude, her father and Hugo indefatigably start for another sea voyage after the new year, leaving Liverpool January 14 and going by sea to Malta, then to Sicily and up through Italy. Hugo and his father returned and

Gertrude made her way into Asia Minor.

Her letters, full of interesting descriptions, are too long to quote, from Malcajik, Smyrna, Magnesia, Burnabat and finally from Smyrna by sea to Haifa.]

[At Malcajik—"Mr. Van Lennep and his family full of help and hospitality." By Smyrna to Pergamos.]

"You should see me shopping in Smyrna, quite like a native only I ought to have more flashing eyes. At Pergamos I went all over the Acropolis and examined temples and palaces and theatres and the great altar of which the friezes are at Berlin."

[Magnesia and Sardis.] "I was fortunate enough to get a secondhand copy of Herodotus in French."

[Sardis] "I was delighted that I had Herodotus so fresh in my mind. . . ."

"It is a madly interesting place."

"Some day I shall come and travel here with tents but then I will speak Turkish, which will not be difficult and I will take only a couple of Turkish servants with me."

[To Butnabat, where she is warmly welcomed by Mr. Whittall and his family. To Ephesus. She then goes on an Austrian boat from Smyrna to Haifa. She finds a temporary abode at Mount Carmel.]

"I am now become one of the prophets-at least I make merry in their room so to speak—and it's a very nice room, I may add, and I am sitting writing at my own writing table with everything genteel about me."

To F. B.

MOUNT CARMEL, 26th March, 1902.

There must be something in the air of Mount Carmel favourable to mental derangement of a special kind—at any rate if you want to commence prophet you take a little house in Haifa, you could scarcely begin in any other way. I have already made the acquaintance of one or two for this afternoon I went down to Haifa—I live on the top of the hill—Haifa is half an hour away—to seek out a teacher. Presently I also approached the window and there was the prophet in his shirt with bare arms working at his trade which I take to be that of a carpenter. . . . I distinctly like prophets—Herr Wasserzug is a charming man, most intelligent about Semitic languages. He sent me off to one Abu Nimrud, a native, 'comme de droit,' of Nineveh, who, he said, was the best man he could recommend. On my way I called on Mr. Monahan. offered me books and advice and coffee. . . . I took a Persian history of the Babis from him and went off hunting Nimrud all over the town. At last I found him in his shop in the bazaar—he agreed to come up and give me my first lesson to-day, but need I say he hasn't come. The next thing was to get a Persian. My old friend Abbas Effendi. . . . I heard that the son-in-law of Abbas, Hussein Effendi, lived here, and I determined to apply to him. Accordingly I made my way to his shop—a sort of little general store like the shop in a small country town—and in this unlikely setting I found a company of grave Persians, sitting round on the biscuit tins and the bags of grain, and Hussein himself leaning over the counter. The upshot of it is that I hope I shall end by getting a Persian to come and talk to me. A horse was the next necessity and horse dealers my next acquaintances—I see one this instant upon the road bringing me up a horse to try. I am excellently lodged in two rooms with a balcony from whence I see all across the bay and Acre at the end of a long stretch of sand, and the Plain of Esdraelon with Kishor, running through it and far away Hermon white with snow,

Later. But for all that I find I shall have to déménager. Abu Nimrud came up this morning and gave me a long lesson but he declared that it was too far for him to come and that he could only get me a Persian on condition that I would come down into the town, so I rode down this afternoon and inspected the two hotels and fixed on one standing in a charming garden where I could get 2 big comfortable rooms; it has the further advantage of being kept by Syrians so that I shall hear and speak nothing but Arabic. . . . Hussein Effendi's brother-in-law is going to teach me Persian.

To H.B.
MOUNT CARMEL, 30th March, 1902.
* * * But mind, if ever you think I'm unbearable, just say it straight out and mention what you can't abide and I'll do my best to mend it. To return to the East. I'm having a comic time, but most amusing. I had a delightful afternoon by myself on Friday and rode out from 1 to 6 on the worst horse in the world. I rode and rode all along the top of Carmel, and though the prophet declares that if you even flee there the Almighty would certainly find you, I think myself that he is mistaken. I can't find anything, not even a village, of which I am told there are some. But I rode over ridge after ridge of rolling hill, and round the top of valley after valley, rocky slopes covered with wild flowers running steeply down into waterless hollows and the whole mountain was heavy with the scent of gorse and the aromatic herbs that my horse crushed through from time to time to avoid an unusually slippery bit of rock in the path. The whole afternoon I saw only 2 houses and 4 people, shepherds with flocks of lop-eared goats—ridiculous ears they have, 10 inches long I should say, an absurd waste of skin. . . . Sometimes I walked and drove my horse in front of me, and by this means I found out that he really could gallop, for he galloped away from me and I concluded not to let him go loose any more. I gathered 2 scarlet tulips, the lovely little tulips with the curling leaf; it is the same as the one of which Hafiz says thus, doubting the promises of Fate it carries always a Wine cup through the wilderness. . . . I am much entertained to find that I am a Person in this country—they all think I was a Person! And one of the first questions everyone seems to ask everyone else is, "Have you ever met Miss Gertrude Bell?" Renown is not very difficult to acquire here.

Monday, 31. To-day I came down into Haifa early with Mr. M. and established myself in my new hotel. I had an Arabic lesson and interviewed a Persian who is to come and teach me every evening after dinner. My hotel is most comfortable, kept by Syrians and I hear and speak nothing but Arabic which is really ideal. I have a large sitting-room—you should see how nice it looks with all my books and things and great pots of mimosa and jasmine and wild flowers.

To H.B.
HAIFA, April 7th, 1902.

This afternoon I paid a long call on the mother and sisters of my Persian—their house is my house, you understand, and I am to go and talk Persian whenever I like. This is my day: I get up at 7, at 8 Abu Nimrud comes and teaches me Arabic—till 10. I go on working till 12, when I lunch. Then I write for my Persian till 1:30, or so, when I ride or walk out. Come in at 5, and work till 7, when I dine. At 7:30 my Persian comes and stays till 10, and at 10:30 I go to bed. You see I have not Much leisure time! And the whole day long I talk Arabic.

To F.B.
HAIFA, April 2, 1902.

I love my two sheikhs. It's perfectly delightful getting hold Of Persian again, the delicious language! But as for Arabic I am soaked and soddened by it and how anyone can wish to have anything to do with a tongue so difficult when they might be living at ease, I can't imagine. I never stop talking in this hotel and I think I get a little worse daily . . . ..

The birds fly into my room and nest in the chandelier!

To F. B.
Tuesday, 22nd April, 1902.

On Monday I went to lunch with my Persians. A young gentleman was invited to meet me-he's a carpenter-and he and I and Mirza Abdullah lunched together solemnly while the wife and sisters waited on us. We had a very good lunch, rice and pillau and sugared dates and kabobs. It was all spread on the table at once and we helped ourselves with our forks at will, dilating the while on the absurdity of the European custom of serving one dish after another so that you never knew what you were going to have, also of whipping away your plate every moment and giving you another! The conversation was carried on in Persian which I speak worse than anyone was ever known to do. I told you that there were 2 American Professors of Divinity in the Hotel? One whose name I don't know is a particularly attractive man, oldish, very intelligent and with a sweet goodness of face and I am sure of character which is very loveable. I was telling Mirza Abdullah about him last night and he said he would like to see him and ask him a question. So I went out and fetched my old American, telling him the sort of person he had to deal with, and Mirza Abdullah (I being interpreter) asked him what he considered were the proofs of Christ's being God. The American answered in the most charming manner, but of course could give no proofs except a personal conviction. Mirza A. said, "He speaks as a lover, but I want the answer of the learned." I felt as I interpreted between them how much the philosophic inquiring eastern mind differed from ours. The value my professor attached to the vivifying qualities of Christ's teaching was certainly lost on the Oriental, and on the other hand Abdullah's dialectics were incomprehensible to the western—at least the starting point was incomprehensible. They talked for about an hour and at the end Abdullah was quite as much at a loss as before to understand why the Professor accepted one prophet and rejected the others and I'm bound to say I quite sympathised with him. He said to me after the Professor had gone: "You must reject all or accept all, but he chooses and can give no reason. He believes what his fathers have taught him." It was a very curious evening. The professor was a perfect angel all the time. One could not help being immensely impressed with the quality of his faith.

[She returns to England at the end of May. She has a pleasant month at home, and early in July we find her in Switzerland again.]

TO F.B.
ROSENLAUI, July 8th, 1902.

I had a most luxurious journey. My 2 guides met me, I dined and made plans and went to bed and slept for 11 hours! . . . We got up to this enchanting place in time for lunch and I was received with rapture by my friend the innkeeper—oh! I must tell you that the guard on the train of the Brünnig line asked me if I were Miss Bell who had climbed the Engelhorn last year. This is fame. There is another climbing woman here—Frl. Kuntze—very good indeed she is, but not very Well Pleased to see me as I deprive her of Ulrich Fuhrer with whom she has been climbing. She has got a German with her, a distinguished climber from Berne, and I sat and talked to them this afternoon when they came in from a little expedition. They have done several things in the Engelhorn but the best thing hereabouts remains to be done and Ulrich and I are going to have an inspection walk the day after tomorrow. Tomorrow we propose to do a new rock which Will probably give us an amusing climb and which will, I hope, be short. . . . The flowers are entrancing—piles of things of which I remember the pictures in my alpine book and forget the names. I wish you would send me that book—Alpine Flora, I think it's called—on one of the shelves above MY writing table at Redcar.

To F. B.
ROSENLAUI, July 11th, 1902.

We had a delightful day on Tuesday, did a charming little rock, up one way and down another, both ways new though the point had been made from a third side by some guides. especially the descent which was quite difficult. We got ourselves landed on to the top of some very smooth rocks, down which we slid on an extra rope with the exciting uncertainty as to whether the rope would reach far enough and as to what would lie below. But the rope was exactly long enough to a foot and led us down to some broken cracks and couloirs by which we descended on to the grass slopes . . . .. Between the two Wellhorns there is an arête of rocks which has never been attempted—it is indeed one of the 4 impossibles of the Oberland—and we intend to do it and we think we can. . . .

Accordingly we got up to-day at midnight, a beautifully starry night, and set off with quantities of spare rope up the slopes to the foot of the Vorder Wellhorn. We hadn't been gone more than half-an-hour before a storm began coming up from all sides at once and we called a halt to see how matters were going to turn out. We lay shivering under a rock for some time while the clouds blew up faster and faster, and lightning began and the thunder and the first drops of rain reached us. Fortunately there were some deserted chalets just below us so I sent Ulrich to see if we could take shelter in them. He came back looking rather dubious and I asked whether there was any one in them. "Dere is pig," he replied. Still pig were better than rain, so we hurried down and fortunately found a hut with nothing in it but some clean hay on which we established ourselves luxuriously. It was half-past 2 or 3 by this time and we lay and waited to see what the dawn would bring, Ulrich relating alpine adventures to pass the time. But the dawn brought more rain and more thunder and we gave up hope, and ran down to the inn where we arrived about 5. I went to bed promptly and slept till 12. And if it clears we are going to begin the same game again to-night.

To F. B.
VORDER WELLHORN, July 14th, 1902.

We have done the first of the impossibles , the Wellhorn arête, and are much elated. We started at 5 yesterday and ran up the Vorder Wellhorn as fast as ever we could, making only a 5 minutes halt while we roped. The arête looked awful from the top of the Vorder Wellhorn. There was a most discouraging bit of smooth rock in it and above that an overhang round which we could see no way. My heart sank—I thought we should never do it. However we set off and when we came nearer we found that these two places were not half as bad as they looked and after 4 hours of very fine arête climbing we lunched at the top of the overhang in the best of spirits. But the worst was to come—a long knife edge of rock so rotten that it fell away in masses as we went along, horrid precipices beneath us so that the greatest care was needed at every step. And it ended in a sharp gap on the further side of which 2 short but extremely exposed chimneys led up to the final slopes. We took nearly an hour over these, I standing most of the time, shivering with cold, at the bottom Of the lowest, while my two guides worked on the tiny ledge above me which was too narrow for us all 3. Finally Ulrich called outt "I have hold of it!" and Heinrich and I scrabbled after him with the aid of an iron nail driven in in the worst place and of a double rope. We ended our day by crossing the Rosenlaui glacier under the séracs, a thing we had no business to do for they hung over us in the most threatening manner, but it Saved us at least 2 hours and we got through without their falling On us. I think if the weather holds, I shall go over to the Grimsel, for the second impossible is now on our minds and we want to set about it as soon as we can.

To H. B.
KURHAUS ROSENLAUI, BERNER OBERLAND July 20, 1902.

I came over here yesterday morning, walking over the Scheidegg, and a most delicious hot day. Yseult Grant Duff met me on the top of the pass and walked down with me. . . . This morning I started out at 5:30 to—well, Ulrich Calls it examining the movement of rocks, it means that you go up and see if a stone falls On You and if it doesn't you know you can go UP that way. It's a new ascent of the Wetterhorn—a mad Scheme I'm inclined to think, but still we'll see how it goes. We went up the steep slopes and up rocks and under a glacier fall, where I examined the movement of a stone on my knee—fortunately a small one, but it hurt for it fell from a long way up—and then we hastily turned back. However, on examination we thought we could get up another way and we intend to try it seriously. . . .

To H. B.
MEIPLINGEN, Sunday, August 3, 1902.

For once I must begin by acknowledging that Donmul's gloomy forebodings came very near to being realised, and I am now feeling some satisfaction in the thought that my bones are not lying scattered on the Alpine mountains cold. Don,t be alarmed, however, they are all quite safe and sound in the Grimsel and if it were not for a little touch of frostbite in the feet I should be merrily on my way to fresh adventures. . . . On Monday it rained and we could do nothing. On Tuesday we set out at 1 a.m. and made for a crack high up on the Wetterhorn rocks which we had observed through glasses. We got up to it after about 3 hours' climbing only to find to our sorrow that the séracs were tumbling continually down it from all directions. We concluded that it was far too risky—indeed it would have been madness to attempt it for we could see from the broken ice on the rocks that the great blocks were thrown from side to side as they fell and swept the whole passage and it was the only place where the cliffs could be climbed at all; we turned sadly back. I record this piece of prudence with pleasure. . . . Next day I came up here. It was a most delicious morning. I left Meiringen at 6 and shared my coach with a dear little American couple who were making a walking tour in Switzerland-by coach mostly, I gathered. There was also a pleasant Englishman called Campbell who was coming up with a rope and an ice axe, a member of the A.C. as I found on talking to him at the halting places. He appears later in the story. Well, we lunched here and set off in the afternoon to the Pavillon Dolfuss, of ill omen, where We arrived at 6. But anything more inviting than the little hut that evening it would be difficult to imagine. It was perfect weather, the most lovely evening I have ever seen in the Alps. Until the sun set at 7 behind the Schreckhorn I sat out of doors without a coat and walked over the tiny alp botanizing while My guides cooked the soup Every sort of Alpine plant grows on the cultivated alp; i found even very sweet pale violets under the big stones. I had it all to myself; I was the lord of all mountains that night and rejoiced exceedingly in my great possessions. The matter we had in hand was the ascent of the face of the Finsteraarhorn: it is a well-known problem and the opinions of the learned are divided as to its solution. Dr. Wilson looked at it this year and decided against it. We have looked at it for 2 years and decided for it and other authorities agree with us in what I still think is a right opinion. The mountain on the side facing the Schreckhorn comes down in a series of arches radiating from the extremely pointed top to the Finsteraar glacier. . . . The arête, the one which has always been discussed, rises from the glacier in a great series of gendarmes and towers, set at such an angle on the steep face of the mountain that you wonder how they can stand at all and indeed they can scarcely be said to stand, for the great points of them are continually overbalancing and tumbling down into the couloirs between the arêtes and they are all capped with loosely poised stones, jutting out and hanging over and ready to fall at any moment. But as long as you keep pretty near to the top of the arête you are Safe from them because they fall into the couloirs on either side, the difficulty is to get on to the arête because you have to cross a couloir down which the stones fall, not to speak Of avalanches; the game was beginning even when we (crossed it an hour after dawn. We left the hut at 1:35 a.m. Thursday. Crossed the séracs just at dawn and by 6 found ourselves comfortably established on the arête, beyond the reach of the stones which the mountain had fired at us (fortunately with rather a bad aim) for the first half-hour on the rock. we breakfasted then followed a difficult and dangerous climb. It was difficult because the rocks were exceedingly steep, every now and then we had to creep up and Out of the common hard chimney—one in particular about mid-day I remember, because we subsequently had the very deuce of a time coming down it, or round the face of a tower or cut our way across an ice couloir between two gendarmes and it was dangerous because the whole rock was so treacherous. I found this out very early in the morning by putting my hand into the crack of a rock which looked as if it went into the very foundations of things. About 2 feet square of rock tumbled out upon me and knocked me a little way down the hill till I managed to part company with it on a tiny ledge. I got back on to my feet without being pulled up by the rope, which was as well for a little later I happened to pass the rope through my hands and found that it had been cut half through about a yard from my waist when the rock had fallen on it. This was rather a nuisance as it shortened a rope we often wanted long to allow of our going up difficult chimneys in turn. So on and on we went up the arête and the towers multiplied like rabbits above and grew steeper and steeper and about 2 o'clock I looked round and saw great black clouds rolling up from the west. But by this time looking up we also saw the topmost tower of the arête far above us still, and the summit of the mountain further still and though we could not yet see what the top of the arête was like we were cheered and pushed on steadily for another hour while the weather signs got worse and worse. At 3 just as the first snow flakes began to fall, we got into full view of the last two gendarmes and the first one was quite impossible. The ridge had been growing narrow, its sides steeper as we mounted, so that we had been obliged for some time to stick quite to the backbone of it; then it threw itself up into a great tower leaning over to the right and made of slabs set like slates on the top with a steep drop of some 20 feet below them on to the Col. We were then 1000 feet below the summit I should guess, perhaps rather less, anyway we could see our way up, not easy but possible, above this tower and once on the top could get down the other side in any weather. It had to be tried: we sat down to eat a few mouthfuls the snow falling fast driven by a strong wind, and a thick mist marching up the valley below, over the Finsteraar joch, then we crept along the knife edge of a col, fastened a rope firmly round a rock and let Ulrich down on to a ledge below the overhang of the tower. He tried it for a few moments and then gave it up. The ledge was very narrow, sloped outwards and was quite rotten. Anything was better than that. So we tried the left side of the tower: there was a very steep iced couloir running up at the foot of the rock on that side for about 50 feet, after which all would be well. Again we let ourselves down on the extra rope to the foot of the tower, again to find that this way also was impossible. A month later in the year I believe this couloir would go; after a warm August there would be no ice in it, and though it is very steep the rocks so far as one could see under the ice, looked climbable. But even with the alternative before us of the descent down the terrible arete, we decided to turn back; already the snow was blowing down the couloir in a small avalanche, small but blinding, and the wind rushed down upon us carrying the mists with it. If it had been fine weather we should have tried down the areête a little and then a traverse so as to get at the upper rocks by another road. I am not sure that it could be done but we should have tried anything—but by the time we had been going down for half-an-hour we could see nothing of the mountain side to the right or to the left except an occasional glimpse as one cloud rolled off and another rolled over. The snow fell fast and covered the rocks with incredible speed. Difficult as they had been to go up, you may imagine what they were like going down when we could no longer so much as see them. There was One corner in particular where we had to get round the face of a tower. We came round the corner, down a very steep chimney, got on to a sloping out rock ledge with an inch of new snow on it; there was a crack in which you could stand and with one hand hold in the rock face, from whence you had to drop down about 8 feet on to steep snow. We fixed the extra rope and tumbled down one after the Other On to the snow; it was really more or less safe because one had the fixed rope to hold on to, but it felt awful: I shall remember every inch of that rock face for the rest of my life. It was now near 6. Our one idea was to get down to the chimney—the mid-day chimney which was so very difficult—so as to do it while there was still only a little snow on it. We toiled on till 8, by which time a furious thunderstorm was raging. We were standing by a great upright on the top of a tower when suddenly it gave a crack and a blue flame sat On it for a second just like the one we saw when we were driving, you remember, only nearer. My ice axe jumped in my hand and I thought the steel felt hot through my woollen glove—was that possible? I didn't take my glove off to see! Before we knew where we were the rock flashed again—it was a great sticking out stone and I expect it attracted the lightning, but we didn't stop to consider this theory but tumbled down a chimney as hard as ever we could, one on top of the other, buried our ice axe heads in some shale at the bottom of it and hurriedly retreated from them. It's not nice to carry a private lightning conductor in your hand in the thick of a thunderstorm, It was clear we could go no further that night, the question was to find the best lodging while there was still light enough to see. We hit upon a tiny crack sheltered from the wind, even the snow did not fall into it. There was just room for me to sit in the extreme back of it on a very pointed bit of rock; by doubling up I could even get my head into it. Ulrich sat on my feet to keep them warm and Heinrich just below him. They each of them put their feet into a knapsack which is the golden rule of bivouac. The other golden rule is to take no brandy because you feel the reaction more after. I knew this and insisted on it. It was really not so bad; we shivered all night but our hands and feet were warm and climbers are like Pobbles in the matter of toes. I went to sleep quite often and was wakened up every hour or so by the intolerable discomfort of my position, which I then changed by an inch or two into another which was bearable for an hour more. At first the thunderstorm made things rather exciting. The claps followed the flashes so close that there seemed no interval between them. We tied ourselves firmly on to the rock above lest as Ulrich philosophically said one of us should be struck and fall out. The rocks were all crackling round us and fizzing like damp wood which is just beginning to burn—have you ever heard that? It's a curious exciting sound rather exhilarating—and as there was no further precaution possible I enjoyed the extraordinary magnificence of the storm with a free mind: it was worth seeing. Gradually the night cleared and became beautifully starry. Between 2 and 3 the moon rose, a tiny crescent, and we spoke of the joy it would be when the sun rose full on to us and stopped our shivering. But the sun never rose at all—at least for all practical purposes. The day came wrapped in a blinding mist and heralded by a cutting, snow-laden wind—this day was Friday; we never saw the sun in it. It must have snowed a good deal during the thunderstorm for when we stepped out of our crack in the first grey light about 4 (too stiff to bear it a moment longer) everything was deep in it. I can scarcely describe to you what that day was like. We were from 4 a.m. to 8 p.m. on the arête; during that time we ate for a minute or two 3 times and my fare I know was 5 ginger bread biscuits, 2 sticks of chocolate, a slice of bread, a scrap of cheese and a handful of raisins. We had nothing to drink but about two tablespoonfuls of brandy in the bottom of my flask and a mouthful of wine in the guides' wine skin, but it was too cold to feel thirsty. There was scarcely a yard which we could come down without the extra rope; you can imagine the labour of finding a rock at every 50 feet round which to sling it, then of pulling it down behind us and slinging it We had our bit of good luck-it never caught all day. But both the ropes were thoroughly iced and terribly difficult to manage, and the weather was appalling. It snowed all day sometimes softly as decent snow should fall, sometimes driven by a furious bitter wind which enveloped us not only in the falling snow, but lifted all the light powdery snow from the rocks and sent it whirling down the precipices and into the couloirs and on to us indifferently. It was rather interesting to see the way a mountain behaves in a snowstorm and how avalanches are born and all the wonderful and terrible things that happen in high places. The couloirs were all running with snow rivers—we had to cross one and a nasty uncomfortable process it was. As soon as you cut a step it was filled up before you could put your foot into it. But I think that when things are as bad as ever they can be you cease to mind them much. You set your teeth and battle with the fates. we meant to get down whatever happened and it was such an exciting business that we had no time to think of the discomfort. I know I never thought of the danger except once and then quite calmly. I'll tell you about that presently The first thing we had to tackle was the chimney. We had to fix our rope in it twice, the second time round a very unsafe nail. I stood in this place holding Heinrich, there was an overhang. He climbed a bit of the way and then fell on to soft snow and spun down the couloir till my rope brought him up with a jerk. Then he got up on to a bit of rock on the left about half as high as the overhang. Ulrich came down to me and I repeated Heinrich's process exactly, the iced extra rope slipping through my hands like butter. Then came Ulrich. He was held by Heinrich and me standing a good deal to the left but only half as high up as he. He climbed down to the place we had both fallen from asking our advice at every step, then he called out " Heinrich, Heinrich, ich bin verloren," and tumbled off just as we had done and we held him up in the couloir, more dead than alive with anxiety. We gave him some of our precious brandy on a piece of sugar and he soon recovered and went on as boldly as before. We thought the worst was over but there was a more dangerous place to come. It was a place that had been pretty difficult to go up, a steep but short slope of iced rock by which we had turned the base of a tower. The slope was now covered with about 4 inches of avalanche snow and the rocks were quite hidden. It was on the edge of a big couloir down which raced a snow river. We managed badly somehow; at any rate, Ulrich and I found ourselves on a place where there was not room for us both to stand, at the end of the extra rope. He was very Insecure and could not hold me, Heinrich was below on the edge of the couloir, also very insecure. And here I had to refix the extra rope on a rock a little below me so that it was practically no good to me. But it was the only possible plan. The rock was too difficult for me, the stretches too big, I couldn't reach them: I handed my axe down to Heinrich and told him I could do nothing but fall, but he couldn't, or at any rate, didn't secure himself and in a second we were both tumbling head over heels down the couloir, which was, you understand, as steep as snow could lie. How Ulrich held us I don't know. He said himself he would not have believed it possible but hearing me say I was going to fall he had stuck the pointed end of the ice axe into a crack above and on this alone we all three held. I got on to my feet in the snow directly I came to the end of my leash of rope and held Heinrich and caught his ice axe and mine and we slowly cut ourselves back up the couloir to the foot of the rock. But it was a near thing and I felt rather ashamed of my part in it. This was the time when I thought it on the cards we should not get down alive. Rather a comforting example, however, of how little can hold a party up. About 2 in the afternoon we all began to feel tired. I had a pain through my shoulder and down my back which was due, I think, to nothing but the exertion of rock climbing and the nervous fatigue of shivering—for we never stopped shivering all day, it was impossible to control one's tired muscles in that bitter cold. And so we went on for 6 hours more of which only the last hour was easy and at 8 found ourselves at the top of the Finsteraar glacier and in the dark, with a good guess and good luck, happened on the right place in the Bergschrund and let ourselves down over it. It was now quite dark, the snow had turned into Pouring rain, and we sank 6 inches into the soft glacier with every step. Moreover we were wet through: we had to cross several big crevasses and get down the sérac before we could reach the Unteraar glacier and safety. For we had felt no anxiety having relied upon our lantern but not a single match would light. We had every kind with usin metal match boxes but the boxes were wet and we had not a dry rag of any kind to rub them with. We tried to make a tent Out Of my skirt and to light a match under it, but our fingers were dripping wet and numb with cold—one could scarcely feel anything smaller than an ice axe-and the match heads dropped off limply into the snow without So much as a spark. Then we tried to go on and after a few steps Heinrich fell into a soft place almost up to his neck and Ulrich and I had to pull him out with the greatest difficulty and the mists swept up over the glacier and hid everything; that was the only moment of despair. We had so looked forward to dry blankets in the Pavillon Dollfuss and here we were with another night out before us. And a much worse one than the first, for we were on the shelterless glacier and in driving drenching rain. We laid our three axes together and sat on them side by side. Ulrich and I put our feet into a sack but Heinrich refused to use the other and gave it to me to lie on. My shoulders ached and ached. I insisted on our all eating something even the smallest scrap, and then I put a wet pocket handkerchief over my face to keep the rain from beating on it and went to sleep. It sounds incredible but I think we all slept more or less and woke up to the horrible discomfort and went to sleep again. I consoled myself by thinking of Maurice in S. Africa and how he had slept out in the pouring rain and been none the worse. We couldn't see the time but long before we expected it a sort of grey light came over the snow and when at last I could read my watch, behold it was 4. We gathered ourselves up; at first we could scarcely stand but after a few steps we began to walk quite creditably. About 6 we got to where we could unrope—having been 48 hours on the rope—and we reached here at 10 on Saturday.

They had all been in a great state of anxiety about us, seeing the weather, and had telegraphed to Meiringen, to Grindelwald, to know whether we had turned up. So I got into a warm bath and then discovered to my great surprise that my feet were ice cold and without any sensation. But having eaten a great many boiled eggs and drunk jugs of hot milk I went to bed and woke about dinner time to find my toes swollen and stiff. Frau Lieseguay then appeared and said that a S. American doctor had passed through in the afternoon and had seen Ulrich and Heinrich and had bound up their hands and feet in cotton wool and told them to keep very warm; so she bound up my feet too-my hands are nearly all right but I think my feet are worse than theirs. Still they seem better now and I don't expect I shall be toeless. They are not nearly as bad as my hands were in the Dauphiné, but the worst of It is that with swollen toes bound up in cotton wool one can't walk at all and I shall just have to wait till they get better. I slept for about 24 hours only waking up to eat, and it's now 4 in the afternoon and I'm just going to get up and have tea with Mr. Campbell, who has, I hear, been an angel of kindness to my guides. They seem to be none the worse except that Ulrich had a touch of rheumatism this morning, and as for me, I am perfectly absolutely well except for my toes-not so much as a cold in the head. Isn't it remarkable! I do wonder where mother is and whether she is anywhere near at hand; if she were I should like to have nursed my toes in her company but I expect I shall be all right in a day or two. I don't mean to move till I am. Isn't that an awful dreadful adventure! It makes me laugh to think of it, but seriously now that I am comfortably indoors, I do rather wonder that we ever got down the Finsteraarhorn and that we were not frozen at the bottom of it. What do you think?

[Captain Farrar of the Alpine Club writes as follows respecting this ascent :

"The vertical height of the rock face measured from the glacier to the summit of the mountain is about 3,000 feet. There can be in the whole Alps few places so steep and so high. The climb has only been done three times including your daughter's attempt, and is still considered one of the greatest expeditions in the whole Alps."

The following In Memoriam notice of Gertrude, Written by Colonel E. L. Strutt, now editor of the Alpine journal, appeared in the A.J. for November, 1926, at which time Captain Farrar was the editor.

"I do not know when Miss Bell commenced her mountaineering career. It was, however, in the first years of this century that her ascents attracted attention, and about the period 1901-1903 there was no more prominent lady mountaineer. Everything that she undertook, physical or mental, was accomplished so superlatively well, that it would indeed have been strange if she had not shone on a mountain as she did in the hunting-field or in the desert. Her strength, incredible in that slim frame, her endurance, above all her courage, were so great that even to this day her guide and companion Ulrich Fuhrer— and there could be few more competent judges—speaks with an admiration of her that amounts to veneration. He told the writer, some years ago, that of all the amateurs, men or women, that he had travelled with, he had seen but very few to surpass her in technical skill and none to equal her in coolness, bravery and judgment.

"Fuhrer's generous tribute on what was probably the most terrible adventure in the lives of all those concerned. 'You who have made the climb will perhaps be able to correctly appreciate our work. But the honour belongs to Miss Bell. Had she not been full of courage and determination, we must have perished. She was the one who insisted on our eating from time to time. The scene was high up on the then unclimbed N.E. face of the Finsteraarhorn, when the party was caught in a blizzard on that difficult and exposed face and were out for fifty-seven hours, of which fifty-three were spent on the rope. Retreat under such conditions, and retreating safely, was a tremendous performance which does credit to all.' The date was July 31 to August 2, 1902; the occasion was a defeat greater than many a victory. 'When the freezing wind beats you almost to the ground, when the blizzard nearly blinds you, half paralysing your senses . . . . when the cold is so intense that the snow freezes on You as it falls, clothing you in a sheet of ice, till life becomes insupportable. . . . .' then, indeed, was Miss Bell preeminent.

"The Lauteraarhorn-Schreckhorn traverse was probably Miss Bell's most important first ascent, July 24, 1902. It is related that she and her guides, meeting on the ridge another lady with her guides making the same ascent from the opposite direction, were not greeted with enthusiasm. In the seasons 1901-1902 Miss Bell was the first to explore systematically the Engelhorner group, making with Fuhrer many new routes and several first ascents. An extract from a letter of the chief Alpine authority, dated December 10, 1911, may be quoted. . . . 'You ask me for some notes on Miss Bell's ascents, and I send all I have. . . . she was not one to advertize, and yet, or probably because of it, they tell me that she was the best of all lady mountaineers. . . . (Signed) W. A. B. Coolidge.'

"The notes contain the following, all relating to the different Engelhorner and all new routes or first ascents
Similistock, August 30, 1901.
King's Peak & Gerard's Peak August 31, 1901.
Vorderspitze & Gertrude's Peak & Ulrich's Peak
& Mittelspitze September 3, 1901.
Klein Engelhorn & Gemsenspitze & Urbachthaler Engelhorn
September 7, 1901
Klein Similistock, July 8, 1902.

"For the reasons stated above, it is difficult to name her other expeditions in the Alps, but a well-known climber has stated that his most vivid recollection of an ascent of Mont Blanc was the effort required to follow Miss Bell.

"Such, briefly and inadequately tendered, are some of the Alpine qualifications of her who must ever be regarded as one of the greatest women of all time., E. L. S."]

To F.B.
London, August 11th, 1902.
I am quite perfectly well. I left Grimsel on the Monday after my adventure and returned to Rosenlaui, walking up, although on rather swollen toes. There I stayed 2 days and then, my time being up, returned home via Bruges where I spent a charming 74 hours. I met the Frank Pembers and the Albert Grays there. . . .

My toes are nearly well; I'm still just a little lame, but it's nothing. I walk about gaily. My best love to Amy. it's horrid cold here.

To F.B.
LONDON, August 13th, 1902.
I am so dreadfully sorry to gather that you have been anxious about me. . . . I am now in boisterous health, as I hope this finds you.

I had a very pleasant dinner with Domnul en tête-à-tête on Monday. We drew out maps and discussed his Persian journey and our hidden plans. He has just been to tea with me—we want to meet in Delhi! I've got a letter from Colonel Baring saying that we are to be put up in the Viceroy's camp. It will be the greatest joke in life. I lunched yesterday with the Storrys. He wants me to write a book for him in a series on art he is bringing out for Gerald Duckworth. He gave me my choice of subject. I think if I did it I would write on Florentines between Giotto and Donatello—the great moment of upspringing when art threw off Byzantium and took on Greece. But I feel very doubtful as to whether I could do it and then when! However, I am to think it over. What do you think? I must tell you the other writers are Furtwangler and people of his sort! Charlie Furse is to do Tintoret, Mrs. Strong Rome, Strzygowski, the greatest living authority, the period before mine. It is very alarming.——

['Domnul,' the Roumanian word for 'gentleman,' is an affectionate nickname for Sir V. Chirol, dating from the Bucharest Days.]

CHAPTER VIII
1902-1903

ROUND THE WORLD THE SECOND TIME

[AT the end of 1902 Gertrude and Hugo started off to go round the world together, their route being India (including the Delhi Durbar), Burma, Java, China and America.

Shortly before their departure the present Bishop of St. Albans, then the Rev. Michael Furse, came to stay with us at Redcar. He was a Don at Trinity College, Oxford, when Hugo was an undergraduate there, and they became great friends. Hugo was devoted to him for ever afterwards. The Bishop now sends us these notes of a talk he had with Gertrude at that time.

"I remember well a walk which I took one evening on the sands at Redcar with his very remarkable and Charming sister Gertrude; it was just before she and Hugo were going off round the world together. In her delightfully blunt and provocative way, she turned on me suddenly and said in a very defiant voice, 'I suppose you don't approve of this plan of Hugo going round the world with me?' 'Why shouldn't I?' I said. 'Well, you may be pretty sure he won't come back a Christian.' 'Why do you say that?' I asked. 'Oh, because I've got a much better brain than Hugo, and a year in my company will be bound to upset his faith.' 'Oh, will it?' I said. 'Don't you be too sure about that. If I Was a betting man I'd give you a hundred to one against it. But even if things do pan out as you think, I am tremendously glad Hugo is going with you, for I should much rather he came to the conclusion that the whole thing was nonsense before he took orders than afterwards! You do your hardest' (which I fear was not the actual word I used, but something much stronger!) 'and see what happens.'"

The Bishop was right. Hugo returned unchanged, and in due course he was ordained in 1909. In 1909 Mr. Furse became Bishop of Pretoria. Hugo followed him to South Africa in 1912 and was with him as his chaplain until the Bishop came back to England for good in 1920.]

To F.B.
December 4th, 1902.

* * * Hugo is the most delightful of travelling companions. We spend a lot of time making plans with maps in front of us. We are chiefly exercised as to how many of the Pacific Islands we shall visit. It is immensely amusing to have the world before us . . . .

[So many descriptions have been written of the Delhi Durbar, and of the well-trodden route which Gertrude and Hugo took afterwards, that it is not worth while giving her letters in extenso, though I have included a few of her comments on her daily personal experiences.]

[Arrival in India]
To F.B.
S.S. "CHINA," December 12th, 1902.

Mr. [Leo F.] Schuster went off by himself and had coffee in Asia, the first time he had set foot on that continent. You can't think how charming and amusing and agreeable the Russells have been. It's added a great deal to the pleasure of the voyage having them. Our servant met us at the quay; he seems a most agreeable party and he's going to teach us Hindustani.

[These lessons seem to have been a success as far as Gertrude at any rate was concerned, because more than once in her subsequent travels she rejoices in being able to talk Hindustani.]

To F. B.
December, 1902.

We have become almost unrecognisably Indian, wear pith helmets—and oh! my Hindustani is remarkably fluent! We no longer turn a hair when we see a cow trotting along in front of a dogcart and we scarcely hold our heads an inch higher when we are addressed as "Your Highness." I called on a Persian to whom my Haifa friends had given me letters,! A Babi. I found him asleep on his verandah (he keeps a printing press), woke him up and had a long conversation with him in Persian. He regarded me with suspicion but treated me with the utmost consideration. I asked him to sell me some Babi books, but he wriggled out of it politely, so I turned to indifferent subjects and had an amusing talk about the plague and things of that kind.

(They go to Government House.]

Lord Northcote is charming, delightful to talk to, and she is even more charming and they were both extremely friendly. My Hindustani is quite enough to carry us through without an interpreter, it's really most convenient.

To H. B.
JEYPORE, December 22nd, 1902.

We had a most cheerful dinner in the station with Mr. Schuster. I feel a considerable affection for him. He is so Cheerful and so equable and he travels about in the lap of luxury. I shared his good fun, his salad, and his delicious coffee. I wish we had been at the last Thursday party. I told You Sir Ian [Hamilton] was a fascinating person.

To F.B.
Delhi DURBAR, December 31st.

A cotton gown, a sun helmet and a fur coat was my simple costume, the only one, I find, which meets the variety of the Indian climate. No one can be dull on an Indian road because Of the birds and beasts. They are so tame that they scarcely get out of the way of your carriage. There is a delightful sort of starling called a maina, with white barred wings, the fat contented bourgeois of the bird hierarchy; the flocks of green parrots are the gay smart people, the vultures sitting—rather huddled up in the early morning cold are the grave Politicians. As for the grey crow, he is the ubiquitous vaut rien [sic] Without which the social system would not be complete. Arthur [Godman] appeared before lunch; he is such a darling, looking older and thinner, and very wise about the country and the people, having seen and observed a great deal and drawn conclusions which are well worth hearing. . . .

[Arthur L. Godman, now Group Captain, R.A.F., was Gertrude's first cousin, being the eldest son of Ada Bell referred to on page 7, who married Colonel Arthur Fitzpatrick Godman.]

The function began with the entrance of the Delli siege veterans—this was the great moment of all, a body of old men, white and native, and every soul in that great arena rose and cheered. At the end came some twenty or thirty Gurkhas, little old men in bottle green, some bent double with years, some lame and stumbling with Mutiny wounds. And last of all came an old blind man in a white turban, leaning on a stick. As he passed us, he turned his blind eyes towards the shouting and raised a trembling hand to salute the unseen thousands of the race to which he had stood true. After that Viceroys and Kings went by almost without a thrill. But still it was a great show. . . .

To F.B.
DELHI, January 2nd, 1903. Visitors' Camp.

We went to tea with Lady Barnes (she has just been knighted) the sister of the Vanbrughs and a most charming woman with whom I have sworn friendship. She is coming to see us in London some day and I'm going to stay with her in Burmah some day. We also made the acquaintance of her husband, Sir Hugh, who is very nearly as charming as she is. Then we went on to congratulate the Lawrences and met Sir Walter Lawrence outside his tent, and he sent us home in one of the Viceroy's carriages, so we were the howling swells. The Russells told me that the first night they were disturbed by the sound of continuous mewing, so much so that Lady A. got up and looked out of her tent and called " Puss, puss!"What do you think would have come if what she had called had really come? The elephants! isn't it deliciously ridiculous! They make a funny sort of mewing sound which from a distance sounds just like cats. I went to a Muhammadan Conference to which I had been invited by Mr. Morison, the head of the Aligarh College. I stepped on to the platform as bold as brass (in my best clothes!) and sat down by Morison who is an enchanting person. . . .

In the train from Alwat to Delhi.

TO F.B.
January 18th, 1903.

My thrice blessed Hindustani, though it doesn't reach to any flowers of speech, carries us through our travels admirably and here we were able to stop where no one has a word of English, without any inconvenience.

[They send for an elephant.]

An elephant is far the most difficult animal to sit that I have ever been on. You feel at first rather as if you were in a light boat lying at anchor in seas a little choppy after a capful of wind—but the sensation soon wears off and you learn to dispose yourself with ease and grace upon the hoodah, and above all U learn not to seize hold of the side bars when the elephant sits down, for they are only hooked and jerk out, landing you, probably (as they nearly landed me) in the dust a good many feet below. We soon discovered that the great tip for good elephantship is to grasp the front bar the moment you get on, for he gets up from in front (and very quickly too for he doesn't like kneeling at all) and the problem is how not to fall over his tail. It's a little disconcerting to find that an Indian, when he wishes to ascribe ideal movement to a woman, calls her "elephant gaited." "An eye like a gazelle, a waist like a lion, and a gait like an elephant."

To H.B.
PESHAWAR, Friday, January 23, 1903.
[At Peshawur they stop to photograph a group of people who are singing to the lute a sort of hymn of praise.]

There were two men outside playing on a sort of lute and singing praises of the Granth, but they can't have been very serious worshippers, for when I stopped to photograph them I heard them interpolate into the song "and the Memsahib came and took a picture "—all in the same squeaky tune.

Aligarh. And here we are safely installed in the Morisons' house. He is one of the most charming of men—a son of Cotter Morison.

[Then follows a description of the Muhammadan College] the only residential College in India.

To H.B.
In the train—as usual! February 2, 1903.

.... I liked Mrs. Morison on further acquaintance. They swear by her in the College and she was very kind to us. Mr. Morison is without doubt the most charming of men. We had an early tea to which he had invited an old Nawab who is a great personage in the College. He was a delightful old man; we conversed in Persian, though I found I could quite well follow him when he spoke Urdu with Mr. M. and Mr. M. can understand, though he cannot speak Persian. . . . Hugo's attitude to his friends is too comic. We heard that one X. was at Hong-Kong. " Good old X. " said Hugo, "I must look him up." I asked who he was. "Oh, he was at oxford with me." "Did you know him well?" "No." I asked whether he liked him. "No—no, I didn't like him. He's not at all an attractive person. Good old X! I'll tell you what—I'll write and let him know we are coming." . . . I got two lovely gowns of Madras muslin, embroidered from the foot to the knee, for 23 rupees, and an old man with a white beard is making them up for me at 4 rupees apiece. I think I shall go to him in future, he is so much cheaper than Denise. Hugo meantime bought flocks of white ducks and a silk coat Of which he is very proud . . . .. I wrote letters to all the people in the Straits Settlements, to tell them we're are coming—lucky dogs!

[At Darjeeling they go up into the Himalayas. They find the Russells and have a cheerful evening with them. . . and then to bed, meaning to get up in the dawn.]

"At 4:30 Hugo came into my room and said, "Get up, get up! the Moons shining on all the snows!" And I jumped out of bed and into a fur coat—for it was bitter cold—and there they were,, white, evanescent, mysterious and limitlessly high dreamy mountains under the moon. We ought to have been wakened at 4, it was most lucky Hugo woke, however we set ourselves to it with some purpose, got into riding clothes, bolted two eggs—I ate my first with sugar, which they had brought in instead of salt, in the hurry of the moment! and some tea, had our horses saddled, and at 5 we were dashing up the road behind the hotel, with two Nepalese saises panting behind us. That was a ride! We dashed on to the top of Tiger Hill, which is about 9,000 ft. high. As we got to the top, I saw the first sunbeam strike the very highest point of Kinchinjunga—Nunc Dimittis—there can be no such sight in the world. Away to the west, and 120 miles from us, Everest put his white head over the folded lines of mountains. . . . The old women of these parts have a plan of lacquering their noses and cheek bones with a brown lacquer, it looks like a frightful skin disease. . . . Our servants on our expedition were as good servants as you could wish to have. We made great friends with them and I vowed I would take them all with me next time, when I come to climb Kinchinjunga.

To H.B.
S.S. "TARA," BAY OF BENGAL, February 22, 1903.

Thanks to your good wishes, we have hitherto escaped from the 96 diseases, the 24 dangers and the 11 calamities. (I'm commencing Buddhist, you see, before I get to Rangoon, and this is the proper Buddhist way of beginning a letter.)

[They travel from Rangoon in a gorgeous railway carriage of which Gertrude enumerates and describes the furniture. In the middle of a description of the scenery: "we have just discovered nine more cupboards."

They stop at a village and go for a walk while their carriage waits for them on a siding].

. . . . At one of the little shops there was a basket of Pineapples, of which we wished to buy one. The lady of the shop was having her midday sleep; her small and entirely naked son roused her when he saw us fingering the pineapples. She just woke up enough to say " Char, anna " (which is 4d.) and then went to sleep again. We paid the 4 annas to the small boy and walked off with the pineapple. On the Irrawaddy.

To F.B.
March 2, 1903.

We came to a very small steam boat. We said "To Pakukku," very loud and clear and our guides seemed to assent. A steep and slippery plank led out to the boat. I took my courage in both hands, crept along it, lifted the awning, and received a broadside of the hottest, oiliest, most machinery laden air, resonant with the snores of sleepers. I lit a match and found that I was on a tiny deck covered with the sheeted dead, who, however, presently sat up on their elbows and blinked at me. I announced firmly in Urdu that I would not move until I was shown somewhere to sleep. After much grumbling and protestations that there was no place to sleep there (which, indeed, was obvious) one arose, and lit a lantern; together we sidled down the plank and he took us back to one of the mysterious hulks by the river bank. It was inhabited by an old Hindu and a bicycle and many cockroaches. We woke the Hindu, and, at the suggestion of our guide, he climbed a stair, unlocked a trap door and took us on to an upper deck where, oddly enough, there were deck cabins with bunks in them. In these we made our beds—it was now 11:30—and went to sleep. What the place was, we haven't to this hour the least idea, but we believe it to have been Maya, pure illusion, for directly we left, it hid itself behind another barge, which was not there before, and has been no more seen. Next morning we caught the small and smelly ferry, and in company with a party of Burmese, steamed down the river to Pakukku . . . .

[They go down the Irrawaddy.]

. . . . and into the monasteries, where I was hailed by an old monk on a balcony, who begged me, by sign and gestures, to come up and take a picture of the pagoda. By great good luck a little monk appeared, who had a smattering of English. I explained to him that I would go and fetch my brother and that we would then take pictures. We had the funniest visit. The monks haven't enjoyed anything so much for a long time; they laughed till their yellow robes fell off their bare shoulders. We all sat cross-legged together under the carved roofs and discussed our various ages and the price of Hugo's watch, while an immense concourse of children gathered round close and closer. I was of no account at all when Hugo appeared, until it came to the picture taking. We had to drive the children away while I photographed the monks, but, at my friend's request, I then took a consolation picture of all the children sitting in a row. The camera may be a horrid modern invention, but it's a universal letter of credit in strange parts. H. questioned the little monk closely as to what he did all day. He replied blandly "Nothing!" One of them was sewing the silk wrapper of a Pali book. They showed us the books, palm leaf books written in gold lacquer, and we made the monk read us a sonorous Pali sentence. He asked us if we could understand and we were obliged to admit that we couldn't, but I don't think he could either. The little monk took us into a second monastery, where we found an extremely old party in yellow, asleep on a chatpoy. He was enchanted to see Us, however, and had all the doors opened that we might see the frescoes on the walls. H. taught the little monk to shake hands when we came away, but he wouldn't shake hands with me. He oughtn't even to have looked at me, according to the rules of the order. . . . Hugo bought a whole orchestra of Musical instruments from a gentleman almost naked except for a pair of spectacles. Our tastes then drew us irresistibly to the monasteries, where we spent a happy twilight hour walking about on gilded balconies and teaching the monks the names, in English, of the beasts carved upon their doors. They can't pronounce the consonants at the end of our words—but we can't pronounce the consonants at the beginning of theirs, so we're quits.

[Gertrude was anxious to see the dancing and was taken by a learned Chinaman to the house of a charming old Burman who had been Theebaw's private secretary. The dance is described. The host produces some of his old court dresses, and the insignia of the Minister's rank, gold ornaments of various kinds. A travelling companion of Gertrude's had accompanied her on this visit.]

"A 12-stringed chain was sent to Mr. Gladstone. I wonder what he did with it?" said the unknown man. "Mr. Morley will tell us that," replied the Chinaman, cheerfully. You might have knocked me down with one of the Burmese lady's tail feathers: the last time I had talked of John Morley's Life of Mr. G. was in the Pollocks' drawing room at Hind Head. One dancer retired to appear as a boy. The change was not overwhelming, for instead of one tight trouser she now wore skirts rather voluminous in front.

To F.B.
BATAVIA, March 16, 1903

We have at last got out of England and are now travelling on the Continent. No one knows what comfort on the sea can be till he travels by a Dutch boat. . . .

[They go to Singapore where they stay with Sir Frank Swettenham. Hugo was very ill here with some sort Of malaria. Sir Frank Swettenham was endlessly kind to him, and kept him and looked after him until he was well enough to go away.]

To F.B.
ASTOR HOUSE, SHANGHAI, April 4th, 1903.

The hotel is most comfortable, when we arrived we found a note left for us by the kind Russells giving us some introductions to people here. It really was very thoughtful of them. We landed on Easter Sunday and had to do all our own getting ashore. The Chinese natives surrounded us and offered to carry our luggage, to carry us, to carry the ship, I fancy, if we would give them a long enough bamboo pole. I adore Chinamen with a passion that amounts to mania. They are the most delightful people in the world. They do everything to perfection. They'll make you a shirt in three hours, a petticoat in two, wash your clothes before you can wink, forestall your every wish at table, fan you day and night When you have the fever—you should have seen the Chinese boys sitting by Hugo's bedside at Singapore and fanning him all day long. . . .

(Please give my love to Sir Ian, when you see him next!)

So we went to a silk shop, and the most delightful gentleman in China showed us for two hours the loveliest stuffs I have ever seen. Kings will leave their thrones in the hope of catching sight of me when I wear a brocade I bought there, and crown princes will flock after Elsa and Moll when they are clothed in some Chinese crêpe I design for them. Hugo addresses all Chinamen as Gnome, but as they don't understand they aren't offended. I like travelling in China. Hugo nods and becks to everyone he meets and they nod back delighted.

[They travel northward through China, sight seeing on the way and being much interested all the time.]

To F. B.
PEKING, 26th April, 1903.
[To Peking, where Claude Russell was then at the Legation, also Sir Walter and Lady Susan Townley.

Gertrude gives a detailed and very interesting description of Peking, of which however so many descriptions have been written already by other travellers that it is not worth while reproducing hers here. She also gives details of the Boxer Rising and contrasts it with the peace of China at that moment (1903). It is Of interest to read this passage in 1927, with an intensified sense of contrast.]

You can't conceive what the horrible fascinating streets of Peking are like. Full, full of people, a high mud causeway down the middle, crowded booths on either side and a strait and uneven way between them and the shops. Your rickshaw dashes in and out, bumps over boulders, subsides into ditches, runs over dogs and toes and the outlying parts of booths and shops, upsets an occasional wheelbarrow, locks itself with rickshaws coming in the opposite direction and at a hand gallop conveys you, breathless, through dust and noise and smells unspeakable to where you would be.

[They see the Temple of Heaven. They dine with the French Minister, M. Dubail, a great connoisseur, and then go shopping with him. Gertrude remarks in her letter to me " I'm so glad I speak French so well, aren't you?]

To H.B.
TAIREN March 20th, 1903.
We may as well back out. I've seen Dalny and I know. We may just as well back out. Five years old and a European town. Roads—you don't know what that means in China—fine streets of solid brick houses, a great port, destitute of shipping as yet, but that will come, law courts, two hotels, factories in plenty, six lines of rails at the station, a botanical garden in embryo, but still there. It contains some deer, an eagle and two black bears—note the symbolism! Do you remember a story of Kipling's in which a Russian officer is well entertained by an English Regiment? He gets up after dinner to make a speech. "Go away, you old peoples," he says. "Go away you—old—peoples!" and falls drunk under the table. That's the speech Dalny is making and I feel inclined to take its advice. In fact there is no alternative. We arrived at 7 a.m. on Thursday, went ashore and breakfasted at the Gastinnea Dalny where the proprietor fortunately spoke German. They take nothing but roubles, being in Russia, and we had to go to the renowned Russo-Chinese bank to change our notes—having paid for our breakfast, our friend, the proprietor, put us into a droschky—a pukha droschky—and we drove round the town. Our driver was a cheerful Kurlander who knew a little German too. He came out last autumn and meant to stay 2 years. "Business is good?" said I, observing his fat and smiling face. "Recht gut," said he, "sometimes one earns 18 roubles a day." No wonder he smiled and grew fat. The railway cutting is being widened, the station is not yet finished. Both were black with thousands of Chinese coolies working for dear life. How

long is it, therefore, between project and completion in Russian hands? Hugo gnashed his teeth, but I did nothing but admire. They deserve to rule Asia-and they mean to rule Asia. Go away, you old peoples!

[They sail for Japan.]

To H.B.
Tokyo, May 23rd, 19o3.

I spent my time in the train learning Japanese so that when we arrived at Miyajima I was able to explain that we wanted to leave our heavy baggage at the station! (At this moment came in a gnome with a most exquisite grey alpaca gown he has just made me an exact copy of one of Denise's but that cost 6 pounds and this 3! I am glad to have it, for Peking dust put a final touch to my dilapidated toilette.) I was delighted to have Lord Lovelace's enchanting letter. He writes like someone in the beginning of last century, touches of politics, social anecdotes, all with a perfect style and in an exquisite hand.

[Gertrude's friendship with Lord Lovelace was always a great pleasure to her. Their companionship ranged over literature, gardening, mountaineering,— whatever else came to hand. I include here one or two extracts from her letters to him, in reply to those she describes.]

To the Earl of Lovelace.
August 5, 1902.

What a series of successes you have had! . . . .. isn't it delightful and wonderful to step on to a hilltop where no one has been before! you have had this sensation very often, I know.

To the same.
July 12, 1902.
[Writing of Alpine flowers.]

No other flowers have the same delicate exquisiteness except indeed those that Fra Angelico puts beneath the feet of dancing saints; but then they are dream flowers. And so are these, I believe growing in delicious dream gardens that exist only for us mountain people.

To the same.
September 28th, 1903.

Oh the tariff—I cannot keep so philosophically remote as you do though I have enough self-control to realise that I value one couplet of Imrul Kais above all the fiscal pamphlets in the world.

To the same.
April 22, 1904.

I have been reading the Buddhist scriptures and making the 'école buissonnière' between and I don't know which is the more profitable occupation.

To H.B.
TOKYO, Sunday, 24th May, 1903.

I spent a delicious morning wandering about temples and gardens under the charge of my rickshaw man. In one of the temples, a wonderful place all gold lacquer and carving set in a little peaceful garden, a priest came up to me and asked if I were an American. I said no, I was English. He bowed and smiled: "So—is that how it is? the English are very good!" I replied in Japanese, in which tongue the conversation was being conducted—"English and Japanese are one." This was greeted with great satisfaction to judge by the expression of my friends, the priests; what they said I could not understand. Aubrey Herbert came to lunch and we all went sightseeing together afterwards, but we were so busy talking that we didn't pay much attention to the sights.

To H. B.
Thursday, 28th May, 1903.

(They meet the Colliers, and Reginald Farrar, "who is a great gardener."]

They and Mr. Herbert all came to see us, and carried Hugo to a tea house to spend the evening in the company of geisha! I wonder how he comported himself. Eric said he appeared to be quite at his ease. . . .

[To Yokohama, then across the ocean to Vancouver. Gertrude's first experience of America.]

To F.B.
LAKE LOUISE, ROCKY MOUNTAINS, June 30, 1903.

Need I tell you that I am now climbing the Rocky Mountains!

We arrived at Glacier after a wonderful morning through the great canyons of the Selkirks. And at Glacier whom do you think I found, pray? 3 Swiss guides from the Oberland, ropes and ice axes and everything complete. So we fell into one another's arms, and they said, "Ach wass! it was Fraulein Bell! how did the Gracious Fraulein enjoy the Finstetaarhorn?" We discussed politics at dinner with our waiter at Vancouver. Says he: "There's only one man understands the Colonies: that's Chamberlain." G.B. loq.: "I think you'll have to pay some of the cost if you want to call so much of the tune." Waiter, loq. "I guess that's so, but they don't seem to think so out here." And he handed me the potatoes.

To H.B.
July 8th, 1903. In the train.

[On the way to Chicago they stop at Moose Jaw—they are delighted with the strips of green, the prairie dogs, the people " A Lancashire man recently come out who is prospering and pleased with everything." They stop to photograph a widow's house and fall into talk with the owner of it.]

She wouldn't live in Moose jaw for worlds; it's to crowded for her. If you could only see Moose jaw, You would realise the force of that statement. It's Just a little more crowded than the desert.

[So to Chicago.] . . . Raymond Robins came to see us. He talked uninterruptedly for one and a half hours. He is rather like Lisa, talks like her, throws back his head and speaks with bursts of eloquence. . . . Hugo and I listened to him, breathless for an hour, and a half. He is a very striking person; I fancy he is going to be a big power. Hugo was so enthralled by his accounts that he is actually going back to Chicago to spend four days with him. I encouraged this notion, for Raymond is exactly the kind of person Hugo ought to be with. He is so entirely outside the bounds of any stereotyped creed. But he was desperately busy the next three days, so we decided that Hugo should come with me to Niagara. as arranged, and then return, by which time R. will be free to show him about. . . .

[They go to] a sort of Earl's Court called Sans Souci, where we dined and saw the shows and enjoyed ourselves. I may say we had then the experience of a lifetime, for we went on a switchback that looped the loop. I can't say it was nice. Hugo says he was distinctly conscious of being upside-down—which we were for the fraction of a second—but I only knew a rush and a scramble and my hat nearly off. Now Hugo and I part company. Lisa meets me in Boston tomorrow afternoon and Hugo goes back to Raymond. . . .

[Gertrude and Hugo landed at Liverpool on July 26th of this year. She was then in England until the following February, when we find her and her father staying at the Embassy in Berlin, after which she returned home.]

CHAPTER IX
1903-1909

ENGLAND, SWITZERLAND, PARIS

[OUR youngest daughter Molly was married to Charles Trevelyan on January 6th, 1904. As Gertrude was then at home with us and also during most of the preceding year, there are no letters to us concerning Molly's engagement in the previous November, or her marriage. Some letters are included here which Gertrude wrote at this time to a young cousin, Edward Stanley, second son of the 4th Lord Stanley of Alderley, afterwards Lord Sheffield.

Edward Stanley went out to Nigeria as Civil Commissioner in 1903. He was a boy of great ability, keen about his work and ready to shoulder responsibility and to face danger. Gertrude cared very much about this young cousin, and kept in touch with him. He was not gregarious, he had not many intimates, and at times when the life in front of him, with its ambitions and possibilities, seemed to him bewildering, he found in Gertrude the most sympathetic of confidantes and correspondents. As usual, none of her letters have the date of the year, and the envelopes of these letters have not been kept, but they seem to have been written between 1903, when he went out to West Africa, and 1908. His early death at his post in the summer of 1908 was one of the great sorrows Of Gertrude's life.]

To N. J. Stanley.

Yes Marcus Aurelius is a good counsellor, if one can follow his advice. I mostly find myself rebelling against it, with an uncanny sense of being too hopelessly involved in the mortal coil to profit by it. What is the use of bending all one's energies to the uncongenial thing? One is likely to do little enough anyway, but if half one's time is taken up persuading oneself one likes it or at least conquering distaste there is Very little left to achieve success with.

Find the thing that needs no such preparatory struggle and then do it for all you are worth if you can. There will always be black or grey moments when it is sufficiently difficult to do even the thing you like.

To the same.

Elsa and I had a delicious day this week in the Eske Valley, at Glaisdale. The woods were full of flowers. We both fell into the river and were wet through and we agreed it was very nice to have reached an age when you can't be scolded and yet still like doing the things you would be scolded for.

To the same.

. . Last night I went to a ball at your house—a very exceptional thing for me to do and enjoyed myself so much that having gone for a moment, I stayed for three hours. A most pleasant party not too crowded, pretty people, a charming hostess and a most cheerful host. London has become very hot and I am glad to think that I shall leave it next week. . . .

I had an amusing dinner the other day sitting between Lord Peel and the Agha Khan. Do you know who he is? He is a direct descendant of the Prophet, supreme head of half the Shiah world, an English subject, enormously rich (his sect allows him 190,000 pounds a year) and a pretender to the throne of Persia. We talked of travel and I said I might be in Bagdad next year. "If you go " said he, "do let me know, I should like to give you letters to my uncles, who look after the shrine at Kerbela. The Marlborough Club always finds me." Isn't that a fine jumble. He explained to Gilbert Russell, whom he knows very well, that he was so rich that 2,000 pounds was to him, as 6pence is to other people. Then," said Gilbert, "could you change me a shilling?"

To the same-

. . . ..Sargent came to dinner this week. Did I tell you I made friends with him last summer? He is delightful, I think. I should like to have about three hours talk on end with him, for one keeps getting into things one can't discuss at a dinner party because there is not time. Last dinner we embarked on composition as understood by the Greeks, which is a most thrilling theme. I think he is wrong, far too modern in his idea of composition. He sets too much store on complexity which is not at all necessarily an admirable quality and may be very difficult to handle—must be. But he is catholic and he has thought things out with a mind that can do a deal of thinking, and to some purpose, and he is extremely keen, so it is interesting to hear his views . . . ..

[In August Of 1904, she again went to Switzerland.)

To H.B.
RIFFELBERG, Thursday, August 11th, 1904.

I came up here this morning and found Geoffrey Young and a cousin of his. Mr. Young gave me much good advice and a general introduction to all the mountains that can be seen from here. He is a very nice creature, charming to look at and I am sorry he is going away. This morning when I was looking at maps outside the Monte Rosa hotel, there came up the old porter and said how gratified they were that I had come to climb in these parts. They had heard so often of my doings in the Oberland and were wondering when I should be coming to Zermatt!

To F.B.
ZERMATT, Sunday, August 21, 1904.

Yes, as you say, why do people climb? I often wonder if one gets most pleasure out of the Alps this way. Some year I shall try the other and come and wander over grass passes and down exquisite Italian valleys and see how I like it.

To F.B.
ZERMATT, Wednesday, August 31st, 1904.

We got our climb yesterday. It is a much better climb than I expected. I left Breuil early on Monday morning. It was very delightful walking up to the hut over the Matterhorn meadows and up easy rocks below the Dent du Lion. The mountain is full of story—here the great Carrel died of exhaustion, there so and so fell off from the rocks above, and when we got on to the little Col du Lion, which separates the Dent from the main mass of the mountain, we were on historic ground, for here Tyndall and Whymper bivouacked year after year when they were trying to find their way up. There is a difficult chimney just below the hut, but there is a fixed rope in it so that one has not much trouble in tackling it. We got up to the hut about 11:15, a tiny little place on a minute platform of rock, precipices on either side and the steep wall of the Matterhorn above. It is very imposing, the Matterhorn, and not least from the Italian hut; the great faces of rock are so enormous, so perpendicular. Unfortunately the hut is dirty, and smelly, as I had occasion to find out, for I spent the whole afternoon lying in the sun in front of it, sleeping and reading. The guides went away for an hour or two to cut and find steps on the snow above and I had the whole Matterhorn to myself—no, I shared it with some choughs who came circling round looking for food about the hut. At 7 we went to bed and I slept extremely soundly till about 1:30, when the guides got up and reported unfavourably of the morning. There was a thin spider's web of cloud over the whole sky, a most discouraging sign, but the moon was shining and we made our tea and observed the weather. By 3 it had distinctly cleared and we started off, without even a lantern, the moon was so bright. I knew the mountain so well by hearsay that every step was familiar, and it gave me quite a thrill of recognition to climb up the Grande Tour, to pass over the little glacier of the Linceul, the snow band of the Cravate, and to find oneself at the foot of the Grande Corde which leads back on to the Tyndall Grat. It was beautiful climbing, never seriously difficult, but never easy, and most of the time on a great steep face which was splendid to go upon. The Tyndall Grat leads up to a shoulder called the Pic Tyndall; it was dawn by this time and a very disquieting dawn too, SO we hurried on for it's no joke to be caught by bad weather on this side of the Matterhorn. However, the sky gradually cleared and we had our whole climb in comfort. The most difficult place on the mountain is an overhanging bit above the Tyndall Grat and quite near the summit. There is usually a rope ladder there, but this year it is broken and in consequence scarcely any one has gone up the Italian side. There is a fixed rope, which is good and makes descent on this side quite easy, but it is a different matter getting up. We took over 2 hours over this 30 or 40 ft.—the actual bad place! & not more than 15 or 20 ft.-and I look back to it with great respect. At the overhanging bit you had to throw yourself out on the rope and so hanging catch with your right knee a shelving scrap of rock from which you can just reach the top rung which is all that is left of the ladder. That is how it is done. I speak from experience, and I also remember wondering how it was possible to do it. And I had a rope round my waist which Ulrich, who went first, had not. Heinrich found it uncommonly difficult. I had a moment of thinking we should not get him up. We got to the top at 10 and came down at a very good pace. The Swiss side is all hung with ropes. It's more like sliding down the banisters than climbing. We got to the Swiss hut in 3 hours and were down here by 4 o'clock. We have heard that two parties who tried to do the Matterhorn from the Italian side this year have turned back because they do not tackle the ladderless rock, so we feel quite pleased with ourselves.

[Gertrude returned to England till November, when she went to Paris to study with Reinach again.]

To F.B.
PARIS, Monday, November 7th, 1904.

it is being extremely pleasant. Yesterday morning I breakfasted with the Stanleys and went with Sylvia to see the Wintter Salon. After lunch I drove out, left some cards and went to see Salomon Reinach, whom I found enthusiastically delighted to see me. There were 2 other men there, an American from the Embassy and one Ricci, who appeared to be terribly learned. We sat for an hour or more while Salomon and Ricci piled books round me and poured information into my ears. It was delightful to hear the good jargon of the learned, and all in admirable English, for they know everything. But bewildering. This morning I read till 11 about Byzantine MSS. which I'm going to see at the Bibliothéque Nationale; then I went shopping with the Stanleys and bought a charming little fur jacket to ride in in Syria—yes, I did! Then I came in and read till 2 when Salomon fetched me and we went together to the Louvre. We stayed till 4:30—it was enchanting. All empty, of course, for it is a Monday; and I think there is nothing more wonderful than to go to a museum with my dear Salomon. We passed from Egypt through Pompeii and back to Alexandria. We traced the drawing of horns from Greece to Byzantium. We followed the lines of Byzantine art into early Europe and finally in the dusk we went and did homage to the Venus, while Salomon developed an entirely new theory about eyelids— Greek eyelids, of course, and illustrated it with a Pheidean bust and a Scopas head. It was nice.

To F.B.
PARIS, November 8th, 1904.

I had the most enchanting evening with Reinach. I got there at 7:30 and left at 11:30 and we talked without ceasing all the time. After dinner we sat in his library while he showed me books and books of engravings and photographs and discoursed in the most delightful manner. He does nothing but work—never goes out, never takes a holiday except to go and see a far away museum. And the consequence is he knows everything. I like him so much. This morning, I went to the Bibliothèque Nationale. Reinach had given me a letter to one of the directors and I was received with open arms. They are most kind. I looked at 2 wonderful Greek MSS.—illuminated—from 12 to 3:30! and I am going back there to-morrow to see ivories and more precious MSS. which they will have out for me. It is perfectly delightful. I should like to do nothing else for 6 months . . . ..

To F.D.
PARIS, Thursday, November 10, 1904.

Yesterday I read all the morning in the Bib. Nat. where i might well spend a great many more mornings. I lunched at home and went afterwards with Reinach and Ricci to a Byzantine Museum not yet open to the public. Most interesting it was. I don't begin to know, but I begin to see what there is to know. I dined with the Stanleys and went with Aunt Maisie to the new Donnay play—absolutely charming. We both enjoyed it. To-day I went to the Louvre in the morning then at 12 with Reinach to St. Germain (NB. I had no lunch at all!), where I read while he was busy and then was shown over it by him and introduced to several large domains of art of which I hadn't suspected the existence! Now I'm going to dine with him and spend the evening in his library. He wishes me to review a new book of Strzygowski's for the Revue Archaeologique—I think I might as well try my prentice hand as it happens to be a Syrian subject which I do just happen to know a very little about. Anyhow it is a jolly task. So to that end I'm going to consult his admirable books.

St. Germain is a nice place, isn't it? I had never been there. Reinach is director of the Museum.

To F.B.
Friday, November 11, 1904.

I have spent the whole day seeing ivories at various museums. As far as Paris is concerned I've seen all the ivories that concern me, and I find to my joy that I'm beginning to be able to place them, so that this afternoon at Cluny I knew a good deal more than the catalogue—which I'm bound to add was very bad. They have some wonderful things here.

This happy result is a good deal caused by having looked through such masses of picture books with Reinach. Last night he set me guessing what things were—even Greek beads—it was a sort of examination—I really think I passed. Reinach was much pleased but then he loves me so dearly that perhaps he is not a good judge. He has simply set all his boundless knowledge at my disposal and I have learnt more in these few days than I should have learnt by myself in a year.

But You can't think what odd things they made about the 3rd and 4th centuries in Gaul. It's a most fascinating study.

CHAPTER X
1905

SYRIA-ASIA MINOR

To F.B.
LONDON, January 4,1905.
I have given Smith & Sons the following addresses—British Consulate, Jerusalem, for 3 weeks beginning from next week, British Consulate, Damascus, for the 3 weeks following; but I will let you know from Jerusalem by telegram. . . .
Aren't I going a long way off? It is not nice at the beginning.

To F.B.
S. S "OATOXA," Wednesday, January 11th, 1905.
Days spent at Port Said are certainly not red letter days. The last I spent here was with Hugo and I wish he were with me now, though I can't think he would desire it, But it is a pleasure to be speaking Arabic again. I feel it coming back in a flood and every time I open my lips expecting toads, pearls come out, at least seed pearls!

To H.B.
BEYROUT, 18 January, 1905/
I'm deep in the gossip of the East! It's so enjoyable. I thought to-day when I was strolling through the bazaars buying various odds and ends what a pleasure it was to be in the East almost as part of it, to know it all as I know Syria now, to be able to tell from the accent and the dress of the people where they come from and exchange the proper greeting as one passes. A bazaar is always the epitome of the East, even in a half European town like Beyrout. I also went to the big mosque and photographed the doors which are rather pretty and made friends with the Imams—great fun it was ! I feel a very fine fellow now that I am the lord of two horses.

To H. B.
FROM MY CAMP, NEAR DUMEIR, January 20th, 1905.
You see I'm off! I got off finally this morning at 12-the first day's start is always an endless matter and I'm thankful to have it over. It was blazing hot and I, having like a prudent traveller kept to my winter clothes, had to push my coat away in my saddle-bags and ride in a shirt. The road is all along the coast, one has a broad blue sea on one side and mulberry orchards on the other. I have a charming camping ground near a river and a full moon besides, and I am dining out of doors at the front of my tent. I mention all this in the hope of giving pain—I strongly suspect you are in the middle of a fog if you are in London. It is a great thought that I shall be many months under this little green roof.
AIN EL KAUTARAH,
January 21st. Today we have had a full day's ride and all goes well. I began

by bathing in the river at dawn-a mighty cold business. I left the servants packing up and rode on alone to Saida where I spent an hour. But the port is charming, with a ruined castle built on an island in the sea and connected with the town by a narrow bridge. I got permission from the chief officer, who was busy having his head shaved completely bald at the time, to lunch there and very agreeable it was. I am beginning to rejoice again in the comfort of my saddle. The first day I generally feel it's rather a toss up whether I remain in it or not. N.B. The horse does the tossing up. He was rather fresh yesterday morning and bucked about through the streets of Beyrout. A strong sense of what was fitting alone kept me from biting the dust of Beyrout.

Sunday, 22nd. A strong wind rose in the night and blew up clouds. In the morning it looked very threatening and was blowing hard. So I jumped up in order to get my tents pitched before the rain came and at 7:30 we were ready. It's no wonder the Phoenicians were seafarers, for it would be difficult to find a more barren stony country than theirs. There is an extraordinary charm in these stony hills and valleys. They look like a land of dead bones,-grey limestone rocks and a few grey fig (you know the whitish colourlessness of them when they are leafless) and a few grey-green olives. But when you come near, the valleys are full of tiny niches which are gardens of anemones and cyclamen, and the rocks are full of beauty, the high-perched villages have an air of romance and the naked hills a wild and desolate splendour.

HAIFA, Wednesday, 25th. . . . .Oh, I've had such a day ! I've lunched with my Persians, I've drunk tea with my horse-dealer, I've spent hours in conversation with my landlord, I've visited everyone I know in Haifa. I'm off tomorrow morning. I doubt if it will be very nice in tents tomorrow, but still!

To F.B.
February 1, 1905.

I had a ride full of vicissitudes from Haifa. The first day was extremely and unavoidably long, 31 miles which is more than one can comfortably take one's animals. Moreover the road lay all across the Plain of Esdraelon (which is without doubt the widest plain in the world) and the mud was incredible. We waded sometimes for an hour at a time knee deep in clinging mud, the mules fell down, the donkeys almost disappeared ("By God!" said one of the muleteers, "you could see nothing but his ears!") and the horses grew wearier and wearier. I got in to camp after dark, at a place called Jenin it was, feeling very tired and head-achy and wondering why. Next day I was worse and by the time I had ridden for an hour I realised that I had a sharp attack of Acre fever, a thing I invariably catch here. It was extremely disagreeable, but I rode on for 6 hours through the most beautiful country-not that I paid much attention to it! till I got to Samaria and then I determined I could go no further. The mules and baggage had gone by another road to Nablus and I had only my cook with me. At the entrance of the town is a great ruined Crusader church, one corner of which has been built up into a mosque. A single bay of the aisle is converted into a room, and hard by in a sort of lean-to there lives the Imam of the mosque. He hurried out and said he could put me up in the aisle room for the night, there was a bed of sorts in it and a few quilts, more or less clean, and then I dropped down and went to sleep. I wish you could have seen the Imam. . . . He was dressed in a long blue robe and had a white turban round his tarbush. He bustled about softly in his ragged socks and made me tea and filled a bottle with hot water to make me warm and finally left me to an uneasy repose. However next day I was almost well. I got up about noon and went out to see the town, which has had great days, and after lunch rode cheerfully into Nablus, which is Shechem. It was bitterly cold and there was a mighty keen wind blowing so I decided not to camp and put up at the Latin Monastery, which was inhabited by two Syrian monks. On

Sunday 30, I started off at 8 and walked into the town which is supposed to be the most fanatical Moslem town in all Syria. There are the remains of a beautiful Crusader church in it. Then I went to the top of Mount Gerizim where the Samaritans hold their Passover and such a view from it too—and then rode to Jacob's well, which is the scene of the interview with the woman of Samaria. The Greeks have built a wall round it and made a little garden in which narcissus were flowering; bits of carved mouldings and capitals lay about between the flowers, all that is left of a mediaeval church, and the grey olives were growing up between the stones. It was very peaceful and charming the most impressive, I think, of all the sacred sites in Palestine. The road lay all down Samaria, over hills and rocky valleys and through olive groves. . . . I got into camp late and had a coldish night; there was ice everywhere when I got up next day. Then 2 hours ride into Jerusalem. In the afternoon I paid some calls and had a long call from Mr. Dickson the consul. He told me that Mark Sykes and his wife were here., so I went off to see them and found them half encamped and half in a Syrian house. They received me with open -arms, kept me to dinner and we spent the merriest of evenings. They are perfectly charming.

I've got a dog, an extremely nice dog of the country. it sleeps in my tent and he is perfectly charming. He is yellow. His name is Kurt, which is Turkish for Wolf.

To F.B.
RAMELEH, Friday, February 3, 1905.

As regards the children's books: it is a pity to send them all away, I think. I remember what a joy ours were to us. Could not they be stored on a shelf in the long gallery? There are not so very many and I think they would be a joy to future children.

[The books were kept, and as Gertrude foresaw have been a great joy to the successive children of the family.]

I have had a few very busy days in Jerusalem. First I have engaged a new cook. The last was not capable enough for me. I was forced to fall back on my muleteers for all service. (One of them, Habib, who is about 25, is turning out an admirable servant, trustworthy and willing and intelligent. He is a Christian from the Lebanon. I have also his father, Ibrahim, who is a good old soul, and a

Dorn, Mahmud, who knows the country into which I am going. They are all good men and I am keeping them on.) The question of a cook was very serious and I had to set about looking for one with great care. Finally I hit on one who seemed satisfactory and learnt from him that he had accompanied Lord Sykes into Asia Minor. So I went off to Lord Sykes and lunched with him and heard a very good account from him. He said he was trustworthy and extremely brave, and on these qualifications I engaged him at once. Mark Sykes also says he can't cook, but it's 5 years since he was with him and we will hope he has learnt. So far I am very well satisfied with him. He has taken over all the arrangements with great skill and I find he never has to be told a thing twice. I hope my camp is now in its final shape and quite complete. I look forward to being very comfortable in a modest way. Not like Lord Sykes! I've seen a great deal of the Sykeses and like them very much.

I have discovered in Jerusalem a German who has started a market garden and collected all the bulbs of the country. I have ordered from him 6 wonderful sorts of iris and a tulip which he is to send to Rounton in the summer. It will be most delightful if they grow. I learned them nearly all for I have seen them flowering at different times. One is the black iris of Moab, and another a beautiful dark blue one, very sweet scented, which grows in Gilead.

To F.B.
JORDAN BRIDGE, February 5, 1905.

We got down to Jericho about 2, but I had resolved not to camp there as I had always had a desire to pitch a camp down by the great Jordan Bridge, the Bridge of the Desert. We stopped to buy corn and straw for our beasts and went on with the muleteers. After about an hour a sharp shower followed and overtook us. By this time we had got to the edge of the strangest bit of all this strange Jordan Valley; it consists of mud hills about 100 ft. high cut into very steep slopes and ravines, and the road—save the mark!—winds on and along the precipitous sides of them. With a very little rain they are turned into hills of soap, inconceivably slippery and quite impassable. We hurried on and fortunately the rain stopped, but only just in time. We had to get off and lead our horses—mine slipped, began to slide down the bank but regained his feet almost miraculously. It lasted only about Half an hour, but it was with many thanks be! that we came to the end of it. People have been known to have been caught in rain in that Sodom and Gomorrah—it's about the site of them, I believe—and to have remained there all night, quite unable to move. We got to the Jordan at 4 and pitched camp in a delightful open place with a little grass and a few tamarisk bushes, just this end of the bridge. A little shrub of spina Christi bushes divides us from the river. The muleteers had made a great fire and we collected round it under the stars listening to the tales of a negro who has appeared from Lord knows where, like a dog turning up where there may be food, and is a bit of a wag in his way. There passed through this morning 900 soldiers on their way to help Ibn Rashid in Central Arabia. It's good luck to have missed them.

At Salt I was busy looking about for some place where I could sleep, and there came to me a charming old party who said I must without doubt be his guest. So here I am installed in the house of Yusef Succur who with his nephew and children waits upon me most attentively and is now going to give me dinner! I have also some other friends here, the sons and daughters of the old man who taught me Arabic at Haifa, and they have all been in to see me and fallen on my neck.

To F.B.
February 7th, 1905.

I passed the funniest evening yesterday. My host was a well to do inhabitant of Salt, Yusef Succur by name (upon him be peace!) He established me in his reception room, which was well carpeted and cushioned but lacking in window panes, and therefore somewhat draughty. He and his nephew and his small boys held it a point of hospitality not to leave me for a moment, and they assisted with much interest while I changed my boots and gaiters and even my petticoat, for I was deeply coated in mud. That being accomplished they brought me an excellent dinner, meat and rice and Arab bread and oranges. When I had finished it was placed before my cook who had joined the party. Then I held an audience. Paulina, the daughter of the old man at Haifa who used to teach me Arabic her brother-in-law, Habib Effendi Faris, the schoolmaster and the doctor all "honoured themselves" ("God forbid! the honour is mine!" is the answer). We drank lots of bitter Bedouin coffee, and at last settled down to business, which was this: How am I to get into the Jebel ed Druze? Finally, Habib Effendi, who was kindness itself arranged to send me out to his brother-in-law Namoud, who inhabits a ruin on a tiny hill called Tneib three hours east of Madeba. Now Madeba is east of the Dead Sea, and you will find it on a map. At 9:30 they left me, and my host, who was a magnificent looking old man, began to lay down the quilts for my bed. Then came my hostess, though they are Christians, her husband keeps her more strictly than any Muslim woman, and she sees no men. She was a very beautiful woman, dressed in the dark blue Bedouin clothes, the long robe falling from her head and bound round the forehead with a dark striped silk scarf. Moreover, her chin and neck were closely tattooed with indigo after the Bedouin fashion. At 10 they left me, and I went to bed and slept like a top till 6. The only drawback to my comfort was that I could not wash at all. You see, I was lodged in the drawing room, and naturally there were no appliances for washing there-if there were anywhere. This morning Yusef gave me a very good breakfast of milk and eggs and bread and honey. Habib provided me with a guide and I set off about 8:30 for a long day's ride. It was fortunately heavenly weather. It had rained last night and rained itself out, we had a perfectly clear sky all day. I love this East of Jordan country. We rode through wide shallow valleys, treeless, uninhabited and scarcely cultivated. Every now and then there were ancient ruined sites, once or twice we met a rider coming from the Bedouin, now and then we saw a flock of goats shepherded by an Arab with an immensely long gun. About 4 we came out Into the great rolling plain that stretches away and away to the Euphrates. The first few miles of it are all under corn. A mile or two in front of us lay the little hill round which my friend Habib has his property. We got in at 5:15 and pitched camp on the edge of the hill, looking south. Namoud was away, but he has been sent for. There are some 50 inhabitants of the ruins who work in Habib's corn land, and a few of the black Arab tents are scattered over the plain. A gorgeous sunset over it all, a new moon and absolute stillness. And I have just enjoyed the greatest luxury of my camp—my evening warm bath! It is all too delightful for words.

Wednesday, 8th. All is well. At 10 last night came Namoud. We fell on each other's necks, metaphorically speaking, and swore friendship and he left with the prospect of good talks next day. It was awfully cold in the night. After waking several times I had to get up and put on all my clothes. To-day was delicious, cold but fine. Namoud appeared after breakfast we had our maps—but my next three or four days Journey appears on no map—and stated exactly how I should get to the Jebel Druze. I am now waiting for my Arab guide and praise be to God! I think I have slipped through the fingers of the Government a second time. It was delightful having a day in camp with this wonderful plain stretched out before me like the sea. Namoud knows every Sheikh of all the Bedouin for miles and miles round, and we had lots of interesting talks about them. He is about thirty-five I should think, a Christian, by origin from Mosul and he is the man I have been looking for for long. We have planned an immense journey for the winter after next, no less than to Ibn Rashid. I think it will come off this time.

Thursday, 9th. To-day we are weather-bound. The rain began this morning on a strong south wind which turned into a real storm—such rain as we seldom have in England and it was absolutely impossible to move. However, we are not badly off. All the horses and mules have been put into a big cave, and as for me, my tent is without doubt the most remarkable edifice that has ever arisen from the mind of man. Though it has streamed all day with a raging wind, not a drop of water has come in; the servants have a big Egyptian tent through which the rain has come a little on the weather side, but not much. This afternoon there arrived half a dozen Bedouins or more, of the tribe of the Beni Sakhr, the biggest tribe here abouts, driven out of their black tents by the rain. N.B. They had left their women behind in the black tents. They came to Namoud for hospitality, and he has lodged them in the big cave in which he and all his people live. I went in for an hour or two this evening and sat with them talking and drinking the bitter black coffee of the Bedouin. The dark fell we were lighted by the fire over which two women were cooking the guests' meal. ("They eat little when they feed themselves, but when they are guests, much—they and their horses," said Namoud).

We sat round the embers of another fire by which stood the regulation three coffee pots and smoked and told tales, and behind us, with a barrier of bags of chopped straw and corn between, some twenty-three cows moved and munched. We made great friends, the Beni Sakhr and I. "Mashallah! Buit Arab," said they: "As God has willed: a daughter of the desert."

Saturday, 11th. And I am still at Tneib. Yesterday it stopped raining, but the weather was still so very doubtful, that we decided not to risk matters by setting out for the desert. For ourselves it does not much matter, but our beasts have to stand out in the rain all night and it is bitter weather for them. So I sent into Madeba for more corn, and myself employed the afternoon in riding out across the plain to a Roman camp called Kartal. On My way home I stopped at the tents of the Beni Sakhr and dined with them. It was a charming party. We sat round the fire and drank tea and coffee and were presently joined by three of the Sherarat, raggeder and dirtier even than most Arabs. They had come from a day or two out in the desert to buy corn from Namoud, much as Joseph and his brethren must have come down into Egypt. The Sherarat are a very big and powerful tribe, but of base blood. The high born Arabs like the Sakhrs won't intermarry with them; but their camels are the best in Arabia. They were very cold—it was a bitter evening—and crouched round the fire of desert scrub. Then came dinner, rice and meat and sour milk, very good. Mahmoud and I ate out of one dish, and all the others out of another. While we were eating we were joined by a fair and handsome young man whom all the Sakhrs rose to salute, kissing him on both cheeks. He was Gabtan, son of one of the Sheikhs of the Daja, the tribe to which I am going as soon as the weather clears. He had heard that Namoud was looking for a guide for me and had come in to take me to his uncle who is the head of all the tribe. He sat down in a corner , ate little and spoke little and very soon after we had finished eating, one of our hosts called Namoud aside and talked long in a whisper to him. He came to us, and said we had better go so we gave the salaam and rode off with Gabtan home to Tneib. It then appeared that there was blood between the Sherarat and the Sakhrs, and the three Sherarat had not known who Gabtan was, but he knew them, and feeling the situation to be strained, our hosts the Sakhrs had hastened our departure. To-day however, the Sherarat have come up for their corn and have spent the morning sitting peaceably enough with Gabtan in Namoud's cave. To-day it has poured nearly all day and is still at it. So we were obliged to remain here—it is boring, but unavoidable. Meantime, I am entirely acclimatised. It's very cold, you understand, and everything in my tent feels damp, bedding, clothes, everything. The match boxes are so damp that the matches won't strike. I feel perfectly warm, and as for catching cold, I don't dream of it. I live in my fur coat, and at night I have a hot water bottle in my bed, a most excellent luxury. To-day Namoud lunched with me that he might eat curry, a delicacy he had never tasted. Then Gabtan and one of the Sakhr came in and drank coffee and smoked. I fortunately have a brand of Egyptian cigarettes they don't like much so the smoking is limited. We laid plans for my journey and Gabtan asked me whether I thought I should have to fight the Turkish soldiery, as if so he would take his rifle. I assured him I did not intend to come into open conflict with the Sultan and I hoped to avoid the soldiers altogether. But he has decided to take his rifle, which I daresay is as well. There was a gleam of fine weather and I went out to -watch the Sherarat buying corn. The corn lives in an ancient well, a very big deep cave underground, and is drawn out in buckets like water—only the buckets are of camels' hair. Then it has to be sifted for it is stored with the chaff to protect it from the damp. This is a mightily long business and entails an immense amount of swearing and pious ejaculations. We all sat round on stones and from time to time we said "Allah! Allah!" "Praise God the Almighty." Not infrequently the unsifted corn was poured in among the chaff. Namoud loq: "Upon Thee, Upon Thee, oh boy! may thy dwelling be destroyed! may thy life come to harm!" Beni Sakhr: "By the face of the Prophet of God, may he be exalted!" Sherarat (in suppressed chorus): "God! God! and Muhammad the prophet of God, upon him be peace!" A party in bare legs and a sheepskin: "Cold! cold! Wallah! rain and cold." Namoud: "Silence, oh brother! Yallah! descend into the well and work."

At four I went into the servants' tent to have tea over their charcoal fire. Namoud joined us and remained till seven telling us bloodcurdling tales of the desert. The muleteers and I listened breathless and Mikhail cooked our dinner, and put in an occasional comment. He is a most cheerful travelling companion is Mikhail. Namoud gave us a warning which I will tell you as it is an indication of the country we are travelling in. Between the Beni Sakhrs and the Druzes there is always blood. There is no mercy between them. If a Druze meets an Ibn Sakhr, one of them kills the other. Now, One Of MY muleteers is a Druze. He has to pass for a Christian till we reach the Jebel Druze, "for," said Namoud, "if the Sakhr here" (my hosts of last night, you understand) "knew he was a Druze, they would not only kill him, but they would burn him alive." Accordingly, we have re-baptised him for the moment, and given him a Christian name.

Sunday, 11th. It was still rather stormy, but I decided to start whatever happened. We got off a little before nine, Namoud, Gabtan and I riding together. In about half an hour we crossed the Mecca railway which is the true boundary between towns and tents. We rode for some two hours across the open plain till we reached the foot of a low circle of Hills, and here we found Gabtan's people, the Daja, a group of six or seven black tents, and were made welcome by his uncle, Fellah Al'Isa, who is a very great man in these parts and a charming person. We went into his tent and coffee making began. It takes near an hour from the roasting of the beans onwards. By this time the mules had arrived, I lunched hastily and rode off with Namoud and Gabtan to see a ruin in the hills. . . ..I came back to tea in my own tent and at six o'clock Gabtan summoned me to dine with the Sheikh Fellah. I hope you realise what an Arab tent is like. It's made of black goats, hair, long and wide, with a division in the middle to separate the women from the men. The lee side of it is always open and this is most necessary, for light and warmth all come from a fire of desert scrub burning in a shallow square hole in the ground and smoking abominably; we had had a discussion as we rode as to the proper word for the traces of former encampments, and at dinner I produced the Muallakat (preMuhammadan poems) and found three or four examples for the use of various words. This excited much interest, and we bent over the fire to read the text which was passed from hand to hand, then came dinner, meat and sour milk, and flaps of bread, all very good. All my servants were "guests" too, but their meal was spread for them outside the tent. I had left one of the muleteers to look after our tents in my absence, and to him too was sent a bowl of meat and bread "for the guest who has remained behind." Dinner over, we drank coffee and smoked cigarettes round the fire, and I spent a most enjoyable evening listening to tales of the desert and of Turkish oppression, and telling them how things are in Egypt. Egypt is a sort of Promised Land, you have no idea what an impression our government there has made on the Oriental mind.

Monday, 13th. To-day the weather has turned out lovely, so we were right to wait those tedious four days. After many farewells and much coffee, I set out with Gabtan a little before eight, and we rode up the low hills across the rolling tops of them. The country was rather like our own border country, but bigger and barer. From time to time we came across little encampments, first of our friends the Daja, then of the Beni Hassan. There was sorrow in the tents of the children of Hassan. Yesterday a great ghazu, a raid, swept over this very country and carried Off 2,000 head of cattle and all the tents of one of the small outlying groups. In one tent we found a Man weeping, everything he had in the world was gone. I could not help regretting a little that the ghazu had not waited till to-day that we might have seen it. Five hundred horsemen, they say there were. We ourselves rode all day till past three, up and down the great sweeps of the hills with the Jebel ed Druze always before us, far, far away to the north. And Gabtan told me tales of ghazus as we went. We are now camped near a big village of houses of hair—the Arabs never say tents—belonging to the Hassanieh. It is a heavenly evening and looking west from my tent door I can see the country, which, if I were in it, I could not have left, and I laugh to think that I am marching along the Turkish frontier, so to speak, some ten miles beyond it, and they can't catch me or stop me. It is rather fun to have outwitted them a second time. I must tell you what will happen to the destitute of the Beni Hassan. They will go round to the rest of the tribe and one will give a camel, and one will give a few sheep and one some pieces of goat's hair for the tent, until each man has enough to support existence—they don't need much. So they will bide their time until a suitable moment when they will gather together all the horsemen of their allies, and ride out against the Sakhr and the Howeitat who were the authors of their ills; and then if they are lucky they will take back the 2,000 head of beasts and more besides. It seems a most unreasonable industry this of the ghazu—about as profitable as stealing each other's washing, but that's how they live. Meantime Gabtan is rather anxious, for the Daja and the Hassanieh are close friends, and the Sakhr are the foes Of both, and this latest exploit may lead to a general commotion. To-Morrow is the great feast of the Mohammedan year, the Feast of Sacrifice. They are going to kill and eat three camels in this encampment. One of these (i.e..,the Camels) is walking about outside my tent, all dressed up. And there has been a great washing—it occurs once a year I have reason to believe. All the tents are hung with white shirts, drying. After sunset there was a mighty firing off of guns. I too contributed—by request—in a modest way, with my revolver, the first, and I expect the only time I shall use it.

BEIT Umm Ej JEWAL, Tuesday, 14th. The Mother of Camels, that is where we are, in short we have arrived, praise be to God. But our ride to-day was not without excitements. The first was a river which the rain had filled very full and which was running with some speed. The water came well up on to the horses' girths and the donkeys almost disappeared. Moreover, the banks were deep, steep mud. Gabtan was invaluable, he put his mare backwards and forwards through the stream and brought each mule safely over. I was truly thankful to see them across. From this point we got into the black volcanic rock of the Hauran, the tents of the Beni Hassan grew scarcer and scarcer, and finally we came out on to a great plain, as flat as could be, stretching away 2 days' Journey to the Druse mountains. Gabtan was anxious, he more than half expected to encounter enemies, for the Arabs of the mountains and the Daja are never on comfortable terms. Moreover we did not know exactly where in that immense plain the Mother of Camels was. So we rode on and on and at last on a little mound we saw some shepherds. At the same moment, two came running across the plain towards us from the right, and as they came they fired—at us— which is the customary greeting to anyone you don't know. Gabtan rose in his stirrups, and threw his fur cloak over his arm and waved it above his head—we riding slowly towards the two as he did so. This reassured them and we were presently exchanging salutes on the best of terms. They directed us on our way, and before long we saw the towers and walls of Umm ej jewal before us. It looks like a great city and when you get near you find it is an empty ruin, streets of houses, three stories high, all of solid beautiful stone, with outer Staircases of stone and arched windows. I have pitched my camp in an open space in the middle, and there are a few Arab tents near me, the Arabs of the mountains. At sunset I was climbing about the ruined streets at some distance from my tents when Gabtan came running after me in a terrible state of mind, saying that if any of the Arabs were to see me in my fur coat, in the dusk, they would take me for a ghoul, and shoot me. Gabtan leaves us here,I am sorry to say. He has been a delightful companion. A gentleman called Fendi, from here, guides us to-morrow.

UMM ER RUMAMIN,
Wednesday, 15. (The Mother of Pomegranates-but there aren't any.) We are encamped in the first Druze village, where we have been warmly welcomed. We had a tedious six hours' ride across the endless stony plain, enlivened by a little rabbit shooting. They were asleep under the stones, the rabbits, it was not a gentlemanly sport, but it fills the pot. The sheikh of this town is an old man called Muhammad and he is of the great Druze family of Atrash, who are old friends of mine. I've just been drinking coffee with him and having a pleasant talk. The coffee was made and served by a charming boy, Muhammed's only son. His mother, too, was an Atrash, and he looks as if he came of a great race. It is very pleasant travelling in this weather, but the nights, after midnight, are bitter cold. This morning the water in my tent was frozen. It is no small matter, I assure you, to get oneself out of bed, and dress before sunrise with the frost

glistening inside one's tent.

Thursday, 16th. Without doubt this is a wonderful world. Listen and I will tell you strange things. I began my day in a most peaceful manner by copying inscriptions and was rather fortunate for I had found several Greek, one Cufic and one Nabathaean-Lord knows what it means, but I put it faithfully down and the learned shall read. Then I breakfasted with Sheikh Muhammad at Atrash. Then I rode off with a friend, name of Sakh, and we had a most pleasant journey to Salkhad. He was a remarkably intelligent young man, and questioned me as to every English custom down to the laws of divorce which I duly explained. He was also very anxious to know what I thought about the creation of the world, but I found that a more difficult subject. So we reached Salkhad and I went straight to the house of the Sheikh, Nasib el Atrash—he is another of the great family—and was made very welcome. Now I must tell you that there is a Turkish garrison here and a Kaimmakam 'et tout le bataclan.' I have not yet had a word in private with Nasib for whenever we begin to talk a Turkish official draws quietly near till he is well within earshot-and then we say how changeable is the weather. When I went to his house again I found the Turkish Mudir who lives side by side with Nasib and acts as a sort of spy upon him. The case is this—I want to go out east to a wild country called the Safah and under the protection of the Druzes I can go, but the Turks don't like this at all, and spend their time telling me how horribly dangerous it is, not a word of all which talk I believe. Salkhad is a little black lava town hanging on to the southern slope of a volcano, and in the crater of the volcano there is a great ruined castle, most grim and splendid. This evening as I dined, deeply engaged in thinking of the intrigue which I am about to develop, I heard a great sound of wild song, together with the letting off of guns, and going out I saw a fire burning on the topmost top of the castle walls. You who live in peace, what do you think this meant? It was a call to arms. I told you the Beni Sakhr and the Druzes were bitter foes. A month ago the Sakhr carried Off 5,000 sheep from the Druze folds in the plain. To-morrow the Druzes are going forth, 2,000 horsemen, to recapture their flocks, and to kill every man, woman and child of the Sakhr that they may come across. The bonfire was a signal to the country side. To-morrow they will assemble here and Nasib rides at their head. There was a soldier sitting at my camp fire. He wears the Turkish uniform, but he is a Druze from Salkhad, and he hates the Turk as a Druze knows how to hate. I said: "Is there refusal to my going up?" He replied: "There is no refusal, honour us." And together under the moon we scrambled up the sandy side of the mountain. There at the top, on the edge of the castle moat we found a group of Druzes, men and boys, standing in a circle and singing a terrible song. They were armed and most of them carried bare swords. "Oh Lord our God! upon them! upon them!" I too Joined the circle with my guide. "Let the child leave his mother's side, let the young man mount and be gone." Over and over again they repeated a single phrase. Then half a dozen or so stepped into the circle, each shaking his club or his drawn sword in the face of those standing round. "Are you a good man? are you a true man? Are you valiant?" they shouted. "Ha! Ha!" came the answer and the swords glistened and quivered in the moonlight. Then several came up to me and saluted me: "Upon thee be peace!" they said, "the English and the Druze are one." I said: "Praise be to God! we too are a fighting race." And if you had listened to that song you would know that the finest thing in the world is to go out and kill your enemy. When it was over we ran down the hill together, the Druzes took up a commanding position on the roof of a house—we happened to be on it at the time, for one always walks for choice on the roofs and not in the streets to avoid the mud—and reformed their devilish circle. I listened for a little and then took my leave and departed, many blessings following me down the hill. . . .

Friday, 17th. I've spent an 'appy day with Nasib. The Ghazu is put off for a day or two by reason of some difficulties between various Druze Sheikhs, and I'm afraid I shall not see the assembling Of the Druzes. . . . Nasib was going to ride out to a village to the south, and I wanted to visit a shrine on a neighbouring hill, so we rode part of the way together, he and I, and some twenty Druze horsemen, all armed to the teeth—including me.

Saturday, 18th. To-day was bitter cold, with some snow. I determined therefore not to move till to-morrow, and this evening is clear and promising. I spent some time making close friends with the Turkish officials, especially with the Mudir who is a charming and intelligent man, a Christian from Damascus. The upshot of which is that I may go wherever I like, and no one will lift a finger except to help me. I hear that Mark Sykes has come into the Jebel Druze with an official escort, so that I might probably have got permission if I had asked for it. But I am very glad I came up through the desert for it has been a most amusing journey and a very valuable experience for a future expedition. You see I have laid the foundations of friendship with several important people—of desert importance that is.

Monday, 20th. We had the devil's own ride yesterday. It was a bright morning with a bitter wind, and I determined to start. So after prolonged farewells I set off with a Druze zaptieh, name of Yusef, and we plodded through the mud and the stones gradually rising into the hills. All went well for the first three hours or so, except that it was so cold that I rode in a sweater (Molly's, bless her for it!) a Norfolk jacket and a fur coat; then we began to get into snow and it was more abominable than words can say. The mules fell down in snow drifts. the horses reared and bucked, and if I had been on a sidesaddle we should have been down half a dozen times, but on this beloved saddle one can sit straight, and close. So we plunged on, the wind increasing and sleet beginning to fall, till at last we came out on to a world entirely white. The last hour I walked and led my horse for he broke through the deep snow at every step. Also I was warmer. By the time we reached Saleh, our destination, it was sleeting hard. The village was a mass of snow drift and half frozen mud and pond. There wasn't a dry spot. So I went up to the house of the Sheikh, Muhammad ibn Nassar, and there I found a party of his nephews who took me into the Makad, which is the reception room, and lighted a fire in an iron stove and made tea. The Makad was a good sized room with closely shuttered windows, by reason of there being no glass, felt mats on the floor and a low divan all round on which carpets were spread for me. Rather a fine place as Makads go. As I sat, drinking my tea and conversing with the nephews—who were delightful intelligent young men—in came the Sheikh, a tall, very old man, and offered me every hospitality he could in the most charming way. Some interest surrounds me, for I am the first foreign woman who has ever been in these parts. Sheikh Muhammad insisted that I should spend the night in his house, and I gladly agreed, for indeed even for a lover of tents,, it was not a promising evening. All the family (males) came in one after another, he has six sons and more nephews than I ever saw, and I established myself on the divan, all the Druizes sitting round in rows, and answered all their questions about foreign parts, especially Japan, for they are thrilled over the war, and explained to them how we lived. They asked particularly after Lord Salisbury and were much saddened to hear he was dead. They knew Chamberlain by name—the real triumph of eloquence was when I explained to them the fiscal question, and they all became Free Traders on the spot.

Two of the sons had been to school in Cple (transcriber's note: Constantinople), and the Sheikh had been honourably imprisoned there for three years after the War, so that they were all a little acquainted with the world, and, as is the habit among the Druzes, wonderfully well informed as to what was passing. Presently came dinner on a big tray, bowls of rice and chicken and a curious sort of Druze food, made of sour milk and semen (which is grease) and vegetables, a kind of soup, not very good. My Zaptieh Yusef and I being the guests, ate together; then the others sat down round the tray. So we re-established ourselves on the divan, drank coffee and continued the conversation till nine o'clock when wadded quilts were brought and spread in three beds, on each side of the Makad—and Yusef, the Sheikh and I coiled ourselves up and went to sleep. But I wish you could have assisted for a moment at that evening party and seen all those white turbans and keen handsome faces of the Druzes, and their interest and excitement at all I said. For my part I slept sound and woke a little before sunrise. The Makad felt rather stuffy so I slipped on my fur coat and went out into the silent frozen village. There is a very attractive old fountain down by the khan, and there I stood in the snow and watched the sun rise and said a short thanksgiving appropriate to fine weather. My servants slept in the khan, they and the horses, all together under the dark shelter. They seemed happy, oddly enough. So I breakfasted with the Sheikh on tea and Arab bread and a sort of treacle they make from grapes, dibbis is its name, and I like it particularly.

We rode off with one of the nephews as a guide, Fais, we are fast friends. We plunged for half an hour or so through snow and ice, and then suddenly left the winter country behind us and had a charming ride all along the eastern edge of the Druze mountains.

Thursday, 23rd. Oh, my dear mother, such a travel I've had! I often wished you could have seen me at it, and wondered what sort of a face you would have made. Listen, then. On Tuesday morning I rode off with my invaluable cook, Mikhail, and the best of my muleteers (and he is as good as anyone could wish)

Habib, on the best of his mules, and six Druzes. I left my tents behind, took some rugs, five chickens and plenty of bread, a fur coat and a camera. This was our modest all for three days. We rode down the Druze mountains for an hour, then for an hour through a shallow winding valley of volcanic rock, then we came out on to the wide desolation of the Safah. It is all covered with black stones. How they got there I can't think. The earth they lie on is yellow like sand, but quite hard, and nothing grows but a few plants of desert scrub, of which there are many kinds, but I won't trouble you with their names at the present time. Once in a while you see a small flock of goats or herd of camels quarrying their dinner, so to speak, and from space to space a few black tents belonging to the Ghiath Arabs, who are a very poor tribe that spend the winter in the Safah and come in spring to the Druze hills. Through this wilderness of stones we rode for three hours and then we met one in rags whose name was Hound of God—it sounds like a pretence mystery tale, but it's the real thing. He was exceedingly glad to see us, was Hound of God, having been a friend of the family for years—at least eighty I should judge. He told us there was a pool of water near, and Arab tents two hours away—we found the water and lunched by it, sharing it with a herd of camels, but in the matter of the Arabs he lied, did Hound of God. We rode on over all the stones in the world and at last, half an hour before sunset, just as we were deciding that we should have to sleep out, waterless, one of the Druzes caught sight of the smoke of some Arab tents. We got there in the dusk and stumbled in over the stones with the camels and the goats which were returning home after a laborious day of feeding. Very miserable the little encampment looked. They have Nothing but a few camels, the black tents and the coffee pots. They eat nothing but bread and all their days they wander the stones in fear of their lives, for the Safah is swept by the ghazus of the big tribes from north to south and they harry the Ghiath as they pass. We scattered, being a big party, Ghishghash, my servants and I went to the house of the Sheikh, whose name was Understanding. His two sons lighted a fire of desert thorns and we all sat round watching the Coffee making. And the talk began to the accompaniment of the coffee pounding, a great accomplishment among them. They pound in a delightful sort of tune, or rather a sort of tattoo. We dined on flaps of fresh bread and bowls of dibbis and then I curled myself up in a blanket and went to sleep In a corner of the tent. The smoke of the fire was abominable but it blew out after a bit, one side of an Arab tent is always open, you know. The fleas didn't blow out. I woke in the middle of the night. There was a big moon shining into the tent, the Arabs and the Druzes were all sleeping round the cold hearth, a couple of mares were standing peacefully by the tent bole and, beyond them, on the stones, a camel lay champing. Then I slept till dawn. Half an hour after the sun was up we were off, the party increased by one of our hosts. . . . And presently I discovered that the narrow track we were riding in was a road as old as time. It was marked at intervals by piled up heaps of stones and at one place there was a stone which had been a well stone, for it was worn a couple of inches deep with the rub of the rope—it must have served a respectable time, for this black rock is extraordinarily hard—

and in another there was a mass of rock all covered with inscriptions, Nabathaean, Greek, Kufic, and one in a babel which I did not know, but it was very like the oldest script of Yemen Sabaean; and last of all the Arabs had scrawled their tribe marks there. So each according to his kind had recorded his passing. At the back of the lava hills we came out into a great plain of yellow clay which stretches for many miles and is called the Ruhbe .... The second night in Arab tents was rather wearing, I must admit, and I felt quite extraordinarily dirty this morning. We started early and I got back to my tents at 4—the bath that followed was one of the most delightful I have ever had. It was an interesting journey, however, hard work but well worth the trouble. I refused a very pressing invitation to dine with my Druze friends, feeling that I really must have a Christian meal, but I went up and drank coffee with them afterwards and we had a long talk which ended in their declaring that they regarded me as one of the family.

BATHANIYEH,
Friday, 24th. There must have been quite ten degrees of frost last night. My sponges were frozen together into a solid mass so that I could not use them, and though there was a bright hot sun the world did not begin to unfreeze till midday. I had a charming ride down from the Druze mountains into the Damascus plain.

Saturday 25th. I got out of the Druze country about four o'clock in the afternoon. Just before I left it I met two Druzes with laden mules coming from Damascus. They gave me a very friendly greeting and I said, "Are you facing to the Mountain?" They said, "By God! May God preserve you!" I said, "I come from there, salute it for me!" They answered, "May God salute you; go in peace." To-night I am camped on the edge of the volcanic country in a village of Circassians and in the matterof pens I don't think there is much difference between me and Caroline Herschell. I wish the weather would be a little warmer.

DAMASCUS, Monday, 27th. Here we are. I arrived yesterday afternoon, alighted at the most fascinating hotel, with a courtyard.

I find the Government here has been in an agony of nervousness all the time I was in the Jebel Druze, they had three telegrams a day from Salkhad about me and they sat and wondered what I was going to do next. The governor here has sent me a message to say would I honour him by coming to him, so I've answered graciously that I counted on the pleasure of making his acquaintance. An official lives in this hotel. He spent the evening talking to me and offering to place the whole of the organisation of Syria at my disposal. He also tried to find out all my views on Druze and Bedouin affairs, but he did not get much forrader there. I have become a Person in Syria!

To F. B.
DAMASCUS, March 3rd, 1905.
I was greeted when I arrived by a distinguished native of the Lebanon, a Maronite Christian, who has constituted himself my cicerone, and has been very

useful, though he is rather a bore. He was directed by the Governor to look after me during my visit and he has fulfilled his instructions to the letter! I wrote to you on Monday, I think. That afternoon I went to tea with the American archaeologists. . . . One of them, Dr. Littman who is an old acquaintance of mine, is a real learned man and I won his esteem by presenting him with a Nabathaean inscription which he had not got, and one in the strange script of the Safah, which he said I had copied without a fault. That was rather a triumph, I must tell you, for I remember as I did it all the Druzes and my Bedouin guide on his camel were standing round impatiently and crying "Yallah, yallah! oh, lady!" . . . . . . Having evaded all the obliging people who offer to escort me everywhere, I dawdled off into the town. I made my way at last to the great mosque—which was a church of Constantine's—left my shoes at the door, with a friendly beggar and went in. It was the hour of the afternoon prayer. In the courtyard, men of all sorts and kinds, from the learned Doctor of Damascus down to the raggedest camel driver—Islam is the great republic of the world, there is neither class nor race inside the creed—were washing at the fountain and making the first prostrations before they entered the mosque. I followed them in and stood behind the lines of praying people some two or three hundred of them, listening to the chanting of the Imam. "Allah!" he cried, and the Faithful fell with a single movement upon their faces and remained for a full minute in silent adoration, till the high chant of the Imam began again: "The Creator of this World and the next, of the Heavens and the Earth, He who leads the righteous in the true path, and the evil to destruction. Allah!" And as the name of God echoed through the great colonnades, where it had sounded for near 2,000 years in different tongues, the listeners prostrated themselves again, and for a moment all the church was silence. . . . Every afternoon I hold a reception and Damascus flocks to drink my coffee and converse with me. That day I lunched in the bazaars, in the fashionable restaurant, unknown to foreigners, and ate fallap and the delicious dishes for which Damascus is renowned. And in the afternoon came the Governor, returning my call, and the usual stream followed him, so that I sat in audience till dinner time. Yesterday I spent the whole morning in the house of the Emir Abdullah. The Abdul Kadir family has a traditional friendship with the Beni Rashid, which is kept up by yearly presents to and fro. They are going to help me in my journeys thither and perhaps I shall take one of them with me. And after dinner I went to an evening party. It was in the house of a corn merchant who is the agent of the Druzes of the Hauran. I found there a Druze of a famous Lebanon family, the Arslan; he is a poet—have I not been presented with his latest ode—and a man of education and standing. I wish I could picture the scene—some eight or ten of the corn merchants, dressed in blue silk robes and embroidered yellow turbans, my friend the poet in European dress, and me, all sitting on the divan in a room blessedly empty of everything but carpets and the brazier. And then coffee and talk and talk and talk till I got up and took my leave about ten o'clock, and went away laden with thanks and blessings.

This has been a visit to Damascus that I shall not easily forget—I begin to see dimly what the civilisation of a great Eastern city means—how they live, what they think; and I have got on to terms with them.

To F. B.
BAALBEK, March 5, 1905.

I have made some curious observations, but think it better to keep them to myself. There is an Arab proverb which says: "Let him who talks by day take heed." And it applies to those who talk by post, The Vali, when he heard I was going to ride to Baalbek, was all for sending a large escort with me, so I hastily declared I should go by train—only pretence. Such are the penalties of greatness. I do trust I shall now be allowed to relapse into the position of a modest traveller of no importance to anyone. I have found out that while I was in Damascus, every time I went out alone I was followed by a man who was commissioned to watch over my safety—it was merely solicitude on the part of the Government and as there were no secrets about my coming and goings it was harmless. So I was followed to the house of Naksh Pendi and was introduced to his favourite wife. She is quite young, a pretty woman, but shockingly untidy with her hair all over her eyes and a dirty dressing-gown, clothing a figure which has already, alas! fallen into ruin. The view from Naksh Pendi's Balcony is, however, immortal. The great splendid city of Damascus with its gardens and its domes and its minarets, lies spread out before you, and beyond it the desert—the desert almost up to its gates, and the breath of it blowing in with every wind, and the spirit of it passing in through the city gates with every Arab camel driver. That is the heart of the whole matter.

To H. B.
BAALBEK, March 6th.

I had almost forgotten how beautiful this place is. Except Athens, there is no temple group to touch it, and I have looked at it with new eyes now that I know a little more than I did about the history of decoration and the genesis of pattern and ornament. But I wish I knew a great deal more still.

To F.B.
KUSEIR, March 8, 1905.

We set off at 8 on our way to Homs. We had a terrible adventure: as we were about to start I found that my dog, Kurt, was missing. I sent Mikhail and Habib looking for him through the town and Habib presently discovered him tied up in the house of one who thought to steal him. Chained up, and Habib with some promptness claimed the dog and appropriated the chain, and upon the thief's protesting, he knocked him down and came away. I can't say I regret Habib's action. It will learn our friend not to be a dog stealer.

To F.B.
Homs, March 9, 1905.

I took a walk through the bazaars, but that was not as pleasant as it might have been on account of the interest my appearance excited. It was an interest purely benevolent but none the less tiresome, for I was never without the company of fifty or sixty people. When I returned, the Kaimmakarn came to see me, and we had a long talk, his secretary piecing out his Arabic and my Turkish. One of the principal inhabitants of Homs, Doury Pasha, to whom I had a letter of introduction from Damascus, has also sent to ask if he may call tomorrow. Oh, Merciful! what fun I am having! Don't you think so?

Friday, 10th. Homs is not Much of a place, but such as it is it has a character of its own. It is all built of black tufa and the best houses have inner courtyards, with a simple but very excellent decoration Of white limestone let into the black either in patterns or in straight courses like the Pisan building. Moreover, the minarets of the mosques and tall slender towers, or Spire, for all the world like an Italian campanile, like the towers of San Gimignano, except that they are capped With a whole cupola, very Pretty and decorative. I spent the morning sight-seeing, with a soldier in attendance so that I was not bothered by the people. Sight-seeing takes a long time in these parts, for when anyone of importance meets you in the streets, he invites you in to drink a cup Of coffee. this happened to me 3 times and gave me the opportunity of seeing the inside of some of the big houses. After lunch I rode down to the river, the Orontes, to see the fashionable lounge, a delicious stretch of meadow and willow trees by the water side. But the trees are not yet in leaf nor the flowers out.

They are all wildly Japanese in this country. There are perhaps 400 people round about my tent.

To F. B.
KALAAT EL HUSN, March 12

I am now staying in perhaps the largest castle known—no, it's not so large as Windsor Castle, but very nearly. It is Crusader—but I must tell you how it all came about. I left Homs at an early hour yesterday—not early enough however to prevent my having a large, eager crowd to watch my departure. It is one of the most difficult things I know to keep One's temper when one is constantly surrounded and mobbed. The aggravation is quite as great when they are friendly; it is the fact of not being able to move without hundreds of people on every side that is so irritating. Only a fixed determination not to afford more amusement than I could help to the inhabitants of Homs kept me outwardly calm. My escort consisted of two mounted Kurds and two prisoners whom the Kaimmakam was sending to the Prison of Husn—my journey afforded a good opportunity Of conveying them. They were hand-cuffed together, Poor wretches! and they trudged along bravely through dust and mud. I proffered a few words of sympathy, to which they replied that they hoped God might preserve me, but as for them it was the will of their lord, the Sultan. They were deserters. we had a very long day, 10 hours, but when we left the carriage road that goes to Tripoli our way lay through such delicious country that every step of it was delightful. It was beautiful weather. The great castle on the top of the hill was before us for five or six hours. The sun shone on it and the black clouds hung round it as we rode up and up through flowers and grass and across running streams. But it was a long way and the animals grew very tired. At sunset we came to the dark tower. I rode through a splendid Arab gateway into a vaulted corridor which covered a broad winding stair. It was almost pitch dark, lighted only by a few loop-holes; the horses stumbled and clanked over the stone steps—they were shallow and wide, but very much broken—and we turned corner after corner and passed under gateway after gateway until at length we came into the court in the centre of the keep. I felt as if I were somebody in the Faery Queen, and almost expected to see written upon the last arch, "Be not too bold." But there was no monster inside, only a crowd of people craning their necks to see me, and the Kaimmakam very smiling and friendly, announcing that he could not think of letting me pitch my tents, and had prepared my lodging for the night. So we went up into the round tower in which he lives and he took me into his guest room, which was commodiously fitted with carpets, a divan and a bed—I supplied the washing appliances and the table-and he offered me weak tea while he engaged me in conversation. He is a man of some distinction, a renowned poet, I believe—but his hospitality outweighs all his other qualities. My men and my horses and me, he has taken us all in and provided for us all. There were two other guests besides me, one an old Moslem woman and the other a Christian lady, the wife of a government official. . . . The Moslem woman was a nice old thing. Her son has recently been murdered in the mountains by a casual robber, and our talk turned mostly upon similar incidents which are very common here. The old lady crouched over a charcoal brazier murmured at intervals: "Murder is like the drinking of milk here. God! there is none other but Thee!" The talk seemed to fit the surroundings. My tower room must have Heard the like of it often. "Murder is like the drinking of water," muttered the old woman. "Oh, Merciful!" At nine they all left me—and one offered to spend the night with me, but I declined, politely, but firmly. To-day is devilish weather, a strong wind and hailstones and thunder storms. . . . I spent a very agreeable evening in the company of my host and hostess. We all dined together and he and I talked. We got on to such terms that he ended by producing his latest copy of verses-and reading it aloud to me. We then fell to discussing the poets with much satisfaction, and he forgot his sorrows, poor man, and became quite brisk and excited. As we have often remarked, there is no solace in misfortune like authorship, be it ever so modest. I could have laughed to find myself talking the same sort of enjoyable rubbish in Arabic that I have so frequently talked in English, and offering the same kind of sympathy and praise to my friend's efforts. Yes., it might just as well have been London, and the world is, after all., made of the same piece.

BURI SAFITAH,

Monday, 13. At dawn it was raining for all it was worth, and I got up and breakfasted in the lowest of spirits. And then of a sudden Someone waved a magic wand, all the clouds cleared away and we set off at half past seven in exquisite sunshine, loaded with the blessings of our host and parting gifts of a more substantial nature, for he insisted on supplying us with our food for the day. At the bottom of the steep hill on which the Castle stands, there lies in an olive grove a big Greek monastery. I got off and went in to salute the abbot, and behold! he was a friend of five years ago, for I had seen him in a place on the road from Palmyra. Great rejoicing and much jam and coffee to celebrate the occasion. Late this evening, just as I was beginning to write to you, there appeared two high officials sent up by the Kaimmakam of Drekish, where I go to-morrow, to welcome me and to put the whole of the forces of the Kaitylmakanilik at my disposal. I hereby renounce in despair the hope of ever again being a simple, happy traveller. The Turkish Government has decided that I am a great swell and nothing will persuade them to the contrary. It is boring to tears, and also very expensive, but what can I do? The only blot on my happiness is that Kurt has finally disappeared. I suppose he was tempted away by someone who offered him food and then stole him. . . . . My Arabic is becoming very fluent, thank heaven! but I wish I talked with more elegance. . . .

HAMAH,

Thursday, 16. A long and tedious ride to-day, across the foothills and the plain to Hamah. I have just had a struggle with the authorities, who insisted on giving me eight watchmen for the night. I refused to have more than two, which is all one ever has anywhere, and the rest have gone away. It is a perfect pest having so many, for in the first place they talk all night and in the second one has to tip them all.

KALAAT EL MUDDIH,

Sunday, March 19, 1905. Apamea, one of the many and a most beautiful place, standing on a great bluff over the Orontes valley. Seleucus Nicator built it and a fine thing he must have made of it, for there is near a square mile of fallen columns and temple walls and Heaven knows what besides. Now think how Greece and the East were fused by Alexander's conquests. A Greek king, with his capital on the Euphrates, builds a city on the Orontes and calls it after his Persian wife, and what manner of people walked down its colonnades, keeping touch with Athens and with Babylon? That is the proposition in all the art hereabouts. The chief characteristics of the person that walked down them to-day-scrambled down them over the huge column boles—was that she was wet. It has rained in heavy showers all day and the deep grass and flowers were dripping wet and I was soaked up to the knees and drenched from time to time from above. One of the difficulties of searching for antiquities is that most of the people don't recognise any sort of picture when they see it, that if you ask a man if there are any stones with the portraits of men or animals on them, he replies, "Wallahi ! we do not know what the picture of a man is like." And if you show him a bit of a relief, however good it is he hasn't the least idea what the carving represents. Isn't that curious?

EL BARCH,

Monday, 20th. I photographed and explored and when I got back to my horses I realised that I had lost my coat. I had taken it off some half an hour after we reached Khirbet Hass and fastened it on to my saddle, it had dropped off and was gone. Mahmud went back to look for it and after an hour and a half came back without it. By this time it was past 6, we had an hour and a quarter's ride over very rough country and clouds were blowing up. So we rode off, picking our way through the stones by an almost invisible path. As ill-luck would have it just as the night fell, the storm came upon us—it became quite pitch dark with drenching rain and we missed our Mecca thread of a way. At that moment Mikhail's ears were assailed by the barking of imaginary dogs and we turned off to gain the spot from which the sound came. So we stumbled on and the moon came out a little and it was clear the path we were on led nowhere. . . .

The Sheikh is a very sprightly old party who was guide de Vogüé 40 years ago and to every archaeologist since his time. He knows them all by name or rather by names his own very far removed from the original. He rode with me this morning. I made a détour with Mahmud and visited two villages, one more beautiful than the other. We had an 'impayable' conversation by the way. It began by my asking Yunis whether he ever went to Aleppo. "Oh, yes," he said, he was accustomed to go when his sons were in prison there. I edged away from what seemed to me delicate ground by asking how many sons he had. Eight; each of his 2 wives had borne him 4 sons and 2 daughters. I congratulated him warmly on this. Yes, he said, but Wallahi! his second wife had cost him a great deal of money. "Yes?" said I. "May God make it Yes upon thee, oh lady! I took her from her husband and by God (may His name be Praised and exalted!) I had to pay him 1,000 piasters (about 10 Napoleons) and to the judge 1,500." This was too much for Mahmud's sense of decency. "Wallahi!" said he, "that was the deed of a Nosairiyeh or an Ismailiyeh!" "Does a Muslim take away a man's wife? It is forbidden." "He was my enemy," replied Yunis in explanation. "By God and the Prophet of God! there was enmity between him and me even unto death." "Had she children?" said Mahmud, "Ey wallah" (i.e. of course), said Yunis, a little put out by Mahmud's disapproval. "By the face of God!" exclaimed Mahmud, still more outraged, "it was the deed of a heathen." "I paid 1,000 piasters to the man, and 1,500 to the judge," objected Yunis—and here I put an end to the further discussion of the merits of the case by asking whether the woman had liked being carried off. "Without doubt," said Yunis, "it was her wish." At noon I came to a wonderful village called Ruweika and lunched in a tomb like a small temple-there was a violent thunder-storm going on all the time.

Sunday, 26th. On Friday I rode east across a rolling plain covered with débris of towns but uninhabited except by half settled Bedouin. It's a curious and interesting thing to see them all along the western edges of the desert taking to cultivating the soil and establishing themselves therefore of necessity in a given place (in some distant age there will be no nomads left in Arabia-but it is still far off I'm glad to think). In the early stages these new-made farmers continue to live in tents, only the tents are stationary and the accompanying dirt cumulative.

To F. B.

KALAAT SINLAN, March 31st,

Aleppo, is a town where it always rains—at least that is my 2 days' impression of it. It has been a great great Arab town. . . .. An endless barren world stretches round, uninterrupted by hill or tree—you can see the Euphrates from the castle in clear weather; you might see Bagdad for anything there is between. I called on the Governor who received me in his harem, of which I was glad, for his wife is one of the most beautiful women I have ever seen. He returned my call in the afternoon. And finally I spent an amusing evening with a native family and talked the most fluent Arabic till a quarter to 11 by the clock! All my leisure moments were occupied in changing muleteers, getting new ones and saying goodbye (with much regret) to the old. It was a necessary step for I could not take Syrians talking nothing but Arabic into Asia Minor. I have got 3 bilingual natives of Aleppo and so far I like them very much. Yesterday morning, what with new muleteers and what with the numbers of people who came to bid me farewell I did not get off till 10 o'clock. When we got Into the low rocky hills the mules went one way and my soldier went another. We reached the place where I had intended to camp at about 4 in the afternoon. There were a few ruined walls there,—the tents of some Kurdish shepherds. We waited an hour and the mules did not turn up. Then the Kurds announced that it was dinner-time and invited us to come and eat. I was very hungry and not at all sorry to share their cracked oats and meat and sour milk. At 6 o'clock there Came in a little boy who stated that he had seen my mules an hour before and that they had gone on to Rahat Simian, a good hour and a quarter away. So I said goodbye to my delightful hosts, who were much concerned at my case, and by dint of riding as hard as we could over the rocky ground we got in just before it became black dark. To our great joy as we got in we heard the mule bells; the others had arrived just before us. We rode through the huge silent church and found them pitching the tents by the light of 2 candles. And now I must tell you where I am. This is the place where St. Simon lived upon a pillar. While the servants pitched my tents I went out and sat upon St. Simon's column—there is still a little bit of it left—and considered how very different he must have been from me. And there came a big star and twinkled at me through the soft warm night, and we agreed together that it was pleasanter to wander across the heavens and the earth than to sit on top of a pillar all one's days.

I have had the most delightful day today, playing at being an archaeologist.

Monday, April 3 rd, 19 o 5. I shall not forget the misery of copying a Syrian inscription in the drenching rain, holding my cloak round my book to keep the paper dry. The devil take all Syrian inscriptions, they are so horribly difficult to copy. Fortunately they are rare, but I've had two to-day. Elsa will sympathise with my desperate attempts to take time exposures in a high wind. Heaven knows what they will be like—something like pictures of an earthquake I should think. By this time even my archaeological zeal had flickered out and I rode into my tents at Basuran, arriving at 2 o'clock, chilled to the bone. I have an enchanting camp tonight in the ruins called Debes. It is quite uninhabited and I have pitched my tents in a big church. I can very seldom induce my servants to camp far from habitation. They pine, not unnaturally, for the sour curds and the other luxuries of civilization. I rather miss the sour curds myself but the charm of a solitary camp goes far to console me!

Wednesday, 5th. We have had such a day's mountaineering! I must say I prefer doing my rock climbing on foot and not on horseback. Today, indeed, I was on foot most of the time, but dragging my unfortunate beast after me up and down walls of rock terrific to the eye. This is no exaggeration. I am pretty well versed in bad roads but till today I did not know what a horse could do. We climbed up and down two mountain ranges. At the second I confess my heart failed me. it was awful—indescribable. I didn't for the moment think we should get up with whole limbs. I jumped and tumbled up the stones and my horse jumped and tumbled after me, and all the time we were on the edge of little precipices quite high enough to break us to bits if we fell over. And when you get to the top of these terrible hills, behold a beautiful country. I lunched and photographed and made friends with the few families of servants who live in some cottages near by and imagine my delight when they turned out to be Druzes! I knew there were a few families of Druzes in these hills and had been looking for them. So we fell on each other's necks, and I gave them all the latest news of the Hauran and one of them insisted on guiding me on my stoney way through the hills. We had a remarkable climb down into the great plain through which flows our old friend the Orontes. And then a no less memorable ride along the base of the hills to my camping ground. It was more exquisitely beautiful than words can say, through gardens of fruit trees and olives with an unbelievable wealth of flowers everywhere.

To Florence Lascelles.
KONIA, April 9.

Darling, You can't think how delighted I was to find your long interesting letter awaiting me here. And the best part of it was the news that you are to be in London in June—Florence, we will arrange for some 6 solid hours, when no one shall interrupt us, and talk without stopping, both of us at once, and then perhaps we shall have got through about one-thousandth of what we have to say. For we have to talk out a whole year, and since you came back from Persia I don't believe we have ever been separated for so long . . . ..

What a country this is! I fear I shall spend the rest of my life travelling in it. Race after race, one on top of the other, the whole land strewn with the mighty relics of them. We in Europe are accustomed to think that civilization is an advancing flood that has gone steadily forward since the beginning of time. I believe we are wrong. It is a tide that ebbs and flows, reaches a high water mark and turns back again.

you think that from age to age it rises higher than before? I wonder—and I doubt.

But it is a fine world for those who are on the top of the wave and a good world, isn't it. . . .

To F.B.
PAYAS, April 14, 1905.

The hot weather has come with a rush. When I got back from Seleucia—in blazing weather—I stayed a day at Antioch in order to see a collection of antiquities in the house of a rich Pasha. He had a MS of the Psalms in Armenian which he showed me and of which I photographed a page or two for the benefit of Mr. Yates Thompson—you might tell him if you see him. He had also some beautiful little bits of Greek bronze which I photographed for Reinach. Yesterday I rode down to Alexandria, :rather a long day-furiously hot. We were on the Roman Road most of the day, crossing the great Pass of Bailan where were the Syrian gates of the Ancients. It was from this pass that Alexander hurried back to meet the army of Darius at Issus—I have been following the line of his march to-day and am now camped on the edge of the Plain of Issus. . . . The plain is very narrow here and fine great mountains rise fteeply up from it. My impression is that the battle must have been fought just about here for the books say that Darius had not room to display his cavalry. . . . I never tell you of the difficulties of camp organization because I think they may be tedious. They are however many, especially now that half my servants talk only Turkish. But to-day a really singular thing has happened. The head muleteer from whom I hired all the baggage horses from Aleppo, has simply not turned up. I haven't the least idea what has become of him—the others suggest that he has either been murdered or imprisoned! He went down into the bazaar after we left Alexandretta and has not been seen since. Fortunately I have the animals nearly up to Konia. I shall go on whether he turns up or not and let him retrieve his beasts from Konia as best he may. I don't regret him at all; he is most incompetent and he treats his subordinates so badly that they leave us at every stage, which is an insufferable nuisance as I have to teach the new men their work—in fragmentary Turkish. The good Mikhail is rather gloomy this evening but I fancy we shall pull through.

April 15 th. It rained floods in the night and continued to do so until this morning. The tents were soaked, the water ran in under the tent walls and I was obliged to retire on to my bed which was the only dry place. Thunder and lightning and all complete. In the middle of it all the good Kaimmakam strolled down to invite me to his house, but I did not go as I should have got wet through on the way. When the rain stopped we had to let our tents dry and by that time it was too late to start and I was obliged very reluctantly to resign myself to a day in camp. In the course of the morning, the missing muleteer turned up. He had in fact been detained by difficulties with a creditor. How he got off I don't know—not by paying I'll be bound—but the incident has had the worst effect on the discipline of the camp, for he re-appeared so overflowing with joy, and I was so much excited and amused that I received him as a sort of prodigal father (he's 60 if he's a day) and his shortcomings are all forgiven for the moment. The Kaimmakam sent a present of 6 oranges and 2 small bottles of Russian beer to console me for my enforced stay!

April 17th. Oh, but I've had a tiring 2 days! What it's like to travel in A roadless and bridgeless country after and during heavy, not tO Say torrential, rains you can't imagine. We started off yesterday in pouring rain, the path was under water, the rivers roaring floods. In the middle of the day we came to a village buried in lovely gardens, the air heavy with the smell of lemon flowers—and here the heavens opened and it rained as I hope never to see it rain again. We had stopped at the house of a Turk to buy a hen—he invited us in till the rain stopped and I took the opportunity to lunch. Meantime a furious roaring stream which we had succeeded in fording, brought the baggage animals to a stand, and while we, unknowing, went gaily on, they made a détour of nearly 2 hours to find a bridge. . . . I was tired and wet and hungry and bad weather travelling is exhausting to the mind and to the body. It was 7:30 before they arrived and we pitched camp in a downpour amid the mutual recriminations of all the servants who had had a hard time too and vented their displeasure On each other. There was nothing for it but to hold one's tongue, do the work oneself, and having seen that the horses were fed, I went to bed supperless because no one would own that it was his duty to light the fire! It was miserable I must say and this morning was just as bad. All the ropes were like iron after the rain and the tents weighed tons and as I splashed about in the deep grass (for I had to watch and encourage every finger's turn of the work) I thought I was a real idiot to go travelling in tents. Then the march—fortunately a short one—through the floods of yesterday's rain. It was very interesting historically for we were going through the Amanian Gates, through which many armies had passed in and out of Cilicia. I was determined not to lose touch with my baggage animals today and when we came to a wide deep river I waited for them and rode backwards and forwards twice through the floods to help them over. When they saw me riding in and out gaily (the water was above my boots I may mention) they took courage and plunged through. And now I hope our troubles are over. We are camped at a place called Osmaniyeh in most lovely country and the sun has come out and our tents are drying and our tempers mending. I think if the rain had lasted another day I should have died of despair—and of fatigue. I'm really in Asia Minor—a most exciting thought. And I have to talk Turkish. There's nothing else for it. I've just been entertaining (in more senses than one) the Kaimmakam in that tongue. I make a preposterous mess of it, but it has to be done. I hope in a week or so I shall begin to scrub along. The chief difficulty now is that though I can put a few questions I cannot easily understand the answers! You know there are moments when being a woman increases one's difficulties. What my servants needed last night was a good beating and that's what they would have got if I had been a mail—I seldom remember being in such a state of suppressed rage!—but as it is I have to hold my tongue and get round them. However as long as one gets through it doesn't matter.

April 18th. The chief interest of this journey is that I find myself talking nothing but Turkish. It's the greatest lark. . . . I've learnt piles to-day. I started off this morning with a soldier who could speak nothing else and I had to make the best of it. It was a lovely shining morning and this country is beyond comparison beautiful. We cantered across a wide delicious plain set round with the great snows of Taurus and the Giaour Dagh—it was an hour after dawn, more heavenly than words can say. Then we came to a deep river across which we went in a ferry boat. I lent a hand to some shepherds who were trying to get a herd of goats onto the ferry—I hope it counts as a virtue to help obstinate goats into a ferry; it's certainly difficult any way. A charming gentleman called Mustapha had attached himself to my party and rode with me all day. So we came to a place called Budsian, which is Hierapolis Cartabala, And here I spent 3 hours. It lies among wonderful crags, the acropolis perched up on top of a great rock and below it a fine theatre, there was a street of columns and 2 very lovely churches. These last I photographed with great care and measured, Mustapha holding the end of the tape. By the time I had finished it was near midday and I eat my lunch at a village near by, where they gave me the most excellent milk and curds, for which they would not let me pay. And so we rode on for 5 hours through charming country to Kars Bazaar, which lies under Taurus and here I have camped. I paid a visit to the Kaimmakam and was further invited to tea with some notables who were sitting in the street Outside the café. There was no one to interpret so I had to do my own talking. I must say they are very clever at understanding. And now I must study the Turkish participles—there are some 30 of them. I don't handle them with any skill.

ANAvARZA,

April 20th. . . . . Yesterday morning I found there were lots of inscriptions to be copied at Kars and a church to be photographed, so what with one thing and another it was getting late before I got off. The mules had gone on ahead—we had to make an immense détour to the north, under the hills, to avoid floods and get to bridges, the rivers being all unfordable. The mules being for once far ahead, missed their way and have gone up on the wrong side of Anavarza with an unfordable stream before them. We were certain something had gone wrong since we did not overtake them but after some indecision I determined to ride on, and following the line of an immense aqueduct, we splashed through the wet plain at sunset into Anavarza. The castle stands on a mass of rock, 2 miles long, which rises like a great island from the sea of plain—it's really a sea at this moment for it is all under water. The rock is some 300 ft. high and in places quite perpendicular; the castle runs all along the top of it and the top is in some places a knife edge, dropping absolutely sheer on either side with just room for a single fortification wall to connect fort with fort. At the western foot of this splendid acropolis lies the city with a double wall of turrets round it buttressed up against the cliff. It was a Greek storing place, a treasury of Alexander's, then Roman, then the capital of the Armenian kingdom-and now a mass of ruin, deeply overgrown with grass. So I rode through the northern gateway of the town not having the faintest idea where I was going to sleep or eat. By good fortune there was a guard-house in the middle of the ruins with a couple of Turkish soldiers in it who supplied me with milk and sour curds. On them and sour native bread I dined: then I spread my cloak on the floor of a little empty room and slept till 6 this morning; in spite Of innumerable mosquitoes. It wasn't really nice however. Roughing it in this weather is more difficult than in the cold. After the long hot day one longs incredibly for one's evening bath and change of clothes. I was most thankful when at 10 this morning the baggage turned up. I shall take great care not to run any risk of its going astray again. I have spent the whole day exploring and photographing and I am going to have another day here in order to have a shot at measuring and planning 3 churches, an extremely difficult business because they are very much ruined and very deeply buried in grASS-

April 21st. Remembering the heat of yesterday I got up at dawn and at 6 o'clock started out to grapple with my churches. The whole plain, my tents included, lay under a thick white mist, but the sun was shining on the earth rock and as I climbed up I saw the great white peaks of Taurus all glittering. It was most beautiful. I took my soldier with me and taught him to hold the measuring tape. He soon understood what I wanted and measured away at doors and windows like one to the manner born. After 5 hours very hard work I found I had arrived at results—more interesting than I had expected. In a word, the churches here are not of the Syrian type which they ought by rights to be, but of the Central Asia Minor type—and I think they will surprise Strzygowski not a little. One very delightful thin happened. One of the biggest of the churches is razed to le ground-nothing but the traces of the foundations remain. I looked round about for any scraps of carving that might give an indication of the style of decoration and found, after much search one and one only—and it was dated! It Was a big stone which from the shape and the mouldings I knew to have been at the spring of two arches of the windows of the apse and the date was carved in beautiful raised Greek letters between the two arch mouldings—"The year 511." I don't know if they used the Christian era here but it must be pretty close to it anyway, for that's about the date one would have expected. Wasn't it a great piece of luck! Two things I dislike in Anavarza. The mosquitoes and the snakes; the mosquitoes have been the most hostile of the two: the snakes always bustle away in a great hurry and I have made no experiments as to what their bite would be like. There are quantities of them among the ruins. They are about 3 ft. long—I wonder if they are poisonous. "Rira bien qui rira le dernier": I have had the laugh of the vultures. After tea I rode round the rocks on the eastern side and met a shepherd boy. So we tied my horse to a stone and the shepherd and I climbed together up the only path which leads to the castle keep. It was rocky enough in all conscience and it wound cheerfully in and out of precipices and led us at last to a little hole in the wall through which we climbed to the highest tower. Like all ruined castles it was more beautiful from without than from within; but the position is glorious and worth climbing for; the walls built on the edge of a straight drop of a couple of hundred feet or more, the great plain all round and the ring of snows beyond. We dislodged the vultures who were sitting in rows on the castle top-they left a horrid smell behind them-and in a small deep window I found a nest with 2 evil-looking brown eggs in it. It is not often that one finds vultures' nests. I have fallen a hopeless victim to the Turk; he is the most charming of mortals and some day when I have a little more of his language we shall be very intimate friends, I foresee. It's blazing hot weather; the wild hollyhocks are out and today I saw the first fat old pomegranate bud. That means summer.

Saturday, 22nd. I shall not soon forget the Cilician plain. The heat of it is surprising and as I told you 'passim' it is most of it under water. We plunged today for ten hours through mud and swamp and sluggish waters, and at last we have come out onto a rather higher bit of country on which the barley is standing in the ear. In a month everything will be burnt up and all the people will have fled to the hills. I don't wonder Anavarza had such a fine necropolis—all the inhabitants must have died off regularly every summer from marsh fever, mosquitoes and snakes. In the blazing middle of the day we came to two very small trees outside a village and I sat down in the shade of them to lunch. No sooner was my coming observed than one of the inhabitants appeared with a large tray of fried eggs, curds and bread for me and my servants. It was pure hospitality-I might give no tips. I could only thank my host sincerely and eat heartily. But though they are the most delightful of acquaintances they are the worst of servants. They will take any amount of trouble for you for nothing, but once you hire them to work, not a hand's turn will they do. At the hands of Turkish muleteers I suffer tortures. They get into camp and when they have unloaded the mules they sit down on one of the packs and light a cigarette with an air of impartial and wholly unconcerned benevolence. I've gone to the length of dislodging them with the lash of my crop, freely applied. It makes no difference; they stroll on to the next pack and take up a position there smiling cheerfully the while.

ADANA,

Sumday 23rd. I rode in here early this morning leaving camp at 3 a.m. to avoid the heat. There was a moon and a high-road and the going was far pleasanter than by day. I got into Adana about 10—there is absolutely nothing of any interest in the town. I went to the house of the Vice-Consul, a very able Greek, and he directed me to the best hotel. . . .The other inhabitants of the hotel are strange Greeks and Turks and parties in turbans and Circassians with rows of cartridges set in their brown frock coats—Oh, the oddest crowd! It doesn't surprise me when I am in tents and part of it, but when I come into an hotel and put on civilised clothes, my surroundings astonish me at times. In the afternoon I called on the Vali, an obliging Kurd who promised me all facilities for my journey and gave me a little bronze lion, Greek I think. I have sent on my camp and tomorrow I am actually going to Tarsus by train! Mr. Lloyd comes too and we spend the day together.

Monday, 24th. We carried out our programme with immense enjoyment. The railway journey which took an hour and a half was quite an excitement to both of us—I haven't been by train since Marseilles. We had a delightful conversation with the statiOn master before we started. He talked English and told us among other things that there were no works of art on the line, only one bridge. We were so busy talking on the journey that we forgot to notice even that work of art. Tarsus is nothing of a place, beautifully situated at the gates of the hills. Mr. Lloyd and I rather enjoyed ourselves however and we finished the day by a dinner-party together in my tent at which Mikhail distinguished himself in the matter of cooking. I have taken on from Mr. Lloyd one of his servants whom he does not want any longer. His name is Fattuh and he is to be general director of the transport and spare hand all round. I think I am wise in taking him for he seems very capable and has an excellent character from Mr. Lloyd, and my transport arrangements have not been going well for the last fortnight.

KARAMAN,
MaY 7th. I daresay it does not often occur to you to think what a wonderful invention is the railway, but it is very forcibly borne in upon me at this moment for I am going to Konia in 3 hours instead of having a weary two day's march across a plain of mud. Yesterday I rode in here some 35 miles. The mountains have no other side, if you can understand me. The road I have come by rose some 6,000 ft. from the sea and did not descend more than 600 on the north side. Inside, the country is exactly what I have often pictured it to myself-a great barren upland with abrupt hills rising out of it. One of my soldiers and I rode on ahead and did the journey in 7 hours. We arrived in a thunderstorm and I went to the hotel and slept for 3 hours till my mules came in. I don't remember having been so tired for a long time. The hotel of Karaman is in the first stage of development from the primitive Khan. Your host provides the roof and every man is his own cook and housemaid. . . . I wonder what the Kaimmakam thinks of the hats of English travellers of distinction. I have worn mine for 4 months in all weathers-you can scarcely tell which is the crown of it and which the brim. . . .

To H. B.
BUSTBIRKLISSE, May 13th, 1905.

If you had read (and who knows? Perhaps you have the very latest German archaeology books you would be wild with excitement at seeing where I am. I must begin at the beginning and tell you about Konia. I stayed 4 days. My friend the German Consul (name of Loytved) is extremely intelligent and his wife very agreeable. The day after I arrived he took me out to see a Greek village in the hills about an hour from Konia, where he said there was a church. It was exceedingly interesting, with a tradition that it had been founded by the Empress Helena. There was a rock cut church in the same village as old if not older, but as it was Sunday and prayers were going on I could not map them, so I came back next day. It was a carpet making village. Loytved and I Went and had jam and water with a delightful Greek family and inspected their carpets on the looms. The old priest told me of another church in a second Greek village and I spent another morning mapping it, it was just as interesting as the first. These villagers have, I should think, been Christian since the days of St. Paul and the Greek population in them is no doubt descended from Greek settlements before the Christian era.

[Then follow descriptions of splendid Seljouk Mosques in ruins.]

Konia contains the mother house of the Dervishes and the founder of the order, Jelal ed Din Zumi the great Persian, is buried there. My visit to his tomb was a real pilgrimage for I know some of his poems and there are things in them that are not to be surpassed. He lies under a dome tiled with blue, bluer than heaven or the sea, and adorned inside with rich and Sombre Persian enamel and lacquer and on either side of him are rows and rows of the graves of the Chelebis, the Dervish high priests and his direct descendants—all the Chelebis who have been ministers and over each is the high felt hat of the order with a white turban wrapped round it. BeYond the tomb are two great dancing halls with polished floors and the whole is enclosed in a peaceful garden, fountains And flowers set round with the monastic cells of the order, so he lies, Jelal ed din Zumi, and to my mind the whole quiet air was full of the music of his verses: "Ah listen to the reed as it tells its tale: Listen, ah, listen, to the plaint of the reed." "They reft me from the rushes of my home, my voice is sad with longing, sad and low." (But the Persian is the very Pipe, the plaintive pipe of the reed, put into words and there is nothing so invades the soul.) I dined or lunched with the Loyeds daily, and he invited selections of banished Pashas daily to meet me. The result was some most interesting talks, for the best intelligence of Turkey is in exile and being in exile speaks out. Some day I will tell you some curious tales. So I have now an enormous circle of acquaintances in Konia and I spent my last afternoon there sitting in the Ottoman Bank and receiving the town. It was almost like Damascus over again. And my clothes arrived from Smyrna! If you had roughed it for 4 months with 2 tiny mule trunks you would realize what that meant. All things are by comparison and one evening when I put on a skirt that originally came from Paris I felt almost too smart to move. I sent my horses On 3 stations down the line and next day took train myself with my camp furniture and some food and Fattuh. We joined the horses on a blazing hot morning and packed our single load onto a hired beast and set off across the plain to Binbirklisse. The name means The Thousand and one Churches and the learned have tried to identify it with the classic Barala, but as then the learned knew nothing of Barala but the name, it doesn't seem to me to matter much whether the identification is correct or no. It lies at the foot of the Kara Dagh, a great isolated mountain arising abruptly out of the plain and whatever it was in classic times, it must have been a very important early Christian city for it is full of churches dating back Strzygowski thinks to pre-Constantine times. There is a lower town down at the foot of the hills and an upper town about an hour from it on a shoulder of mountain, and fate and my zaptieh ordered by good luck that our road should lead us to the upper town first. I fell in love with it at once, a mass of beautiful ruins gathered together in a little rocky cup high up in the hills—with Asia Minor at its feet. We arrived at mid-day and I established myself in a ruined church to lunch and then the brilliant idea seized me that I could make my headquarters up in the hills and not at Maden Sheher, which is the real Binbirklisse down in the plain. I had no tents with me and it was necessary to find out whether there was a possible place to sleep. The village consists of some 15 Turkish families who have built themselves shanties out of the ruins, but it is Turkish custom that any village however small shall contain a guest room for travellers and we went off to inspect. Yes, of course, said the sheikh of the village, there was an'oda'in his own house and I was most welcome to it. As soon as I saw it I knew that my best dreams were fulfilled. It was a little bare mud built room, with the name of God scratched up on the walls and before the door a platform looking out over the great plain and the slopes of Kara Dagh. I turned out the felts and mats in it put in my own furniture and it has proved ideal. It has had the further advantage that while the lower town has been thoroughly mapped, the upper was almost untouched and I have had the pleasure of doing it myself. The first day I rode down to Maden Sheher and spent the day there, photographing and learning from Strzygovski's book what was the nature of the architecture here. The churches were most interesting, but the place horrid, intolerably hot and with execrable water, so that it was a real delight to come back to my mountain and my beautiful spring in the evening. This was a fortress city of churches and monasteries. It has been most fascinating to work through a whole town and find the same architectural features occurring or being slightly modified by the originality of the builder. And then it has been very amusing to be for 4 days a Turkish Villager. It gives me great pleasure when I come in to tea to find my friend and host, the sheikh, saying his afternoon Prayers on a felt mat spread out at his door (he has got his orientation wrong; he prays looking west which can't Possibly be the direction of Mecca, but I daresay it's all one), and the women weaving coarse cloth in the shadow of the wall and the men driving their wooden ploughs through the stones that are the arable land of the village. Everyone takes me as a matter of course but the dogs who still bark furiously whenever I pass. And then my house is so nice with its mud walls and the name of God written up on them: Allah Allah. And my servants are so charming. And then Fattuh, bless him! the best servant I have ever had, ready to cook my dinner or push a mule or dig out an inscription with equal alacrity—the dinner is what he does least well—and to tell me endless tales of travel as we ride, for he began life as a muleteer at the age of ten and knows every inch of ground from Aleppo to Van and Bagdad. This morning I ascended Kara Dagh, and on horse back! It's a huge volcano the crater of which is about half a mile across, a ring of rocky peaks round the lip of it and the great plain stretching away to snow ranges behind. There were patches of snow still on Kara Dagh with crocuses on the edges of them and there were snowdrops in the oak scrub of the higher slopes, and a whole hillside of orange red tulips lower down and the most beautiful frittillary in the world, a bright deep yellow with brown spots. So you see it has made a delightful end to my travels, Binbirklisse. I do regret that I must go down to-morrow, but my work is finished and we have eaten up all our food. To-day we succeeded in buying a hen from the Sheikh—there are only 4 in the whole village and I thought it rather greedy of me to eat one of them, but Fattuh said stoutly that they would have 3 left and that was enough. The hen thought otherwise. It took sanctuary in every ruined church in turn and was finally run to earth in a tomb where Fattuh shot it with my gun!

    May 15th. Today I came down from my mountain top. I left at the first streak of dawn and rode for an hour before the sun rose. . . .

May 16th. I was up at 4 today and at 5 I rode off to the hills to see one of the great sights of Asia Minor, the Hittite sculptures at Loriz. It was delicious riding at dawn up towards the snow of Taurus and more delicious still when after a couple of hours we entered a wonderful valley with a rushing stream flowing that I did not know, until we came to the village of Loriz at the mouth of a splendid rocky gorge. Above the village the river rushes out from under the rocks, a great stream as clear as crystal and just below its source there is the famous rock on which the sculptures are. Two figures, a god with curly hair and beard and pointed shoes and Phrygian cap adorned with a crown Of horns, in his hands the fruits of the earth, corn and bunches of grapes, which he offers to a smaller figure, a king standing before him with hands uplifted in prayer. Behind the two run several lines of that strange script which no one can read, and beneath the rock rushes the clear water of the river. So I sat down under the walnut trees and considered that fine piece of symbolism of 5000 years ago: the river bursting from the mountain side and bearing fruitfulness to all the plain below and the god standing at its source with his trails of grapes and his swathe of corn. And then one came from the village and brought me eggs and milk and honey and the biggest nuts in the world and I feasted by the edge of the river. And if I had known the Hittite language I would have offered up a short thanksgiving in that tongue to the god with the curly hair and the tiara of horns who had brought such good things out of the naked earth. And then I rode back to Eryli—blazing hot it was—and took the train and came back to Konia. The Consul and his wife met me at the station and dined with me at the hotel and I found there besides Professor Ramsay, who knows more about this country than any other man, and we fell into each other's arms and made great friends. . .

[This was Gertrude's first meeting with Sir William Ramsay, and it led to their interesting partnership in Asia Minor two years later.]

(Extract from Sir William Ramsay's Preface to "The Tbousand and One Churches." "In 1905 Miss Gertrude Bell was impelled by Strzygowski's book to visit Bin Bir Kilisse; and, when I met her at Konia on her return, she asked me to copy an inscription on one of the churches, in letters so worn that she could not decipher it, which she believed to contain a date for the building. Her belief proved well founded and the chronology of the Thousand and One Churches centres round this text. I sent her a copy of the text, the imperfect—result of four hours' work, but giving the date with certainty; longer study was prevented by a great storm; and I printed in the Athenaeum the impression made on me by a hurried inspection of the ruins, mainly in order to reiterate in more precise form my old hope that an important architectural and historical investigation might be performed by an architect and an epigraphist, combining their work for a month or two on the site. This letter attracted her attention; she wrote suggesting that we should undertake the task; and as no one else seemed likely to do so, my wife and I arranged to join her in 1907. . . ."

Sir William Ramsay, once more home from Asia Minor in 1927, writes me this further letter of appreciation of her work with him.

13 Greenhill Terrace, Edinburgh.
24 June, 1927.
DEAR LADY BELL,
. . . . I should be glad if you would add an expression of my admiration for the thoroughness and alertness of Miss Gertrude Bell's examination of Bin Bir Kilisse on her first short visit. The important inscription was almost totally concealed in a little cave. During our work in 1907 I spent about a fortnight on that inscription and finally succeeded in deciphering it completely, and it appears in our joint work with the help of her eyes.
I am, Yours faithfully,
W. M. RAMSAY)

CHAPTER XI
1905-1909

LONDON-ASIA MINOR-LONDON

(IN the following June Gertrude was in London again, enjoying herself there as usual. She spent the summer at Rounton. She was extremely keen about the garden and especially greatly absorbed in starting a rock garden which afterwards became one of the show gardens of the North Riding. It was exquisitely situated, formed round a lake, from the shores of which was a view of the wide amphitheatre of the Cleveland Hills.

In the autumn she went to Paris to study with Reinach again.]

To F. B.
PARIS, October 24, 1905.

On Saturday I came over by the 10 o'clock train and arrived rather late, so I sent a word to S. Reinach that I would appear after dinner. . . . I went in and found him and Mrs. S. R., who extremely friendly. She is a pleasant woman. After a bit Reinach and I went into his library and I showed him my plans And photographs and we settled some details about publication and illustrations. I came back to my hotel at 11—it's only a steP from the Reinach's. This morning, a heavenly bright frosty day, I went to Reinach's at 9:30 and waited till 11:30 when Dussaud the Syrian traveller came to see me, we had a most delightful hour's talk. I'm going to his house to-morrow to look over some Nabathean and Safaitic inscriptions and discuss what is to be found in Nejd. After he went we lunched, I then took a little stroll with the two Reinachs in the bright sunshine. We walked towards the Bois. R. and I came back at 3 and I looked through travel books and inscriptions till 6. It is perfectly enchanting having everything at one's hand, and R. to suggest and lay more books before me. He is delighted with the first article and is going to send it to press at once. To-night he has asked Yves Guyot to dinner because I said I wanted to see him, so we shall have a little 'relâche' from archaeology. . . .

I don't feel I could be doing this work under better conditions.

[Gertrude and her father left Plymouth on December 16th, 1905—Gibraltar, Tangiers, Spain, Marseilles, Paris, etc., and so to London.

We have no letters from Gertrude in 1906. That year she seems to have spent between London and Rounton, enjoying mightily having people to stay during the summer, seeing the rock garden grow and writing her book of travels—The Desert and the Sown—which came out the following year.

Among her special friends who stayed with her that summer were Major (now Sir Frederick) O'Connor, Aubrey Herbert, Sir Hugh and Lady Barnes, Lady Arthur Russell, Elizabeth Robins, the William Tyrrells, Sir Valentine Chirol and Mr. and Mrs. Wilton Phipps.

On December 20th of that year she and her father left London and went via Marseilles to Cairo. There her father was ill. They returned to England at the beginning of February, 1907, and early in April she is in Asia Minor again

The technical results of Gertrude's work with Sir William Ramsay were shown in the book they wrote together, " The Thousand and One Churches," published in 1909, in which the plans and measurements of the more important churches and architectural remains were given.

From her letters from Asia Minor in 1907, therefore, I have taken extracts relating to her personal experiences only, on the road. Although travel in Asia Minor is not so adventurous as crossing the deserts of Arabia, it has an adventurous and picturesque side of its own. In Asia Minor she was again befriended by the kind Whittall family.]

To F.B.
CAIRO, Tuesday, January 1, 1907

The great event is Hugo's arrival yesterday. [Hugo had been to Australia.] He is extremely cheerful and full of interesting tales. We talked all the afternoon and he came up into my room and talked till dinner time. It's quite delightful having him. We dined with the Cromers—Lady C., Lady Valda [Machell] and I were the only women so I sat on the other side of Lord C. and had a quite enchanting talk with him. He is the nicest person in the world, without doubt. He was very eager to know if there was anything I wanted and when I said I wanted to have a good talk with a learned sheikh, he was much concerned about it, saying to Mr. Machell across the table, " Look here, Machell, you must find us a good sheikh. Just think who is the best." So they are thinking. The immediate result was that they arranged that we should see the Azhar to-day. It is the great university of the Mohammedan world, where they are sometimes rather tiresome about letting women in. However, I found a friend on the doorstep, and we fell into one another's arms and he took us all over. Indeed, we were invited to dine there by an old party from Bagdad who lives there and I'm invited to breakfast on Saturday if I like, so anyway I feel I may come and go as I Please in the Azhar. Hugo talked to Lady Valda all the morning yesterday, and I to Sir W. Garstin, who is very pleasant and interesting, so we all enjoyed ourselves. Father and I had a charming dinner with the Machells, too; Sir W. G. was there also. Yesterday we lunched with the Bernstorffs and we are going to their box at the opera to-night. On Friday, Father and I spent the whole morning with Ernest Richmond, seeing Coptic churches—most pleasant.

To F.B.
CAIRO, Friday, 12th January, 1907.

I had an interesting talk with Moritz while he was teaching me to take squeezes of inscriptions after a manner of his own (an excellently simple one, by the way).

To F.B.
SMYRNA, April 4th, 1907.

I hope I shall get off on Monday. My preparations are really all finished but I have to wait and hear about the head man for my diggings whom Mr. Richard Whittall is engaging for me. As this is the most important matter of all I cannot leave without settling it. Then to call on all my Whittall friends. They have the bulk of the English trade in their hands, bran offices all down the southern coast, mines and shooting boxes and properties scattered up and down the S.W. coast of Asia Minor and yachts on the seas. They all have immense quantities of children. The sons, young men now in the various Whittall businesses, the daughters very charming, very gay. The big gardens touch one another and they walk in and out of one another's houses all day long gossiping and laughing. I should think life presents itself nowhere under such easy and pleasant conditions.

To F.B.
MAGNESIA AD MEANDRUM, Wednesday, April 9, 1907.

I've just been visiting the ruins of this town in the company of a pleasant Greek who talked Turkish, so we managed to have a little conversation. But it is such a bore not talking the language properly. I must hurry up and learn. Of course, one ought to know Greek too, but for the moment I feel one new language is a good deal more than I can manage. I've just been giving my friend the Greek tea in my carriage. The station master came in and joined the party. The station masters on this line are supposed to know English and accordingly as he entered he said cheerfully, " Goodbye!"

To F.B.
MILETUS, Friday, April 12, 1907.

Often when one sets out on a journey one travels by all the roads according to the latest maps, one reaches all the places of which the history books speak. Duly one rises early and turns one's face towards new countries, carefully one looks and laboriously one tries to understand, and for all one's trouble one might as well have stayed behind and read a few big archaeology books. But I would have you know that's not the way I have done it this time. I said to myself: I will go and see the Greece of Asia, the Greece Grote didn't know. And I have found it. The seas and the hills are all full of legends and the valleys are scattered over with the ruins of the great rich Greek cities. Here is a page of history that one sees with the eye and that enters into the mind as no book can relate it.

To F. B.
MILETUS, April 12, 1907.

In this sort of travel one goes on very short commons. One starts early and one gets in late; there is no time to cook, and there is no meat to be had if one could cook it. So I have lived mostly on eggs and rice and sour milk, not a bad diet of its kind if you have enough of it, and to-night's dinner (soup and a chicken) was the best meal I have had for some days. . . .

I gave up thinking .. . . . . for the crossing of that river was itself sufficient matter for thought. There was no bridge—if there had been one it would have been broken—the water was deep and the ferry-boat was a buffalo cart. The river came nearly over the buffaloes' backs; we had to take everything off the horses and lead them behind us—the buffaloes didn't care, they plodded steadily on and held up their noses to keep them out of the water. Now a buffalo can't hold up his nose very far; a little more and they would have been drowned, but they did not think of that. At the other side we changed horses and rode 25 miles into Aidin, all good going till we came to the Meander valley where it was the very devil. Before we reached it, as we rode along the high road, there came a sound of crying and presently we saw a heap of something on the broad road. It was a dead man, lying as he had fallen with a tattered coat thrown over his face, and beside him a ragged child, a little girl sitting all alone in the sun, and wailing, wailing—you have never heard the east Mourning, it is always the same and always more melancholy than any other sound. A man passed just before we reached the child, he merely drew his horse aside and rode on. Eh! a man more or less in the world, and a gypsy at that. We stopped and questioned her. They had sent on news to Aidin, her brother had gone, she didn't know when they would come. And so she took up her dirge again. We rode on to the ferry over the Meander and tried to hire a cart to bring in the dead man's body, but no one would go—no, he must stay there till his people came, that was the custom. The girl? She could stay too to keep the dogs off and if night fell and she was afraid she would come in to the nearest village. Yes, someone would go and watch with her if I would give him two mejidis. But I knew that was no good as he would come away the moment my back was turned. So I rode on too; the child will come into the village at nightfall and the man is dead and does not care how long he lies alone. But I felt a beast, all the same. We crossed the Meander in a ferry—the bridge was broken, I need scarcely say, and the high road beyond was all under water. So we splashed for an hour along a narrow cobbled path running between bottomless swamps. We came to Aidin about 5, it is against the hills and all shining in the sun. But what makes it chiefly memorable is that I got Elsa's telegram here saying she was engaged to Herbert Richmond, and am thinking of it with such mixed feelings. But there it is, and there's nothing else for it but to put up with it and try not to think what a difference it will make. I can't come home now because I can't leave Ramsay in the lurch and I shall hear no more from you till I get to Konia, bother it! I've written to Elsa since there is no way of telegraphing.

To F.B.
BODJELI, April 24th, 1907.

I have got your letter telling me of E.'s engagement. Yes, in a way it's easier perhaps not to be at home. it is unsatisfactory for the family rather, still I rather wish I were with you all the same. Meantime I shall continue to tell you of my adventures, if you have time to think of them! One rides for hours over beautiful well watered country without seeing an inch of ploughed ground. We are riding towards a high Snowy range of mountains, at the foot of which Aphrodisias lies. The town must have been distinguished above all other places for the elaborate beauty of its architecture; every doorway was covered with scrolls of fruit and flowers with birds and beasts entwined in them.

I slept! Oh, if you could have seen where I slept! It was in the khan, a tiny room separated by a rough wall of planks from the 30 or 40 muleteers and camel drivers who were lodging there for the night. It was quite empty, however, and I put my camp bed in and was as happy as possible, —One wall was all window— I closed half of it with a shutter when I went to bed, and until then I sat and watched the village unloading its camels, cooking its evening meal over wood fires lighted in earthenware bowls, saying its evening prayer on a little raised platform in front of the khan and after having seen the temple under the moon I went to bed and no number of talking, smoking muleteers could have kept me awake. Fattuh, however, was not at all happy. He did not think it a suitable lodging for my Excellency. . . .

To F.B.
ISDARTA, April 28th, 1907.

I don't suppose there is anyone in the world happier than I am or any country more lovely than Asia Minor. I just mention these facts in passing so that you may bear them in mind. We rode and rode over the hills and down to the edge of a great lake of Buldur. Bitter salt it is and very blue, and mountains stand all round it, white with snow, and the fruit gardens border it, pink and white with peach and cherry. And SO we Came to Buldur, a fine town standing in a rich land, and there we pitched camp in a green field at the edge of the tOwn. All the authorities came down in turn—begged me not to spend the night in the wilderness and entreated me to share their flea-y houses and told me that my next day's journey was quite Out of the question because of the snow and the mountains and I don't know what, till finally I said I was going to bed and sent them all away. Said Fattuh: "What sort of Soldiers are these? They fear the cold and they fear the mountains and they fear the rivers-perhaps they fear the rabbits and the foxes." And he went away shaking his head mournfully over the degeneracy of the Turkish army and muttering in Turkish "Nasl arkar! nasl arkar! what sort, what sort of soldiers!" To-day I started off at 5:30 and, leaving Fattuh to bring the camp by the straight road, I took a soldier and rode into the hills, a wonderful, wonderful ride. . . .

It is now night and the moon has not yet risen. Fattuh has gone to look for horses and I am left with the soldier who is our guard to-night. I think he feels rather anxious at being left alone here in the dark for he has crept in close to the light of my tent and has been telling me, half in Turkish and half in broken Arabic, of his 10 years in Yemen and of how, praise be to God! he did not die there though he was wounded twice.

Tuesday, April 30th. We have not made much way to-day as the crow flies because the road along the eastern shore of the lake is not yet finished and we had very rough going which delayed the baggage animals. It was instructive to see how road making is conducted in Turkey. It's a very hilly road, up and down and in and out over the mountains. They had one old man and three younger ones with a few little boys working at one end and at the other unfinished end there were some 30 men who were engaged in baking and eating bread on the hill-side. Also they take no count of the streams that cross the road continuously, the country being mountainous as YOU Will understand. These streams therefore wash away the work as soon as it is done. I think it will be some time before this road is joined up.

Wednesday, May 1st. I haven't really done much to-day though I have taken a good deal of trouble about it. I had to find a fountain with a Latin inscription of which Ramsay wanted a new copy. I found it, inscription and all complete, and worked two hours at the latter without a very satisfactory result as it was much broken and lay too near the splash of the fountain so that I could not take a good rubbing. The oldest and most decrepit soldier in the world was told off at Egerdir to bear me company. He knows nothing of the country and our intercourse was confined to something like the following: Me: "Where does this road go to?" He: "Effendim, I do not know." Me: "What is the name of that village?" He: "Effendim? I could not say." Me: "How far is it to so-and-so?" He: "Effendim, I have not been." The result of which is that I have to find all my own routes by asking the people by the wayside. . . .

I started at 5:45 taking with me an intelligent villager of Tokmajik the place where I had spent the night. He knew the country and was a satisfactory guide and an agreeable companion. He had been a soldier and had served mainly in Crete, an island of which he thought highly. We took a path hitherto untravelled over the hills, past two villages unknown to Kiefert (there were unfortunately no inscriptions in them though there were old worked stones) and dropped down on to the northern end of the Lake of Egerdir. There was a place which Ramsay had begged me to try and visit on the eastern shore of the lake. It is a place of pilgrimage where the Christians come once a year, in September, from all the countryside, and the probability is that it was a holy site long before the Christian era, sacred to Artemis of the Lake who was herself a Pisidian deity re-baptised by the Greeks. I found the Place, about 2 miles down the lake, and a very striking place it Was. The rocks drop here straight into the lake and at their foot there is a great natural arch some 15 feet wide through which glistens the blue water of the lake. In the rock above is a small rock-cut chamber into which I scrambled with some difficulty and found a slab like a loculus in it. It may have been a tomb at some time but I think more probably the slab was sacrificial; at any rate the Christians use the chamber now to celebrate their yearly mass. So we rode back along the beautiful grassy shores of the lake, where the Yuruks were watching their flocks and herds, and all round the swampy northern end of the lake. Almost joined to the shore by beds of immensely tall reeds there is a little island which no one had yet succeeded in visiting. I, however, found a fisherman's hut in the swamp and near it a very old and smelly boat, so I hired the three fishermen for an infinitesimal sum and rowed out to the island with Nazmi, my Tokmajik man. it was completely surrounded by ruined Byzantine walls dropping into the water in great blocks of masonry; here and there there was a bit of an older column built into them and they were densely populated by snakes. There was only one thing of real interest, a very curious stele with a female figure carved on it, bearing what looked like water skins, and two lines of inscription above. She might have been Artemis of the Lake itself and perhaps the inscription said so, but unfortunately the whole stone was covered by 18 inches or more of shimmering water. It had fallen into the lake and there it lay. I did all I knew to get the inscription. I waded into the water and tried to scrub the slime off the stone, but the water glittered and the slime floated back and finally I gave it up and came out very wet and more than a little annoyed. It was provoking after I had taken so much trouble, wasn't it? However at any rate now we know that it's there and someone can go and fish it out. So we punted back through the reeds. One of my boatmen had been through the Russo-Turkish war—Nish, Plevna, he rambled on about all the things he had seen and done while we brushed through the reeds, looking sometimes for fish in the traps they had set, and sometimes for birds' eggs, and I sat in the sun and dried myself. It was so hot that I was quite dry before I got into camp. Then we rode north up the plain and explored a village for inscriptions as we went. There was a large farm here left by an agreeable Greek who helped me in my search and invited me into his house where his wife gave me milk; and at last at a quarter to seven we got to Kundanly where I found my camp pitched and my dinner ready. In and around Kundanly have been found (mainly by Ramsay) a very curious series of inscriptions relating to an anti-Christian Society of the second century. It was called the Society of those who showed the Sign, and the Sign was probably some act of worship of the Emperor and the old gods. I had all the published inscriptions with me and I hunted round this morning for a couple of hours and found a new one in a Turkish house—very short and I fear not very important, but I took a rubbing to the surprise and joy of the inhabitants, and shall give it to Ramsay. It was very hot again to-day. Got into camp at 3, since when I have done nothing but sleep and eat and write my diary. To-morrow is an off day and I can't say I regret it. It's very laborious being the careful traveller I don't think I do it well either. There are probably lots of things that I don't see because I don't know how to look. I remember Ramsay's telling me that the first journey he made in Asia Minor he found nothing at all. And you see I only find things under water! Fattuh loq: "Never in my life did I see such a town! May God send them to their fathers and may their women be taken captive! I paid 5 piastres for your Excellency's beans. No meat in all the town and may it be destroyed!" I: "And the chicken is less good than the chicken of Tokmajik." Fattuh (with indignant reminiscence of his culinary experiences at Tokmajik) "That chicken she eat 4 piastres of fire wood and then I cooked her 3 hours at Kundanly—God send all chickens to their fathers!"

In the afternoon I called on the Kaimmakam—I must tell you about the Kaimmakam. Fattuh went down into the town early. The barber's shop is as you know the fashionable lounge and there he found the Kaimmakam, the Binbashi, the Imam the Kadi and a few more all sitting together. In the afternoon I go to the Kaimmakam; the Kaimmakam, the Binbashi, the Imam the Kadi, etc., are still all sitting together drinking coffee and smoking. An hour later comes a message to say that the Kaimmakam, the Binbashi, etc. wish to call on me. SO up they came, six of them, all in a serried row and sat in my tent and drank more coffee and smoked more cigarettes. It's my private conviction that that's all they can do, any of them, and they all do it together every day. They appear to have given their advice collectively as regards the hiring of a cart for my luggage and even the buying of candles and rice, so to-day they have been unusually busy. I've bought another horse, this time for 10 pounds, which is not dear. I like the look of him very much. The first one has turned out excellently, and I think this one is even better. Now I'm provided. In this transaction I did not seek the advice of the Kaimmakam, the Binbashi, the Imam or the Kadi.

Tuesday, May 7th. We've had laborious travelling, but it has all ended successfully. We left Yalorach early on Sunday, 6 a.m. I had hire a cart for my luggage. I had always been told by the authorities on the subject that that was the proper way to travel in Asia Minor. Now I know it isn't. One has to learn these things for oneself. So we set out, and I was riding my new horse which was as wild as a hawk and as timid as a lizard, so I had enough to think of for the first hour or two. (He is settling down now he has got into good hands and is becoming a capital little animal, I think the best horse for travel I have ever had.) In four and a half hours we came to a dullish place called Karagash. We went to the khan and determined to wait anyhow till the cart arrived and then set out again. We waited and waited and at noon we lunched and then there came a most furious thunderstorm with sheets of rain and batterings of hail and at length came news that the cart had broken down and the man had gone back to fetch another. By this time the road was deep in water and mud, and the end of it was that the luggage arrived at 5 and there was no more thought of travel for that day. On the whole perhaps it was as well, for it rained without stopping till 7 so that we should have got very wet. So I ate some of the curious soup that Fattuh makes out of the Lord knows what and went to bed. I may mention that my room was crowded with bugs and fleas, but I had my own bed at least. There were no horses to be got at Karagash, no horses, so there was nothing for it but to hire another cart next day and again we set out at 6 o'clock full of hope. For the first hour or two the road was deep in mud but presently we came to a little pass and the ground hardened and cleared. Here Fattuh stopped to wait for the cart and I rode on with my soldier. At 10:15 I got to Kassaba, another miserable little hole, again I went to the khan and again I waited. This time after an hour and a half came a message sent by Fattuh to say that the cart had stuck in the mud and he had gone back to Karagash for another. I ordered eggs and bread and curds and lunched and did my best to be patient and at 1:30 up came Fattuh triumphantly with two carts, having pulled the first out of the mud with buffaloes and then driven it into Kassaba. But I was not going to be put off again with half a day's journey, so I left the carts and Fattuh to rest for an hour and rode on over the flat plain by Bey Sheher lake. It is not so fine as the other lakes though the mountains drop steeply into it on the W. side, but it is very typical of this country and of no other. A melancholy land, in spite of its lakes and mountains, though I like it. You leave the bright and varied coast line which was Greece, full of vitality, full of the breath of the sea and the memory of an active enterprising race, and with every step into the interior you feel Asia the real heart of Asia. Monotonous, colourless, lifeless, unsubdued by a people whose thoughts travel no further than to the next furrow, who live and die and leave no mark upon the great plains and the barren hills-such is central Asia, of which this country is a true part. And that is why the Roman roads make so deep an impression on one's mind. They impressed the country itself, they implied a great domination, they tell of a people that overcame the universal stagnation. It was very hot and still and clouds of butterflies drifted across the path and there was no other living thing except a stork or two in the marshy ground and here and there a herd of buffaloes with a shepherd boy asleep beside them. At the end of the lake a heavy thunderstorm gathered and crept along the low hills to the east and up into the middle of the sky. And so we came to the earliest record of what was probably one of the earliest trade roads in the world and the forerunner of the Roman road; and here the clouds broke upon us in thunder and lightning and hail and rain and I saw the four Hittite kings, carved in massive stone, against a background of all the fury of the storm. They are seated at the edge of a wide pool, a spring bubbling out of the hillside, from which a swift river flows away to the lake; and above them are figures with uplifted hands, as though they praised the god of Gotat waters.

KONIA,

Saturday 11th. . . . ..I'm writing to Elsa about plans (I can scarcely bear the idea of not being at her wedding). Ramsay arrives in tbree days and I've got a hundred thousand things to do so I'll write no more now.

To F.B.
MADEN SHEHER, May 21, 1907.

My donkey goes at dawn to-morrow to fetch the post and I must write you a word, though 10 hours hard riding, which is what I have been doing to-day, is not a good preparation for letter-writing. The habit of building everything on the extreme top of hills is to be deprecated. It entails so much labour for subsequent generations. It was very hot to-day. I lunched in the house of a charming Circassian, who lives in a Circassian village on the other side of the hills. He gave me coffee and some curds to add to my own lunch and we made great friends. He has invited me to come and stay. All the other Circassians sat round the while. Yesterday I had a hard day. I had found the afternoon before, a ruined site with a very perfect church on the top of a hill near my camp, and in the church was a half-buried stone which I thought was probably the altar. So I took up some of my men with picks and crowbars and had it out and it was the altar. Then I photographed and planned the whole site, a good 5 hours' work. I came back to my tents for lunch and an hour's rest and then we rode off to another further hill and there I found a church and chapel, much ruined but of an interesting plan, so I worked at them all the afternoon. I meant to draw them out to scale when I came back but I was too tired and they are still waiting to be done. The truth is there is too much work here for one person, but I am very much enjoying my solitude, and the work is mighty fun too if one could only do it a little better. As yet I haven't touched this place, thinking that Ramsay had better have the responsibility. If he doesn't come there are one or two things I must do and the rest I shall leave to someone cleverer. My Cast! oh my cast! it's more professional than words can say. I'm longing to do another when I can find time. My larder is splendidly supplied with hares and partridges which the villagers bring me. It's as well, for they won't sell their lambs as nearly all their sheep died in the cold winter they have had. Fattuh rode out to a village 5 hours away and brought back a lamb across his saddle bow. We kept it against accidents, such as the Ramsay family appearing unexpectedly, and it browses round my tents in a charming fashion.

To F.B

MADEN SHEHER, Saturday, May 25, 1907.

I really must begin a diary to you. The Ramsays arrived yesterday. I was in the middle of digging up a church when suddenly 2 carts hove into sight and there they were. It was about 3 in the afternoon. They instantly got out, refused to think of going to the tents, Lady R. made tea (for they were starving) in the open and R. oblivious of all other considerations was at once lost in the problems the church presented. It was too delightful to have someone as much excited about it as I was! . . . . They have brought their son Louis with them who is deeply learned on birds and beasts and has a commission from the British Museum to collect the small mammalia of these parts.

Now I must tell you something very very striking. The church on the extreme point of the Kara D., at which I worked for 2 days before R. came, has near it some great rocks and on the rocks I found a very queer inscription. The more I looked at it the queerer it became and the less I thought It could be Christian or anything that I knew, so I took it down with great care, curious rabbit-headed things and winged sort of crosses and arms and circles, and with some trembling I showed it to R. The moment he looked at it he said, "It's a Hittite inscription. This is the very thing I hoped most to find here." I think I've never been so elated. We now think nothing but Hittites all the time.

Now this is the manner of Asia Minor: there is never a shrine of Christian or Moslem but if you look long enough you will find it has been a holy place from the beginning of history and every church on the top of the hill stands on a site where the Hittites worshipped. We began to find queer things, a tower of a very ancient sort of fortification, and then we found cuttings in the rocks which puzzled us for a long time till I, who had seen the same before in Syria, discovered that they were winepresses, and the long and the short of it is that we think we have a Hittite settlement at Maden Sheher and that this was the entrance fort. Of course we may get no more evidence and the thing will have to remain as a supposition, but the inscription on the top of the Kara D. is a fixed point.

[Then followed excited days of visiting churches, planning, deciphering, guessing.]

.....I haven't told you half enough what gorgeous fun it's being! You should see me directing the labours of 20 Turks and 4 Kurds! We are going to get something out of it, you'll see.

To F.B.
MADEN SHEHER, May 29, 1907.

I got a long letter from you today dated May 19, enclosing some photographs from Hugo (for which I am deeply obliged) and describing the plans for Elsa's wedding. I fear I have definitely given up all hope of coming back for it. I am in for this business and I must carry it through. I get up at 5 and breakfast before the Ramsay family have appeared and go off before 6 to wherever we are digging, and stay there till 12 superintending and measuring as we uncover. Then I come back to the tents for an hour, for the men have an hour off in the middle of the day and after lunch I go back to the diggings and stay there till 5 or later. R. generally appears on the scene about 7 or 8 in the morning and about 3 in the afternoon Then he has inscriptions to find and read and the map to make and he can't physically do more. I shall have all the measuring and planning to do and I'm at it some 12 hours a day on and Off. Nor can it be otherwise for that's the part that I have undertaken. Of course it's great great fun, but it's also very hard work, you understand. And there is no one to do it but me. Therefore I can't leave and that's an end.

To F. B.
MADEN SHEHER, May 29th, 1907.

One of the difficulties of the commissariat here is the water. I have to send 2 hours up the hill for it daily and I find I can't supply the needs of the whole camp with one donkey load and the poor donkey can't go more than once a day. So Fattuh is going to Karaman to morrow to buy another donkey and more water tins. Housekeeping in the wilderness takes a great deal of thinking about! But I must say the difficulties are considerably alleviated when all your guests are as amenable as mine are.

Friday, May 30th. We've had a very long day clearing out a round church which is a difficult architectural problem, and oh! Horrible to measure. I'm tired now and I shan't write any more.

To F. B.
MADEN SHEHER, June 4, 1907.

I haven't kept to my good resolutions in the matter of a diary letter but the fact is I'm so very busy.

I've been working all today from dawn on the big apse on which I first began. It still remains a complete puzzle and one I fear will not be elucidated. I shall give it a day off so as to think about it and then do another day's work on it. The walls we have uncovered seem to have no meaning and they are such bad work that it's a stretch of the imagination to suppose that there is any consecutive idea in them. Anyway it's not a church, of so much we are certain; and the guesses of all our Predecessors have been wrong, but what to guess ourselves is the problem. The learned world is agog about my Hittite inscription. We shall have to go up and do some more work there. It's all very, very nice-I'm enjoying it thoroughly.

To F.B.
DAILE, June 8, 1907.

Today we have had the greatest exodus known since the days of the Jews. We have moved all our camp up to the yaila, the summer quarters. It took 11 camels and 4 donkeys to transport us. Now this is the place that I first came to two years ago. It is on a shoulder of the Kara Dagh, 1000 ft. above Maden Sheher and it is entirely composed of churches, chapels and monastic foundations. A few Turkish hovels are' accommodated in the ruins-in one of them I stayed two years ago. The people are overjoyed at my return and gave me a most cordial welcome. They sent down to me while I was at Maden Sheher to say they hoped I was coming up and I hired from them all the camels for the transport. One of the most interesting parts of our job has been the tracing of the first settlement of the mountain. It began with my Hittite High Place; there we found several vestiges of an ancient town at Maden Sheher and today Sir W. has seen 3 Hittite inscriptions on an outlying spur of the mountain-he went there while we were moving camp. Of these and of the High Place we are going to take casts so as to have absolutely perfect impressions of them. Isn't it a good thing I learnt to take casts, by the way! Without that we could not have got perfect impressions of these things for the stone is so rough that it is extremely difficult to get anything like a good rubbing. We are getting so much material that it will certainly make a book. Our plan is that Sir W. shall write the historic and epigraphic part and I the architectural. I think it will be well worth doing, for this is the first time that an accurate study has been made of any one district in these parts, hitherto people have onlY travelled through and seen what they could see and gone On. We shall certainly be able to contribute a great deal to the knowledge of such settlements as this must have been. I look forward to a delightful winter at home drawing my plans and writing my part of the book. I should have been helpless here without Sir W. and the more I work with him the more I like him and respect his knowledge. In fact, it's being a magnificent success, quite everything I hoped it would be.

It will be a very dull book, you understand, but I intend it to be magnificently illustrated. I wonder if Heinemann will do it for me!

It will be very pleasant to have the Barneses at Mt. Grace-I hope they will come.

To her Brother.
DAILE, June 14, 1907.

I must answer at once your delightful letter with the descriptions of Penrhos all so characteristic! His Lordship! I can see him with the Times Atlas listening to my letter! You would be surprised to see the scene in the middle of which I am writing. Thirty-one Turks are busy with picks and spades clearing out a church and monastery. At intervals they call out to me " Effendim, effendim! is this enough?" or "Come and see this-this is good!" or something. They are perfectly charming people up here and I have got the pick of my men from Maden Sheher and we are all on the most friendly terms. It is about 7 a.m. and I have been at work for an hour. If you find some earth in my letter it's the dust of Byzantines which flies round me.

To H. B.
DAILE, June 14, 1907.

I'm charmed to hear the rock garden looks nice. I'm glad we have an addition to the stable. I hope the foal will turn out well. I am horribly bored at not being at E.'s wedding. I shall always regret not having seen her married, but I think I am right in deciding to stay and finish this job. I hope You think so. I really haven't a moment to think of anything but my work and it accumulates with an almost malignant rapidity. I tremble to think of the amount of drawing I have before me now.

To F. B.
KARADAGH, June 17, 1907.

Of course you can't write to me much. I'm busy too in a modest way. . . . I believe this is the very first time anyone has set Bout to explore thoroughly a single district in central Asia. See what we have got out of it! Two great sites and a vast amount of unexpected Byzantine remains. We spend much time discussing our book, which is to be a great work, please God! Oh, it's delightful, delightful! I only do so hope you think I was right to stay Out here, I could scarcely bear it if you didn't—at a breath from you I would come back by the next train. I hate being away, you understand, but I am deeply absorbed by this work. it grows more and more exciting as one gets further into it.

To F.B.
DAILE, June 21, 1907.

Torrents of rain are streaming down onto my tent, the first heavy rain we have had for 5 weeks and more. I hope it won't go on very long or it will probably run in under my bed where I keep all the long rolls of my big plans. We have had rather a disagreeable few days as regards weather; first 2 days of great heat (I was digging with 30 men on one of them and had to be out the whole day long in the sun). Then we had 2 days' wind which is the most intolerable thing possible and almost prevents us from working at all, as one can scarcely dig or measure and if one goes to one's tent to draw, one finds it a kind of dust heap inside. Last night the wind brought up a thunderstorm and it rained a good deal in the night and this morning it was quite grey and cool. Sir W. and I profited by this to go down to Maden Sheher to finish up some odds and ends. I think we have still about a week's work here and it's the most important work of all for we are now beginning to get our views and our information into some kind of shape. This consoles me a little for I should have had to have been going away now to get home in time for Elsa's wedding. I am become quite the architect I must tell you. I have pages and pages of mouldings all beautifully drawn out and MY plans are most elaborate, I don't think anyone has ever published any of these Anatolian mouldings before—our book will be very 'bahnbrechend,' you'll see! . . . . I'm so glad the new motor is a success. Dear me! it will be very pleasant to be back again in the bosom of my family. Still, I'm very happy.

I propose to stay at home for a good long time after this.

To F.B.
DAILE, Tuesday, June 24, 1907-

We are coming to the very end of our time here. The Ramsays leave on the 26th and I on the 28th. Well, we have accomplished a great deal. This last week has been the most useful of all. It makes me quite sad to think that in all probability I shall never come back here. We have been a sort of small providence, what with our work and the market we have offered. I don't suppose so much money has passed hands in the Karadagh since the time of the Byzantines.

My simple annals must seem very paltry to you in the midst of all your festivities. Yes, it is very very nice to be completely absorbed in the thing one is doing and to have no interruption in it. I rather shiver to think what a tremendous work it will be writing all this. It will take months, I think. I am not going to lecture at all—I've refused to go to Redcar. I must get this book done or someone else will nip in and take the wind out of our sails. I'm afraid I shall not be back till the beginning of August, but as I've stayed so long it would be silly to scamp things for the sake of a week more or less. . . .

To F. B.
KARAPUNA, June 30, 1907.

Yesterday I took the road again. A great plain is a wonderfully beautiful thing. It stretched away and away from my tent door as far as the eye could see, as level to the horizon as it was level under my feet. It looked like an immensely wide floor made ready for some splendid spectacle. To-day we rode over it again for 3 hours to Karabanar, a small town at the foot of the Karajadagh. There lives on the plateau the largest beetle I have been privileged to see. Black and green is his colour and he is the size of a mouse.

I lunched in the khan, waiting for my luggage cart. They gave me quite a nice bare room to myself; publicity, however, was ensured by a window which opened into the room next me. Then the KaiMMakam and another came to call.

Thank Heaven I can now talk enough Turkish not to be left speechless with Kaimmakams and the rest. We were in the thick of making arrangements to go straight on into the hills.

When I arrived I had asked if there were pack horses. "As many as you like can be found," said the innkeeper. Presently he returned to say there were none. "Then," said I, "I will take a cart to the village at the edge of the hills." Most excellent," said the surrounding company, "the cart will draw you to the hills and then you will get camels." "Camels are to be found, then?" said I. "Many," said they. Then arrived the Kaimmakam and the Other, and I explained that I was leaving at once for Salur with my luggage in a cart. They heartily approved this plan. Over the coffee the Other let fall a remark to the effect that I should find no people at all as they had all gone up to yaila. "Then how shall I find camels?" said I. "Effendim ," said he, "there will be no camels." Finally I resolved to take camels from him and after waiting for 4 hours the camels have appeared. An incident similar to this occurs daily when travelling in Asia Minor; the wonder is that one gets through at all. . . . There go the camels with a Haide! father! pull, my soul! hasten, hasten!" from all onlookers.

They pulled very well and we got in here at 5:30. . . . . .

I must tell you that this expedition into the Karajadagh is rather an adventure. No one has as yet explored the mountain. We have come into the heart of it and pitched tents and so far all is well. The whole of the upper part of the mountain is entirely deserted. It's extraordinarily lonely. There are said to be robbers about.

I have no less than 6 men here, including the 2 camel drivers, so I don't feel at all anxious even if they should be still in these parts.

Wednesday, July 3 I am so dreadfully torn this week by considering exactly what you are doing and wishing I were doing it too. I feel terribly outcast when I think of you and long 50 times a day to be at home. However, there it is and next week I shall feel better, after it's all over and done with. Yesterday I had a very long day. We started out, Haidar and my gipsy, Aziz is his name, and I, and rode up to a hill on the top of the crater above us. It was cold, absurdly enough, a north wind which increased all day till it became a horrid nuisance. There were two men on the uplands above the crater, one with a herd of deer and one with a herd of cattle from the villages below—we saw no other living soul all day. And there was a cruciform church with monastic buildings and fortifications and all complete! I do not doubt that this is the chief and central shrine of the Karajadagh so I am content. No one has been here before—it's a most curious sensation to step into these great ruined places and to be the first person of the same civilization which they stand for since the last monk fell or fled before the Seljuks. Up in the mountains there was the absurd cuckoo which shouted all day above my camp. I don't like hearing the cuckoo in deep summer; he is sadly reminiscent of the delicious beginnings of things—"where are the joys of spring? Oh, where are they!" The kite who screams above my tents here is better.

Friday, July 5. Yesterday I had a long, hot and tiresome day. We spent the whole morning going from village to village along the side of the Karajadagh looking for ruins and inscriptions. The manner of proceeding is this: you arrive in a village and ask for inscriptions. They reply that there are absolutely none. You say very firmly that there are certainly inscriptions and then you stand about in the hot sun for 10 minutes or so while villagers gather round. At last someone says there is a written stone in his house. You go off, find it, copy it, and give the owner two piastres, the result of which is that everybody has a written stone somewhere and you have to look at them all, 99 per cent. of them being only a lintel with a cross on it. As you leave they all tell you that though there are not many written stones here, in the next village, or in the village on the next mountain 10 hours away, or in the one you have just left behind you there are at least a hundred. I know this village of the hundred inscriptions so well now that I hear of it without any emotion, even when I have left it behind. At 11 o'clock I determined that I would do no more of this pottering work, so we rode down to a village in the plain, where we expected to find the tents and lunch in the shade. No tents, no shade, no people, for they had all gone to the yaila. At last we found a deaf old man who told us that there was a magnificently cold place to lunch in by the mosque and thither we went. It was the mosque porch. I distinguished myself by climbing wearily on to a sort of erection of planks in the corner. Haidat arriving with the lunch looked horrified at seeing me there and begged me to come down at once for it was the village hearse. So I came down, thinking that it probably hadn't been much disinfected since the last man who died of smallpox was carried on it to his grave, and for the evil omen that I had brought upon the party Heaven sent a sacrifice in the shape of a young swallow who dropped out of his nest above me on to the pavement and died at once, poor little dear.

Transport is rather difficult in this country. The camel drivers we had brought from Karapuna declared last night that they were going no further than the Karajadagh, but as we had no other means of carrying our packs but their camels only, we put force upon them and insisted that they should take us across to Hassan Dagh lest nameless evils should befall them. So they went, and they went 8 hours, poor people, the usual camel march being 5. We started before 5 in the morning so that it might be cool for them, and by great good luck it was a grey cloudy day with scarcely a glimpse of sun, and we rode across the waterless flat plain without any trouble and up the low foot hills that lie before Hassan Dagh.

Saturday, July 6th. An aged man appeared this morning at the tents and professed to know all the ruins round about, so Fattuh engaged him as guide-in-chief for the day. His name was Ali as I had presently cause to know. After breakfast I went down to the village and drew the church and by dint of wading about in dark and horrible stables and poking into the dark and horrible houses that had been built in the aisles and apse I got it out all complete and it proved extremely interesting. Then I came in and changed all my things, for the houses and the stables were, as always, alive with fleas. Very great travellers would no doubt think nothing of this, but I find it an almost intolerable vexation, yet one can't leave a church unplanned because there are fleas in it. Then I questioned the aged man as to what I should ride out and see. He said: "Many churches there are, a very great many." "Where?" said I. "over there," said he, "that side," waving his hand vaguely round the mountains, "there is one ." "What is his name?" said I (there's no neuter in Turkish). "Ali," said he. "Not your name, the church's name." "Chanderlik," said he. "Aren't there any in the other direction?" said I, for the way he seemed to be pointing was my route for to-morrow. "Not any at all," said he. A bystander, "Many, a great many; over there there is one." "What is his name?" said I. The bystander, "Ali." "Not his name, the church's name?" "Uleuren there is, and Karneuren and Yazlikisle a. . . ." so on and so on. (Euren means ruin and kisle means church.) Ali indignantly, "No churches! Ruins muins" (you repeat the word changing the first letter to 'm' when you want to say "and so forth") "euren meuren,"said he louder and louder, "all destroyed, mestroyed pulled down, broken, all ruins." "It's ruins I want to see," said I. "All ruins," he said, "all broken, moken, no marble churches, all marble and so forth, not any at all." "My soul," expostulated a fellow townsman, "there are two at Uleuren." "No marble churches," said he (there aren't any, anywhere, I may mention)" all ruins, all broken." However we went to Uleuren and I found two churches and a long inscription. Ali was not a success as an archaeologist and I declined to employ him further. Nor did he want to come.

We are now going round to the north side of the mountain where I am told there are a million if not a billion churches or something of the kind. I hope there may be one or two. I know how you are spen ding this Sunday -how I wish I were with you! I also wish so many flies were not spending Sunday with me.

Wednesday, July 11th. I thought of you a great deal on Monday and very much longed to see Elsa looking as pretty and as happy as I am sure she did look. I shall love to see the wedding photographs and hear all the tales. Now that it is all over I am glad I did not come back, for you see I should have been landed with my work half done and a horrible feeling that I could not go ahead properly for want of knowledge.

The long expected robber turned up in the night and I was awakened by my servants' firing at him. They missed him, but he missed our horses.

The following preposterous conversation has just occurred:
G.B. loq: Oh! Fattuh, to whom does this poplar garden belong?
F.—To a priest, my lady.
G.B.—Doesn't he mind our camping in it?
F.—He didn't say anything.
G.B.—Did you ask him?
F.—No, my lady.
G.B.—We must give him some backshish.
F.—At your Excellency's command.
A pause.
F.—My lady.
G.B.—Yes?

F.—That priest is dead.

G.B.—!!! Then I don't think we need bother about the backshish.

F.—No, my lady.

The trouble is they don't use speech for the same purpose in the East as we do in the West.

It was piping hot, and we rode over barren rocky uplands and made our horses go their best pace—so good a pace that in 3 hours instead of the promised 4 we got to the great church that I had heard of. I should think it is 10th Cent. All round it the rock is honeycombed with the rooms and halls of a monastery with columbaria and churches. MY heart sank when I saw it for I knew I could do nothing at it under 3 hours and it was the hottest day we have had. However, I eat my lunch under the dome and then we set to work and we got it done in the three hours, the church only, I had not time to touch the rockcut things though they ought to be properly examined. And then we rode down the hills and across an endless plain.

Saturday, July 13. I was very glad to have a day off. I spent the whole morning in my tent drawing out some of all the work that has collected in the last few days. It was blazing hot.

Sunday, July 14. From Akserai we had 3 days of absolutely uninteresting travel across the great plains to Konia. I resolved that nothing should induce me to ride, it's too boring and too hot, so we sent the animals on with Haidar and my Turkoman, very early in the morning and Fattuh and I started off with the baggage at 5:15 in two carts. They are springless wooden carts covered with a hood of plaited straw with a cloth thrown over it. I should think less luxurious carriages do not exist. We packed all the luggage into one and put a quantity of rugs and waterproof sheets on to the floor of the other in which we journeyed, and it really wasn't so bad. At any rate! we were out of the glare and much less hot than we should have been riding.

Tuesday, July 16th. Everything comes to an end, even the road from Akserai to Konia. We got in at 10 o'clock this morning. I found quantities of letters from you and Father and Hugo and Moll, and was delighted to have them.

Domnul gives me the first description of the wedding. It Sounds all very very successful.

ON BOARD THE "IMOGEN," OFF CONSTANTINOPLE,
July 27, 1907

I'm having a mighty fine time, I must tell you. The Ambassador was more than cordial. Then he insisted on carrying me off to Therapia with him—the Embassy is there now. So I flew back to my Hotel and packed and went down to the quay. Up came Hugoenin, the Director of the German Ryl. So I introduced myself to him, and he pushed me and my box into his launch and steamed up the Bosphorus till we met Sir Nicholas coming down to fetch me. This morning I went into C'ple and did a lot of business and then came back to Therapia to lunch. Now I have gone off with the O'Conors on their yacht to sail about these waters till Monday. It is perfectly delightful and they are both extraordinarily kind.

To H.B.
PERA PALACE, CONSTANTINOPLE, Thursday, August 4, 1907.

Today I accomplished the most important object of my visit here—I saw the Grand Vizier. He is a very great man, is Fetid Pasha. . . .

There are troops of professors and people of that kind here who have all been to see me. I find it vastly entertaining.

I expeCt I shall be in London about the 7th or 8th and I should be most grateful if Marie could be sent up to meet me there. I shall have to stay a day or two to get some clothes.

To F.B.
LONDON, Friday, August 9, 1907.

Today I lunched with Sir Edward and Mr. Haldane—Willie [Tyrrell] told Sir E. I was here and he quickly asked me to lunch. It was most interesting and delightful. I'll tell you about it.

Sir Frank [Swettenham) is coming to tea and I dine with Domnul and spend the balance of the evening, after he goes to the office, with Willie T.

Sir Henry C. B. hasn't sent for me yet—I'm a little surprised, aren't you? So different from my habits in Constantinople.

To F.B.
CAMBO, NORTHUMBERLAND, Wednesday, September 4, 1907.

I dOn' think I ever saw anything more adorable than Moll's children. There's no question about Pauline's being pretty, I think she's quite charming. We have just been spending an hour with them in their garden trying to photograph them. I don't know that it will be a great success for there was no sun an one of them was always crawling busily out of the picture, so that all you saw was the end of its legs. Then I photographed Moll with them, she looks so beautiful with them hanging about her. Now we are going to take Pauline with us and look at the Wallington garden.

To H. B.
LONDON, Saturday, October, 1907.

I have had a wild 24 hours. I worked at the Geog. Soc. All yesterday and in the evening I went to Red Hill, getting there at 8. A young man (one of my fellow students-I think his name is Fairweather) met me at the station and we walked up on to the Common where we met Mr. Reeves. Then we took observations on stars for two hours. It was wonderfully calm and warm but the moon was so bright even the big stars were a little difficult to see. However, I took a number of observations and shall work them out on Monday. I got back after midnight, very hungry, and this morning I was back at Red Hill before 10 and spent three hours taking bearings for a map with Mr. Reeves. That has to be plotted out too on Monday at the Geog. Soc.

[I wrote to Mr. Reeves in May, 1927, asking him to tell me something of Gertrude's studies with him. I give here an extract from his reply.

ROYAL GEOGRAPHICAL SOCIETY.

May 21St, 1927.

Dear Lady Bell, ". . . . She came to me for instruction in surveying and astronomical observations for determining positions just before starting on her great journey in Arabia 1913-14. I have never had anyone to teach who learned mor rapidly and took a more intelligent interest in the subject, we had to deal with. . . .

"Miss Bell's prismatic compass route traverse Made on her remarkable journeys after she left me, was Plotted from her field books, and adjusted to her latitudes here by our draughtsmen. I need not say that her mapping has proved of the greatest value and importance. Her field books are here in our possession and will be greatly treasured."

All the following year, 1908, she was at home absorbed in writing "A Thousand and One Churches," the work she wrote in collaboration with Sir William Ramsay recording their architectural experiences in Asia Minor.

Early in 1909 she made one of her most important desert expeditions, to the castle of Ukhaidir. It is deplorable that there are no letters from her to be found about her very important undertaking of the reconstruction by plans and measurements of this immense castle. She subsequently wrote a book published by the Clarendon Press in 1914. The book is a quarto volume 13 inches by ten inches of 168 pages of letterpress, two maps and 93 plates which included 15 ground plans of her own planning and 166 photographs taken by herself besides photographs and plans from other sources. It is dedicated to Dr. Walther Andrae.

As there are no letters remaining about Ukhaidir I quote from Gertrude's preface. it is too important an enterprise for her record of it to be omitted altogether. M. Massignon, the French traveller, was the first to make any record of Ukhaidir, although it had been visited by other travellers several times.]

"The next visitor to the palace was myself. I left AleppO in February, 1909, and reached Ukhaidir on March 25, travelling by the East bank of the Euphrates and across the desert from Hit via Kubaisah and Shethathâ. . . . I published a paper on the vaulting system of the palace in the Journal of Hellenic Studies for 1910 and I gave a more detailed account of the building, in the following year (Amurath to Ammrath, p. 140). I returned to the site in March, 1911, in order to correct my plans and to take measurements for elevations and sections. Going thence to Babylon, I found that some members of the 'Deutsche Orient-Gesellschaft' who were engaged upon the excavations there had been to Ukhaidir during the two years of my absence and were preparing a book upon it. Their book appeared in 1912 and is referred to frequently in this volume. For their generosity in allowing me to use some of their architectural drawings, I tender my grateful thanks, together with my respectful admiration for their masterly production.

"I feel indeed, that I must apologize for venturing to offer a second version.

... But my excuse must be that my work which was almost completed when the German volume came out, covers not only the ground traversed by my learned friends in Babylon, but also ground which they had neither leisure nor opportunity to explore; and further, that I believe the time has come for a comparative study of the data collected by myself and others such as is contained in this book....

"With this I must take leave of a field of study which formed for four years my principal occupation, as well as my chief delight. A subject so enchanting and so suggestive as the Palace of Ukhaidir is not likely to present itself more than once in a lifetime, and as I bring this page to a close I call to mind the amazement with which I first gazed upon its formidable walls; the romance of my first sojourn within its precincts; the pleasure, undiminished by familiarity of my return; and the regret with which I sent back across the sun drenched plain a last greeting to its distant presence."

[She was in England during the latter half of 1909 and again enjoyed at Rounton the company of a succession of congenial visitors among them Sir Frank Lascelles, Sir George Lloyd, P. Loraine, Lady Arthur Russell, Sir Edwin and Lady Egerton, G. W. Prothero, Sir Valentine Chirol, Sir Ernest Shackleton, etc.

Gertrude, as may well be imagined, was the pivot of these gatherings and was always inventing exciting things to do, sometimes, indeed, too exciting for some of the guests. I have a vivid recollection of her insisting when the Egertons were with us on having a picnic on the top of the hill behind Mount Grace. Sir Edwin Egerton, a retired Ambassador, no longer very active, perhaps, had protested against going for a picnic and declared there was nothing he disliked more than sitting on the ground. Gertrude however insisted on his going. But she made many arrangements for his comfort, and when Sir Edwin arrived at the hill top, he found a table and chair awaiting him, his cover laid, and everything complete....

But in spite of the influx of guests that came and went, and her absorption in her own work in the intervals, she managed to go away on one or two visits.]

To F.B.
August 17th, 1909. [P.S. only.]
I'm drawing my castle [Ukhaidir] and it is coming out beautifully. I can scarcely bear to leave it for a moment.

To F.B.
September 13th, 1909.
I've finished the chapter for Strzygowski-only blocked out of course, there is a lot more work to be done on it, but the worst part is over and what is more I think it's rather neat. I've been so absorbed in it that I haven't had a moment to think of anything else. Now I'm going for a walk on the moors to forget about it till after tea.

I fear I shall have to come straight home and not go to Moll yet. Next week I must write an article for Mr. Prothero and even if I get home on Friday it leaves me very little time. I would rather go to her after it's done, when I shall be through this overwhelming batch of work that has to be done in such a hurry.

She writes from Ardgowan, Greenock, in September, she was staying with Sir Hugh and Lady Alice Shaw Stewart.]

To F. B.
ARDGOWAN, September 15th, 1909.

Mr. prothero, would rather not have my article till Jan. an immense relief to me, especially as the Hellenic Soc. want me to lecture on November 9th and that will take a vast preparation. By the way Mr. P. talks of being in Yorkshire early in October, and I've asked whether he cannot come to us, saying I know you would endorse the suggestion. He is in Scotland This is one of the most beautiful places I ever saw. There is an amusing party, the Gerald Balfours, Rayleighs, Bear Warre and others. The men go shooting every day. As for Lord Rayleigh I think he is very alarming, but he took me in to dinner yesterday and told me most exciting things suited to my understanding about radium. He opens doors into a wonderful unknown world which I shall never be able to walk in however. My hostess is delightful. . . .

[Hugo was ordained at Ripon on September 19th, 1909.)

I don't think I shall go to Ripon. I do feel so entirely out of that atmosphere. Of course don't say that to Hugo, I would not wound his feelings for the world, and if you think I shall do so by not going, I will.

To F. B.
LONDON, October 5th, 1909.

I went straight to the office and had an interview with a very capable lady who used to be the organising secretary of one of the Suffrage societies and has seen the error of her ways and wants to work for us. I fancy she will make an excellent and very sensible speaker and I intend to follow the matter up.

When I came in I found a telegram from George Lloyd Asking me to lunch to-day so I rang him up and asked him to dine with me. He came back yesterday. I asked Willie T. to come too but he was busy and is coming in after dinner. So I shall have a good all round view of the crisis.

[During this year the women's suffrage agitation took greater proportions. Gertrude was strongly opposed to it. I have found no letters from herself about it but Lady Jersey who was Chairman of the Women's Anti-Suffrage Committee sends me the following note, respecting Gertrude's connection with it.

From the Dowager Countess of Jersey.

"In the summer of 1908 Gertrude became interested in the movement against the extension of the Parliamentary Franchise to Women, and joined Mrs. Humphry Ward, myself and others in the formation of a Women's Anti-suffrage League. The women received throughout practical assistance from men, among whom Mr. John Massie was the able advisor and Hon. Treasurer. After two or three years Lord Curzon and Lord Cromer formed a larger League into which the Women's Society was ultimately merged.

"In the initial steps and until her departure for her great Arabian journey,

Gertrude displayed her usual delightful energy and powers of organisation. . . . It is impossible here to name the many keen women who rendered devoted assistance. It was soon realised that defence was harder than attack. . . . But in Gertrude at least there was never any want of spirit, and her unfailing good temper and direct common sense encouraged and inspired those who sometimes felt the task of opposition a hard one.

"In the Great War Gertrude's unrivalled experience of the East immediately marked her out for important spheres of action and her colleagues in the Anti-Suffrage cause had regretfully to abandon the hope of welcomIng her back to their counsels; they however are among the many who, while mourning her death, are proud of her life of achievement."]

CHAPTER XII
1910-1911

ITALY-ACROSS THE SYRIAN DESERT

(IN these letters from Rome, Gertrude is again in places too well known to make it worthwhile to give her descriptions of them. I quote however some personal extracts, which show her keenness and thoroughness of study.

She goes from Rome to Spalato.

She goes to Dalmatia and then back to Spalato where she is shown the palace of Diocletian by Monsignor Bulic, Director of Antiquities, "the most charming old man imaginable."

She goes to Zara, Polo, Ravenna, deep in study everywhere with experts, and then feels she must turn homewards.]

To F. B.
ROME, February 28th, 1910.

I have decided to stay on here another week with Eugénie (Mrs. Arthur Strong]. I have got a very nice room in her pension. But I shall miss Father dreadfully. We have had the most interesting ten days together and I hope he has enjoyed them as much as I have. He is such an ideal companion. With the archaeologists he is in his element, and he disconcerts the learned by extremely perdinent questions! but they are all delighted with him and I think he puts them upon their mettle and that they are far more interesting when he is there. We have made several new friends. The head of the German school Dr. Delbrück is extraordinarily able and we are going to spend a long morning together on Thursday in his library and discuss vaults. But our chief friends are the dear Wyndhams, who are darlings both of them. Robert Hichens turned up. at my lecture this afternoon—Oh, I think the lecture went quite well and I had a very distinguished audience of professors. Dr. Ashby at the head of the British School spends his time in trotting round with us.

Well it's all being quite as amusing as we meant it to be.

To F.B.
ROME, March, 1910.

It is most kind of you to agree to my staying here, and I want to tell you that I feel an awful beast about the dinner party. But at the same time I do think another fortnight here will be of immense value to me. Even in this last week I have begun to get hold of things. To-day I worked at Architectural decoration all the morning, partly out of doors and partly in the German Institute where I went to read for an hour before lunch. In the afternoon I joined Miss Van Demen at the Baths of Caracalla and looked at them all the afternoon. They are very difficult and I have not got them quite straightened out so I shall have another day at them tomorrow. I can't tell you what a delightful sensation it is to begin to understand these things. I feel so excited about them that I can scarcely bring myself to come in to lunch. I came back at 5 for Eugénie's lecture, a very good one and very helpful to me.

To F.B.
ROME, March, 1910.
When my literary remains come to be published the letters from Rome will not occupy an important place.! ween have not a minute to write but I must seize spaces between archaeologists to tell you what I am doing. . . . Yesterday morning I spent three hours with Delbrück who gave me the most wonderful disquisition I have ever heard on the history of architecture. It was a regular lecture. He had prepared all his notes and all his books to illustrate what he was saying. He is a very remarkable man and as he talked I got the hang of things that had always remained mysteries to me. He ended by saying that it was absurd that I should be so ignorant of the Roman monuments and by telling me that I ought to come here for 6 weeks to study. He is perfectly right and I'm contemplating quite seriously whether I will not come in Oct. and Nov. and study. I would like to do it before I go back to the East. It is a bore but after all 2 months is a short time in one's life. If it would give one a real hold of Roman problems it would be infinitely well spent. We'll talk of this when I come home.

To F.B.
ROME, 1910.
. . . . I went to the Capitol Museum and worked at ornament over which I grew so excited that I flew up to the Terme and went through all the ornaments there with immense satisfaction. . . . . .

To F. B.
1910.
You were really very kind not to mind my staying in Rome. I felt when I got your letter about the dinner party that I ought to come home at once, and I shall think of you tomorrow evening. Meantime my regrets are tempered by having learnt so much. I have been working like a slave and have got to the bottom of Diocletian's baths this last day or two. I have also been working at ornament and find to my joy that the moment one begins to look at it with care a regular sequence is apparent and the things that all seemed an immense muddle fell into a quite comprehensible history. All this has left me very little time for anything else. . . .

To F. B.
ROME, 1910.
I called on a delightful old Italian, Signor Sordini. We sat and talked of East and West with the completest accord and tnade great friends—all in Italian, mind you. I talk it disgracefully badly however and I know I constantly call people Thou in my anxiety to call them It [sic.]

To H.B. and F.B.
RAVENNA, 1910.
. . . . As for London, no, I don't expect I shall be there much. I must fall back to the book and I think that can be written best at home. You see I don't want to waste any more time than I can help—the book! . . . .

[This was 'Amurath to Amurath.'

Before going to England she goes to Munich to See the exhibition of pictures. There she receives a letter from W. Heinemann.)

To F.B.
MUNICH, 1910.
. . . . Then I came in to grapple with a letter from Heinemann who wants me to reply by telegram to the terms he offered me for my book and to agree to have it ready early in November. I have agreed, but I expect we shall have the devil's own hurry over it and so I have written to him.

The exhibition is wonderful. I am very glad that I am alone here so that I can really work at it.

To F.B.
MUNICH, 1910.
I have had these evenings when I have been alone to write an article on the Persian and Arab Poets for Mr. Richmond. I hope it is all right. I think it is, and I am glad to have it off my mind.

To F.B.
january 9th, 1911.
Two things I want in Rome.

You know the round church of Santa Costanza) outside the walls? Next to it is the little basilica of St. Agnese which has in the inside a double storey of columns on either side of the nave. The capitals of the lower story are acanthus captals with tiny garlands hung over the corners. I want a photograph of one of these, showing the garland clearly, for it is the only example I know in Rome of the garlanded capital of the early Christian monuments at Diarbekr and in the Tur Abdin. The photograph does not, I think, exist. But Eugénie's photographer would take it for me for a few francs. I shall want it as a point for comparison when I write my forthcoming work about the Tur Abdin.

The second thing is in the Museum of the Terme. I was shown it by the curator, Paribene, who took Eugénie and me around. It is Part of some architectural fragments from a tomb of the Antonines found some way out of Rome, near Tivoli, I think. When I saw these fragments, they were not yet being exhibited to the public. Paribene said they had to be sorted and set up. The interesting thing about them was that some of the decoration was the acanthus spinosus, the fat jagged acanthus, not the broad, flat-leaved one. Now the earliest example I know of the acanthus spinosus, except this tomb, is at Spalato—50 years later than the fragments at the Terme. It is undoubtedly an

Asiatic motive (the plant itself is Asiatic) and it points to a school of Asiatic stone-cutters having existed in Rome in the time of the Antonines—so I think. If Paribene would be so kind, I should like to have a good photograph of one of these fragments, showing exactly that particular kind of acanthus decoration. It is rather an important point which I should like some day to use. Here again, the photographs would probably have to be taken specially for me. Eugénie knows the fragments in the Terme—we saw them together—and she could get permission from Paribene to have them photographed, if she would be so good. . . .

(this letter from Gertrude was written on board ship on her way to the East on February 9th 1911. Her father and I were in Rome. It shows her thoroughness of study, and her determination to verify every detail of architecture. The photographs she asked for were sent to her.)

To F. B.
BEYRouT, January 16th, 1911.
. . . ..I went off to the Jesuit College where I was received with open arms by the two librarians. We had a long talk and I told them all I was going to do, and they gave me some useful introductions to bishops in the Tur Abdin. And then we went over the printing establishment. I found one compositor setting up the Arabic text which Sir Charles Lyall is bringing out, much perplexed over some indecipherable English words which I succeeded in reading for him. He only knew Arabic you see. They are sending me a lot of their publications, the two fathers of the library (I always send them my books) so they will arrive at Rounton some time and must be kept for me. With all this I have spent a most delightful morning, as you may imagine. You remember I told you that my delightful Sheikh was in prison on a charge of murder. Fattuh tells me they succeeded in getting him out, by a free use of my testimony to his character! I'm delighted. He'll be able to murder someone else now. What a country! Already I feel my standards of virtue entirely changed.

To F.B.
DAMASCUS, January 18, 1911.
. . . . I thought I had better begin to see about my journey so I went off to the quarter where the sons of Abdul Kadir live. They are the great people here and if any one knows the desert, it is the Amir Umar, Abdul Kadir's son, and the Amir Takir, his grandson. I found them both in the Amir Takir's hous, and we had a long talk, the upshot of which is that the Amir Takir is going to seek out a sheikh of the Wahed Ali, who is now in Damascus, and we are all to meet and discuss matters. The Emir Ali is the eldest son of Abdul Kadir. He is a great big splendid looking man with hair and beard as black as coal, and that directness of address which is very typical of the Abdul Kadirs.

Now I must tell you another old friend has turned up, Selim Tabit. I found him waiting for me when I came in and we went to a neighbouring hotel where he lodges and found there the Amir Umar and the Amir Takir whom I presently took aside and conversed at length about my journey. All is going well, and in a day or two I hope we shall see our way clear. It's still pretty cold, but the weather is improving. I have just come in from dining with Selim Tabit. He is, I must say, a very amusing companion. He told me the gosssip of Syria by the yard and as the dinner drew to a close it occurred to me to ask after my old friend, Muhammad Pasha Jerudi. "Oh," said Tabit Bey, "he has just come in from Jerud—shall we go and see him?" So we stepped round to old Jerudi's house. He was sitting all alone in a great coat, running a rosary through his fingers and with nothing else to amuse him. The night was bitter cold and the room, which was all window, was warmed by a charcoal brazier. So we sat down and Tabit Bey talked uninterruptedly for an hour and a half. I doubt if Jerudi can read, but anyway Selim is better than any newspaper. He related what was happening in Macedonia and what in the Yemen, the latest news from the Jebel Druze and from Persia. It interested me just as much as it interested jerudi and by the time we left I found that I had even forgotten that I was shivering with cold.

So you see Damascus is as delightful as ever.

To F.B.
DAMASCUS, January 27th, 1911.

I shall not be able to post a letter to you for a long time because I shall not be in the way of a post-office, but when I get to Hit I will send word to our consul in Bagdad and ask him to telegraph to you, "Arrived Hit." then you will know that all is well and that I shall be in Bagdad about a fortnight later.

To F. B.
DAMASCUS, February 1st, 1911.

. . . .The first reviews of my book have come. . . . But now the reviewers all stick at the archaeology (well, they will have to bear it) and not one of them has said anything about my fellow travellers, Cyrus and Julian, whom I think I treated rather well. There is little satisfaftion to be got out of reviewers, whether they praise or blame,

To F. B.
DAMASCUS, February 7th, 1911.

We have been blocked up by snow on all sides, all the rlys.stopped, no posts, no nothing. At last the spring has come and we are off. I'm glad you did not send a photograph to the Daily Graphic. I have had an interesting time, though too much of it. I've done some work at inscriptions, for van Berchem and I've seen all the world. The best of all is the delightful old Arab Sheikh who has helped me with my journey. I pay him calls at his house after sunset and find always some twenty or thirty people there from every corner of the Moslem world. One night I was sitting there as usual when he rose and said to the company: "Will you pray?" It was the hour of the evening prayer. His great nephew brought out white felts from an inner room, spread them on the floor facing Mecca and all the guests stood up and prayed. After telling me all the news of the desert he asks me whether I think there are diamond mines there and whether gold—questions difficult to answer.

To F.B.
DUMEIR, February 9th.

We're off. And now I must tell you the course of the negotiations which preceded this journey. First as you know I went to the sons of Abdul Kadir and they called up Sheikh Muhammad Bassam and asked him to help me. I called on him the following evening. He said it was too early, the desert camels had not come in to Damascus, there was not a dulul (riding camel) to be had and I must send out to a village a few hours away and buy. This was discouraging as I could not hope to get them for less than 15 pounds apiece, I wanted five and I should probably have to sell them for an old song at Hit. Next day Fattuh went down into the bazaar and came back with the news that he and Bassam between them had found an owner of camels ready to hire for 7 apiece. It was dear but I closed with the offer. All the arrangements were made and I dispatched the caravan by the Palmyra road. Then followed misfortune. The snow closed down upon us, the desert post did not come in for three weeks and till it came we were without a guide. Then Bassam invented another scheme. The old sheikh of Kubeisa near Hit (you know the place) was in Damascus and wanted to return home; he would journey with us and guide us. So all was settled again-

But the sheikh Muhammad en Nawan made continuous delays, we were helpless, for we could not cross the Syrian desert without a guide and still the post did not come in. The snow in the desert had been without parallel. At last Muhamma en Nawan was ready. I sent off my camels to Dumeir yesterday (it is the frontier village of the desert) and myself went to sleep at the English hospital whence it was easier to slip off unobserved. For I am supposed to be travelling to Palmyra and Deir with four zaptiehs. This morning Fattuh and I drove here, it took us four hours, and the Sheikh came on his dulul. The whole party is assembled in the house of a native of Kubeisa, I am lodged in a large windowless room spread with felts, a camel is stabled at my door, and over the way Fattuh is cooking my dinner. One has to put on clogs to walk across the yard, so inconceivably muddy it is, and in the village one can't walk at all, one must ride. I got in about one and lunched, after which I mounted and went out to see some ruins a mile or two away. It was a big Roman fortified camp. And beyond it the desert stretched away to the horizon. That is where we go tomorrow. It's too heavenly to be back in all this again, Roman forts and Arab tents and the wide desert. All the women here address me as Hajji. It is very gratifying. Every few minutes someone comes into my room and enquires after my health. I reply politely: "Praise God!" and he leaves me. We have got for a guide the last desert postman who came in three days ago, having been delayed nine days by snow. His name is Ali.

Syrian Desert February 10th. There is in Dumeir a very beautiful temple, rather like one Of the temples at Baalbek. As soon as the sun was up I went out and took some photographs of it, but I was ready long before the camels were loaded; the first day's packing is always a long business, Finally we got off soon after nine, a party of fifteen, myself, the sheikh, Fattuh, Ali and my four camel men, and the other seven merchants who are going across to the Euphrates to buy sheep. In half an hour we passed the little Turkish guard house which is the last outpost of civilisation and plunged into the wilderness. Our road lay before us over a flat expanse bounded to the N. by the range of barren hills that trend away to the N.E. and divide us from the Palmyran desert, and to the S. by a number of distant tells, volcanic I should think. I rode my mare all day, for I can come and go more easily upon her, but when we get into the heart of the desert I shall ride a camel. it's less tiring. Three hours from Dumeir we came to some water pools which are dry in summer and here we filled r skins, for where we are camping there is no water. There was a keen wind, rising sometimes into a violent storm which brought gusts of hail upon us, but fortunately it was behind us so that it did not do us much harm. Late in the afternoon another hail storm broke over us and clearing away left the distant hills white with snow. We had come to a place where there was a little scrub which would serve as firewood, and here we camped under the lee of some rising ground. Our companions have three big Arab tents, open in front, and we our two English tents, and oddly enough we are quite warm in spite of the rain and cold wind. I don't know why it is that one seldom feels cold in the desert; perhaps because of the absence of damp. The stony, sandy ground never becomes muddy. A little grass is beginning to grow and as you look over the wide expanse in front of you it is almost green. The old sheikh is lamenting that we are not in a house in Damascus (but I think one's first camp in the Hamad is worth a street full of houses); "By the head of your father!" he said, "how can you leave the garden of the world and come out into this wilderness?" Perhaps it does require explanation.

February 11 th. But to-day's experiences will not serve to justifY my attitude. When I went to bed a hurricane was blowing. I woke from time to time and heard the good Fattuh hammering in the tent pegs, and wondered if any tent would stand up in that gale and also what was going to happen next. an hour before dawn Fattuh called to me and asked if I was cold. I woke in surprise and putting my hand out found the waterproof valise that covered me wet with snow. "It is like the sea," cried Fattuh. Therefore I lighted a candle and saw that it had drifted into my tent a foot deep. I dug down, found my boots and hat and put them under the valise; I had gone to bed as I stood and put all my extra clothing under the Wolsey valise for warmth so that nothing came to harm. At dawn Fattuh dragged out the waterproof sheet that covers the ground and with it most of the snow. The snow was lying in great drifts where the wind had blown it, it was banked up against our tents and those of the Arabs and every hour or so the wind brought a fresh storm upon us. We cleared it out of our tents and settled to a day as little uncomfortable as we could manage to make it. In the afternoon seven Arabs of the Heseneh rode in in a furious sleet storm. I was busy cutting firewood at the time. We built up the fire in Sheikh

Muhammad's tent, gave them coffee and dates and sent them on a little comforted. They had spent the night out, on the way to a distant camp. At last, atsunset the wind dropped, the barometer rose and we pray for the weather tomorrow. Most of the snow has melted already, and left the desert spongy.

February 12th. We have got out into smooth waters at last. You can imagine what I felt like when I looked out of my tent before dawn and saw a clear sky and the snow almost vanished. But the cold! Everything in my tent was frozen stiff—yesterday's damp skirt was like a board, my gloves like iron, my sponges—well, I'll draw a veil over my sponges—I did not use them much, Nor was my toilette very complicated as I had gone to bed in my clothes. The temperature after sunrise was 30, and there was a biting wind blowing sharply from the west. I spent an hour trudging backwards and forwards over the frozen desert trying to pretend I was warm while the camels were loaded. The frozen tents took a world of time to pack-with frozen fingers too. We were off soon after eight, but for the first hour the wet desert was like a sheet of glass and the camels slipped about and fell down with much groaning and moaning. They are singularly unfitted to cope with emergencies. For the next hour we plodded over a slippery melting surface, for which they are scarcely better suited, then suddenly we got out of the snow zone and all was well. I got on to my camel and rode her for the rest of the day. She is the most charming of animals. You ride a camel with only a halter which you mostly tie loosely round the peak of your saddle. A tap with your camel switch on one side of her neck or the other tells her the direction you want her to go, a touch with your heels sends her on, but when you wish her to sit down you have to hit her lightly and often on the neck saying at the same time: "Kh kh kh kh," that's as near as I can spell it. The big soft saddle, the 'shedad,' is so easy and comfortable that you never tire. You loll about and eat your lunch and observe the landscape through your glasses: you might almost sleep. So we swung on through an absolutely flat plain till past five, when we came to a shallow valley with low banks on either side and here we camped. The name of the place is Aitha, there is a full moon and it is absolutely still except for the sound of the pounding of coffee beans in the tents of my travelling companions. I could desire nothing pleasanter.

February 13 th. Don't think for a moment that it is warm weather yet. At 5:30 to-day (which was the hour of my breakfast) the thermometer stood at 20, but there was no wind. We were off soon after six. The sun rose gloriously half an hour later and we began to unfreeze. It is very cold riding on a camel, I don't know why unless it has to do with her extreme height.

We rode on talking cheerfully of our various adventures till after ten which is the time when my companions lunch, so I lunch too. The camels were going rather languidly for they were thirsty, not having drunk since they left Damascus. They won't drink when it is very cold. But our guide, Ali, promised us some pools ahead, good water, he said. When we got there we found that some Arabs had camped not far off and nothing remained of the pools but trampled mud.

The extraordinary folly of Bedouin habits is almost past belief. They know that the pools collect only under a sloping face of rock; if they would clear out the earth below they would have good clear water that would last them for weeks; not only do they neglect to do that but they don't even clear out the mud which gets deeper and deeper till there is no pool at all. So we had to go searching round for another pool and at last we found one about a mile away with a very little water in it, but enough for the riding camels, my mare and our water skins. It is exceedingly muddy however. We got into camp about four not far from some Arab tents. This is our plan of action: first of all we all set to work to put up our tents, my part of the proceeding being to unpack and set up my camp furniture. By the time I have done that and taken off my boots Fattuh has tea ready. My companions scatter over the plain with axes to gather firewood which is a little dry plant called Shik, six inches high at the highest. We speak of it as the trees. A few strokes with the pick makes the square hearth in the tents and in a moment a bundle of shik is blazing in it, the sheikh has settled down to his narghileh and coffee making has begun. We never stop for five minutes but we pile up a heap of shik and warm our hands at the bonfire. We seek out for our camping place a bit of low ground. When we get near the place Ali purposes to camp in, the old sheikh is all for stopping. "This room is fair," says he looking at a little curve in the bank. "Wallahi oh sheikh," says Ali "the next room is better; there are more trees." So we go on to the next allotted chamber. It is a wonderfully interesting experience this. Last night they all sat Up half the night because my mare pricked her ears and they thought she heard robbers. They ran up the banks and cried out "Don't come near! we have soldiers with us and camels." It seemed to me when I heard of it (I was asleep at the time) a very open deceit but it seems to have served the purpose for the thief retired. As we rode this morning Ali detected hoof marks on the hard ground and was satisfied it was the mare of our enemy.

February 14th. What I accuse them of is not that they choose to live differently from us: for my part I like that; but that they do their own job so very badly. I told you of the water yesterday now I will give you another instance. Everybody in the desert knows that camels frequently stray away while feeding, yet it occurs to no one to put a man to watch over them. No when we get into camp they are just turned off to feed where, they like and go where they will. Consequently yesterday at dusk four of our baggage camels were missing and a riding camel belonging to one of the Damascene sheep merchants and everyone had to turn out to look for them. I could not do anything so I did not bother and while I was dining the sheikh looked in and said our camels had come back—let us thank God! It is certain that no one else could claim any credit. But the riding camel was not to be found, nor had she come back when I was ready to start at 4:30 this morning. We decided to wait till dawn and that being two hours off and the temperature 30 I went to bed again and to sleep. At dawn there was no news of her, so we started, leaving word with some Arabs where we were gone. She has not yet appeared, nor do I think she will. I was very sorry for the merchant, who now goes afoot, and very much bored by the delay. For we can't make it up at the other end because the camels have to eat for at least two hours before sunset. They eat shik; so does my little mare, she being a native of the desert. At ten o'clock we came to some big water pools, carefully hollowed out "in the first days" said Ali, with the earth banked up high round them, but now half filled with mud and the banks broken. Still they hold a good deal of water in the winter and the inhabitants of the desert for miles around were driving their sheep and camels there to drink. We too filled our water skins. We got into camp at three, near some Arab tents. The sheikh, a charming old man, has just paid us a long visit. We sat round Muhammad's coffee fire and talked. It was all the more cheerful because the temperature is now 46—a blessed change from 26. My sponges have unfrozen for the first time. We have got up into the high flat plain which is the true Hamad, the Smooth, and the horizon from my tent door is as round as the horizon of the sea. The sharp dry air is wonderfully delicious: I think every day of the Syrian desert must prolong your life by two years. Sheikh Muhammad has confided to me that he has three wives, one in Damascus, one in Kubeisa and one in Bagdad, but the last he has not seen for twenty-three years. " She has grown old, oh lady—by the truth of God! and she never bore but one daughter."

February 15th. We were off at five this morning in bitter frost. Can you picture the singular beauty of these moonlit departures! the frail Arab tents falling one by one, leaving the camp fires blazing into the night; the dark masses of the kneeling camels; the shrouded figures binding up the loads, shaking the ice from the water skins, or crouched over the hearth for a moment's warmth before mounting. "Yallah, yallah, oh children!" cries the old sheikh, knocking the ashes out of his Narghileh, "Are we ready?" So we set out across the dim wilderness, Sheikh Muhammad leading on his **white** dulul. The sky ahead reddens, and fades, the moon pales and in sudden **splendour** the sun rushes up over the rim of the world. To see with the eyes is **good,** but while I wonder and - rejoice to look upon this primeval existence, it **does not** seem to be a new thing; it is familiar, it is a part of inherited memory. **After** an hour and a half of marching we came to the pool of Khafiyeh **and since there** is no water for three days ahead we had to fill all our empty skins. But **the pool** was a sheet of ice, the water skins were frozen and needed careful **handling for if** you unfold them they crack and break-and we lighted fire and set to **work to thaw** them and ourselves. I sent the slow baggage camels on, and with **much labour** we softened the skins and contrived to fill them. The sun was now **up and a** more barren prospect than it revealed you cannot Imagine. The Hamad stretched in front of us, flat and almost absolutely bare; for several hours we rode over a wilderness Of flints on which nothing grew. It was also the coldest day we have had, for the keen frosty wind blew straight into our faces. We stopped once to wait for the baggage camels, and warmed ourselves at a bonfire meanwhile, and again We stopped for half an hour to lunch. We watched our shadow catch us up and march ahead of us as the sun sank westward and at three o'clock we pitched camp in the stony waste. yet I can only tell you that we have spent a very pleasant day. The old sheikh never stops talking, bless him, he orders us all about when we pitch and break up camp, but as Fattuh and I know much more about the pitching of our tents than he does, we pay no attention. "Oh Fattuh," said I this evening when he had given us endless advice, "do you pity the wife in Bagdad?" "Effendim," said Fattuh, "she must be exceedingly at rest." Still for my part I should be sorry not to see Sheikh Muhammad for twenty-three years.

February 16th. After I had gone to bed last night I heard Ali shouting to all whom it might concern: "We are English soldiers! English soldiers!" But there was no one to hear and the desert would have received with equal indifference the information that we were Roman legionaries. We came to the end of the inhospitable Hamad to-day and the desert is once more diversified by a slight rise and fall of the ground. It is still entirely waterless, so waterless that in the spring when the grass grows thick the Arabs cannot camp here. All along our way there is proof of former water storage-I should think Early Moslem, marking the Abbassid post road. The pools have been dug out and banked up, but they are now full of earth and there is very little water in them. We are camped to-night in what is called a valley. It takes a practised eye to distinguish the valley from the mountain, the one is so shallow and the other so low. The valleys are often two miles wide and you can distinguish them best by the fact that there are generally more "trees" in them than on the heights. I have made great friends with one of the sheep merchants. His name is Muhiyyed Din. He is coming back in the Spring over this road with his lambs. They eat as they go and travel four hours a day. "It must be a dull job," said I. "Eh wallah!" he replied, but if the spring grass is good the master of the lambs rejoices to see them grow fat." He travels over the whole desert, here and in Mesopotamia, buying sheep and camels; to Nejd too, and to Egypt, and he tells me delightful tales of his adventures. What with one thing and another the eight or nine hours of camel riding a day are never dull. But Truth of God! the cold!

February 17th. We were running short of water this morning. The water difficulty has been enhanced by the cold. The standing pools are exceedingly shallow so that when there is an inch of ice over them little remains but mud; what the water is like that you scrape up under these conditions I leave to the imagination Besides the mud, it has a sharp acrid taste of skins after forty-eight hours in them—not unhealthy I believe, but neither is it pleasant. So it happened that we had to cut down rather to the south today instead of going to the well of Kara which we could not have reached this evening. Sheikh Muhammad was much agitated at this programme. He expected to find the camps of tribes whom he knew at and near the well, and he feared that by coming to the south of them we might find ourselves upon the path of a possible raiding party of Arabs whom he did not know coming up from the south. Ali tried to reassure him, saying that the chances were againsst raiding parties (good, please God!) and that we were relying upon God. But the Sheikh was not to be comforted. "Life of God! what is this talk! To God is the command! we are in the Shamuyyeh where no one is safe—Face of God!" He is master of a wonderful variety of pious ejaculations. So we rode for an hour or two (until we forgot about it) carefully scanning the horizon for ghazus; it was just as well that we had this to occupy us, for the whole day's march was over ground as flat as a board. It had been excruciatingly cold in the early morning but about midday the wind shifted round to the South and we began to feel the warmth of the sun. For the first time we shed our fur coats, and the lizards came out of their holes. Also the horizon was decorated with fantastic mirage which greatly added to the enjoyment of looking for ghazus. An almost imperceptible rise in the ground would from afar stand up above the solid earth as if it were the high back of a camel. We saw tents with men beside them pitched on the edge of mirage lakes and when at last we actually did come to a stretch of shallow Water, it was a long time before I could believe that it was not imaginary. I saw how the atmospheric delusion worked by watching some gazelles. They galloped away over the plain just ordinary gazelles, but when they came to the mirage they suddenly got up on to stilts and looked the size of camels. It is excessively bewildering to be deprived of the use of one's eyes in this way. We had a ten hours' march to reach the water by which we are camped. It lies in a wide shallow basin of mud, most of it is dried up, but a few pools remain in the deeper parts. The Arabs use some sort of white chalky stone—is it chalk?—to precipitate the mud. We have got some with us. We boil the water, powder the chalk and put it in and it takes nearly all the mud down to the bottom. Then we pour off the water.

February 18th. We were pursued all day by a mad wind which ended by bringing a shower of sleet upon us while we were getting into camp. In consequence of the inclemency of the weather I had the greatest difficulty in getting the Sheikh and the camel drivers to leave their tent and they were still sitting over their coffee fire when we and the Damascene merchants were ready, to start. Inspired of God I pulled out their tent pegs and I brought their roof about their ears—to the great joy of all, except those who were sitting under it. So we got off half an hour before dawn and after about an hour's riding dropped down off the smooth plain into an endless succession of hills and deep valleys—when I say deep they are about 200 feet deep and they all run north into the hollow plain of Kara. I much prefer this sort of country to the endless flat and it Is quite interesting sitting a camel down a stony descent. The unspeakable devilish Wind was fortunately behind us—Call upon the Prophet! but it did blow!

February 20th. We marched yesterday thirteen and a half hours without getting Anywhere. We set off at five in a delicious still night with a temperature of 36—it felt quite balmy. The sun rose clear and beautiful as we passed through the gates of our valley into a wide low plain—we were to reach the Wady which is the father of all valleys in this desert, in ten hours, and the little ruin of Muheiwir in half an hour more and there was to be plentiful clear water. We were in good spirits as you may imagine; the sheikh sang songs of Nejd and Ali instructed me in all the desert roads. We rode on and on. At two o'clock I asked Ali whether it were two hours to Muheiwir? "Nore," said he. "Three?" said I. "Oh lady, more." "Four?" I asked with a little sinking of heart. "Wallahi, not so much." We rode on over low hills and hollow plains. At five we dropped into the second of the valleys el Ud. By this time Fattuh and I were on ahead and Ali was anxiously scanning the landscape from every high rock. The Sheikh had sat down to smoke a narghileh while the baggage camels came up. "My lady," said Fattuh, "I do not Think we shall reach water to-night." And the whole supply of water which we had was about a cupful in my flask. We went on for another half hour down the valley and finally, in concert with Ali, selected a spot for a camp. It was waterless, but, said he, the water was not more than two hours off: he would take skins and fetch some, and meantime the starving camels would eat trees. But when the others came up, the Father of Camels, Abdullah, he from whom we hired our beasts, protested that he must have water to mix the camel meal at night (they eat a kind of dough) and rather against r Judgment we went on. We rode an hour further, by which time it was pitch dark. Then Muhiyyed Din came up to me and said that if by chance we were to meet a ghazu in the dark night, it might go ill with us. That there was reason in this was admitted by all; we dumped down where we stood, In spite of the darkness Fattuh had my tent up before you could wink, while I hobbled my mare and hunted among the Camel loads for my bed. No one else put up a tent; they drew the camels together and under the shelter they gave made a fire of what trees they could find, Fattuh and I divided the water in my flask into two parts; with half we made some tea which he and I shared over some tinned meat and some bread; the other half we kept for the next morning When I shared it with the sheikh. We were none of us thirsty really; this weather does not make you thirsty. But my poor little mare had not drunk for two days, and she whinnied to everyone she saw. The last thing I heard before I went to sleep was the good Fattuh reasoning with her. "There is no water," he was saying. "There is none. Ma fi, ma fi." Soon after five he woke me up. I put on my boots, drank the tea he brought (having sent half to the poor old sheikh, who had passed the night under the lee of his camel) and went out into a cheerless daybreak. The sky was heavy with low-hanging clouds, the thermometer stood at 34, as we mounted our camels a faint and rather dismal glow in the east told us that the sun was rising. It was as well that we had not tried to reach water the night before. We rode to-day for six and a half hours before we got to rain pools in the Wady Hauran, and an hour more to Muheiwir and a couple of good wells in the valley bed. For the first four hours our way lay across barren levels; after a time we saw innumerable camels pasturing near the bare horizon and realised that we must be nearing the valley: there is no water anywhere but in the Hauran and all the tents of the Deleim are gathered near it. Then we began to descend through dry and stony watercourses and at midday found ourselves at the bottom of the great valley, and marched along the edge of a river of stones with a few rain Pools lying in it. So we came to Muheiwir which is a small ruined fort, and here we found two men of the Deleim with a flock Their of sheep—the first men we have seen for four days. there camp is about three miles away. Under the ruined fort there are some deep springs in the bed of the stream, and by them camped, feeling that we needed a few hours' rest after all our exertions. The sheikh had lighted his coffee fire while I Was taking a first cursory view of the ruin. "Oh lady" he cried "honour us." I sat down and drank a cup of coffee. "Where" said he, looking at me critically, "where is thy face in Damascus and where thy face here?" And I am bound to say that his remark was not without justification. But after ten days of frost and wind and sun what would you have? The clouds have all cleared away—sun and water and ruins, the heart of man can desire no more. The sheikh salutes you.

February 21st. We got off at four this morning and made a twelve hours' stage. It was freezing a little when we started, the moon rode high on the shoulder of the Scorpion and was not strong enough to extinguish him—this waning moon has done us good service. It took us two hours to climb up out of the Wady Hauran. I was talking to Muhiyyed Din when the sheikh came up, and said "Oh lady, speech before dawn is not good." He was afraid of raising some hidden foe. Reckless courage is not his characteristic. We have camped under a low bank, selecting carefully the east side of it so that our fires can be seen only by the friendly Deleim to the east of us. We are nowhere tonight—just out in the open wilderness which has come to feel so homelike. Four of the sheep merchants left us yesterday hearing that the sheikhs with whom they deal were camped near at hand, for each man deals every year with the same sheikh. If you could see the western sky with the evening star burning in it, you would give thanks—as I do.

February 22nd. An hour's ride from our camp this morning brought us to the small desert fortress of Amej. . . . But Muhiyyed Din and the other sheep merchants found that their sheikhs were camped close at han and we parted with much regret and a plentiful exchange of blessings. So we rode on till at four o'clock we reached the fortress of Khubbaz and here we have camped beneath the walls where Fattuh and I camped two years ago. It feels almost like returning home. It blew all day; I must own that the desert would be nicer if it were not so plagued with wind. The Sheikh and Ali and one of the camel drivers sang trios for Part of the afternoon to beguile the way. I have written down some of the sheikh's songs. They are not by him, however, but by the most famous of modern desert poets, the late Emir of Nejd.

February 23rd. The morning came grey and cheerless with an occasional scud of rain. We set off about six and took the familiar path across barren watercourses to Ain Zaza. The rain fell upon us and made heavy and sticky going, but it cleared before we reached the Ain and we lunched there and waited for the baggage camels till eleven. Kubeisa was only an hour and a half away, and it being so early I determined to refuse all the Sheikh's pressing invitations that we should spend the night with him, and push on to Hit, three and a half hours further. The baggage camels were informed of the change of plan and Fattuh and I rode on in high spirits at the thought of rejoining our caravan that evening. For you remember the caravan which we despatched from Damascus was to wait for us at Hit. But before we reached Kubeisa the rain came down again in torrents. Now the ground here is what the Arabs called 'sabkha,' soft, crumbly salt marsh, sandy when it is dry and ready at a moment's notice to turn into a world of glutinous paste. This is what it did and since camels cannot walk in mud I was presently aware of a stupendous downfall and found myself and my camel prostrate in the sticky glue. It feels like the end of the universe when your camel falls down. However we both rolled up unhurt and made the best of our way to the gates of Kubeisa. And here another misfortune awaited us. The rain was still falling heavy, Abdullah, Father of Camels, declared that his beasts could not go on to Hit across a road all sabkha and even Fattuh admitted that, tired and hungry as they were, it would be impossible. So in great triumph and with much praising of God, the Sheikh conducted us to his house where I was seized by a pack of beautiful and very inquisitive women ("They are shameless!" said Fattuh indignantly) and conducted me into the pitch dark room On the ground floor which is the living room. But the sheikh rescued me and took me upstairs to the reception room On the roof. Everyone we met fell on his neck and greeted hin, With a kiss on either cheek and no sooner were we seated upstairs and a bonfire of trees lighted in the middle of the room, than all the worthies of Kubeisa began to assemble to greet him and hear the news. At the end they numbered at least fifty. Now this was the room in which I was supposed to eat and sleep—there was no other. I took Fattuh aside—or rather outside, for the room was packed to overflowing—and said "The night will be troublesome." Fattuh knitted his brows and without a word strode down the stairs. I returned to the company, and when the room grew too smoky with trees and tobacco, sat outside talking to the sheikh's charming son, Namân. The rain had stopped. My old acquaintances in Kubeisa had all been up to salute me and I sat by the fire and listened to the talk and prayed that Fattuh might find some means of escape. He was as resourceful as usual. After a couple of hours he returned and said "With your permission, oh Muhammad. We are ready." He had found a couple of camels and a donkey and we were off. So we took a most affectionate leave of the Sheikh and left him to his narghileh. Half the town of Kubeisa, the female half, followed us through the streets, and we turned our faces to Hit. The two camels carried our diminished loads, Fattuh rode the donkey (it was so small that his feet touched the ground and he presently abandoned it in favour of one of the baggage camels and sent it back) and I was supposed to ride my mare. But she had a sore heel, Poor little thing, and kept stumbling in the mud, so I walked most of the way. We left at 2:30 and had two and a half hours before sunset. The first part of our way was hard and dry; presently we saw the smoke of the Hit pitch fires on the horizon and when we had passed between some low hills, there was the great mound of Hit and its single minaret in front of us. There remained an hour and a half of journey, the sun had set and our road was all sabkha. The camels slipped and slithered and tumbled down: "Their legs are like soap,,, explained the camel boy. If the rain had fallen again we should have been done. But it kept off till just as we reached Hit. The mound still loomed through the night and we could just see enough to keep more or less to our road-less rather than more-but not enough to make out whether stone or mud or sulphur pools lay in front of us. So we three great travellers, Fattuh, the mare and I, came into Hit, wet and weary, trudging through the dark, and looking I make no doubt, like so many vagabonds, and thus ingloriously ended our fine adventure. The khan stands outside the town; the khanji is an old friend. "Ya Abud!" shouted Fattuh "the caravan, our caravan, is it here?" "Kinship and welcome and may the earth be wide to you! They are here , The muleteers hurried out, seized my bridle, seized my hand in theirs and laid it upon their forehead. All was safe and well, we and they and the animals and the packs. Praise God! there is no other but He. The khanji brought me tea, and various friends came to call, I dined and washed and went to bed. And so you see, we have crossed the Syrian desert as easily as if it had been the Sultan's high road, and we have made many friends and seen the ruins we went out to see, and over and above all I have conceived quite a new theory about the mediaeval roads through the desert which I will prove some day by another journey. And all that remains is the hope that this letter, which is the true history of all, will not be lost in the post.

February2 4th. We have repacked our loads and are off this day on the road to Ramadi.

To F.B.
RAMADI, February 27th.

We did not leave Hit yesterday till one o'clock, having a good deal of repacking to do. Then I rode off with a Zaptieh over the sandy wastes that surround Hit and presently Came in view of Euphrates and put up a thanksgiving at the blessed sight of him. We rode on for three hours til we came to a little valley, full of water after the rains, and then we stopped to direct the baggage animals to the bridge and I heard for the first time the sound of my own caravan bells. We camped a quarter of an hour further under a cliff by the river's edge near a few mean huts of the Dulaim and a patch of green Corn, with the sound of the water wheels in our ears, and the Euphrates lying big and calm under the sunset. There is no river to be compared to him. Neither is it possible to describe the comfort of a fully appointed camp. Praise be to God! as Fattuh frequently exclaims, there is nothing that we lack. we had a march of about seven and a half hours-not very interesting, the familiar barren landscape of the lower Euphrates. All the palm trees have been killed by thesnow; there are miserable brown patches instead of the old vivid green. Kubeisa and Hit were scarcely to be recognised. It is a great misfortune. We camped about half a mile outside Ramadi on the Rakkahyyeh road (which we take to-morrow) and Fattuh went off into the town to buy corn and things. I was sitting reading in my tent when suddenly I heard unusual sounds and stepping out saw my muleteers in the grip of about fifteen rascally young men who had picked a quarrel with them, thinking they were alone, I rushed into the fray, feeling rather like the lady in the Nonsense Book (only I had no stick) and soon put an end to the business, for the roughs were alarmed when they saw a European. But after they had gone Mahmud discovered that his watch was missing and Fattuh, presently returning with Government in the shape of a couple of officials, found that a revolver had been taken from one of the saddle bags. So we lodged a complaint but whether the things will be recovered or not I don't know. It is a bore, but wasn't it surprising? A Deleim sheikh who is camped near us came down to offer his assistance and we have two of his men as watchmen to-night as well as two soldiers. So we ought to be all right. Anyhow I shall be less promPt by night for I shall be asleep.

February 26th. There were no suites to last night's incident except that the Commissaire Effendi (whatever that post may be) paid me a second visit and after offering me his watch and revolver-this was merely formal—begged me not to lodge a complaint with Nazim Pasha of whom they are all mortally afraid, I gave the promise the more readily as I never had any intention of pursuing the offender-no more copy for the Daily Mail if I can help it! Moreover, the combined value of the two things did not amount to thirty shillings. We have taken a short cut to Ukhaidir via Rakkahyyeh; it saves at least a day, probbably two. Our path lies through the most pitiless desert I have ever seen, a pebbly sand like a hard sea beach, and sometimes not even hard. The pebbles are all water worn; I expect this waste was once the bottom of the sea and I can't help thinking that it had better have remained there, for it is unfit to meet the eye of the sun. The reports about water were extremely varied, there was said to be a salt well at Abu Furukh which the horses would drink and plenty of fresh water in the valley of Roda. We fortunately met a caravan from Rakkahyyeh which said there was no water at Roda (this left me indifferent, for I had made Fattuh fill a skin with Euphrates water, and when we got to Abu Furukh we found a good fresh pool in the sandy water course. I relate this tale in full so that you may realize how difficult it is to get trustworthy information, our two zaptiehs were as ignorant as ourselves. But I am now instructed; I always carry water. So we watered our horses at Abu Furukh and filled five skins for their evening provision. We came into camp among sandhills near Roda and since we have marched nine and a half hours today I think we can only have about eight before us, so we need not fear. It is impossible to get meat; I subsist entirely upon the hen, sometimes in the form of eggs and at other times in that of boiled chicken.

February 27th. We got up at six this morning and reached Rakkahyyeh at noon. Bidding farewell to our two soldiers, who had been bidden to accompany us only to Rakkahyyeh, we pushed on to Shethatha and got into camp at 4:30—a long march. While we were pitching our tents the Sheikh of the town sent us an invitation to pass the night in his house and I replied that I was exceedingly grateful, which means No thank you. There is a hot wind and the temperature was 70 at sunset, the highest we have had. We bought a wild duck of a man in Rakkahyyeh marsh, the same appeared for dinner to-night. I said: "Oh, Fattuh this duck is very good. May God conquer her women!" He replied: "how much we laboured With her! She would not cook." "She has turned out well," said I. "A double health!" said Fattuh, "May God destroy her dwelling!"

March 1st. Yesterday morning broke grey and threatening and presently it began to rain. My men went off to buy necessary provisions in the bazaar while I devoted an hour or two to the darning needle. By the time my caravan was ready it was near noonday and the rain was coming down in torrents. Ukhaidir was only three hours off and I would not stay. It took us however an intolerable four and a half hours, mostly in streaming rain. We plunged for an hour through the slippery paths of the oasis, in mortal danger of tumbling into the irrigation streams, and for the rest of the time we plodded through the Soppy desert, heavy going for man and beast. The rain had almost stopped when we reached the beloved castle, but we were wet through. I carried a letter to Sheikh Sukheil of the Zagarit, a subtribe of the Shammar, who was camped near the castle, and sent out news of my arrival to his tents. He came at once with some twenty others and found us pitching our tents in the dusk outside the castle gate. We stabled our horses in the great hall, and the Sheikh and three others stayed with us all night as watchmen. This morning we moved our tents into the inner court and put our horses into two vaulted rooms that lead out of it. The pair of Arabs who were our guides yesterday have gone back to Shethatha and we are left with the men of the Zagarit who are extremely friendly and agreeable. I have had a hard day's work correcting a few details in my old plan and beginning the measurements for an elevation. We have three men to watch over us tonight and being within the castle walls I think we are safe from attack—at least I hope so; one is never very safe at Ukhaidir. My friends of last time have left and the castle is empty of all but us. I wish they had cleaned up a little before they went away; it is very dirty.

March 3rd. I worked for eleven hours yesterday at elevations and had therefore little time to think of anything else. The Zagarit are thoroughly enjoying our visit. They sit in an expecttant circle round Fattuh's tent, waiting for any stray handful of dates or cigarettes that he may give them. They bring their needlework and establish themselves for the afternoon. i found the men of the tribe employed upon some new shirts (of which they stood in great need) when I came in for a hasty lunch. "Don't your women make your shirts?" said Fattuh. "Wallahi, our women do nothing but keep quiet" they replied. And I'm not sure that one can ask more of woman. They came down in the morning, a few of them, to look at me, but they don't interrupt me—I just go on working. This morning we rode out with the Sheikh at 6 o'clock. I went castle hunting and he rabbit hunting. His equipment was the more picturesque for he came hawk on wrist, with his greyhound at his heels. While we were saddling our mares the greyhound foraged about for stray bones; when the hawk saw her eating he was very angry and screamed to her for food, but the sheikh would not let me give him any till we came back. He was a most charming bird. Unfortunately we found no rabbits, but as far as I was concerned the expedition was quite successful, for about an hour from Ukhaidir we came to the old plaster factory, from which I make no doubt they brought the plaster for the building of the castle, all standing and quite interesting. So I planned and photographed it and we got home at ten. The quarry is said to be about an hour in the other direction. The Mudir of Shethatha came with a large party to see how I was getting on—very friendly of him. I handed him and his friends over to Fattuh who entertained them in the proper manner with coffee, After lunch the Mudir came and sat with me for a little and then they all rode away. It was a delicious day, the first fine day we have had here. I made a map of the site with a plain table and though it isn't amazingly good I feel unreasonably proud Of it. You see it iss the first. My plan of two years ago, on the other hand, is wonderfully accurate. I have corrected one or two mistakes, but they are so insignificant that really they do not matter much. However I have the satisfaction of feeling that one or two points on which I did not feel quite clear are now explained. Also I have done a lot more work at details of construction.

March 4th. We left Ukhaidir this morning. I wonder whether I shall ever see it again and whether I shall ever again come upon any building as interesting or work at anything with a keener pleasure. We are now bound for Nejef, but you are not to think that we are taking any common road to it. On the contrary, we have cut straight across the desert, for I had heard of a couple of ruins, one at least unvisited, which I longed to see, Sukheil and Nasir. We rode for three hours over intolerable sand, then climbed a low hill and got on to an immense level which was a little better going. At the top of the hill I looked back and saw Ukhaidir for the last time. An hour or so further on we came to the first ruin, Mujdeh which proved to be a very interesting round tower, built of brick and finely wooded. I expect it was a beacon and I should Date it somewhere in the 9th century. It did not take long to plan it, and I caught up the baggage horses, lunching on my mare as I went to save time. We saw standing up above the horizon the next ruin, Khan Arsham, so flat is the plain. All the desert was scattered over with the flocks and tents of the Beni Hassan and we found some of the tribe camped under the ruined khan. It was hot, the first hot day we have had, and I was feeling rather tired after eight and a half hours hard marching— but the khan brought back my energies. For it is a really Splendid ruin of I should think the 9th century, about The time of Samarra, and it opens up all kinds of interesting questions as to old roads and as to the date of Ukhaidir itself. I set about the plan without delay and worked on till the light failed and the camp fires of the Beni Hassan gleamed out red all over the plain. It is a wonderful sight the desert in the spring. And this is our last sight of it. Tomorrow we return to high roads and soldiers and the rest of it. Well, even high roads, when you must take them, have their advantages, especially in the matter of water. We brought ours from Ukhaidir to-day and the horses are so thirsty after their hot march that there is not enough for me to have a bath. A misfortune! tomorrow, please God. All the Zagarit were very smart this morning in their new shirts. They do not, however hem them up at the bottom, which makes them look rather ragged round the ankles. As we crossed the desert today the deserted encampments where the snow had fallen a month ago were marked by the corpses of sheep and donkeys. None of these Arabs had ever seen snow. The Mudir of Shethatha told me that the people there when they woke and saw it lying on the ground, thought it was flour.

March 5th. The day broke grey and threatening and I was in mortal dread of rain which would have made the heavy desert sand quite impassable. I don't know what we should have done, for we had neither oats nor water, but I suppose we should have got through somehow. However we were not put to the test, for the rain held off. I had still an hour's work to do at the Khan and we did not get off till seven. We parted with two men of the Zagarit and took as guides two men of the Beni Hassan. The map was of course a "perfect and absolute blank" and I had only a hazy idea where we were—and how long it would take us to reach the road. I guessed we must be five hours from the first khan and I was only a quarter of an hour wrong-it took us four and three quarters of an hour to reach it. Our land-mark after the first hour was the Tower of Babel. One of the Arabs sighted it first, an almost invisible speck on the North East horizon, it grew and grew till we could see it rising above a sea of palms, and finally when theY were still three hours away we saw the palm trees round Hamad which was an objective. I confessed I breathed a sigh of relief when we reached it and found ourselves upon the Nejef road. Here we parted from the Beni Hassan who had been most cheerful companions. They are better by day than by night. The men of the tents near Khan Arsham roved round our camp all last night and if my men had not kept good watch we should have found ourselves with seriously diminished possessions this morning. The road was almost as sandy and barren as the desert. Nejef and Kerbela are you know the greatest Shiah shrines in the world and the whole of Persia comes on pilgrimage to them. The inhabitants (mostly Persian) are exceedingly fanatical; no Sunni is allowed to live within the walls of Nejef, nor may he enter the great mosque where the Khalif Ali is buried. The road between the two towns is provided with immense khans for the accommodation of pilgrims and by one of them we have camped. Its name is Muzalla; there are a few houses near its walls in a dry canal, soldiers, chickens and most of the other luxuries of civilisation—at least so it seems to us who come to it fresh from difficult travel in the desert. I warned my Sunni muleteers to be on their guard and found that they had forestalled my prudence by becoming Shiahs for purposes of convenience. "My lady " said they, "we heard the men here call upon Ali as we call upon Allah, and when they asked us what we were, we said we were Shiahs come from Aleppo to pray at the grave of our Lord." Muleteers, having a wide experience of men and customs, are generally able to cope with new conditions, and since they don't mind passing as Shiahs, I do not think that my soul need feel the weight of the deception. We are all very cheerful at having got safely through the last few days. They were not easy. And do you realise that I have only been one day on a road since I left Damascus? Fattuh and I feel some satisfaftion when we look back on the events of this journey. "We are," says he, "Praise be to God, skilled in travel—God made us!"

March 6th. We were premature when we rejoiced last night over the end of our desert journey. I had determined to send my caravan into Nejef and to ride out myself to see some curious caves cut in the cliff that forms the western boundary of our old lake, now dry but still called the sea of Nejef. Accordingly I took an Arab as a guide, Sheikh Selman of the Beni Hassan. As we rode out across the desert, he said: "Do you want to go to Rakban?" "What is Rakban?" said I. "it is a castle of the first time" said he "but you cannot reach Nejef from it to-day." In a flash my mind ran out to the Lakhrnid castles which none of us has been able to trace; in another flash I had turned round, stopped my caravan, told the men to buy corn at the khan and to come out with me into the desert. They accepted the order as cheerfully as if I had invited them into a garden. The golden dome of Nejef gleamed at us invitingly on the horizon, but even more invitingly gleamed those delusive castles of Ibn Mundhir. There was a high wind and by the time we reached the cliffs of the Sea of Nejef, it had raised a dust storm. We climbed down them and crossed the floor of the sea in driving sand. Five hours from Musella we reached some water pools, bitter salt but the horses drank there. I meantime lunched hastily and grittily in the unspeakable sand. An hour further we came to a pool less bitter and I left my men to fill the water skins and rode on with the Sheikh. Presently the black mass of the castle appeared in front of us. I plunged on through the sand, reached it and found it to be nothing but a mud-built enclosure, not 50 years old. "Oh, Selman," said I "this castle is not old." "Oh lady," he said, "before my beard was grown I saw it here." It said much for the temper of my camp that when my men came in and I told them we had had all our trouble for nothing, no one was angry. So we camped-it was half past three-and I can see that the Lakhmid castles, if any of then, still exist, are not for me. But what was I to do? I could not leave a ruin unvisited.

To H. B.
BABYLoN, Friday,&10th.
I have been so busy travelling the last three days that I have put off letter writing till I got here. On the 7th We retraced our steps through the sand as far as Amm el Gharrof and then journeyed by a good firm path along the bottom of the sea to Nejef which we reached at mid-day. It is a walled town standing on the edge of the cliff of the dry seaand surrounded on the other sides by a flat plain. Above the walls rises the golden dome of Ali's tomb which is the place of pilgrimage of all the Shiah world and outside the walls the town is encompassed on two sides by the graves of the Faithful who are brought from far to be buried here. We pitched our tents on the third side and after I had lunched I went to call upon the Kaimmakam who instructed the chief of the police to take me sight-seeing. But there was little to be seen; I might not go into the mosque, nor even pass very close to the doors of it (even as it was the people eyed me angrily and one man jumped out of the crowd and tried to stop me from going neaarer the mosque); the bazaars were without interest, and presently I returned to our tents where I received a number of visitors, sheikhs of the mosque and official personages. At night, however, I came into conflift with the officials who wished to place a guard of thirty soldiers round my tents. I protested with oaths and the guard was withdrawn. The reason for these precautions was that there are nightly disturbances in the cemeteries. The Arabs bring in their dead by night and try to bury them without paying the sum of 10 s. which the town exacts as a fee for every grave; the soldiers shoot at them and they shoot back. We heard this shooting going on, together with the vibrating cry of the women, but we were far from the cemetery and no one troubled us.

Next day I sent my caravan direct to Kifil and taking an aged soldier with me (he was useless as a guide for he knew The way to nowhere) I rode out for an hour or two south to the ruins of Khawarnek which really was one of the

Lakhmid castles. Nothing remains but mounds, but I was interested to see the site. My old zaptieh, Abbas, was extremely conversational, but as he was also toothless it was difficult to understand all that he said. I rode off with a guide, and lunched on top of the Tower of Babel. You know what it was? It was an immense Babylonian temple dedicated to the seven spheres of heaven and the sun god. There remains now an enormous mound of sun-dried brick, with the ruins of a temple to the North of it and on top a great tower of burnt brick, most of which has fallen down. But that which remains stands up, like a finger pointing heavenwards, over the Babylonian plain and can be seen from Nejef to Babylon. I left Babylon with many regrets, then I rode on to Hilleh, meeting my caravan at the gates of the town. And as we rode through the bazaar an officious policeman took upon himself to seize my rifle from Fattuh, saying that the carrying of rifles is forbidden. I went at once to the head of the police and Pointed out that every Arab in the desert carries a rifle and that as we had come through the desert I had to carry arms; Moreover I had permission to do so. But he would listen to no reason so I betook myself to the Kaimmakam and found him to be an intelligent and cheerful soldier from Bagdad who Promised at once to have the rifle restored.

Sunday, 12th. Bagdad lies on the east side of the river but the bridge had been swept away by the floods, so Fattuh and I having left our horses at the khan with the baggage horses (which had come in hours before) stepped into a 'guffa' and floated down the Tigris to the Residency. The Lorimers were most friendly and gave me a large and very welcome tea. I think it possible that I may not be able to get letters again till Diatbekr, but you will hear pretty regularly from me and if I am a long time on the road I will send you a telegram through the Diarbekr Consul.

To H.B.
BAGDAD, March 18, 1911.
(This for the private ear of my family). Mr. Lorimer says that he has never met anyone who is in the confidence of the nations in the way I am, and Mr. Lorimer, I should wish you to understand, is an exceptionally able man!

To F.B.
21st March, 1911.
.... Mr. Lorimer and I steamed up the river in the launch and called on Sir William Willcocks. He is a twentieth century Don Quixote, erratic, illusive, maddening—and entirely loveable. . . . I left Bagdad early on Sunday morning. I do owe an immense debt of gratitude to the Lorimers. No two people could have been kinder. The road to Khanikin, which I am now following, is the quickest way to the Persian frontier. We had a journey of 11 hours the first day to Bakuba (it is 35 miles from Bagdad and very dull it was: absolutely flat, barren country, a waste of hard sand on which little or nothing grows. Moreover there was a strong wind). We reached Bakuba at nightfall and camped outside the village not far from the banks of the Diala river. Next morning I rejoiced to see

those banks set thick with blossoming fruit trees and when we had crossed the river, by a bridge of boats, and ridden through the town, we found the plain on the other side of it a great stretch of young spring wheat and the irrigation trenches deep in grass. So that day's ride, though the country was as flat as ever, was a great deal pleasanter. And it was only 9 hours. We camped in a green field outside the village of Shabraban—you realize that during our whole journey we have never yet seen grass covering the earth? Before us stretched the low range of the Hauran, nearer akin to real mountains than anything we have met since the Syrian snows dropped down below the lip of the Hamad. To-day we crossed the Hamrin; there were flowers in its Dry watercourses; at noon we reached the village of Kesrabad (Kizil Robat the maps call it) and rode on another 3 hours into a second stretch of low hills wherein we camped by a big guard house. It is a delicious camp, all green with grass and flowering weeds, and I have a cup full of yellow tulips on my dinner table.

Tuesday, March 28th. Most wonderful of all were the mountains of Persia, range beyond range and white with snow. So we rode gaily along the broad road scattered with tiny mud-built huts where you can drink tea and buy bread and dates and hard-boiled eggs, and towards noon we came to Khanikin which lies on either bank of the Heliwan river. The storks had arrived before us; they were nesting on every house top. Sami Pasha's relations in Bagdad had given me a letter to a Kurdish chief of high repute, Mustafa Pasha, and to his house I went. I accepted his invitation—there was nothing else to be done—and was lodged in a tiny room at the top of the house side by side with a pair of storks. Mustafa Pasha was sitting in his reception room when I arrived, with a number of friends. They most of them spoke Arabic, but between themselves they spoke Kurdish, which bored me for I wanted to hear what they were saying. We spent a couple of hours in this fashion, the Pasha transacting business from time to time and receiving innumerable letters. This is also typically oriental. Every man would appear to carry on an unlimited correspondence with the other inhabitants of his town or village, which is the more surprising as they all seem to visit each other every day. I was beginning to feel rather hungry when fortunately the Pasha called out to his servants to bring food. Some 8 of us went into the next room where we found a table spread bountifully with a variety of meats and we ate from the dishes with our fingers as best we might. It was all very good, if messy. I nearly had a 'fou rire' in the middle, when looking round upon the party with which I lunched I remembered Herbert's picture of me, so wonderfully exact was the likeness....

Towards sunset the Pasha invited me to come into the harem and I spent some time with his two wives and his other female relations. They were extremely pleasant and I don't doubt that they were glad to see me, for they never go out of the house. " We are imprisoned in the courtyard)" they said. Their furthest excursion is to take the air on the roof. When the Pasha was exiled he left them behind and they spent all those years alone in Khanikin. Next day I was talking to one of my muleteers, a Moslem, and I told him how Mustafa Pasha's ladies never went beyond the courtyard. "Wall' ahi!" said he, "that is how it should be." And then he told me that his mother (his father is also a muleteer) had never been outside their house in Aleppo until last year, when she went to Mecca with her husband. What a great adventure the Hajj muft seem to them, who see the world for the first time! . . . .

(She then rides north again with a man Mustafah Pasha had sent to them with directions to see to their safety.]

About 1 o'clock we reached Kasri Shirin which stands beautifully on the river Helwan, a straggling street climbing the hillside, the great fort of Kerim Khan standing on top. It was to Kerim Khan that I was specially recommended, and I took a short cut up to his fortress, forgetting that I ought to pass through the Persian custom house which is managed by a Belgian. You see I had become so accustomed to neglecting custom houses. I interviewed the Khans (there were a great many of them) and told them I was going to work in the ruins. They bade me very welcome and I galloped after my caravan. The ruins, I must tell you, are a couple of great Sassanian palaces and it was these that I had Come all this way to see. I found my servants camping near the first palace and a little upset because two bullets had whizzed past their ears while they were riding up to it. However, I told them that Kerim Khan would look after us, and after that I forgot all else in the excitement of working at the palace. A good many people came out to see me in the course of the afternoon and they all assured me that we should be greatly troubled by thieves if we spent the night there. I remained sceptical as to the thieves, but there was no doubt about the rifle bullets, and it is almost as annoying to be shot by accident as on purpose. The last incident of this eventful evening was the arrival of a mild-looking man with a message from Kezim Khan. He said that the Serkar had heard that I had had some dispute with the head of the Custom House and desired to know whether I was in any difficulty for he would be glad to settle it by having all the custom house people shot. It was merely a complimentary expression of good will, though so picturesquely couched. I sent back my salaams and thanks And said there was no need for extreme measures as I had made It up with the head of the Custom House. I worked for the next two days at the palaces without so much as turning round. I went out to the ruins at 6 a.m. and remained there till 9 p.m. and I never stopped for a moment drawing, measuring and photographing except when Fattuh sent or brought me lunch and tea. It is almost more than the human frame can bear when you have got to struggle through such an undertaking single-handed and I wished several times that the Sassanians had never been born. . .

I'm glad I've seen Kasri Shirin; it is one of the most beautiful places I have ever been in and I shall never forget the exquisite look of it all as I worked from dawn till dusk. . . .

Next morning we had a difficult job to tackle, the crossing of the Diala, bridgeless and in flood. We rode through the first arm of it; it was not very deep, up to a tall man's waist; but it was very swift. In the middle I heard shouting above the turmoil of the waters and looking round caught the terrified eye of my donkey who had been swept off his feet, thought his last hour was come. One of the ferrymen with us rescued him, as well as the muleteer whom he had spilt in mid stream, and they were both brought safely over. The second arm was too deep to ford. We crossed in a craft called a kelek, 19 inflated skins tied together and floored over with reeds. It looked very frail in those swift waters but it served our purpose and in 4 journeys took us and our loads over. The last kelek load was the donkey, bound hand and foot, with Fattuh sitting on his head and one of the muleteers on his tail. The horses had to swim. Two of the ferrymen stripped naked and got on to the 2 bare-backed mares—the others were driven in behind them and I watched, with my heart in my mouth, while the rushing water swept them down. May God be praised and exalted! they all clambered out safely on the other side....

[She crosses the Zab again, where she changes Zaptiehs and buys provisions.]

....We rode off with our new Zaptieh but once outside the town I found that he was heading for Mosul, whereas I wanted to go to Kalat Shergat. I protested and he declared that he knew no other road to K. Shergat. So I rode back to the mayor and with the aid of a very imperfect map (War Office!) I explained that I did not wish to go a day's journey out of my way. He came with me, good man, to the Mudir, and I restated my case. The Mudir was much perplexed; one day more or less seemed to him a small matter to fuss about. He asked to see the map, but since he looked at it upside down we were not much further forward. He got more satisfaction out of my permit from Kerkuk which was the next thing he asked to see. It stated in the clearest language that I was to do anything I liked—the officials treat me with unparalleled generosity and kindness—and that everyone was to help me to that end. I then suggested that I should take the Zaptieh and add to him a man of the town as guide. The Mudir agreed with relief and told the mayor to find a guide. The mayor and I went down into the street and there met an aged party whom the mayor clapped on the back and taking him by the hand ticked off on his fingers all the places to which he was to lead me, ending with Shergat. The old man did not seem to be the least surprised—it is a two days' journey, you must realise. He tucked up his skirts, made A suitable reply in Turkish and marched off down the street, I following. "In the peace of God! and give him two mejidehs (7s.) when you get to Shergat," said the mayor. "Upon my head!" said I, "We salute you," and rode away.

Sunday, April 2nd. My old guide is a great source of satisfaction to me. He has no visible means of support: he does any odd job that turns up and if someone happens to need a guide he is always ready to meet their wishes. "Khanum Effendi" (we talk Turkish), "I had not a penny left. And then you came. God is merciful; you came! There is no God but God!" When we began our march this morning he repeated the profession of faith uninterruptedly under his breath for an hour, and he never neglects the appointed hours for prayer, though he has to run with all his might to catch us up afterwards. I make the caravan go slowly while he prays, so that he has not to run so far. He has a wife and two small children. How they live is not stated. We had a 9 hours' march to-day and it was hot, but he walked all the way with unceasing cheerfulness except when my kind muleteers mounted him on their animal for an occasional half hour. He takes special pride in telling me the names of all the villages. "Khanum Effendi, that so-and-so—write, write!" So I get out my map and put it in.

Monday, April 3rd. Safely arrived at Kalat Shergat where Dr. Andrae and his colleagues have given me a very warm reception.

To F.B.
APril 14,1911.

I spent three enchanting days at K. Shergat and would gladly have stayed longer. Three of the four who were there two years ago I found this year and two others whom I had not seen before. One of them, Herr Preusser, had visited two of my Tur Abdin churches and is publishing them, so we had a great time comparing plans. But chiefly I found this year, as I found two years ago, great profit from endless talks with Dr. Andrae. His knowledge of Mesopotamian problems is so great and his views so brilliant and comprehensive. We went over the whole ground again with such additional matters as I had brought from Kasri Shirin, and as he had derived from two more years of digging. He put everything at my disposal, photographs and unpublished plans, and his own unpublished ideas. I don't think that many people are so generous. Also they taught me to photograph by flashlight- provided me with the material for doing so, which I shall find very useful in some of my pitch-dark churches. And we went over the last two years' work stone by stone and discussed it in all its bearings. K. Shergat was looking its best. I love it better than any ruined site in the world. The only drawback of my visit was that I was so reluctant to go away, and I carried a heavy heart over the high desert to Hatra—which is a long way! But one can't be heavYhearted at Hatra; it is too wonderfully interesting. It was (perhaps you know?) the capital city of the Parthian kings about whom we know so little. The Parthians were an eclectic folk; their arts sprang up on ground that had already been strongly Hellenised by the Alexandrids; and they learnt, no doubt, from the Romans, with whom they were always at war. They worked out these new ideas upon old oriental foundations, and the palace at Hatra is the one building left out of all their cities where you can see the results at which they arrived, for it stands to this day. We arrived late on a gray and stormy afternoon and were received with acclamations by the Turkish army. I shall write a long article for some leading journal when I get home, and call it "Pacification of the Desert," for it should be known how well and wisely the Turks are handling matters here.

After I had done my work we paraded the army—cavalry, infantry, and artillery, and I photographed them all, to their great satisfaction and to mine. The drawback of Hatra is The water; it's all salt. The town stands about half an hour from the river Tharthar, which is so bitter salt that no one drinks it but the Arabs: we drank from wells, but they were exceedingly nasty. When I left I was escorted for a couple of hours by half-a-dozen officers, who galloped with me across the beautiful grass plains; we drew up on a mound and waited for the caravan, and then we took a tender farewell of one another, and I went on more soberly with my own men. We followed the Tharthar valley and fortunately in an hour or two came to a rainwater pool, at which we filled a skin. It was even more horrid than the Hatra salt water, sticky, greasy standing water, tasting strongly of decayed grass. But we had nothing else. There were Arab camps and flocks all along the shallow valley and we camped at evening near some of these. There was abundant grass, but we had no fresh water for the horses, and all but my mare refused to drink the Tharthar water. I could not wonder, for it tasted like the sea. We had a difficult journey next day. Fattuh was verY ill and we had a march of nearly 11 hours which we could not shorten because there was no fresh water. We passed a rain pool in the morning, watered our horses and took a skinful with us, but the day was hot and the men thirsty, and by five o'clock there was scarcely any left. At last we saw Arab tents ahead and knew that there must be drinkable water near at hand. We put up our tents near them, boiled water and made hot compresses for Fattuh and forced him to lie down while the muleteers made shift to cook some sort of dinner. The Arabs were very sympathetic and brought us some curds and milk, but the water they had was next to undrinkable, drawn from standing rain pools. We joined company with a body of the Shammar who Were on their way northwards from Riza Bey's gathering of the clan at Hatra. They were moving camp when I came up to them and the whole world was alive with their camels. Now the Shammar are Beda; only the Shammar and the Anazeh are real Bedawin, the others are just Arabs. Akh-el bair we call the Beda, the People of the Camel. They never cultivate the soil or stay more than a night or two in one place, but wander ceaselessly over the inner desert. It was delightful to see their women and children travelling in the camel howdahs and their men carrying the long spears that are planted before the tent door.

Fattuh having called in a native doftor who bled him copiously he rather surprisingly recovered. . . .

We got back to our tents just as a very heavy shower of rain fell and congratulated ourselves on having escaped the worst of it, when suddenly a hailstorm battered on to my tent roof. I began hastily to fasten the door and before you could wink a hurricane of wind swept down upon us and every tent was flat. My books and papers went flying out into the universe, Fattuh and Abud flying after them, while I, half blinded with wind and hail, strapped up our open boxes. It only lasted for a minute or two, but we were all wet through, We gathered ourselves together and began putting up the tents again. The casualties were extraordinarily small: a tent pole, an eyeglass and a comb, and a good many odds and ends of papers—nothing very important. The two muleteers came running down from the town where they (fortunately for themselves!) had been buying corn, the tents were got up again, the sun came out and we changed and spread out our wet things to dry. It was an extremely disagreeable experience, but what we should have done if it had happened at night, I can't think! You may imagine how we lay awake and listened to every gust of wind!

Monday, April 17. There is a charming passage in Sir Edward Grey's book on flyfishing in which he praises the various moods of Nature. "Rain," says he, "is delightful," and I remember when I read it, thinking of warm May rain on our opening beech leaves at home and thoroughly agreeing with him. But one begins to feel rather differently about it when one is camping in pitiless torrents. It rained like the devil on Saturday night and like ten thousand devils on Sunday. The wind howled through my tent ropes till it sounded like a hurricane on board ship and the rain thundered against the canvas. I thought my tent would go down more than once, but my excellent servants kept the pegs firm by piling stones on to them. The storks were less fortunate: their house was blown away . . . ..

[She then goes on by Nisibin to Mardin, and so into the mountainous region of the Tur Abdin, exploring ruins, planning, photographing, over the rocky ridges of the Tur Abdin across the valley and down into a rocky gorge.]

. . . .And at the foot of the cliff rolled the Tigris, in full flood, between the broken piers of a huge stone bridge. The first thing we learned was that there could be no crossing of the Tigris till it had run down. The ferry boat is a raft on skins, on which you can't put horses and neither raft nor the horses could cross in that flood. We'were delayed for two days, but they were not wasted days . . . ..

[More photographing of inscriptions in fifteenth century mosques and minarets.]

I managed to piece together a very pretty piece of Arab History. . . ..

On the afternoon of the second day the river had dropped so far that I gave the order to cross. The landing place on the opposite side was nearly a quarter of a mile below the bridge—it looked a very long way off and the rush of the water against the piers of that bridge was anything but encouraging. So the horses thought, for when we drove them into the water they struggled about in the deep backwater by the bridge and eventually returned to us. Then we devised another scheme. We tied two of them to the raft, which was loaded with the pack saddles, and drove the rest in again They, seeing the raft swirling down the stream, and two of their companions with it, swam after it, all but 2 who again were swept back to our bank. These 2 we tied to the raft on its final journey, when I also crossed, and so we all got over in safety—but I shall long remember the rather too exhilarating sensations of that ferrying, the raft darting down the flood and the two horses panting and groaning in the water beside it.. . .

[After 12 hours' ride she reaches Mayafarkin where she makes a day's halt.]

I found, first, the most splendid ruined mosque I have ever seen, secondly, the remains of a huge basilica of the fifth century and thirdly, a great domed church of the sixth or seventh century. I have had two days' hard work at these three. I feel very triumphant over them. They have not been published, and no one knew any more than I did when I arrived, what a wealth of material there was at Mayafarkin. Moreover, the mosque will never be done again as I have done it, for they are busy rebuilding it and the old work will disappear under the new, and under whitewash and other abominations. I felt as if I was receiving its dying will and testament as I worked at it, and I only hope I have written down every word. We have suddenly jumped into summer. The temperature is 70 in the shade, the trees have all rushed into full leaf, and the corn stands high in the fields. The ruined bastions of Mayafarkin, walls, towers of unrivalled Arab masonry rise out of all this sea of green; the storks nest in every tower and the world is full of the contented clapping of their beaks. The Kaimmakam's wife sent a special message asking me to visit her, and when I arrived she greeted me, rather disconcertingly, with "Addio!" It was the prelude to a very voluble conversation in Turkish, of which I picked up what I could, and was much amused. A native Protestant pastor gave me great help in reading the inscriptions. He had learned a little English at Mardin, so from time to time I talked English laboriously. G.B.-"Is it more cold here or at Mardin?" Pastor.-"Yes." It then became very difficult to take up the thread of the dialogue.

Saturday, May 6th. When the 1st of May came I had a great 'sehnsucht' for the daffodils and the opening beech leaves at Rounton—it's not all beer and skittles travelling, you know. The splendid finds at Mayafarkin consoled me a little, but I still have an overpowering desire to see my family. However the work here must be done first—one does not pledge oneself to ancient buildings for nothing. I feel out here more like the Heathen than ever, for the passion for stocks and stones becomes a positive worship. . . . Poor Maurice! his collar bone is really too brittle. I have the most delicious post-card from Pauline—angel!

To F. B.
Sunday, May 14, 1911.

I left Diarbekr on Thursday and had 2 long days' journey to Wirausheber. Wirausheber was the headquarters of Ibrahim Pasha the famous Kurd who was in league with Abdul Hamid. Before I left Wirausheber I called on Ibrahim Pasha's widow—or one of his widows—Khanza Khatun, a very remarkable woman. She was renowned for her beauty-though she is now old, you can see the traces of it in the fine shape of the face and in the splendid carriage of the head. Her deep-set eyes have some of the old fire in them and as she came out to greet me she looked like "one who wins and not like one who loses." We sat together on a carpet outside the house by the edge of a spring, among willow trees: it was early morning, the women were cleaning the sour curds in skins hung from the willow branches. The men of her household stood back while we discussed her position, and the possibility of the sons' return. She manages all the estates, which are still very large, during their absence. She wore a long European man's coat over her dress, and an Arab cloak over that; on her head the male keffiyeh, silk kerchief, bound over the head with a thick roll of black silk. I looked back, after I had bidden her farewell and mounted. She stood under the willow trees with shrouded head and gazed after me with her deep-set eyes—a very striking figure. "Thijah!" murmured Fattuh, as we rode away, "She is a man!" I must relate to you another silly talk with Fattuh. He made for me in Diarbekr some very good little mutton sausages. "Oh, Fattuh," said I, thinking to improve my Arabic, "What is the name of these?" "Effendim," said Fattuh, "these? Their name is sossigio."

URFA,

Thursday 18. We had two long and rather difficult days from Ras al Ain to Harran. We could get no corn at Ras al Ain and therefore had to do the journey on grass, which meant stopping 2 hours in the middle of the day to let the horses feed-

and there was really nothing for them to feed on. Then there was also trouble about a guide; my soldiers knew nothing of the desert way and I set out from Rasal Ain with only a compass to direct me, and a map. But the good old head of the Circassians, Hassan Bey, sent a boy after me and it was as well he did, for though we should probably have found a way through, the water was scanty in the extreme and not easy to find. The first day we met no people and saw only the very smallest traces of former habitation. The second day we passed a very interesting fortress. Lack of food obliged us to push on. Then we came to a large ruined town, quite deserted and full of dead sheep. There was a large encampment of Arabs not far from it and near there we stopped and pastured our horses. Soon afterwards we reached the Crest of the high ground and saw the great mound of Harran before us, two or three hours away in the fertile plain. We got into camp at 7 p.m. having started that morning soon after 5 a.m. It is said to be the place where Abraham met Rebecca, at any rate, it was out of this origin that the Jewish tribes migrated to Canaan and the huge village mouns scattered over the plain are an indication of its early importance. I had come there to see the ruins of a very splendid mosque of the early Abbassid period. We camped in the great court and I spent nearly 3 hours next morning photographing it stone by stone. It was wonderfully interesting. There is no town now, only a collection of mud-built huts inhabited by half-settled Arabs, and the mound with an immense ruin field round it, all enclosed by the remains of a fine stone wall. There was a very ancient moon cult here, as old as Abraham probably; the Emperor Julian came to propitiate the goddess before he set out on his fatal campaign. So we rode into Urfa over the fertile plain, and were not sorry for once to have done with desert and with marches 12 hours long. The town lies on the lower slopes of the hills and I camped above it in a terraced garden which was once a café but has fallen into disuse, fortunately for us. I have spent the day here: it's a beautiful place and like Harran and Hierapolis it goes back into the dimmest mists of Oriental history, of which it preserves the memory in the sacred pool stocked with unmolested fish which may not be caught.

It has become really hot and this morning we set out before sunrise, while it was still cool. But we did not avoid heat and it is still at 6 p.m. 87 in the shade. I do not mind it,bUt it makes the horses languid. Birejik is one of the most famous of the Euphrates passages. Here Crassus passed over the river to his defeat at Harran: the eagles of the 5th Legion turned backwards from the bridge of boats, but he would not heed the omen. To-morrow I go to Carchemish in the hope of finding Mr. Hogarth there.

Just after I had written to you the Kaimmakam came over to call on me and told me that Mr. Hogarth had left but that Mr. Thompson was still at Carchemish. Accordingly I went there-it was Only 5 hours' ride—and found Mr. Thompson and a Young man called Lawrence (he is going to make a traveller) who had for some time been expecting that I would appear. They showed me their diggings and their finds and I spent a pleasant day with them.

[This is Gertrude's first meeting with T. E. Lawrence. She then returns to Aleppo and is back in England in June.]

CHAPTER XIII
1913-1914

JOURNEY TO HAYIL

To H. B.
LONDON, October 28th, 1913

Last night I went to a delightful party at the Glenconners' and just before I arrived (as usual) 4 suffragettes set on Asquith and seized hold of him. Whereupon Alec Laurence in fury seized two of them twisted their arms until they shrieked. Then one of them bit him in the hand till he bled. And when he told me the tale he was steeped in his own gore. I had a great triumph on Monday. I got Edwin Montagu to lunch to meet Major O'Connor and the latter talked for one and a half hours of all the frontier questions—admirably E.M. sat and listened For one and a half hours and then summed up the whole question with complete comprehension. I was enchanted. He is not only able, E.M., he is the real thing—he's a statesman. . . .

[On November 13th she starts for the East via Marseilles.]

To F.B
ALEXANDRIA, November 20, 1913.

Alexandria is not much of a place but it makes me feel as if I were dropping back into the East. Oh my East! My cab driver yesterday showed all the solicitude of one's oriental servants, took me for a drive along a very smelly canal because I was tired of looking at catacombs and insisted on my drinking a cup of coffee under the trees to fortify me before I went to the museum! It did fortify me, or else he did.

To F.B.
DAMASCUS, November 27th, 1913.

Yesterday I sent round to Muhammad al Bassam to tell him I was here. . . . he came to see me at once and spent half the morning with me. He is my great support in all plans and arrangements. It looks as though I have fallen on an exceedingly lucky moment, everyone is at peace. Tribes who have been at war for generations have come to terms and the desert is almost preternaturally quiet. Bassan knows Of some good desert camels, riding camels, going cheap it Damascus, an almost incredible stroke of good luck as I thought I should have to transport myself somewhere into the wilds and haggle for camels there. In short I scarcely like to trust to all this good fortune but I hope it will turn out to be true. I am not quite certain yet whether I shall go to the Druzes or the Anazeh first. I shall have no difficulty in going to either but there may be some little complication in passing from one to another; nothing however that cannot be overcome. Muhammad says that it is perfectly easy to go to Nejd this year. If I found it so I should certainly go. I will let you know anyhow from Madeba— look for it on the map east of the north end of the Dead Sea. Go on writing here and I will keep in touch with you as long as possible.

Now Fattuh and I must go and talk about camels. It is heavenly weather.

To H.B.
DAMASCUS November 29th, 1913.

I sent you to-day a telegram which I fear will rather surprise you asking you to make the National Bank telegraph 400 pounds to my credit through the Ottoman Bank London to the Ottoman Bank here. I telegraphed to you because I did not know whether if I telegraphed straight to the National Bank they would think the request sufficient without receiving it in writing, but I hasten to explain to you (which I could not do in the telegram) that this is not a gift for which I am asking. I wish to borrow the money from the N. Bank The position is this: As far as I can make out and I have had a good deal of information from many sides, there never was a year more favourable for a journey into Arabia than this. The desert is absolutely tranquil and there should be no difficulty whatever in getting to Hayil, that is Ibn al Rashid's capital and even much further. Moreover I have got to-day exactly the right man as a guide. He was with Mr. Carruthers 3 years ago. I heard of him with the highest praise from him. To-day he turned up at Bassams and Bassam at once told me that I could not have one who is better acquainted than he with all the Arab tribes. To have got him is a piece of extraordinary good luck. He is the man of all others whom I should have chosen. So much for the chances of success in this business. As for the expenses, you see this time I have to begin by buying everything I shall need here. As far as I can make out we shall need 17 camels (we have bought one or two already) and they cost an average Of 13 pounds a piece including their gear. Bassam says I must reckon to spend 50 pounds on food to take with us, 50 more for presents such as cloaks, keffeyehs for the head, cotton cloth, etc. It is obvious that this is wise advice because the things are wortth much more there than they are here and a kerchief which costs only 5 shillings here is a respectable present in the desert. That comes altogether to 321 pounds. Bassan says I ought to take 80 with me and to give 200 to the Nejd merchant who lives here in return for a letter of credit which will permit me to draw the sum in Hayil. I think both these sums are reckoned very liberally but I don't like to provide myself with less money lest when I get into the heart of Arabia (Inshallah) I should not be able to do anything for want of funds. You will see that I have now come to a total of 601. I could not possibly explain all this in my telegram so I attempted to explain nothing but I hope you will not say No. It is unlikely that you will because you are such a beloved father that you never say No to the most outrageous demands. Perhaps it is a pity that you don't. I am practically using all my next year's income for this journey, but if I sit very quiet and write the book of it the year after I don't see Why I shouldn't be able to pay it all back. And the book ought to be worth something if I really get to Nejd and beyond. On the whole I hope you will think it is worth it since the conditions are so good. I shall try to keep in some sort of touch with you. At the end of the first 3 or 4 weeks I shall have no difficulty in sending you letters by the Hadj railway, and I shall make arrangements to have my letters sent to me from here. After that I fear I shall not be able to hear from you though I shall try to get one lot of letters at Hayil. I think there is no doubt I shall be able to get news out to you, It ought to take about a month from my station near the Hadj railway to Hayil that is to say you will hear from me after the lapse of some 2 to 2 and a half months. And if I go further South I will try to send out news from somewhere on the Persian Gulf. Anyway wherever I can possibly find a messenger I will send a letter. I must tell you that there have been very good autumn rains so that we ought to find plenty of surface water and also grass.

I feel much better after four days here and I am beginning to drop into the East.

One thing more I must tell you. I have arranged with Mr. Cumberbatch that if I reach anywhere where I can I will telegraph to him and he will communicate with you. But of course there is no such place till I get to the coast somewhere. Also I shall write to him from here and tell him exactly what I intend to do and let him know that if at any time you or he want information about me the best person from whom to get it is Bassam. M.C. could communicate with him privately. He has all the news of the desert, he knows exactlY what I am doing and he is sure to know more or less where I am. But don't go to him with questions unless news of Me is greatly overdue.

Dearest beloved Father don't think me very mad or very unreasonable and remember always that I love you more than words can say, you and Mother.

You know things are working out much better than I expected they would but don't talk about Nejd to outsiders in case it does not come off.

To F. B.
DAMASCUS, December 5th, 1913.

I don't think I shall be off till next Friday, 12th, so that puts all the dates I gave Father a week later. There are such a lot of things to buy and arrangements to make. Meantime I spend my days quite pleasantly. To-day was fine and I worked with my theodolite all the morning on the roof and went for a walk in the afternoon. We walked up on to a hillside and climbed to a top of an eminence whence we had a glorious view over Damascus and its gardens, still brown and gold with autumn leaves and then straight into the desert where I am going. I saw the little volcanic hills to the S.E. where I shall make the first stages of my journey and I wished I were already among them.

I have called on a good many of my Mohammedan friends and have been received with open arms. They are all extremely kind and cordial. There are one or two I still want to see but the mud has made visiting difficult except in houses near at hand. I have got much fatter than when I came, idleness partly, I suppose, and partly an abundant diet of sour curds which is without doubt the best food in the world.

I wonder what you are doing and where you are—it is difficult to think of you making preparations for Xmas. My love to Maurice.

To F.B.
DAMASCUS, December 12., 1913.

My camels should have got off to-day but we were delayed by a tiresome contretemps. Fattuh has an attack of malaria and I shall be obliged to wait another day or two. . . . I dined in the native bazaar quarter the Maidan with my old guide Mohamed al Mardwi. An enormous party was assembled to meet me including the agent of Ibn al Rashid. The latter was a curious figure, young very tall and slight, wrapped in a gold embroidered cloak and his head covered with an immense gold bound camel's hair robe which shadowed his crafty narrow face. He leant back among his cushions and scarcelY lifted his eyes, talking in a soft slow voice the purest classical Arabic, but after a bit roused himself and told marvellous tales of hidden treasure and ancient wealth and mysterious writings in central Arabia of which you may believe as much as you please. The men on either side of me murmured from time to time "Ya Satif! Ya manjud," Oh Beneficent, oh Ever Present! as they listened to this strange lore. Finally we ate together that bread and salt might be between us and then-why then we all came back together on the electric tram!

To F.B.
December 15th, 1913.

A misfortune has befallen us. Fattuh fell sick a week ago and we fear it is typhoid. Fortunately his wife is here. I have put off my departure from day to day and now I'm going-my camels left to-day and I sleep with the Mackinnons and start to-morrow. I still hope that in three weeks or so when I near the railway F. may be able to join me and he of course never doubts for a moment that he is coming. But it is a horrible bore. I've got a boy to take his place—take his place indeed! He seems bright and quick, I like him and I do not doubt that after a day or two my camp will fall intO order. . . .

To F.B.
20th December, 1913.

I got off safely on the 16th from the kind Mackinnons, drove out a couple of hours, picked up my camels, loaded water and went off into the desert. We camped early about an hour or more S. of Dumeir and it was as well we did so, for the first night in camp always means a good deal of sorting out, and when you have no single man with you who has ever travelled with a European you can guess what it Is like. I had to show them everything, and find everything myself, Fattuh not being there, who had packed all. They did not even know how my English tents went up, nor how to boil an egg. But they are all most anxious to please me and most willing to learn, and by dint of patience and timely instruction I'am getting things into shape. It rained and blew the night of the 16th and all the day of the 17th, impossible to travel if the devil had been behind us (and I was a little afraid that the Damascean authorities might look for us) so there we sat and shivered and overhauled our packs. I ve learnt by now to bear rainy days in camp when you are never for one moment warm or dry and the hours seem endless. We sent to Dumeir for firewood for the men, chopped straw for the camels and cotton cloth for me, with which I sat at my needle and made bags for all our provisions. It is long since I have sewed so diligently. Next day was fine, but what with wet tents and unaccustomed men we took 2 and a half hours to break camp—I despaired, but kept silence until later, and the second morning we were under one and a half hours from the time I woke till the time we marched and that is as good as anybody can expect. I have good servants, you see, and besides I know the job and they soon find that out. We struggled on the 18th for an hour through the mud and irrigation canals of the Dumeir husbandry—a horrible business with the camels slipping and falling. At last we were out in the open desert, with the rising ground of the stony volcanic country, the region of Tells, under our feet, and mud forgotten. We marched through it all yesterday and all to-day, a barren region Of volcanic stones and tells. We have sighted but one camp of Arabs in all our Way. A man rode out from it to see who we were and we found them to be one of the half-cultivator tribes from near Damascus. For water we have an occasional rain pool, very muddy, but I still have drinking water with me from Damascus, and bread and meat and eggs and butter, so that hardships have not yet begun. It was bitter cold last night; the temperature fell to 28 and I woke several times shivering. When we set off to-day in a dense mistt the sparse grass and shrubs were all white with frost and we ourselves blue with it. But one takes no harm. The mist did not lift till near mid-day, which made mapping most tedious as I could take no long bearings, but we came into camp early in the afternoon (having started early) in glorious sunshine and I am now writing in the long afterglow of a cloudless sunset. Already I have dropped back into the desert as if it were my own place; silence and solitude fall round you like an impenetrable veil; there is no reality but the long hours of riding, shivering in the morning and drowsy in the afternoon, the bustle of getting into camp, the talk round Muhammad's coffee fire after dinner profounder sleep than civilization contrives, and then the road again. And as usual one feels as secure and confident in this lawless country as one does in one's own village. We have a Rafiq, a comrade of the Ghiyatah with us—we fetched him from Dumeir to stand surety for us if we met his tribe. We ought by rights to have a man of the Beni Hassan, with whom our Ghjyatah is useless since they are deadly foes and if we come across the B. Hassan we will take one along. Good, please God! the earth is ours and theirs and I do not think we shall trouble one another. Such good mushrooms grow here. I have them fried for dinner.

December 7th, JEBEL SAIS. We have reached our first goal and a very curious place it is, but I will begin at the beginning. It was horribly cold last night. The temperature dropped to 19 and it was impossible to keep warm in bed. N.B.-I am not cut out for Arctic Exploration, it is clear. Anyhow I kept waking up to shiver. The men's big tent was frozen hard and they had to light fires under it to unfreeze the canvas, otherwise it would have torn when they packed it. But the sun rose gloriously, clearing away the mists, just as we marched, and in half an hour we were all warm. We sighted J. Sais at 8 and reached it at 12, marching over almost flat ground covered with volcanic stones—a desolate country which must be a furnace in summer. But the rains have filled all the water pools and the grass and shrubs are growing. On our way Muhammad saw two men in the distance and was much perturbed, but they were probably only, shepherds of the Saiyadand—anyway I did not bother about them. I have got men enough with me who will recognise or be recognized by all these tribes. J. Sais is a big and very perfect volcano with a sort of deep moat round the W. and S.sides, ending to the S.E. in a lake, now full of water. I took some photographs while the men pitched camp and then climbed with my Ghiyatah guide to the lip of the volcano to take bearings. "Oh! Hammad," said I, as we breasted the stony slope, "who can have lived in this strange place?" "By God," "we would learn from you. But, indeed, oh lady, there is no guide to truth but God." It was a wonderful view from the top—desert, desert and desert; wide stretches of yellow earth, great shining water pools, and miles and miles of stones. We scanned the whole world for Arab tents, but saw none anywhere. With that I ran down the hill and had just time to plan all the ruins before sunset. There remains a little photography and taking of angles for to-morrow morning. I have not for a long time enjoyed anything so much as this afternoon's work. Content reigns in my camp and all goes smoothly.

December 22nd. A preposterous and provoking episode has delayed us today. We had marched about 2 hours when we sighted camels and the smoke of tents. We took them to be (as indeed they were) Arabs of the Mountain, the Jebel Druze, with flocks. I told you that we tried in Dumeir to get one of the Jebel Druze Arabs as a companion and failed—and we suffered for it. Presently a horseman came galloping over the plain, shooting as he came, into the air only. He wheeled round us, shouting that we were foes, that we should not approach with weapons, and then while he aimed his rifle at me or other of us Muhammad and Ali tried to pacify him, but in vain. He demanded of Ali his rifle and fur cloak, which were thrown to him, and by this time a dozen or more men had come galloping or running up, some shooting, all shouting, half dressed—one of them had neglected to put on any clothes at all—with matted black locks falling about their faces. They shrieked and leapt at us like men insane. One of them seized Muhammad's camel and drew the sword which hangs behind his saddle with which he danced round us, slashing the air and hitting my camel on the neck to make her kneel. Next they proceeded to strip My men Of their revolvers, cartridge belts and cloaks. My camel got Ub again and as there was nothing to be done but to sit quiet and watch events that's what I did. Things ooked rather black, but they took a turn for the better when my camel herd, a negro, was recognised by our assailants, and in a minute or two some sheikhs came up, knew Ali and Muhammad, and greeted us with friendship. Our possessions were returned and we rode on together in quiet and serenity. But to avoid the occurrence of such events, or worse, we are to take with us a man from their tents, and to that end we have been obliged to camp near them that a suitable companion may be found. The sheikhs have drunk coffee with me, enjoyed a long conversation with all of us and been so good as to accept my backsheesh in token of our gratitude in being rescued from the hands of the shepherds. And they have given us a comprehensive letter to all the Arabs of the Mountain. Good, please God, but I feel not a little impatient at the delay.

December 23rd. It rained hard till 8 o'clock this morning and the desert turned into paste. But it dries quickly and by 10 we were off, at the bidding of my impatience. All went well, however. We had no more rain though it remained cold and grey. We have with us to guard us against the Arabs of the Mountain the oldest old man you could wish to see. He crouches upon a camel by day and over the camp fire by night. He seldom speaks and I can scarcely think that any one would respect a party introduced by so lifeless and ragged a guarantor. We are camped in a strange bleak place under a gloomy volcanic hill.

Winter travel has its trials. We got off an hour before dawn in a sharp frost. No sooner had the sun risen than a thick mist enveloped the world and hung over it till 10:30 faith, but it was cold! far too cold to ride so I walked for some four hours, the mist freezing into a thick hoar frost on my clothes. We had passed out of the black hills before sunrise and we walked on and on over an absolutely level plain with the white walls of the fog enclosing us. It was not Unpleasant—though I wonder why? One turns into nothing but an animal under these conditions, satisfied with keeping warm by exercise and going on unwearied and eating when one is hungry. But I was glad when the sun came out and we could see our way again. I got bearings back to the hills of our camp so that my map will not suffer. This business of mapmaking, far from being a trouble, is a great amusement, and alleviation in the long hours of riding and walking. The light came upon us just as we entered a wide and shallow valley up which we shall march until we reach our goal—the fort of Burqa which has been heard of but never seen.

BURQA,
December 24. We sighted the keep of the fort at 10 this morning and reached it at 1 o'clock—I with an excitement scarcely to be kept in bounds. Burqa has proved most interesting. There is a good Kufic inscription which I have deciphered—it is dated in the year 81 A.H. and as inscriptions of the first century A.H. are very rare, it is exceptionally important..

December 25. What paart of Xmas Day have you been spending? I have thought of you all unwrapping presents in the Common Room and playing with the children. But you were certainly not breakfasting out of doors in a temperature of 28, which was what I was doing at 7 a.m. It was so cold that I could not take rubbings of my inscriptions till late in the morning, because it was impossible to keep the water liquid, I have worked hard all day, planned, photographed, taken a latitude. Late in the afternoon I discovered that the boulders were covered with Safaitic inscriptions and I copied them till night fell. They are pre-Muhammadan, the rude inscriptions of nomad tribes who inhabited these deserts and wrote their names upon the stones in a script peculiar to this region. So you can picture the history of Burqa—the Byzantine outpost with Safaitic tribes camping round it; the Muhammadan garrison of the

7th century; then a gentleman who passed along in the 8th century of the Hejira and wrote his name and the date upon the walls; then the Bedouin laying their dead in the courtyard of the fort (it is full of graves) and scratching their tribe-marks on the stones; and lastly we to read the meagre tale. Well, I have had a Profitable day. I have not had time to think whether it has been merry. Bless you all.

December 26. I should like to mention that it was 25 when I breakfasted this morning. The wonder is that one minds it so little. I walk for an hour or two every morning so as to unfreeze after the painful process of getting up and packing before dawn. We have been doing to-day the very thing I dreamt of doing. We have been following an ancient road, not metalled, but marked all the way by Safaitic inscriptions.

Heaven be praised, it is 10 degrees warmer to-night than it was last night. What with sun and frost I am burnt out of all knowledge and, as you may imagine, feel like the immortal gods for health. Nor do I believe that they sleep half so well as I, nor eat so much.

December 27th. I copied inscriptions for another two hours this morning and then we broke up camp and set off. But the devil took possession of the old old man who is my rafiq and he set off independently or went to sleep somewhere or I don't know what. Anyhow after half-an-hour's searching we discovered he was not with us, and having spent an hour in looking for him, he turned up from quite a different direction, and we all cursed him, poor old thing, for wasting our time and energies. It was a horrid march to-day in the teeth of a wind and over endless stones with no apparent path through them. Heaven send us better ground to-morrow.

December 28th. The last prayer was not answered. We marched oVer stones all day, and marched far, being waterless. At 4 in the afternoon we reached a khabra nearly dry and after some time we espied the smoke of Arab tents far off and camped hastily, hoping that they would not notice us. At night we watched their distant fires flickering and sinking. No doubt they watched ours for we had not been more than a couple of hours on our way to-day before we heard sounds which meant our neighbours were stirring. We left Abu Ali, my old old man—on top of a stony ridge to tackle them and ourselves descended into low ground and halted. Presently a horseman topped the ridge and greeted us with the customary rifle shot, but Abu Ali met him and found him to be of his kin. So all was well. Meantime we had lighted a fire, round which we sat with the newcomer, gave him food and tobacco and exchanged with him information as to the movements of tribes. He told us we should meet the Serdiyyeh moving camp and half an hour later we did meet them and went through the usual formulae. It happened to be the chief Sheikh, Ghalib, whose people we had met, and he joined us and insisted on our camping with him that night. There was no help for it since we shall have to take a rafiq from him to guarantee us with his tribe further on. So I have spent the afternoon sitting with him, sitting with the women, drinking coffee, doctoring a man with a horribly bad foot—my only remedy was boric ointment which can work neither harm nor good, but if I had said I could do nothing they would not have believed me. And now I am going to dine with Ghalib, who has killed a sheep for us. In return for which I shall give him a cloak. The new moon is just setting in a wonderful clear sky, the fires are all alight in the Arab tents; it's all very lovely and primeval, but I prefer a solitary camp.

December 31st. Yesterday we rode all day over stones. At noon we reached a Roman outpost, a little fort on a hill top. I sent my camels on, and keeping two men with me planned and photographed the place. We got into camp late, but since we were without the baggage camels we trotted our camels wherever the ground permitted. It was a nice camp by some springs-the joy of clean water! This morning we moved into Qasr Azraq, which stands among palm trees, surrounded by a multitude of springs. I had ridden on with one man, whom I left with my camels while I went into the castle alone. It is inhabited by Arabs, but in the front room I found a Druze who greeted me with the utmost cordiality and gave me coffee I then began to plan the castle when immediately I was surrounded by Arabs all shouting at the top of their voices that if I wrote a line they would burn my book. I took them all down to my Agent, Ali, the postman of 3 years ago (they had shut the great stone gate of the castle to keep me prisoner the better while they haggled with me). We sat down under the palm trees and I smoked and left Ali to explain, with the result that before long they declared themselves to be entirely at my service. I've worked at this place all day and shall have another day at it to-morrow. I really don't know if it was worth the trouble, but I dislike leaving things undone in far away places. I rather think I have got one new Greek inscription. I must take a rubbing of it to-morrow and see what can be made of it. So the year ends.

January 2, 1914. They were all outlaws and outcasts at Azraq and, as Ali observed, as we rode away this morning "The world would be more restful if they were all dead."

It was really warm to-day for the first time. I dined after sunset with my tent all open. But there seems to have been no rain here and the question of water may present difficulties. We can carry—and are carrying to-day—water for 4 nights, if we are careful with it—no baths and very little washing, I fear! After dinner I sit for an hour or so at the men's camp fire and they tell tales of raiding and of desert journeying. The fire lights us as we sit in a circle and one after another takes up his story. The negro camel herd, if he is not asleeP in a corner (for he takes the first watch at night), looks Over the shoulders of us gentry with his face one gleaming smile as the detailed adventures grow more and mor blood curdling. When I get up to go they all rise and send me away with a blessing. I often look round the circle and think how closely I resemble Herbert's picture of me.

JanuarY 5 th. I have had 3 days of very hard work at Kharaneh, another of the Umayyad pleasure palaces. Nothing so interesting has come into my way since Ukhaidir. It is not my discovery, but I have done much more at it than anyone else; in fact, it has not been studied at all as yet. Besides the wonderful architectural details I have got heaps of Kufic graffites which I hope Moritz will be able to study from my copies and photographs. One at least is dated A.H. 92. The difficulty here has been water, as we feared. My men have scoured the country round, but 4 waterskins was all the neighbourhood offered. But with what we brought with us we had enough for three nights here which was all I wanted and we still have to-morrow's supply in case we come across none on our march. Lack of water has unfortunately frustrated my admirable plan of sending in to Madeba while I worked here. As we don't know when the next supply will be found we could arrange no rendezvous. It means, too, no washing and I begin to feel that I shall never be clean again. However Karaneh is worth it all—delays and dirt and everything. I have worked these days from 6:30 a.m. till 5 p.m. with an hour off for lunch at 11. Darkness at either end prevented longer hours. But it has been glorious. So now we march west, towards Madeba, and camp where God ordains.

January 6th. My letter goes and I fetch letters.

To H. B.
january 9th, 1914.

As I said before, paf! I'm caught. I was an idiot to come in so close to the railway, but I was like an ostrich with its head in the sand and didn't know all the fuss there had been about me. Besides I wanted my letters and Fattuh. Well, I've got both. Fattuh turned up yesterday morning, just arrived from Damascus, still looking pale and thin (and no wonder), but with a clean bill of health from Dr. Mackinnon. And do you know I really believe that his coming makes up for all the misadventure? I have missed him dreadfully, my faithful travelling companion. Never in the world was anybody given more devoted friendship and service than he gives me. He was in the seventh heaven at being with me. Well meantime none of the 4 men whom I had sent in to Madeba and Ziza to buy stores had returned. In the Middle of the morning one of the camel drivers arrived with chopVed straw, and after the camels and I had lunched on all the luxuries Fattuh had brought from Damascus) I rode off to Mshetta, which is only an hour from my camp. As we came back Ali, the camel driver, looked up and said "Are those horsemen or camel riders going to Our tents?" I looked, and they were horsemen and, what is more, they were soldiers, and when we rode in they were sitting round our camp fire. More and more came, to the number of 10, and last of all a very angry, rude (and rather drunken) little Jack-in-Office of a Chaowish, who said they had been looking for me ever since I left Damascus. There it was. We put on a good countenance and when the Chaowish stormed we held our tongue. I sent off at once telegrams to Beyrout and Damascus to the two Consuls, but I had to send a man with them to Madeba and the Chaowish intercepted them—and put the man, one of my camel drivers, into the Ziza castle, practically a prisoner. Thither he presently sent Fattuh also, on some imaginary insult (F. had said nothing) and then he ransacked our baggage, took possession of our arms, and posted men all round my tent. All this which he had not the slightest right to do I met with an icy calmness for which God give me the reward; and later in the evening he began to feel alittle alarmed himself and sent to ask me whether I would like Fattuh back. But I refused to have Fattuh routed out again for the night was as icy as my demeanour and I shivering in bed, had some satisfaction in thinking of how much those unwelcome guardians of ruins were shivering outside. The temperature was 22. There was a frozen fog. To-day we have waited for the Kaimmakam of Salt to turn UP or send permission for us to go elsewhere. He is the nearest authority and I only wish he would come. The Chaowish left us in the early morning to the care of 6 Or 7 soldiers and turned up in the evening very affable. We have spent the day not unpleasantly, gossiping with the soldiers, mending a broken tent pole, and also in very long periods of gossip in Fattuh's tent, one member of the expedition or another dropping in to share in the talk. And I am busy forging new plans for I am not beaten yet. But I fancy this road is closed and I shall probably have to go up to Damascus and start afresh via Palmyra. The Bagdad Residency is the best address for me. It's all rather comic. I don't much care. It's a laughable episode in the adventure, but I do not think the adventure is ended, only it must take another turn. I have done some interesting work in the last 3 weeks—just what I meant to do, but I have not enjoyed the thing much up to now and my impression is that this is not the right road. I think I can do better. Anyhow I will try. God ordains. Fattuh observes cheerfully, "I spent the first night of the journey in the railway station, and the second in prison, and now where?"

Saturday, January 10th. So far all is well. The Kaimmakam not having arrived I came down to Amman and here I found him on his way to me, a charming, educated man, a Christian, willing and ready to let me go anywhere I like by any road I please. The Commandant here, a Circassian, ditto. But there comes in a question of conscience. I do not want to get the Kaimmakam into any trouble by taking advantage of his kindness so I have telegraphed to Damascus for permission to visit the ruins round Ziza and if I get that (I see no reason why I should not), I shall have relieved my friend of all responsibility and shall be free, as occasion offers, to go my own way. I am bound to say that I shall be glad when the permission comes. It was curious riding through hilly ways and cultivated country to-day after three weeks of desert. But such weather! Wind and sleet and it's blowing like the devil to-night. They wanted me to sleep in the serai, but I preferred my tent. This is such a wonderful place. If only it is fine to-morrow I shall like seeing it again. I was here with the Rosens 14 years ago. But it has been a heavy road for the laden camels, up and down hill. The camel is not a mountain bird in this part of the world. They all know me in these parts. I have met here a nephew of Namoud, the man who helped me into the Jebel Druze in 1905—vide "The Desert and the Sown." And they are all as nice as can be. Altogether the misadventure is rather fine so far. What will Damascus say? Well, I shall know to-morrow. But I can take no other course than that which I have taken.

January 11th. The reply has not yet come from Damascus, but the Kaimmakam thinks they can't refuse the permit so I wait with an easy mind. I am sending letters up to Damascus to-night and this shall go with them. I have spent the day receiving—and returning)—visits from the notables of Amman and it has been very amusing. Also I took a long walk with the Kaimmakam in the afternoon and had an interesting talk with him. He is a very nice man, but these Christians always give me a hopeless feeling. They walk blindfold and won't look facts in the face. It is not easy for them to work with the Muhammadans, but if you think they meet them half way—well, it isn't so. Yet this is a capable man and intelligent. I have liked being with him and with the good old Circassian magnate. I expect I shall be here to-morrow too. There was no sun to-day, but to-night it is fine again and I have a good deal of photography to do to-morrow.

To F.B.
AmmAN, January 14, 1914-

My troubles are over. I have to-day permission from the Vali to go when I like. The permission comes just in time for all my plans were laid and I was going to run away to-morrow night. They could not have caught me. However, I am now saved the trouble—and amusement! of this last resource. The delay has had the advantage of giving Fattuh a few days to pick up strength. He looks and is much better than when he joined me but one does not recover from typhoid in a twinkling of an eye. Now I think he will be able to travel without fatigue. To-morrow I camp again at Ziza in order to pick up two rafiqs—one of the Beni Sakhr and one of the Sherarat who will serve us as guarantors when we meet their tribes as we probably shall in a few days.

I have made the acquaintance of all the leading inhabitants of Amman! To-day I attended a Circassian wedding and drank tea with the protestant congregation which numbers 15 families.

To H. B.
january 19th, 1914

I must begin a chronicle, though Heaven knows when it will be sent off. We left Amman on the 15th, I have given the authorities at Amman an assurance that the Ott. Government was not responsible for me. This amounted to little, for wherever I went without gendarmes the government had the right to wash its hands of me. And I could not take gendarmes into the desert. I rode up that day to the farm of some Christians in the hill above Lina, where I was given a regal entertainment. Also Nimrud, the man who helped me in 1909, came up and spent the night there. I was delighted to see him.

I must tell you that I was in some trouble about my muleteers. The men I had brought from Damascus were very uncertain as to whether they would come on with me—I think they really dreaded the perils of the road. While we were at Amman we had fetched another man from Damascus a nephew of my old guide, Muhammad, his name is Said. It Was as well we did so, for on the 16th, just as I was starting, the three Agail threw down their camel sticks and declared that they would not come. I had Said and my negro camel herd, Fellah, an excellent boy. My hosts pressed into my service a fellah, a peasant, on their farm (his name is Mustafa), and I engaged as third man an Agaili, who had followed us from Amman in hope of getting work. His name is Ali, not to be confused with Ali Mausar, the postman guide of 1911, who is still with me and will never, I think, leave me. Besides these, I have Salim, another nephew of Muhammad's, whom I took at first in Fattuh's Place; he is an admirable servant and a very nice, well-educated man, I like him immensely. And finally, I have Fattuh, the lynch pin of the whole party.

So we set out. My hosts provided me with two Rafiqs a man of the Sherarat of whom I have not seen much, and a man of the Beni Sakhr, Sayyah, who is a delightful companion. They themselves rode with me till beyond Lina and then by the Mecca railway, they, Nimrud, and I, and various slaves and retainers made a hearty lunch and I parted from them with a feeling of gratitude. They clasped me by the hand, embraced Muhammad and Fattuh, and sent us forth with many deep voiced blessings. I crossed the Mecca railway and turned my face to Arabia.

We rode next day across the undulating country of the Beni Sakhr and passed occasional herds of camels and flocks of sheep. A young sheikling of the Sikhur joined us, he and his slave, and spent the night with us as guests, the sacred word. He was a charming boy, cousin to the great Sheikh Hathmel, and he was very anxious to come on with us, he and his slave.

Next day we went on our way over hills and wide shallow valleys, entirely covered with flints, and came in the afternoon to the palace of Tubah. It had been sufficiently planned by Musil, but very insufficiently photographed, and I spent a very profitable afternoon working at it. We camped among the ruins and found a good clear water pool in the sandy bed of the valley on which they stand, but the men were rather anxious that night, as the desert to the east of us was "empty" i.e., there were no Sukhur beyond us, and they feared the possibility of an Anazeh raiding party, making for the grazing camel herds we had passed in the morning. This thought did not, I need scarcely tell you, keep me awake-I should sleep but little in the next few weeks if I were to be disturbed by such things—and when I woke I found there had been no raiding party and my goods were safe and sound.

It was 34 when we started before dawn, and 70 when we camped at two o'clock. It is difficult to adjust one's toilet to a thermometer which behaves in this fashion. We have ridden through flint country all day, no water in the valleys, and consequently no people. We brought our water with us from Tubah. We are camped in a dry valley bed, not far from the great land-mark of all this country, the three pointed hills which are called the Thlaithuwat: the blessing it is to Have a point for my compass bearings is more than I can say! Since there is no water there is not much fear of raiders, but we keep watch for casual robbers, who, if they found us watchful, would turn out as guests, and if they found us sleeping, would lift our camels. "Beni Adam!" as Muhammad says, "Sons of Adam!" I listen all day as we ride to tales of raid and foray. But it is a fine country, this open desert, and I am enjoying myself mightily.

January 21st. We rode all day across flint strewn desert on the 20th. About mid-day two camel riders came up behind us and proved to be Jadan, the great

Sheikh of the Agaili, and one of his men. They had spied us as we passed under the Thlaithuwât, and taking us for a raiding party, had followed us to see where we were going.

"We took you for foes," said he.

"No, praise be to God," said I, " we are friends."

he rode on with us for an hour, for company, and then turned back to reassure his people. And we came at two o'clock to the last of the castles, Bair, as yet unplanned and unphotographed. The plan is a very old type and the place may be 8th century. It is very famous on account of its wells, and in summer and autumn, if the Sukhur are not camped here, all the ghazus pass this way. I have therefore heard more raiding stories here than ever before, and I will tell you one.

Muhammad, Sayyah (my rafiq) and I were sitting on the top of the biggest well, which is about twenty meters deep, and M. observed that when he first knew Bair this well was filled in. A party of the Isa had fallen here on the Sukhur and killed a horseman. The Sukhur killed Of the Isa two canel riders. The Isa were thirsting and the Sukhur, before they made off, threw the two dead men and their camels into the well and rolled in a few big stones on top, so that the Isa might not drink and follow them.

"Haram," said I, "it is forbidden."

"No," said Sayyâh, "their thought was good."

"The Arabs are devils," observed Muhammad.

"Devils," said Sayyâh.

"They are the very devil," said I, and with such conviction that Sayyâh looked up and laughed. You may take that as an example of our usual conversation.

Friday, 23 rd. We have marched for two days across exceedingly featureless country, indeed, for most of to-day there was nothing on which to take a bearing, but my camel's ears, which are not a good line. We march for an hour or two across flintstrewn uplands, glistening black, and then down and up the banks of a deepish valley—dry, of course—and then into the upland again. All the valleys here run approximately East and West.

Last night we had some rain, and the first deep valley to which we came there were small standing pools, which the camels drank greedily. We are carrying water, and since we are rather uncertain whether we shall reach pools to-morrow, we are using it sparingly, No baths and little washing of any kind. It has turned cold after the rain, not frosty, but a nipping wind—rather nice, however.

Yesterday we picked up a stone with a Safaitic inscription, a great deal further south than I expected to find such things. It is a desolate land—barren beyond all belief. But in the valleys we find dry bushes, on which the camels Pasture-

sunday, 25th. We changed our course a little yesterday, for seeing how dry and barren the world was, we decided that the Sukhur must have moved off east and that it was no good looking for them. We reached the western edge of the flint plateau.

Then we dropped down into a sandy valley and saw in the sand many footprints of camels, coming and going. But what Arabs had passed this way we did not know.

We camped in a hollow, where our fires could not be seen, and Ali, Sayyâh, and I went off scouting for Arabs. We climbed very cautiously up a high tell and from the shoulder surveyed the landscape through my glasses. But there was no soul in sight

Today we set off in a frosty dawn and marched on down the valley. Ali and I walked on for an hour and waited in a sandy hollow for the camels, and the foot-prints were all round us in the sand. "They are fresh," said Ali. The valley ended in A wide, open plain, set round with fantastically riven hills black and rusty red as the volcanic stone had weathered. The light crept round them as we marched across the plain. They stood in companies watchin us, and in the silence and eptiness were extraordinarily sinister. Suddenly Sayyâh called out "There is smoke." A tall spire of smoke wavered against a black hillock. I must tell you that we were waterless and thirsty—the camels had not drunk for four days. We were not at all sure when we should find water, neither did we know in the leasft what Arabs had kindled the fire whose smoke we watched, but the consensus of opinion was that it was a ghazu—raiders. These are the interesting moments of desert travel. We decided that it was best to go up and see who was there; if they were enemies, they would be certain to see us and follow us anyway; if they were friends they would give us news of the tribes and water. The latter question, however, we solved for ourselves—we found the pool for which we had been looking. We watered the camels, leaving the men to fill the water skins, Muhammad, Ali, Sayyâh and I went on to examine that questionable smoke; we crossed a little ridge, and on the farther side saw flocks of sheep and the shepherds of the Howaitât who came up and greeted us and gave us news of their sheikhs. All was safe and we went on into the hills and camped. Tomorrow I hope we shall be guests of the Howaitât. The big camps cannot be far away, for the only water in this district is the pool we found this morning, with the exception Of one stnall well in the hills to the east. The Howaitât are great people. They raid all across to the Euphrates and have a resounding name for devilry—reckless courage.

Tuesday, 27th. Yesterday we rode into the hills. On our way back we met a camel rider who told us that a very regrettable incident had occurred the night before. A man who was camping with the Sukhur had attacked a small camp of the Howaitât—he had an old grudge againft the dwellers in it—and carried off sheep. The Howaitât pursued him and killed him; in revenge his brother shot three of the pursuers and fled to the tents of the Sukhur. This news caused my Sukhur rafiq, Sayyâh, to feel very anxious as to the reception he might meet with in the tents of the Howaitât and I tried to comfort him (with some success) by assuring him that under no circumstances would I desert him. But all turned out well. We reached the tents of Harb, one of the sheikhs of the Howaitât, and were received with all kindness, Sayyâh included. Harb killed a sheep for us and we all dined with him that night. To-wards the end of dinner another guest arrived, who proved to be Muhammad Abu Tayyi-the Abu Tayyi are the great sheiks of the Howaitât. He is a magnificent person, tall and big, with a flashing look—not like the slender Beduin sitting round Harb's fire. He carried the Howaitât reputation for dare-devilry written on his face-I should not like to Meet him in anger.

Today we have sent the camels down for water; all this country drinks from the pool at which we filled our water skins on Sunday, and we dare not go on without a good provision. Accordingly, I have had rather a long day in camp, sitting and talking to Harb and his people, drinking coffee, talking again, photographing—they love being photographed—I took a latitude at noon, which is much to the good. Muhammad al Marawi and his nephew, Said, my camel driver Sayyâh, goes back from here, and I shall send this letter in the hope that it will ultimately reach a post and give you assurance that I am safe and flourishing. We take a Howaitât from here, and as the Howaitât are all along our way, we reckon we ought to be sufficiently protected. I have decided to go to Taimah—you will see it on the map—so as to get news of Nejd there. It is a town of the Rashids. I count it some eight easy marches from here. I expect I shall be able to write you from there.

I've bought an ostrich skin and two eggs! They live about here but I haven't seen a live one yet.

To H. B.
February 4, 1914.

I have really delayed too long in beginning my next letter To you. Since I sent off the last by Sayyâh (I wonder if you will get it?) we have changed our plans several times and I still hesitate to pronounce that we are on the road to Nejd, though I think we are. At any rate we are in Arabia, in the very desert and no doubt about it. But you must hear. When it came to the point of leaving Harb's tents I found that the question of who was to come as our new rafiq was by no means settled. On the contrary, all the Arabs and all my men were gathered round the camp fire with faces the one longer than the other. It seemed that the desert before us—the way to Taimah—was "khala," empty, i.e., there were no tribes camping in it. It would be, they all assured me, infested by ghazus who would fall upon us by night and undoubtedly rob us, if not worse. Whether this were true or no I had no means of judging, but I take it to be against the rules of the game to persist in taking a road against which I am warned by all; moreover there was the conclusive difficulty that we could get no rafiq to lead us along it. Therefore, after prolonged consultations, it was decided that we should strike east, go to Jof, throw ourselves on the kindness of the Rualla and make our way south, if possible, and, if not possible, east to Bagdad. We set out next morning with Harb's brother, Awwad, as rafiq, for Jof and the Wadi Sirhan in pursuance of this plan. I did not add anything to my letter, though Sayyâh was not yet gone, because the future seemed so doubtful, and it was as well I did not. I should have said we were going to Jof and it would have been no truer than that our way lay to Taimah. Riding over the last hills—they were very delicious, full of herds of camels—we came presently to the big tent of Audah, the great sheikh of the Howaitât; Audah was away, as we knew, raiding the Shammar, but we stopped for coffee and photographs and then rode on east. But it happened that a man who was among the coffee drinkers had given Awwad the information that some of the Ruwalla were camped in the Wady Sirhan. Now as any man of the Ruwalla whom he might chance to meet would cut his throat at sight it was clear that he could not conduct us to the Wadi Sirhan and I was again rafiq-less. I sent him off to the tents of Muhammad, Audah's brother (he turned up in Harb's tents the first night we were there—a formidable personage) to fetch a Sherari of repute who had no blood feud with the Ruwalla, and we came into camp and waited results. He returned in an hour accompanied by Muhammad himself and several others who all stayed to dine and sleep. Muhammad brought in a lamb and a very beautiful ostrich skin, and further, over the coffee cups, he told me of a ruin in the Jebel Tubaiq which, if I would come back with him to his camp, he would take me to see. Now I was very reluctant to turn back, but a ruin is a ruin, and moreover it is my job to determine what kind of ruin it may be. So next day we rode back with Muhammad, my men inclined to grumble and I not a little inclined to doubt my own wisdom. We had got our Sherari guide, Musrud, and might have gone on if we wanted. But after all I was right. In the first place the ruin was worth seeing. It has a Kufic graffito and all complete and to get to it I rode five hours across the Jebel Tubaiq, saw and photographed a pre-Muhammadan High Place (so I take it to be) and got a far better idea of these exceedingly interesting hills. They are full of wild beauty and full of legend; they deserve a good month's study which I may perhaps give to them some day, and we such friends With the Howaitât. For I made great friends with Muhammad. He is a good fellow and I like him and trust him. In the 3 days I spent with him—one, indeed, a very long one, was spent in riding over the hills and back—I saw him dealing out justice and hospitality to his tribe and found both to be good. Of an evening we sat in his big tent—he is an important person, you understand—and I listened to the tales and the songs of the desert, the exploits of Audah, who is one of the most famous raiders of these days, and romantic adventures of the princes of Nejd. Muhammad sat beside me on the rugs which were spread upon the clean soft sand, his great figure wrapped in a sheepskin cloak, and sometimes he puffed at his narghile and listened to the talk and sometimes he joined in, his black eyes flashing in question and answer. I watched it all and found much to look at. And then, long after dark, the "nagas," the camel mothers, would come home with their calves and crouch down in the sand outside the open tent. Muhammad got up, drew his robes about him, and went out into the night with a huge wooden bowl, which he brought back to me full to the brim of camel's milk, a most delectable drink. And I fancy that when you have drunk the milk of the naga over the camp fire of Abu Tayyi you are baptised of the desert and there is no other salvation for you. I saw something of the women, too—Muhammad's wives and sister. Yes, those were interesting days. They were prolonged beyond my intention for this reason. The day I visited the ruin we had sent our camels to water at a khabra and bring us water. Do you know what khabra is? It is a rain pool. Now this khabra proved to be so far away that the camels took 18 hours on their way there and back, and one never came back at all. It sat down and it would not get up and they left it 6 hours away. That's what camels do; if they are tired and don't mean to move, nothing in this world or the next will induce them to stir. It was clear that we could not abandon a camel. We despatched a man in the middle of the night to feed and fetch her and waited another day. During that day we changed all our plans once more. Muhammad al Marawi came to see me and said he thought if we went to Jof we should have great difficulty in getting on to Nejd, since the Ruwalla are foes of the Shammar, moreover Musrud, our Sherari rafiq, was prepared to take us south—to Taimah, if we liked, or if we liked better, S.E. and direct to Nejd. The ghazus, the perils, the rifle shots at night, seemed to have vanished into thin air. I questioned Musrud very closely, made up my mind that the scheme was feasible and told my men that the less said about it the better. Nominally we were still going to Jof—one becomes very secretive in these countries. The camel messenger came back that night and reported that he had persuaded the camel to move on three hours— we did not mind her non-appearance, for our new road lay in her direction. The real danger ahead, as I made out, was the lack of camel food. If we found no pasturage in the desert to the south (we had only six days' aliq with us—aliq is fodder-) we should be faced by starvation for the camels and with I did not know—what for us. But the reports, if they were to be believed, of the country ahead were good and as all other chances of getting to Nejd seemed so remote I resolved to take the risk. Muhammad gave us half a load of corn, his crowning act of hospitality, and I gave him a Zeiss glass in return for all his kindness. We set out and rode 3 hours to the southern edge of the Jebel Tubaiq, dropping down by a rocky gorge into the plain below, where we camped. Here we found our camel, more or less recovered, and fit to go on next day. The " trees " were greening and there was plenty of good pasturage. Before us lay the country in which we now are, a country of red sandstone and the resulting sand. But the early winter rains have been good and the sparse thorny bushes growing in the sand have sprouted into green, all the rain pools are full and (so far) raiders non-existent. We have with us not only our Sherari rafiq, but still better a man to conduct us into the heart of the Shammar country—not a man, a family. We met them in our last Tubaiq camp, at the foot of the hills, a Shammar family who wanted to return to Nejd. Without us for company they would not dare to take this direct road, and we are no less grateful than they, for if we meet a Shammar ghazu we are guaranteed against them. So here we are, camped in red gold sand among broken hillocks of red sandstone, with all the desert shrubs grey green and some even adventuring into colourless pale flowers. They smell sweet and aromatic. "Like amber" said Ali, sniffing the wind as we came into camp this afternoon. And the camels have eaten their fill. We march slowly, for they eat as they go but I don't mind. I never tire of looking at the red gold landscape and wondering at its amazing desolation. I like marching on through it and sometimes I wonder whether there is anywhere that I am at all anxious to reach.

February 7th. Three days' journey have not brought us along very far. There is such abundance of green shrubs and flowering weeds that the camels stop and graze as we go, and yesterday we came into camp very early so as to give them a good feed. A day or two more of this sort of country will make a wonderful difference to them. Yet it is nothing but sand and sandstone, long barren hills and broken sandstone tells. But the early rains have been good and to-day there were places where the bare desert was like a garden. It is very delightful to see. Also the rain which fell upon us the day we left the J. Tubaiq was very heavy over all this land. We find the sandstone hollows full of clear, fresh rain water and scarcely trouble to fill our water skins, so plentiful is the supply each night. It is wonderfully fortunate. Yesterday we had an absurd adventure. Besides the Shammar family we have a couple of Sherarat tents with us, the people miserably poor (they seem to be kept from the ultimate starvation which must overtake them by small gifts of flour from us) possessing nothing but a few goats and the camels which carry them. These goats had gone on with their herd before dawn; just before the sun rose the Shammar and Sherarat followed on their camels and I went behind them on foot for I Wanted to take bearings from a little ridge ahead. We had been camping in a very shallow valley. Musrud was with me. We may have walked about 100 yards when all those in front of us turned round and hurried back to us. " They are afraid," said Musrud. "They have seen an enemy." Ghadi, the chief Sharnmari came riding up. "What is it?" I asked. "Gom," he answered, "foes." "How many?" said I. "Twenty camel riders," he answered, and shouted to my men "To the valley, to the valley!" We crouched all the camels behind the sand heaps and tamarisk bushes, got out our arms and waited. Nothing happened. Presently Ghadi crept back to the ridge to scout. Still nothing happened. Then Fattuh, Musrud and I went across to the ridge and swept the world with my glasses. There was nothing. We waved to the others to come on and marching down the hills in complete security, came to the conclusion that the 20 camel riders could have been nothing but the Father of goats who was found presently pasturing his innocent flock ahead of us. At night I announced that I intended to take a rafiq of the Beni Maaz, the Goat Tribe, and this not very brilliant witticism threw the whole company round the coffee fire into convulsions of laughter.

February 10th. On Feb. 8 we fell among thieves-worse than the goats. An hour or two after we had struck camp we met some of the Howaitât who told us that Sayyah, Sheikh of the Wadi Sulaman was camped a few hours to the east. Since it was pretty certain that he would hear of our presence we thought it wiser to camp with him that night and take a rafiq from hin, -otherwise, you understand, he would probably have sent after us in the night and robbed us. He received us with all courtesy, but it was only pretence. Presently the oneeyed ruffian came into our camp, examined all our possessions and asked for everything in turn. We thought at first to get off with the loss of a revolver, but it ended by my having to surrender my Zeiss glass also to my infinite annoyance.

He swore that no Christian had ever visited this country and none should go, that he would send no rafiq with us so that he might be free to rob us, and finally he proposed to said and Fattuh that they should aid him to kill us and share the spoil. He got no encouragement from them and I do not know that any of the threats were more than words. I clung to my glass as long as I could, but when at last Said, who knows the Arabs, advised me to yield lest things should take a worse turn, We got our rafiq, Sayyâh's cousin, and are therefore assured against "the accursed of both parents." We took also two men of the Faqir, another tribe whom we may meet. They are said to be still more unfortunate in their ancestry than the Wadi Sulaiman. One of their sheikhs was camping with Sayyah and he sent his brother and another with us. This brother, Hamid, is a very pleasant fellow traveller, and I have no fault to find with Sayyâh's cousin Zayyid. But Sayyah has a name for roguery. It was typical of him that he mulcted our Shammar companions Of 3 mejidehs before he would let them go on with us. They had no money and could not pay, but Muhammad al Marawi stood surety for them and I shall of course give them the ransom, poor souls. We had a very dull day's journey yesterday over rolling pebbly sandhills, nothing whatever to be seen, except that once we crossed the tracks of an ostrich. To-day has been rather more varied, hills on which to take bearings, and we have come into camp in a valley bottom full of green plants for the camels. We have recovered from the depression into which Sayyah's conduct threw us and we are in good hopes that we shall not meet any more sheikhs.

February 12th. We rode yesterday over a barren pebbly waste and came down through sand hills to a desolate low lying region wherein we found water pools. We watered our camels and filled our water skins and then turned our faces S.E. into the Nefad which lay but an hour from us. The NeftLd is a great stretch of sandhills, 7 or 8 days' journey across. Our path lies through the S.W. corner and I am glad to see this famous wilderness of sand. It is the resort of all the tribes during the winter and spring when an abundance of vegetation springs from the warm sand, but there is no permanent water except at the extreme borders and in summer it is a blazing furnace. This is the right moment for it. All the plants are greening and putting forth such flowers as they know how to produce and our camels eat the whole day as they march. But the going is very heavy—up and down endless ridges of soft pale yellow sand. occasionally there are deep gulleys hollowed out by the wind and we make a long circuit to avoid them, and from time to time the sand is piled up into a high ridge or head—a 'tas,' it is called in Arabic—which stands out yellow over the banks for its precipitous flanks are devoid of vegetation. Towards midday we came to a very high tas and I climbed to the top and saw the hills near Taimah to the west and the first of the mountains of Nejd to the S.E., Jebel Irnan. When I came down Fattuh greeted me with the news that one of the camels had sat down and they could not make her stir. Muhammad, Fellah and I went back with some food for her, thinking she might be weary with walking in the deep sand and that with food and coaxing we could get her on, but when we reached herve we found her rolling in the sand in the death agony. Muhammad said "She is gone. Shall we sacrifice her?" I said "It were best." He drew his knife and said "In the name of God. God is most powerful." With that he cut her throat. She was, he explained, sick of a malady which comes with great suddenness. Fortunately she was one of the 3 weak animals we have with us. I should have been obliged to sell her at Hayil and she would not have fetched more than a pound or two. She is no great loss as far as that goes, but I am deeply attached to all my camels and grieve over the death for reasons of sentiment.

February 15 th. We continue our peaceful course through the sands of the Nefûd, for according to all the information which comes to us from the Arabs we meet encamped it is the safest road, and I, who am now so close to Hayil, have no other desire but to get there without being stopped. We are now skirting Within its southern border and from every sandhill top we see the mountains of Nejd. Yesterday we camped early in order to water. We had seen no water since the khabra. The well Haizan was an hour and a half from our camp and I rode down with the camels to see the watering. Wells are very scarce in the Nefûd. They are found only on its borders and are very deep. Haizan lies at the bottom of a great depression enclosed by the steep sandbanks of the Nefûd. Our well rope was 48 paces long. We carried two stout sticks with us and a little wheel with which we made a pulley for the rope. There was an Arab camp near ours and the Sheikh, Salim, was there with some of his people watering their camels. They used a pulley like ours. It was interesting to watch and I took a lot of photographs. There were some who objected at first to my photography and asked what it was for. I asked the Shammar who was with us and the two brothers who have come with us from the J. Tubaiq whether I ought to stop, but they said no, it did not matter. And so I went on and no word was said. When you consider what a strange sight I must be to these people who have never seen a European it is remarkable that they leave me so unmolested. Desert manners are good.

February 19th. Marching through the Nefûd is like marching through the Labyrinth. You are for ever winding round deep sand pits, sometimes half a mile long, with banks so steep that you cannot descend. They are mostly shaped like horseshoes and you wander along until you come to the end and then drop down into low ground, only to climb up anew. How one bears it I don't know. I should think that as the crow flies we barely covered a mile in an hour. But there is something pleasant about it too; the safe camping grounds among the Sands, the abundance of pasture, the somnolent monotony. But we have done with it. We came out of it to-day. Two days ago we were held up by heavy rain. It began just as we broke up camp. We marched for two hours, by which time all the men were wet through and I was far from dry. The clouds stay on top of the sandhills like a thick fog and at last my rafiq declared that he could see no landmarks and could not be sure of our direction. No Arabs march in rain and I had to give way. We pitched camp and dried ourselves at an immense wood fire. It rained and hailed and thundered most of the day and night and all the world rejoiced. "To-day the sheikhs will sacrifice a camel," said my rafiq. The camels will pasture in the Nefûd for 3 months after this rain. Last night we got to the first

Shammar camp—the Shammar are the Arabs of Nejd—and took as a rafiq the oldest and raggedest sheikh in the world. Beduin are not noted for strong and steady judgment, but he is one of the most birdwitted whom I have met. And this morning we reached the barren sandstone crags of Jebel Misma, which bound here the Nefûd, and passed beyond them into Nejd. As we topped the last sand bank the landscape which opened before us was more terrifyingly dead and empty than anything I have ever seen. The blackened rocks of Misma drop steeply on the E. side into a wilderness of jagged peaks set in a bed of hard sand and beyond and beyond stretches the vacant plain, untilled and unpeopled and scattered over with isolated towers and tables of sandstone. We have camped once more on the skirts of the Nefûd for the sake of the pasture, and tomorrow we go down into the plain.

Sunday, February 22nd. it proves to be a very pleasant place that dead country. The sandstone hollows were all full of water and there was plenty of pasturage. We marched gaily over a hard floor all day and camped in the midst of hills on a sandy floor between high cliffs. We had some Shammar for neighbours about a mile away. Yesterday we had a dull journey over an interminable flat and up sandbanks to another little camp, but this time high up in the heart of the little range. Somewhere in the sandbanks we passed the boundary between the sandstone country and the granite. I had noticed that the strange shapes of the sandstone hills were not to be seen before us and when we came to our camp in Jebel Rakkam behold the rocks were granite. I climbed into the top of one of the peaks and found flowers ggrowing in the crevices, small, white and purple weeds and thistles and a dwarf asphodel-not a great bounty, but it feasted the eyes in this bare land. And to-day we passed a tiny village with corn plots round it—the first we have seen since Ziza. There were only 6 Or 7 Of them. And thereafter we were overtaken again by the Nefûd which puts out a long finger to the south here, and marched by hollow ways of sand in a very hot sun. We are camped in sandhills to-day.

February 24th. We are camped within sight of Hayil and I might have ridden in today, but I thought it better to announce my coming and therefore I sent on Muhammad and Ali and have camped in the plain a couple of hours or so from the town. We finished with the Nefûd for good and all yesterday, and today we have been through a charning country—charming for Arabia—of great granite rocks and little plains with thorny acacia trees growing in them and very sweet scented desert plants. We passed a small village or two, mud houses set in palm gardens and all set round with a mud wall. I hope the Hayil people will be polite. The Amir is away and an uncle of his is left in charge.

March 7th. And now I must relate to you the strange tale of my visit to Hayil. I broke up camp at sunrise on the 25th and rode towards the town. When we had been on the road for about an hour we met Ali on his camel, all smiles. They had seen Ibrabim, the uncle in charge. He was most polite, said I was welcome and there were three slaves of his household come out to receive me. With that he pointed to 3 horsemen riding towards us, one of whom carried a long lance. So we came up to the walls of Hayil in state, skirted them and entered the town by the S. gate. At the doorway Of the first house stood Muhammad al Rashid, great uncle of the present boy. I walked up a long sloping passage—not a stair, a ramp—to an open court and so into a great room with a roof borne on columns and divans and carpets round the walls. It was the Roshan, the reception room. Here I sat and one of the slaves with me. These slaves, you must understand are often very important personages. Their masters treat them like brothers and give them their full confidence, Also when one of the Rashids removes the reigning prince and takes his place (which frequently happens) he is careful to murder his slaves also, lest they should revenge the slain. The men then went away to see to the lodging of the camels and the pitching of the tents in the wide courts below. (There are five courts to my domain, all mudwalled and towered. It was here that in the old days, before the Mecca railway, the Persian Hajj used to lodge.) Thereupon there appeared upon the scenery two women. One was an old widow, Lu-lu-ah, who is caretaker here, as you might say. The other was a Circassian, who was sent to Muhammad al Rashid by the Sultan as a gift. Her name is Turkiyyeh. Under her dark purple cloak—all the women are closely veiled here—she was dressed in brilliant red and purple cotton robes and she wore ropes of bright pearls round her neck. And she is worth her weight in gold, as I have come to know. She is a chatterbox of the first order and I passed an exceedingly amusing hour in her company. She had been sent here to spend the day and welcome me. After lunch Ibrahim paid me a state visit, slaves walking before him and slaves behind. He is an intelligent and (for an Arab) well educated man. He was clothed in Indian silks and carried a gold mounted sword. He stayed talking till one of the slaves announced that the call to afternoon prayer had sounded. Then he rose and took his leave. But as he went he whispered to old M. al Murawi that as the Amir was away and as there was some talk in the town about my coming, a stranger and so on, he was bound to be careful and so on and so on—in short, I was not to leave the house without permission. I spent most of the afternoon sitting in the women's court and talking to Turkiyyeh who was excellent company. My camels badly wanted rest; there is no pasturage near Hayil and we decided to send them away to the Nefûd with one of my men and a couple of Hayil Men whom Ibrahim had provided. I sold 6 camels—the Amir being away raiding and with him all available camels, they are fortunately much in request at this moment—6 which were badly knocked up by the journey, and sent the remaining 13 away next morning. And then I sat still in honourable captivity and the days were weary long. On the 27th Ibrahim invited me to come and see him in the evening—I had expressed a wish to return his call. After dark he sent a man and a couple of slaves and I rode through the silent empty town to the Qasr, the fortress palace of the Amirs. I rode in at the gate, and was conducted by troops of slaves to the Roshan, the great columned reception room, where I found Ibrahim and a large company sitting on carpets round the walls. They all rose at my entrance. I sat at Ibrahim's right hand and we talked for an hour or more while the slaves served us first with tea and then with coffee. Finally they brought censers and swung them before each one of us three times and this is the sign that the reception is ended. So I rode home, tipping each of the many doorkeepers as I left. I had sent silken robes to all these people,—Ibrahim and the chief slaves and the absent Amir—to him a Zeiss glass and a revolver also. I was now living upon the money which I had received for my six camels and it became necessary to ask for the 200 pounds which I had deposited with the Amir's agent in Damascus. It was met by the reply that the Letter of Credit was made out to the Amir's treasurer who was away raiding with him and that the money could not be paid to me till he returned. Now the Amir will in all probability be away for another month. I did not contemplate remaining in Hayil for a month; even if I had been free to go and come as I chose. Moreever I was persuaded that the Amir's grandmother, Fatima, who is a very powerful person in his court, had been left in charge of the treasury and could give (or withhold) as she pleased. But I could not risk being left here penniless. I had just 40 pounds. I told my men that it must suffice, that I should call in my camels, take the 8 best and go with Fattuh, Ali and Fellah to Bagdad, while the rest of the men would wait another week till the camels were rested and return to Damascus via Medina and the railway. The money I had would just suffice for all of us and for the tips in the house here. So it was agreed and after two more days I asked for a private audience with Ibrahim, went again to the Qasr at night, saw him and again heard from him that no disbursement could take place in the Amir's absence. I replied that if that were so, I much regretted that I should have to leave at once and I must ask him for a rafiq. He said the rafiq was ready and anything I wished should be given. That morning I must tell you, he had returned the gifts I had sent to hin and to his brother Zamil, who is away with the Amir. Whether he did not think them sufficient or what was the reason I do not know. I took them back with me that evening, said I had been much hurt and must request him to receive them, which he did. He had lent me a man in the morning and I had ridden out with one of his slaves to a garden belonging to him and beyond the town. For this I thanked him and we parted on the best of terms. Next day I sent a messenger out for my camels—they proved to be two days away-and again I sat still amusing myself as best I might and the best was not good. I had no idea what was in their dark minds concerning me. I sat imprisoned and my men brought me in rumours from the town. Ali, in particular, has two uncles here who are persons of consideration; they did not care to come and see me, but they sent me news. The general opinion was that the whole business was the work of Fatima, but why, or how it would end, God alone knew. If they did not intend to let me go I was in their hands. It was all like a story in the Arabian Nights, but I did not find it particularly enjoyable to be one of the 'dramatis personae.' Turkiyyeh came again and spent the day with me and next day there appeared the chief eunuch Said—none more powerful than he. He came to tell me that I could not leave without permission from the Amir. I replied that I had no money and go I must and would, and sent this message to Ibrahim and Fatima. But he answered that going and not going was not in our hands. I sent hasty messages to Ali's uncles and in the afternoon one of their nephews came to see me—an encouraging sign. That night I was invited to the Qasr by the women. The Amir's mother, Mudi, received me and Turkiyyeh was there to serve as introducer of ambassadors. It was more like the Arabian Nights than ever. The women in their Indian brocades and jewels, the slaves and eunuchs, and the great columned rooms, the children heavy with jewels—there was nothing but me myself which did not belong to medieval Asia. We sat on the floor and drank tea ate fruits—vide, as I say, the Arabian Nights passim. Thereupon passed another long day. At night came Turkiyyeh- the women only go out after dark. We sat in the big Roshan here and drank tea, served by one of my slaves—for I also have two or three. A single lamp lighted us and the night wind blew through the chinks of the shutters. No windows are glazed. I tol her all my difficulties, that I had no money and could get none, that I sat here day after day and that they would not let me go. Next day I was invited by two boys of the sheikhly house—I won't tell you all the relationships, though I heard them all—to spend the afternoon in a garden near at hand. I went and there were the two boys and all the other Rashid male babies—all that have not been murdered by successive usurping Amirs, and of course many slaves And the eunuch Said. We sat on carpets in a garden pavilion, as You may see in any Persian miniature you choose to look at, and I again put forward my requests, which were again met by the same replies on the part of Said. I ended by declaring that I wished to leave the next day and asked for a rafiq. Thereat we wandered through the gardens and my hosts, the two boys, carefully told me the names of all the fruit trees (which of course I knew) and the little children walked solemnly hand in hand in their long brocade robes. And then we drank more coffee and at the afternoon prayer I left. After prayers came Said and told Muhammad al Murawi that I must understand that nothing could be done till permission came from the Amir. I went to the men's tent and spoke my mind to Said without any Oriental paraphrases and, having done so, I rose abruptly and left them sitting—a thing which is only done by great sheikhs, you understand. The camels came in at dusk and I, thinking that in the end I should have to stay here for another indefinite time, was beginning to plan where to send them out to graze, when after dark came Said and another with 200 pounds in a bap, and full permission to go where and when I liked. The rafiq was ready. I replied with great dignity that I was very much obliged and that I did not intend to leave till the next day for I wished to see the Qasr and the town by daylight. And today I have been shown everything, have been allowed to photograph everything and do exactly as I pleased. I gave 10 pounds in backshish in the Qasr. As I was returning I was given an invitation from Turkiyyeh and I went to her house. She says she explained the whole position to Fatima and I think that the 'volte-face' is due to her, but however it may be I am profoundly thankful. I go to Bagdad. After careful enquiries I feel sure that the road south is not possible this year. The tribes are up and there is an expedition pending from here. They would not, therefore, give me a rafiq south and I should have considerable difficulty in going without their leave. So Hayil must suffice for this year. Moreover I have learnt a good deal about travel in this country and I know that none of the southern country can be travelled 'a la Franca.' If ever I go there I must go with no more baggage than I can carry on my own camel.

Sunday, March 22nd. We are within sight of Nejef. I have camped an hour from the town because I know there is no camping ground near it and I should probably have to put up in the Government sarai, which is tiresome. Also I very much want to get through to Bagdad without questions or telegrams. Oh, but it is a long dull way from Nejd! I wanted to come up by the old pilgrim road, which has a certain historic interest and is also the shortest, but the morning I left Hayil came a slave with a message to say I was to travel by the western road as the eastern was not safe. As I did not much mind the one way or the other I acquiesced. Two days out we met the Amir's messengers bringing in a tale (which they served up to us) of a highly successful raid, the flight of all the Anazeh before the Amir and the capture of Jof. They said the Amir was a few days further on. But when we had crossed the Nefûd for 4 days and come near the place where he was reported to have been he had left and crossed over to the eastern road and was said to be off raiding some tribes further east. I did not intend to turn back for him and it would have been useless for I might have taken days to find him so I went on my way in all tranquillity. We rode for ever over immense levels not a valley or a hill to be seen and so little water that we were almost always too short of it to spend it in washing. As long as we were with the Shammar and that was for the first 10 days, we were perfectly safe with a rafiq from Hayil. He rode with us for 8 days and we took on another Shammari for the next 2 days. Then the fun began. We had to get through the Shia tribes of Iraq, all out in the desert now for the spring pasture and all accursed of their two parents. The first we reached were the Beni Hasan and we spent a Very delicate hour, during which it was not apparent whether they meant to strip us or to treat us as guests. Ultimately they decided on the latter course. We camped with them, they killed a lamb for us and gave us two rafiqs next day. That day luckily we saw no one and camped in solitude. Early on the following morning we sighted tents and our rafiqs were reduced to a state of quivering alarm for they will kill each other just as gaily as they kill you. One of them, however, was induced to ride up to the tents, which he found to be those of an allied tribe. He brought back two new rafiqs for he and his companion flatly refused to go on. So We rode on for 6 hours or so and then again we sighted tents and-'même jeu!' The rafiqs even talked of turning back and leaving us. But again we made one of them go up and enquire what Arabs they were and as great good luck would have it they were the Ghazâlat who are the only people of any real importance and authority in these parts. We camped with them and took on an excellent rafiq—a well-known man—his name is Dawi. With him we have felt comparatively safe, but if we had not had him with us we should have been stripped to the skin twice in these last two days. The first morning we came down to water at some horribly stagnant pools we found a large company of the Madan filling their water skins there. The Madan are possibly the worst devils known. They offered DAwi 30 pounds if he would abandon us for they could not touch us as long as we had a sheikh of the Ghazalat with us for fear of the Ghazalat, you understand. And yesterday afternoon we met a large caravan of

Madan coming up from Meshed and in a moment we were surrounded by stalwart armed men who laid hold of our camels and would have made them kneel. But Dawi called out to them and when they saw him they let go and drew off. This morning a casual person who was tending flocks sent a rifle bullet between the legs of our camels. Dawi ran out and expostulated with him before he sent another and we protested loudly at the treatment he had accorded us. "An enemy does not come riding across the top of the plain in full daylight!" said Ali " and if you feared us the custom is to send a bullet over the heads of the riders till you have found out whether they are friends or foes." He admitted that he had broken the rules and, for my part, I rejoiced that he had broken none of the camels' legs. Even to-night I don't upon my honour know whether we are safe camping out here two hours from the town, but the men seem to think it is all right, and anyhow here we are! The edges of the desert are always stormy and difficult. The tribes are not Bedu but Arab, a very important distinction, for they have not the code and the rules of the Beduin. But these Shia people are a great deal worse than any one we have met upon our whole way. Having penned these lines it occurred to me to go and ask Ali whether he thought we were safe for the night. He replied that he did not and that his mind was far from being at rest. (He had chosen the camping ground himself, I mention.) I enquired what he thought we had better do. He thought we had better go on to a village. It was then two hours before sunset. We packed the dinner, which was cooked, into our good camp saucepans, struck camp and loaded all in half an hour and off we set! It was a most absurd proceeding, but I thought it would be still more absurd to have a regrettable incident on this last night of our desert journey. Just at sunset we reached a small village of wattle huts and here we have camped. The villagers have received us with much courtesy and to the best of our belief we are in security at last.

To H. B.
BAGDAD, March 19th.

Yes, we were safe and we got here without further incident. I drove from Meshhed to Ketbela—Nejef and Meshhed are the same—dined and spent the evening with our vice-consul and drove into Bagdad next day. I have fallen on my feet with some new acquaintances, Mr. Tod, the head-man of Lynch's company and his darling little Italian wife. I am going to stay with them when I come back from Babylon. I go to Babylon for a couple of nights to-morrow. They wanted me to come to them at once, but I thought I would have a few dayys of complete freedom here first. I have seen all my native friends; they precipitated themselves and gave me a welcome which warmed my heart. Bagdad has grown a 'weltstadt!'

I may stay here another week or so when I come back from Babylon. Then across the Syrian desert to Damascus—quite safe and easy. . . . I have written to Louis Mallet suggesting myself to him. I should like to tell him my tales and hear his. I love Bagdad and this country much better than Damascus and Syria and I do not know when I shall be here again so that I gladly stay a day or two longer.

Besides I shall get another mail, which is good—perhaps 2. It's queer and rather enjoyable at first, the sense of being in perfect security, but one ksoon loses the realisation of it.

To H.B.
23rd April, 1914.

Behold I'm 11 days out from Bagdad and I have not begun to tell you my tale. I have been put to it to get through the long days and I have been too tired at the end of them to write. I drove out from Bagdad to Feluja, on the Euphrates, having arranged that my camels were to leave Bagdad the previous day and meet me at Feluja. The day they left Ali made an unjustifiable request—that I should take a cousin of his with us, the cousin wishing to escape military service. I refused and Ali struck. Fattuh got him and the camels off with great difficulty late at night; in consequence they had not arrived when I reached Feluja, and when they came Ali had brought the cousin with him! ai was very angry, Ali was in the Devil's own temper and I dismissed hin on the spot to find his way back to Bagdad with the cousin. He has given me a great deal of trouble. I have put up with a great deal for the sake of long acquaintance, but gross insubordination I won't stand and there is an end of him. MY party therefore was Fattuh, Sayyif and Fellah (the negro) and I was left without a guide for the Syrian desert. I am travelling very light with two small native tents, a bed on the ground, no furniture, no nothing—for speed's sake. We pitched our tiny camp half-an-hour out of Feluja in the desert by your Dulaim tents—it was blazing hot, and what with the heat and the hardness of the ground (to which I have now grown accustomed) I did not sleep much. Next day we rode along the high road to Ramadi on the Euphrates, where lives the chief Sheikh of the Dulaim. I went straight to him. He received me most cordially, lodged me in his palm garden, gave me a great feast and a rafiq from his own household, Adwan, a charming man. It was blazing hot again and noisy, dogs and people talking, and I slept less than ever, We were off before dawn and struck south west into the desert to the pitch springs of Abu jir. We arrived in a dust storm, the temperature was 90 and it was perfectly disgusting. The following day was better, as hot as ever) but no dust storms. We rode on west into the desert. Two days more, west and slightly north, with the temperature falling, thank Heaven, brought us up on to the post road and here we fell in with the sheikh of the Anazeh and I took a new rafiq from him, Assaf is his name, and very reluctantly said goodbye to Adwan. We rode down the following day to muhaiwir in the Wadi Hauran, where I had been 3 years ago. The world was full of Anazeh tents and camels—a wonderful sight. It meant, too, that with my Anazeh rafiq I was perfectly safe. And in two more days we came to the great Sheikh of these eastern Anazeh, Fahad Bey, and I alighted at his tents, and claimed his hospitality. He treated me with fatherly kindness, fed me, entertained me, and advised me to take a second rafiq, a man of the Rwalla, who are the western amazeh. I spent the afternoon planning a ruin near him—a town, actually a town in the heart of the Syrian desert! Only the fortified gate was planable, the rest was mere stone heaps, but it throws a most unexpected light on the history of the desert. There was most certainly a settled population at one time in these eastern parts. We had violent thunderstorms all night and yesterday, when I left Fahad, a horrible day's journey in the teeth of a violent wind and through great scuds of rain. To-day, however, it has been very pleasant. I have been following the old road which I came out to find and am well content to have my anticipations justified. We came to a small ruin in the middle of the day which I stopped to plan. Fahad told me that the desert from the camp to Bukhara is 'Khala,' empty, i.e., there are no Beduin camped in it. I like solitary camps and the desert all to myself, but it has the drawback of not being very safe. With our two rafiqs no Anazeh of any kind will touch us, but there is always the chance of a ghazu. Very likely they would do us no harm, but one can't be sure. However, so far I have run my own show quite satisfactorily and it amuses me to be tongue and voice for myself, as I have been these days. But I am tired, and being anxious to get through and be done with travel, we are making long marches, 9 and 10 hours. Oh, but they are long hours, day after day in the open wilderness! I have come in sometimes more dead than alive, too tired to eat and with just enough energy to write my diary. WE are now up nearly a couple of thousand feet and I am beginning to feel better.

On the 24th we began the day by sighting something lying on the desert with an ominous flutter of great wings over it. Assaf observed that it was 3 dead camels and 2 dead men, killed ten nights ago—ghazu met ghazu, said he. . . . On 25th we came at midday to an encampment of Seubba, a strange tribe of whose origin many tales are told. We halted at their tents to buy some butter and I was glad to see and photograph them. They are great hunters; one man was clad in a lovely robe of gazelle skins. They pressed us to camp with them, but we rode on for a couple of hours and camped by ourselves. On the 26th . . . . In the middle of the morning we met a man walking solitary in the desert. We rode up to him and addressed him in Arabic, but he made no answer. Assaf, my rafiq, said he thought he must be a Persian dervish. I spoke to him in Turkish and in what words of Persian I could muster, but he made no reply. Fattuh gave him some bread which he accepted and turned away from us into the rainy wilderness, going whither? But we rode on towards the mountains and missed our way, going too far to the north, till at last we came upon some tents and herds, an Anazeh tribe, and they directed us. We were in sight of Palmyra, lying some 10 miles from us in a bay of the hills. Seeing it thus from the desert one realizes the desert town, not the Roman,—Tadmor, not Palmyra. We are terribly bothered by wind, both marching and in camp, when it sheets us in dust. We march very long hours, and oh, I'm tired!

May 2nd. We rode through the mountains, a beautiful road but I was too tired to enjoy it much. Also we made very long hours, ten and twelve a day. On the 30th we went in to Adra an camped there, on the very spot where I mounted my camel the day I set out from Damascus, four months and a half ago. Next morning, yesterday, through gardens and orchards to Damascus. I rather think I shall catch a boat to C'ple on the 8th, getting there on the 12th, stay there a week or less and come on by train, getting to London about the 24th.

[This arrival at Damascus on her return journey marks the end of Gertrude's travels in the desert with her caravan.

Dr. David Hogarth, President of the Royal Geographical Society, gave an account on April 14th, 1927, before the Society, of Gertrude's adventurous expedition to Hayil from which I quote the following.

"Her journey was a pioneer venture which not only Put On the map a line of wells, before unplaced or unknown but also cast much new light on the history of the Syrian desert frontiers under Roman, Palmyrene, and Ummayad domination. . . . But perhaps the most valuable result consists in the mass of information that she accumulated about the tribal elements ranging between the Hejaz Railway on the one flank and the Sirhan and Nefûd on the other, particularly about the Howaitât group, of which Lawrence, relying on her reports, made signal use in the Arab campaigns Of 1917-1918.

"Her stay in Hayil was fruitful of political information especially concerning both the recent history and the actual state of the Rashid house, and also its actual and probable relations with the rival power of the Ibn Sauds. Her information proved of great value during the war, when Hayil had ranged itself with the enemy and was menacing our Euphratean flank. Miss Bell became from 1915 onwards, the interpreter of all reports received from Central Arabia."

Dr. Hogarth also said in reference to her return across Hamad to Damascus from Bagdad:

"To another European woman, in the days before desert motor services had been thought of, such a journey would have seemed adventurous enough. But to Miss Bell, who had been into Nejd, the crossing of the Hamad seemed something of an anti-climax.

". . . .The jaded traveller, writing in April 1914 her diary and letters at Bagdad, had no suspicion that, in little more than a year, the knowledge and experience acquired during the past four months would become of national value. Nor could she foresee that, even after the war Northern Nejd would return to the obscurity from which she had rescued it. Up to this year of grace, 1927, her visit to Hayil, thirteen years ago, remains the last that has been put on scientific record by a European traveller . . . . . ."

CHAPTER XIV

1914-1915-1916

WAR WORK, BOULOGNE, LONDON, CAIRO.

To F.B. EMBASSY, CONSTANTINOPLE,
May 15, 1914.

I ought to have telegraphed yesterday for I arrived on the evening of the 13th. . . . I have entirely recovered from the exhaustion of the Syrian desert. . . . If you are at Rounton I should come straight there. Sir Louis is perfectly delightful. He is tremendously full of his job and we have talked for hours.

[Gertrude was then in England for the rest of the summer. At the outbreak of war she was at Rounton. During September 1914 she went round to various places in the North Riding of Yorkshire giving addresses on the war, and cheering people on. She was an admirable speaker, and her addresses always aroused enthusiasm.

After this she went for a time to Lord Onslow's Hospital at Clandon, and afterwards, by the initiative of Lord Robert Cecil (now Lord Cecil), to Boulogne, where she worked with Flora and Diana Russell in the office for tracing the Missing and Wounded.]

To H.B. BOULOGNE,
November 26, 1914.

Ian Malcolm has brought a motor over with him so for the moment that's all we want. But I can't be certain that we may not want one later, for this whole thing is merely in course of organisation, a new branch is in prospect and I wish you could hold your hand till I see what happens. It Is fearful the amount of office work there is. We are at it all day from 10 till 12:30 and from 2 to 5 filing, indexing and answering enquiries. Yesterday after five I went to see Mrs. Charlie Furse at the central Ry. station where she has her out station and afterwards we went together to one of the big hospitals at the Casino and talked to some of the men of the wards. A lot came in with frost bite last week; now it's warm and that won't occur. The Red X won't let any women make the enquiries at the hospitals, which is very silly, as it would give us all occasional change of work, but of course I shall gradually make friends with C.O.s and sisters and go in after to wherever I like. Mrs. Furse lunched with Diana and me to-day, an interesting woman, she is doing her job awfully well. Will you ask General Bethune to send us out as complete a list as he can of the Territorial Battalions—something corresponding to the Army List for Regulars. Also can I have some sort of London Address book for the office? An old telephone directory would do.

To F.B. BOULOGNE,,
November 27, 1914.

. . . . I sometimes go into our big hospitals and talk to the men. It is immensely interesting to hear their tales. There are a good many Germans to whom I talk. Our men are exceedingly good and kind to them and try to cheer them as far as they can with no common language. I generally go for a walk by the sea from 8:30 to 9 a.m.—it's the only time I have. We lunch in a tiny restaurant with soldiers of all sorts and kinds, the oddest world. Everybody takes everybody else for granted.

To F.B. BOULOGNE,
November 28, 1914.

I hear to-day that you have your convalescents 20 of them (where have you put them all). Now would you like me to come back? I am quite, quite ready to come. I don't approve doing other things when you are wanted in your own place. If you send me a telegram I will return at once and no more said. I should not be happy here if I thought you needed me.

Please telegraph and I'll come home at once.

To F.B. HOTEL MEURICE, BOULOGNE,
November 30, 1914.

.... We are very busy to-day making up double card catalogue which has to be done over and above our work mostly in the luncheon hour and after tea when the office is supposed to be shut. It will take days I fear but when it is done the office will be in far better order. ...

To F.B. BOULOGNE,
December 1, 1914.

In time I think we ought to have one of the best run offices in France we are already scheming to get into closer touch with the front which is our weak point. Lord Robert asked the Adj. General to let us have a representative and he refused categorically. Now we have a great plan for getting lots of Army Chaplains for it is quite clear we shall have to make our own channels for ourselves. Also I have several other ideas in my head to put into execution gradually. I'll tell you about them as they evolve.

We have had the most pitiful letters and we see the most pitiful people.

Don't let all this discourage you at all from bringing me home if you want me.

To H.B. BOULOGNE,
December 5, 1914.

.... Would you please ask the County Association office to send me the latest arrangements about Soldiers and Sailors allowances—what is given to the widows and orphans if the man is killed and what to the man if he is disabled. The orders have been so many that I have not kept them in MY head and we want them for reference.

To F.B. BOULOGNE,
December 6, 1914.
 I've got a great deal of work done these last days and I very nearly cleared away the mountain of mistakes which I found when I came.

To H. B. BOULOGNE,
December 19th, 1914.
 You know we have a head office in London under Lord Roberts at 83 Pall Mall. Sometime when you are near there you might go in and see him and find out if he is satisfied with the way we run the office here.

To H.B. BOULOGNE,
December 26, 1914.
 Diana and I took a half holiday yesterday and walked along the coast in frosty sun.

To H. B. BOULOGNE,
December 30 1914.
 ... Do you mind my being here, dearest father. I feel as if I had flown to this work as one might take to drink, for some kind of forgetting that it brings, but, you know it, there is no real forgetting and care rides behind one all the day. I sometimes wonder if we shall ever know again what it was like to be happy. You sound terribly overworked. . . . .
 I try to look in the face the thing that may be before us-but it won't bear speaking of. I shall see Maurice when he comes over and before he goes to the front. I may very likely have a day or two with him, that's what I hope.

To F.B. BOULOGNE,
january 1, 1915.
 A happier New Year. What else can I wish you? Diana and I caught ourselves wondering last night whether the next 31st Dec. would find us still sitting at our desks here. We saw the New Year in after all. It happened this way.
 Yesterday morning there 'débouchéd' in our office Mr. Cazalet, who is working with Fabian Ware out at the front. Mr. Cazalet brought a tangled bundle of letters and lists which we had been working to compare with ours and to be put straight for him. We had 24 hours for the work before he returned to the front. It was just like a fairy story only we hadn't the ants and the bees to help us in a mountain of work. Diana ran out got a great ledger and proceeded to make it into an indexed ledger which we couldn't find here.
 We had two hours off from 7 to 9 to dine with her cousin who has come out to look for a missing son—dead I tnuch fear. At 9 we went back to the office. By 9:30 everything was sorted out and I began to fill in the ledger, Diana keeping me supplied, we could not have done it if I had not prepared all that was possible beforehand. At midnight we broke off for a few minutes, wished each other a better year and ate some chocolates. At 1 a.m. a young man of an

acquaintance seeing our lights burning came up to know if he could help us but he could not and so sent him away with thanks. By 2 a.m. we were within an hour or two of the end so we came home to bed I was back at 8:15 prepared the ordinary days work, shortened it a little, the rest will stand over for tomorrow got through my part with the men when they came in and leaving Diana to clear up the rest returned to the ledger. BY 12:30 it was finished with just an hour to spare and I took it to Mr. Cazalet. It had been an exciting time but we won it and now this really important thing is set going. There now remains a card index of names to write for him but we have a week for that.

To H.B, BOULOGNE,
january 6th, 1915.

We are going to start an office at Rouen I think and hope. The Russells will take charge of it and I am to have Tiger Howard here. I had a long talk with Mr. Fabian Ware tonight—he appears to be very grateful for our lists and things and delighted to heap all his information upon us which is the one thing I want. As for Lord R. he is quite delightful. And he is satisfied with the way things have been done here-I think more than satisfied which is a great relief to my mind. He contemplates making this more and more of a centre and I think it will become the real distributing place of information for which, geographically it is best suited. They all seem to want that and I need not say I'm ready to take it all. The more work they give me the better I like it.

To F.B. BOULOGNE,
January 12, 1915.

. . . The Rouen office is settled. Flora and Diana are together taking charge of it alternate fortnights . . . ..

To H.B. BOULOGNE,
February 10, 1915

. . . . Katie Freshfield turned up. She is a V.A.D. part of a detachment which is going up as orderlies to the Cross Hospital at G.H.Q. They are delayed here for the moment and she and another girl came in at an early hour to dust our office.

[From Boulogne Gertrude was summoned back to London by Lord Robert Cecil. The office in London for tracing the wounded and missing was in a state of chaotic confusion and Lord Robert opined that Gertrude would be the best person to put it straight-which she did, and succeeded in organising it on efficient lines.

In November she was sent for to Cairo. Dr. David Hogarth, then in close connection with Col. T. E. Lawrence, who was taking an active part in the Revolt in the Desert, felt that Gertrude's knowledge of the tribes of Northern Arabia would be invaluable. Through his intervention therefore and that of Capt. Hall (now Vice-Admiral Sir Reginald Hall) in London, it was Proposed to Gertrude that she should go to Cairo at once. She went there in November 1915.)

To F.B. CAIRO,
November 30th, 1915.

I telegraphed to you this morning after my arrival and asked you to send me by Lady B. another gown and skirt. I have not yet been to see the MacMahons but I must leave a card on them to-day. For the moment I am helping Mr. Hogarth to fill in the intelligence files with information as to the tribes and sheikhs, It's great fun and delightful to be working with him. Our Chief is Col. Clayton whom I like very much. This week Mark Sykes passed through and I have seen a good deal of him. I have just heard that Neil Malcolm has arrived from Gallipoli—I think he is chief staff officer here; I have written to him and asked him to dinner if he is not too great for such invitations.

We had a horrible journey—almost continuous storm. Helen Brassey and I survived triumphantly and took comfort in one another's society. She is a very charming creature. We reached Port Said after dark on Thursday night. Capt. Hall, the brother of our Capt. Hall (he is head of the Railway here) made every possible arrangement for my comfort and Capt. Woolley, ex-digger at Carchemish and head in the Intelligence Dept. at P. Said came on board to meet me. Next morning I came up here. Mr. Hogarth and Mr. Lawrence (you don't know him, he is also of Carchernish exceedingly intelligent) met me and brought me to this hotel where they are both staying. Mr. Hogarth, Mr. Lawrence and I all dined together; at our table sit two Engineers Col. Wright (brother of Hagberg) and very nice and Major Pearson. Occasionally we have Mr. Graves into dinner—he was Times Correspondent in Constantinople in former days. I knew him there. Now you know my circle-it is very friendly and pleasant, but Mr. Hogarth leaves next week which will make a terrible gap in it. You will write to me here in future Won't you and will you have the Times sent out to ne—the edition which appears three times a week. I'm glad I came but I long for news of you.

To F.B. CAIRO,
December 6th, 1915

Mr. Hogarth leaves tomorrow, to my great sorrow. He has been a most friendly support and I have scarcely Yet found my own feet yet. They have given me some work to do on Arab Tribes their numbers and lineage. It is a vague and difficult subject which would take a lifetime to do properly I should think it will be about a month before I can get it into any sort of shape, but it rather depends on what information one can collect. I haven't begun yet for I have been doing odds and ends of jobs for Mr. Hogarth which have taken all my time. Far the nicest people who I have met are the MacMahons with whom I dined last night. They are both charming, so pleasant and agreeable. They gave me a standing invitation to come in whenever I liked and I am going to have a long talk with him one of these days.

To F. B. CAIRO,
December 13th, 1915.

. . . .. The days pass quickly here. I am quite happy and beginning to feel a little more as if I were getting hold of things. I do the same thing every day all pleasant but not matter for good letter writing. I have an Arabic lesson from 8:15 to 9:30 then I walk up to the office and work at tribes or annotate telegrams—the latter is great fun. Back to lunch and then to the office again and I seldom get home much before 7. . . . . but usually I dine here with Col. Wright, Mr. Lawrence and a party of people, we all share the same table. And it is not till after dinner that I go back to Arabic and do a little work for next morning. I wonder if you sent me out a purple evening chiffon gown by Lady Brassey—I telegraphed for it, but I haven't heard anything of it or her yet. Also a new white skirt from Ospovat which I found I hadn't got. I am rather short of clothes for a prolonged stay in Cairo. It is heavenly weather—almost too nice for wartime I feel. Still I think I'm right to be here. . . ..

[She stayed in Cairo for 6 weeks, during which time she met one person after another who interested her, either old friends or new acquaintances.]

To F.B. ON THE NILE,
December 25th, 1915.

You don't mind my staying, do you? as long as they have a job for me. Of course if you want me I will come home. I rather wish I had brought out more clothes. Could you possibly send out to me the blue shot silk gown with a little coat and its own hat trimmed with feathers? And if you are sending anything I should like too the purple satin day gown with a cape—Marie knows which I mean—and a mauve parasol, I have lots I know. I don't know whether things sent by parcel post would be likely to reach me. Both gowns would fold up so small that they could almost be sent by letter post—not a hat however. Perhaps if you were to ask the kind Captain Hall he could contrive to send out a small box for me, by bag even. I should be very grateful—and the sooner the better.

To F.B. CAIRO,
january 1, 1916.

A second year of war—and I can only wish you as I wished you last first of January that we may not see another. Never another year like the last. Its probable that I may go on for a few days to India towards the end of the month. I have had long and very interesting letters from Domnul and an invitation from the Viceroy who wants to see me. it comes rather conveniently for there are certain matters on which we should like to have the V's sympathy and co-operation. I should not stay more than a week. It seems a long way to go from Saturday to Monday but my chiefs are inclined to think it would be worth it. I will telegraph to you if this plan takes form. Mr. Hogarth writes to me that he is coming back as soon as possible which will be very nice. Also he might bring me out some clothes!

To H.B. CAIRO,
january 3, 1916.

My tribe stuff is beginning to be pulled into shape and will make quite a respectable book when finished-a respectable basis for further work at any rate. I love doing It—you can't think what fun it is. In fact I have come back to it with such renewed zest that I can scarcely tear myself away from it. . . . . They are immensely kind all these people and it is most useful to be able to draw on their knowledge and experience. I'm getting to feel quite at home as a Staff Officer! It is comic isn't it.

To H. B. CAIRO,
January 16th, 1916.

I rather hope I may hear this week from Domnul in reply to a cable I sent him saying I might come out to India at the end of the month. My chief here is warmly in favour of the idea. They would very much like me to stay a fortnight or so at a halfway point on my way back—I won't 'préciser' further and if Lord H. views the idea with favour as I believe he might I should certainly do so and I think it would be very useful in many ways. There is no kind of touch between us except telegrams and it would be a great advantage if we could establish more direct and friendly relations. I feel a little nervous about being the person to carry it out, but the pull one has in being so unofficial is that if one doesn't succeed no one is any the worse.

To F.B. CAIRO,
January 19th, 1916.

Here is the letter about my summer clothes. It seems a great deal but I know it isn't more than I had last year—they only just lasted me through. Lady MacMahon sent me a lot of things from Egypt. I'm feeling awfully tired and done up. I don't know what's the matter. I've been working a great number of hours and getting through dreadfully little, having anamia of the brain. I'm going to try a course of morning rides to see if exercise will do any good. I feel just like I was before I had jaundice, yet it would be unnatural to have jaundice again! Its jaundice of the imagination this time.

To H.B. CAIRO,
JanuarY 24th, 1916.

I can't write through censors and I must therefore send you a private word by bag enclosed to the Hogarths to tell you what I'm doing—it is of course only for you Mother and Maurice. . . . When I got Lord H's message through Domnul I suggested that it might be a good plan if I, a quite unimportant and unofficial person were to take advantage of the Viceroy's invitation and go out to see what could be done by putting this side of the case before them and hearing that. My chief has approved. I cabled to Domnul and received from him an enthusiastic reply. So I'm going. I don't suppose I shall be in India more than ten days or a fortnight. I shall go straight up to Delhi to Lord H. If they will let me I would very much like to go to Basrah for a week or two on my way back. I shall very probably spend a few days at Aden before I return here as there is a good deal of information about tribes and the people which we want from them and don't seem to get. I feel a little anxious about it, but take refuge in my own extreme obscurity and the general kindness I find everywhere. I shall find Domnul at Delhi which will make everything easy, otherwise I don't think I should have the face to set out on a political mission.

To F.B. CAIRO,
January 25th, 1916.

Your news about Maurice filled me with such immense relief that I can scarcely believe anything so fortunate should be true. It seems odd to regard an operation in that light. The knowledge that he is safely at home makes me feel indifferent as to going to India which did seem a fearfully long way from home. . . . I don't much like going away from here. I've fallen into the way of it, friendly and pleasant._11 days of solitary journey is a formidable prospect but I've nO doubt it will be very nice when I get there and I'm looking forward to seeing Domnul. Anyhow I think I ought to go and that's an end. I have practically finished the Tribal book I have been doing as far as it can be finished here, but I look forward to getting lots of fresh material in India.

To H. B.
CAIRO, January 18, 1916.

I'm off finally at a moment's notice to catch a troop ship at Suez, I really do the oddest things. I learnt at 3 p.m. that I could catch it if I left at 6 p.m. which did not allow much time for thought. I'm charged with much negotiation—and I hope I may be well inspired.

[An officer who was at Cairo at the time said afterwards that he "never saw anyone mobilise as quickly as Miss Bell."]

CHAPTER XV
1916-1917

DELHI-BASRAH

To F.B.
S.S. "EURIPIDES," February 1, 1916.
    We reach Karachi on the 6th and I'm cabling to Domnul to let him know. It is an extraordinary quick voyage. The cat and I are the only two people not in uniform on board. There is a chaplain called Wood who is a friend of Hugo's and was ordained on the same day. I have foregathered with him a little. He has asked me to come and talk to the troops this afternoon about Arabia or anything—they get so bored poor dears, I shall love to do anything to amuse them. The adjutant has also asked me to give a conference on Mesopotamia to the officers which I shall like less. They are the 23rd and 24th Rifle Corps coming out to do Garrison duty in India in order to relieve younger troops. I'm luxuriously comfortable with a large cabin and a big room next to it usually the nursery where I go and work all the morning and again after dinner. It's the first time I've ever succeeded in doing any work on the sea, the weather is deliciously warm.

To F.B.
VicE-REGAL LODGE, DELHI, February 11 th, 1916.
    .... But in order properly to appreciate dust you must go by train across the desert of Sinde. We reached Delhi at 7:30 a.m. I hadn't an idea what was to happen to me, nor whether anyone knew I was coming and behold when I got outg coated in dust on an icy cold morning, there was Domnul On the platform and a Vice-Regal motor waiting outside. YOU may imagine my joy.
    [Then followed some very interesting days at the Vice-Regal lodge discussing the situation with the Viceroy, seeing Mr. Baker and Mr. Lutyens, hearing of the new Delhi.]
    Later. I've just come in from another dinner party at Vice-Regal Lodge. At the beginning of dinner the V. sent me a scribbled card to say that it was all settled about my going on and that I was given permission to go much further up the river than I had originally thought of doing. It is interesting, deeply interesting, but oh, it's an anxious job. I wish, I wish, I knew more—and was more. And I am rather overwhelmed at meeting with so much kindness and confidence.
    I shall be here another week, I suppose, but as to that I shall do what I'm told.
    I know you will both think that this is right. Tell Maurice and Herbert. Otherwise I always think the less said the better.

To H.B.
VICE-REGAL LODGE, DELHI, February 18th, 1916.
 .... No one has helped another as you helped me, and to tell you what your love and sympathy meant is more than I know how to do.
 .... As at present arranged I leave Delhi on the 23rd, and spend a day or two at Lahore and start from Karachi on the 27th. What will happen after that I have no idea. The V. is anxious that I should stay at Basrah and lend a hand with the Intell. Dept. there, but all depends on what their views are and whether I can be of any use. That hangs on me, I feel—as we have often said, all you can do for people is to give them the opportunity of making a place for themselves. The V. has done that amply. He has been extraordinarily kind, and indeed all the people here have been delightful. Mr. Grant has placed all their archives at my disposal and I have spent my time reading the Arabian files—and learning much from them. Besides reading the files I have seen all the people concerned with Indian Foreign Affairs and talked to them about Arabia till I am weary of the very word—they must be too, I should think. I think I have pulled things straight a little as between Delhi and Cairo. But nothing will ever keep them straight except a constant personal intercourse it ought not to be difficult to manage and I am convinced that it is essential.

To F.B.
Vice-REGAL Lodge, DELHI, February 18th, 1916.
 .... The Viceroy took me one afternoon, to see the new Delhi. It was very wonderful seeing it with him who had invented it all, and though I knew the plans and drawings I didn't realise how gigantic it was till I walked over it. They have blasted away hills and filled up valleys, but the great town itself is as yet little more than foundations. The roads are laid out that lead from it to the four corners of India, and down each vista you see the ruins of some older imperial Delhi. A landscape made up of empires is something to conjure with.
 [Extract from letter written to Captain R. Hall (now Vice Admiral Sir Reginald Hall, G.C.B.) from the Vice Regal Lodge, Delhi, Feb. 20th, 1916.)
 DEAR CAPT. HALL, ...Before I went to Basrah I remember your putting your finger on the Bagdad corner of the map and saying that the ultimate success of the war depended on what we did there. You are one of the people who realised how serious are the questions we have to face. . . . I have had a most useful fortnight here. . . . I have got on terms of understanding with the India F.O. and the I.D. It is essential India and Egypt should keep in the closest touch since they are dealing with two sides of the same problem. . . .
GERTRUDE BELL.

To H.B.
KARACHi, February 26th, 1916.
 I can't remember where I left off in my last letters. I spent the remaining days at Delhi ardently reading all their files and got through the most important of them. A man came down from Simla to see me and spent a long day

discussing how we should best cooperate intelligence work, so that the same ground should not be covered twice over by Egypt and by India. That was most profitable and I sent my scheme to Cairo for an approval which I think I shall get. It seems obviously reasonable that we should not work in watertight compartments but it's not an idea which dominates official dealings though I find everyone curiously ready to accept it when once it's mooted. The result is that I'm now enrolled as one of the editors of the Gazeteer of Arabia which is being compiled at Simla and I very much fear that I shall have to come back and see Col. Murphy there before I return to Egypt—whenever that may be. My last night at Delhi I dined with Mr. Grant of the Indian F.O., and had a long evening's talk with him which was very useful. He also would like to see me on my way back and he wants me to come with a sort of informal report for the benefit of the new Viceroy. If I have anything to say, therefore, I expect I shall have to go back and say it, but it depends on how long they keep me at Basrah and on how much they let me see and hear.

TO H.B.
March 3rd, 1916.

We are within half an hour of Basrah. I've come on a transport. It interests me immensely coming into this country from this direction, which I have never done before. We have been steaming up the river all the morning through a familiar landscape of palm groves and Arab huts, with apricot trees blooming here and there in untidy mudwalled gardens—I'm so glad to see it all again and I feel as if I were in my own country once more and welcome it, ugly though it is. Now it remains to be seen whether they find a job for me or send me away without delay.

I wish I knew how Maurice is and were certain that he is not going back to France yet.

To F.B.
BASRAH, March 17, 1916.

Monotonous days pass so quickly that I never realize it,s mail day till it is upon me. I am still with the Coxes but I only dine, sleep and breakfast here—for I go in to lunch next door to G.H.Q., which saves time and trouble. Next week I am to be lodged there also. Sir Percy is most charming, Well read and interesting. But I can't decently impose upon their kindness much longer—I've been with them a fOrtnight already. Mr. Dobbs also is a great standby. I go walking with him of an evening.

I'm still wading through the stuff which they have got here but tomorrow I have a man who is coming to see me and give me information, an Arab of Central Arabia, and I expect to have rather an amusing talk with him.

No mail in yet. One pines for news.

To H.B.
BASRAH, March 18th, 1916.
.... And I fall to asking myself what I am really doing here—really nothing, though I work at it like a nigger all day long. At the end of a week I look back and think I've perhaps put in one useful wordand perhaps not; I can't be certain. And if I went away it wouldn't matter, or if I stay it wouldn't matter. However I've thrown in my lot with it—and I would as soon be here as anywhere. They are fussing in Egypt to know how long I'm going to stay. I don't know whether they want me to come back, but I've written to say I think I had better stay on a bit till we see what happens. But I don't mind either way. I have an unhappy feeling all the time of trying to take a hand in things which are too big to be guided. They move on inevitably and you can't stay them with your little knowledge and your feeble will.

To F.B.
BASRAH, March 9, 1916
I wish I ever knew how long I was going to stay in any place or what I were likely to do next. But that is just the kind of thing which one never can know when one is engaged in the indefinite sort of job which I am doing. There is, however, indeed a great deal of work to be done here. I have already begun to classify the very valuable tribal material which I find in the files at the Intel. Dept., and I think there are pretty wide possibilities of adding to what has been collected already. It is extraordinarily interesting; my own previous knowledge though there was little enough of it, comes in very handy in many ways—as a check upon, and a frame to the new stuff I am handling. And I can't tell you how wonderful it is to be in at the birth, so to speak, of a new administration. Everyone is being amazingly kind. I have been given a lodging next door to Headquarters in the big house on the river which belongs to Gray, Mackenzie & Co. That is most convenient, for I have only to step across the bridge a little creek to get to my work. Today I lunched with the Generals—Sir Percy Lake, General Cowper, General Offley Shaw and General Money, and as an immediate result they move me and my maps and books onto a splendid great verandah with a cool room behind it where I sit and work all day long. My companion here is Captain Campbell Thompson, exarchaeologist—very pleasant and obliging and delighted to benefit with me by the change of workshop, for we were lodged by day in Col. Beach's bedroom (he is head of the I.D.), a plan which was not very convenient either for us or for him. The whole of Basrah is packed full, as u may understand when it has had suddenly to expand into the base of a large army. Finally I have got an Arab boy as a servant. His name is Mikhail. Sir Percy Cox came back last night—he has been away at Bushire—and he also is going to help me to get all the information I want by sending on to me any Arabs whom he thinks will interest me. Therefore if I don't make something of it, it will be entirely my own fault. I'm thankful to think that M. won't be back in France at any rate till the end of April. The relief it is to know that he is not fighting! The situation night develop very rapidly here

and there is a feeling of changing tide which is exciting and disturbing. My days are, however, very uneventful. I work at G.H.Q. from 8:30 to 12:30, come in to lunch, and go back there from 2 till near 6. Then, it being sunset, wonderfully cool and delicious, I walk for half an hour or so through palm gardens it's more like a steeplechase than a walk for the paths are continuously interrupted by irrigation channels, over some of which you Jump while over the others you do tightrope dancing across a single palm trunk. I shall fall in some day, and though I shall not be drowned, it will be disgustingly muddy.

To H.B.
BASRAH, March 24, 1916.
. . . .I sometimes try to picture what it will be like when we are all at home together again and daren't think of it lest the Gods should be taking heed. We are now on the edge of important things and we hold our breath. If we don't succeed it will be uncommonly awkward. I don't know that there is much point in my being here, but I'm glad I came because one inevitably understands much more about it. And I'm glad I have got to know Sir Percy Cox. He is a very remarkable person, not the least remarkable thing about him being his entire absence of any thought about himself. He does his job a gigantic job and thinks no more about it. I wonder if Elsa is back at Rounton yet. Very soon the wild daffodils by the little pond will come out and nod their heads to the east wind. It is 3 years since I saw them.

To F.B.
BASRAH, April 9, 1916.
. . . . This week has been greatly enlivened by the appearance of Mr. Lawrence, sent out as liaison officer from EgYPt We have had great talks and made vast schemes for the government of the universe. He goes up river tomorrow, where the battle is raging these days. . . . I have nearly finished my tribe handbook, but I want go up to Nasariyeh before it is put into it's final form, for I know it needs checking from there. For that I must Wait to see the result of Kut.

To H. B.
BASRAH, April 16, 1916.
ow Kut holds out still I can hardly guess, but it does and we may yet get through in time. But one feels dreadfully anxious. . . . Even Basrah has a burst of glory in April. The palm gardens are deep in luxuriant grass and corn, the pomegranates are flowering, the mulberries almost ripe, and in the garden of the house where I am staying the roses are more wonderful than I can describe. It's the only garden in Basrah, so I'm lucky.

To F.B.
G.H.Q., BASRAH, April 27, 1916.
Nothing happens and nothing seems likely to happen at Kut—it's a

desperate business, Heaven knows how it will end. Meantime I have been having some very interesting work and as long as it goes on, I shall remain. One is up against the raw material here, which one is not in Egypt, and it is really worth while doing all these first hand things. I don't mind the heat there has been nothing to speak of the thermometer so far seldom above 90, and I rather like it. But I wish I had some clothes; my things are beginning to drop to pieces; I wonder if you are sending me out any, and if they will ever arrive. I think I shall write to Domnul in Bombay for some cotton skirts and some shirts. One wears almost nothing, fortunately, still it's all the more essential that that nothing should not be in holes. I generally get up nowadays about 5:30 or 6 and when I haven't got to mend my clothes, bother them I go out riding through the palm gardens and have half an hour's gallop in the desert which is Very delicious. Then back to a bath and breakfast and across the road to G.H.Q. by 8:30, I work there till about 5:30, with half an hour off for lunch after which if I haven't been out in the morning I go for a little walk, but it's getting rather too hot to walk comfortably much before sunset. Then read a little or do some work which I have brought in with me, have another bath, dine at a quarter to 9 and go to bed.

The days pass like lightning. Last week I went out for a night to Zubair. We have a political officer there, Captain Marrs, very nice and intelligent. I was put up at the post office in a room with a mud floor furnished with my own camp bed a chair a bath and a table lent by Captain Marrs, but the Sheikh of the town insisted on entertaining me and we went in to him for all our meals and unlimited gossip about the desert with which he is always in the closest touch since the caravans come in to Zubair. . . .

I was also much obliged to Father for his very interesting statistics about the falling mark, and for the article on the Mesop. campaign in the Economist. I fear the latter is nothing short of the truth, but the blame needs a good deal of distribution. I don't hold a brief for the Govt. of India, but it is only fair to remember that K. drained India white of troops and of all military requirements, including hospitals and doctors, at the beginning of the war, that the campaign was forced on them from England, and that when it developed into a very serious matter—far too big a matter for India to handle if she had had command of all her resources—neither troops, nor artillery, nor hospital units, nor flying corps, nor anything were sent back in time to be of use. And what was perhaps still more serious was that all their best generals had gone to France or Gallipoli many of them never to return.

Politically, too, we rushed with the business with our usual disregard for a comprehensive political scheme. We treated Mesop. as if it were an isolated unit, instead of which it is part of Arabia, its politics indissolubly connected with the great and far reaching Arab question, which presents Indeed, different facets as you regard it from different aspects, and is yet always and always one and the same indivisible block. The coordinating of Arabian politics and the creation of an Arabian policy should have been done at home—it could only have been done successfully at home. There was no one to do it, no one who had ever thought of it, and it Was left to our people in Egypt to thrash out, in the face of strenuous opposition, from India and London, some sort of wide scheme, which will, I am persuaded, ultimately form the basis of our relations with the Arabs. Well that is enough of Politics. But when people talk of our muddling through it throws me into a passion. Muddle through! why yes so we do—wading through blood and tears that need never have been shed.

To H.B.
G.H.Q., BASRAH, May 14, 1916. :

You will tell me, won't you, if you think I ought to come home. I will do exactly what you think right and what you Wish, but if you do not send for me I shall stay here as long as they will let me I might be recalled to Egypt, where they are fussing to have me back, but I am persuaded that for the moment I am much more useful here and indeed I am beginning to feel that I am being really useful. I should have to go a long way back to tell you how many gaps there were to fill. I have got hold of the maps and am now bringing them out in an intelligible form, but that is only one among the many odd jobs which I do. Also the natives here are beginning to know me and drop in with news and gossip. Finally, and I think most important of all, there is the difficult gap between Mesop. and Egypt to bridge and I hope I am going to be the person who is charged with the task. Sir P. Cox wants me and as I have a great respect and admiration for him and get on with him excellently I believe I can keep the matter going without friction. There is so much, oh so much to be thought of and considered so many ways of going irretrievably wrong at the beginning, and some of them are being taken and must be set right before matters grow worse. I know these people, the Arabs; I have been in contact with them in a way which is possible for no official, and it is that intimacy and friendship which makes me useful here That is why I want to stay; but when I have letters from home telling of sickness and sorrow I can scarcely bear to be away from you.

George Lloyd [now Lord Lloyd] has just come out to work with Sir Percy. It will make a great difference to me to have him. I hope he will find time to ride with me sometimes in the morning, when we can talk things over and help each other. But if I become the Egyptian link, I shall probably go into Sir Percy's office too, and that is where I ought to be. MY work is political, not military. The sole drawback is that it is a quarter of an hour from where I live and one can't come backwards and forwards in the middle of the day. Also it is not so luxurious as G.H.Q., where we sit under electric fans all day and really don't feel the heat. The moment you get away from a fan you drip ceaselessly, but I suppose one will get accustomed to that. I am absolutely fit, and don't suffer at all from the climate.

To H.B.
G.H.Q., BASRAH, May 4th, 1916.

for some days before it actually happened it was clear that Kut must fall. . . . Aubrey [Herbert] is, I gather, helping to arrange the exchange of prisoners, his knowledge of Turkish being very useful. The Admiral has just come down here; I have not seen him yet. And today the Army Commander and all G.H.Q. staff return from up river. I must then find out what they wish me to do. If they will let me, I shall stay for the work is extremely interesting and I think I can make a good deal more of the sort of jobs I have been doing if they give me a free hand to recast a lot of their Intelligence publications. I am now engaged in getting into communication with Ibn Rashid, whom it is rather important to preserve as a neutral if we can do no more. He is only about 4 days off and Sir Percy Cox has approved warmly of my sending him a letter. A curious game, isn't it, but you can understand that it is exciting to have a hand in it. The climate is, of course, infernal, but oddly enough I don't mind it. I ride 3 or 4 mornings a week, going out about 5:30, and then come in to a room with all doors and windows closed and electric fans spinning—really quite comparatively cool. The temperature hasn't run up to 100 yet, but it is very close and stuffy with a perpetual south wind—if you can call it a wind, it seems to me perfedly still. This is always the weather in May and they say it is more trying than the hotter months when the N. wind sets in.

To H. B.
G.H.Q., BASRAH, May 21, 1916.

The question of my position with regard to the correspondence with Egypt is not yet definitely settled but I think it is practically certain that I shall be appointed. I shall have to come more strictly under official control and I should not be able to leave this country without very good cause shown, like any other person with a Job here. But I should have no hesitation in giving undertakings of that kind, knowing that you would approve. The thing is to be of the best use one can and I feel certain that this position would give me far greatter opportunities and that I can put them to profit. Things are moving very quickly here as you will probably learn long before this letter reaches you and the political side has become of immense importance, and will be of more importance still.

Well, I come back to your pamphlet and find I haven't said half enough how good and witty and wise I think it, and God bless your soul how can any born man think otherwise?

To F.B.
G.H.Q., BASRAH, May 26th, 1916.

. . . ..I have a lace evening gown, awhite crape gown, a stripy blue muslin gown, two shirts and a stripy silk gown, all most suitable, and the last superlatively right. Thank you so very much. I ride pretty regularly in the mornings for an hour and a half setting Out at 5:30, and feel much better for plenty of hard exercise. One comes in wet through, has a bath and breakfast, and begins work at 8 or a little before. After that YOu can't with any comfort go out in the sun till towards evening. The shade temp. is not much over 100. You keep all door's and windows shut and electric fans spinning, and except for about an hour in the afternoon you don't feel it. One sleeps on the roof. The temp. drops to a little above 90 and probably to 80 or so before dawn. It is quite comfortable.

I went yesterday afternoon, after 5, in an electric launch up the Shatt-al-Arab turned into the new Euphrates channel a few miles above Basrah. The floods are out, and the whole country is under water. We left the channel and went across several miles of shallow water with occasional Palm groves standing in it, derelict villages made of reed matting, and even the reeds themselves sticking up where the water was very shallow. All stewing in the blazing heat. And in the middle of it was a solitary buffalo, knee deep in mud and water, eating the reed tops. Whether he was there because he liked it, or whether he was there by mistake, I don't know. He looked quite happy, but if ever he wanted to lie down, he would have to walk for days it is slow going to find a dry place to lie on. The Ark and all the rest become quite comprehensible when one sees Mesopotamia in flood time. . . .

[She goes up to Nasariyeh by river with Generals McMunn and Cooper—describes the flooded country on the banks of the Euphrates, always in a burning heat with a scorching wind.]

To H.B.
June 12, 1916.
. . . .I could wish Maurice were not so well. The thought of his going back to France—he is probably there by now—is horrible. How dreadfully you will miss him.

Much as I enjoyed my little journey I was very glad to get in under a house roof again, for the last few days were verY hot. I found a great deal of work when I returned. It's not easy here—some day I'll tell you about it. But the more difflcult it is the more I feel I ought to stay.

To H.B.
G.H.Q., BASRAH, June 15th
I'm delighted to hear that M. doesn't go back to France yet, but how will he like a Welsh regiment, I wonder. your encouragement to me to remain here came just at the right moment and I have decided to let them appoint me official Correspondent to Cairo. A routine order is now to be issued ,making me part of I.E.F. "D," the Indian Expeditionary Force "D," and I believe I'm am to have pay, but fortunately I need not wear uniform! I ought to have white tabs, for I am under the Political Department. It's rather comic isn't it. It has its disadvantages, but I think it's the right thing to do. The news this week has been of Mecca, deeply interesting, and one up to Egypt and my beloved chiefs there, from whom I am now entirely detached for the moment. I expect the immediate results will not be very great—we must beat the Turkish army before anything very striking can happen—but the revolt of the Holy Places is an immense moral and tolitical asset. I've had a busy week and I expect I shall be busier when I take up my new work. I shall like very much coming into closer contact

with Sir Percy Cox. He is going to give me a room in his office where I shall go two or three mornings a week—as often as is necessary. The other days I shall go on working at G.H.Q., which is next door to where I live. Sir Percy's office is a quarter of an hour away you can't realize what that means until you've stepped out into the sun here anywhere near the middle of the day. The heat from the ground burns you like the breath of a furnace. We've had a very hot and heavy fortnight, and the north wind, long overdue, doesn't come, curse it. The result is that there's an astonishing amount of sickness, all the clerks and typists going down first so that you can't get your work done. I am absolutely well. I never have the smallest touch of fever or even feel tired—a little slack at the end of the hot day, which isn't surprising seeing that one gets up soon after 5. I sleep like a top, My bed is on the roof; I've discarded all mattresses and sleep on a bit of fine matting with a sheet Over it. After midnight it gets cooler and one wakes for a moment and pulls a second sheet over oneself.

Mr. Dobbs has come back. He's a great addition to my small world. I like him so much and he is so interesting and so clever. George (Lloyd) is still here, but I fear he has nearly finished his job. He will be a great loss. It's the queerest life, you know-quite unlike anything one has ever done before. I love the work, and the people are all very kind. On the Whole I like it all.

But I feel rather detached from you—I wish I could sit somewhere midway and have a talk with you once or twice a week.

To H.B.
BASRAH, July 3, 1916.

I have entered on my new duties, to my great satisfaftion and amusement. I go every morning at 9 to the Political Office—it's about 10 minutes' walk—and work there till 12:30. They give me a cup of coffee in the middle of the morning. Then I have a cab to fetch me and come back to lunch, after which I rest for half-an-hour and go to G.H.Q., where I either find some job waiting for me, or I write things from the notes I have made during the morning. I hope that it will all work out very well and that it will be satisfactory to the Egyptians. There's no denying that the weather is confoundedly hot. We have had some bad days, temperature over 111, and very damp. Hot nights, too. One swears at it, but I'm perfectly well so I haven't any business to complain. There is a terrible amount of sickness, however, among people who have to be out of doors and who are not luxuriously lodged and fed. To carry on a campaign under these conditions is no small matter, for not only are your soldiers enduring more casualties than in the worst battle, but your staff vanishes like sand before the sun—clerks, typists, servants, they go down before you can wink, and you are left to do the things for yourself.

To F.B.
G.H.Q., BASRAH, July 9, 1916.

.... You both tell me of Maurice's new command and Father of his attempts to get him out to the front, which I devoutly hope will prove fruitless.

My work at the Political Office continues to be delightful, and I think it will prove valuable. I had a touch of fever this week and was off for a day, but am now perfectly recovered it was no more than the attack which I was nursed through by the old man in the mosque, you remember, and I may congratulate myself on having got through half the hot weather with quite exceptional immunity from all ills. Oh, but it's a great game we're playing here, or we will play, and some day I shall have so much to say about the general principles of it. They are so simple and so obvious and so apt to be neglected.

We've had some rather better days this last week; temp. something over 100 instead of something over 110, which makes a great difference. It's Ramadhan and the Mohammadans are abstaining from food and water all through the daylight hours. It must be awful in this weather, for scarcely any work can be got through. How can you unload ships and tow boats up stream when you are starving and athirst?

To H.B. and F B.
G.H.Q., BASRAH, July 15th, 1916. . . . .

. . . ..Last night I woke at 1 a.m. to find the temp. still over 100 and myself lying in a pool, My silk nightgown goes into the bath with me in the morning, is wrung out and needs no more bother. Yes, it has been deuced hot, and will be for another 6 weeks at least. I'm all right, but its trying, there's no denying it. It's the first hours of the night, absolutely still, damp and close which I find the worst. But sometimes I think it Pretty horrid to be wet through all day. It's uncommonly difficult to tackle one's clothes! Don't forget, Father, to let me have your paper on Trade Unions. I've always time and the greatest interest for your observations on these matters. But I don't think you can argue Free Trade now on its economic merits—there's bound to be too much passion in the whole question now and for some time to come. Perhaps some day the world will come back to common sense. It won't be yet. I must tell you in confidence that I'm being useful here, more useful than I could be anywhere else because I've got better qualifications for this sort of job than for any. It's not of a world shaking character, but for all that it's worth doing and it would not be done if I didn't stay. That's what holds me up every now and then when I think the nights and days really almost too disagreeable. I'm going to be rather desperately solitary next month. George will be gone, Mr. Dobbs is going on leave, Mrs. van Ess and her husband to Nasariyeh and elsewhere for a month to see about schools. That sweeps away nearly all my circle at one stroke, but General McMunn remains and I find him a great standby and a mighty comfort. There are times when one gets into a sort of impasse, a helpless feeling that there's so much to be pulled straight in human affairs and so little pulling power. One permanent source of satisfaction is my chief, Sir Percy Cox. He is so delightful to work with, so generous to me about all I want to do and so kindly appreciative. I have a very real affection for him. But he is taking on too much, more than any mortal man could accomplish and though it's wonderful how evenly good his health is, I'm always afraid that he may break down under it.

After Mr. Dobbs goes there'll be no one capable of taking his place. . . . The administration here owes him a very great deal. Upon my soul, it's a comfort to come up against real sound good sense combined with administrative capacity. One needs it in a country of this kind which is all beginnings. The real difficulty under which we labour here is that we don't know, and I suppose can't know till the end of the war, exactly what we intend to do in this country. You are continually confronted with that uncertainty. Can you persuade people to take your side when you are not sure in the end whether you'll be there to take theirs?

To H.B. and F.B.
G.H.Q., BASRAH, july 23rd.

I had a letter from Maurice besides the one enclosed by Father. Thank Heaven he's out of it for the moment. And still more thanks that he is not out here. it's Hell at the front and nothing short of it. Sir Victor Horsley's death will make people realize perhaps that the climate is warm whereas the daily death from heatstroke of people who are not 'de connaissance' doesn't filter through. The precautions which might have been taken to mitigate the fury of the summer, such as the supplying of plentiful ice machines, were not taken. Even here we are short of ice, at Amarah or the front, God help you. And it's difficult to do anything now for there's barely enough transport to keep the troops supplied with food. There has been a little breath of north wind on and off for the last few days, but not enough even to keep the nights cool. One comforts oneself by thinking that in 6 weeks or SO we shall be through the worst of it. At least in Sep. it's said to be cool at night. George has gone and I miss him bitterly. He has done good work but even better than his work is the atmosphere of sanity he brings with him. It's difficult at times to see straight and to think straight. One gets bewildered—and there are enough materials for bewilderment—and when the thermometer is persistently over 110 one can't pull oneself together, with the result that things won't fall into scale and the prospect is blocked by a molehill. If you knew what it's like running offices here, with all your clerks and typists going sick and no one to replace them.

Goodbye, my dearest parents. I'm liking my work with Sir Percy very much and indeed I like it all, as well as I should like anything. But I shan't be sorry when the temp. drops 20 degrees.

To H.B.
G.H.Q., BASRAH, July 29th, 1916.

. . . . As for Free Trade, you know what I think. The question must for the moment cease to be a purely economic one and the wise thing is to 'reculer pour mieux sauter.' At least if not to draw back, to draw in. Is this too much the wisdom of the serpent to suit you? You're too good to play the part of Don Quixote, you know—don't break your lance on the windmill wings of passion; it will be wanted strong and bright when the tempests have ceased to turn those wheels round. But whatever you do I shall continue to think you the most beloved Father.

Lord! it's been hot here. The actual temperature is hotter up river but they say that the dryness there makes it more bearable. It's bearable all right here, but so nasty. Everything you touch is hot, all the inanimate objects—Your hair—if that's inanimate—the biscuit you eat, the clothes you put on. The temp. of the river is 94 and one's bath water, drawn from a tank on the roof, never under 100 except in the early morning. But it doesn't steam—the air's hotter.

To F.B.
G.H.Q., BASRAH, August 9th, 1916.

I've been, I'm ashamed to say, on the shelf with fever this week. I'm all right again but feeling like a limp rag. The stiffening will come back in a day or two. I shall not let this happen again if I can help it. A small daily dose of quinine ought to keep it off. We really have got the north wind at last, which means cool nights even if it doesn't much alter the temperature of the days. Cool nights make a world of difference; the temp. before dawn drops sometimes to 77. One feels deliciously frozen! A fall Of 30 from the daytime temperature isn't bad. The dates are all yellow; they will be ripe very shortly. I'm a great deal too woolly to write.

To H.B. and F.B.
G.H.Q., BASRAH, August 11th, 1916.

How warmly I shall welcome Richard Pennessy! [Colonel Pope Hennessy.] It's almost too good to be true. We have had a north wind for the last 10 days, with cold nights, though it doesn't seem to make much difference to the days. I'm much better, nearly well—I'm thankful it's not a week ago when I felt too ill even to write to you. I have been steadily at work ever since and am now beginning to feel like a person again.

Yesterday we had a most entertaining man at the Political Office. He is a famous camel doctor and I had heard of him up and down Arabia. He knows every man in the desert and every man knows him. He can go anywhere with perfect security thanks to his remedy for mange, whatever it is. We had a most amusing gossip about the desert. A man Of that kind is a great asset as a bearer of news—or a carrier of messages. I think the Turks are not having much of a time in Mesopotamia. Ottoman Govt. seems to have vanished from every place except Bagdad and a few of the other towns. The tribes do exactly what they like and there is no attempt to control them. We ought to have a look in one of these days. But I wonder what it will be like trying to bring back some kind of order when there has been nothing but the wildest license. I hear from the front that things are much better, more food and more variety of it, cooler nights and the health of the troops greatly improved; heaven be praised! We are through the worst of this summer now, but when I look back on July I fall to wondering how the army weathered it. It was awful.

I rejoice in the thought that M. is still in England and I am glad to hear he's happy.

TO H.B.
G.H.Q., BARAH, August 19th, 1916.

I write to one parent, but it's meant for both. I'm heartily well again and enjoying immensely a bout of cooler weather, the temp. 101 instead of 107 (you can't think the difference it makes) and cool not to say cold nights. It's heavenly. Even if we go back to another spell of great heat it can't last long. Meantime I've taken to riding again which is very delicious.

My paper on labour met with Sir P. C.'s approval and he sent it up to the W.O. not of course as coming from me but as a memorandum from his office. I was pleased, however. I've been engaged this week in drawing up a memorandum about Musqat where the political situation is both curious and interesting. That's the sort of job I do, sandwiched in with tribe notes and things I pick up from Arabs who come in to see us. It's all very amusing work. The I.G.C. asks me what part I intend to play in the future administration of this country! I think I shall have to keep an eye on it, you know, from time to time! I suppose I shall be able to keep an eye on all the developments in the Near East through the Arab Bureau. . . .

To F.B.
G.H.Q., BASRAH, Augast 27th, 1916.

I went out last week along the light railway 25 miles into the desert—it's the Nasariyeh railway—and found myself in the middle of a big Shammar encampment, hearing all the desert gossip in the familiar manner. It was so curious to travel 50 minutes by rail and find yourself in another universe. General Maude, our new Army Commander, has just arrived. I've made his acquaintance, no more.

I continue to like my work very much and to be extremely thankful for it.

To F.B.
BASRAH, September 20th, 1916.

I didn't write last week because I was having jaundice and truly miserable. It was a mild bout and I'm better but I am going this afternoon for change of air to a sort of big rest house attached to our officers' hospital a few miles down river. It seems a sensible thing to do and I hope a few days will set me on my feet again and restore me to my usual complexion.

It's so provoking to be laid up when there's such a lot of work to do. The thing is growing and this week came a letter from the W.O., to whom I send articles through the Intell. Dept., saying I was sending just what they wanted and would I send more. So that's all right. It makes me want to be back more than ever. Everyone is immensely kind; the Consulting Physician of the Force comes to see me and the woman who is Inspector General of all the hospitals looks after me. I'm ashamed of bothering them about such a silly little ailment.

Will you please send me a winter hat. Something of this kind in dark violet. Either of these would do. Also I would immensely like a soft black satin gown which I could Wear either by day or night crossed over in front, skirt down to the ground. I would like Marte (Conduit St.) to make it because she will make me something pretty. She doesn't usually make anything but evening gowns, but if you told her it's for me and where I am I know she would do it for me.

To H.B.
BAIT NAMAH, 10 September, 1916.

I'm still in hospital but I've made a very rapid cure (I was pretty bad when I came) and I hope they will let me go back to Basrah in a day or two. I've been quite extraordinarily comfortable and the kindness of everyone is past belief. It really was very pleasant to find oneself here with all the trouble of looking after one's own self lifted off one's shoulders. I've done little or nothing but eat and sleep and read novels, of which I found plenty here. Oh yes and I've read all Gilbert Murray's translations of Greek plays—glorious they are—which I also found, one of the doctors being brother to Charles Roberts! I must tell you this hospital is in a great huge modern Arab house which we commandeered, very beautiful and splendid. There are two large courts with orange trees in the middle of them, and in one of them they have set aside a ward for convalescent nurses from the other hospitals. That's where I am. There are always 5 or 6 other people in my ward but I have a corner bed with a screen round it, and for the last few days I have scarcely been in the ward at all. I sit all day in the verandah (and for the last 3 days I've been working all the morning). After lunch I have a bath and read till tea and then I go down and sit in the shade by the water's edge. I dine on the verandah and sleep on the roof under the stars.

Do you know I've never been so ill as this before. I hadn't an idea what it was like to feel so deadly weak that you couldn't move your body much nor hold your mind at all. When once I began to mend and to eat I didn't mind it. . . .

Would you give Bain the bookseller an order for me. He is to send me every month from 4 to 6 new books, novels and poetry, nothing very serious, he knows exactly the kind of thing I like. Tell him I left England last November and have read nothing that has come out since so he will have plenty to go on with. He might send one or two regularly every week. New poetry I love to have and Bain knows perfectly well the sort of novel I like Anthony Hope at one end of the scale and the Crock of Gold at the other

To H.B.
c/o BASE POST MASTER, M.E.F., BASRAH, November 4th. 1916.

I've just been out for a long walk with Mr. Bullard (Revenue Dept.) the first time I've walked a step since May. It is still too dusty to be a very nice form of exercise; riding is better. At the Political Office I am beginning to reap Profit from the long slow collecting and classifying of information—a job I'm always busy with. They send me down all the telegrams and reports that come in from the provinces with a request for a note on the people, tribes and places mentioned. With any luck I can find and place most of them now it's a great satisfaction. It's so nice to be a spoke in the wheel, one that helps to turn, not one that hinders.

To F.B.
BASRAH, November 16th, 1916.

I had a pleasant 5 days away from Basrah. I went up to Qurnah and made that my headquarters, living on my launch but spending most of the day in the A.P.O.'s home. I saw innumerable sheikhs and got all the information I wanted. The weather is perfection. The rain hasn7t come yet—it ought to have come but I'm in no hurry for it. The temperature hangs about 80, with cool damp nights. This morning I was out riding as the sun rose and in the desert half an hour later—the air clear as crystal, you count the tamarisk trees at Shaaibah, 8 miles away. It was wonderfully beautiful. From all of which you may gather that I am extremely well, as indeed I am. I wonder what letters of mine went down in the Arabia and whether I asked for anything in them! I know I did ask about that time for a winter hat, smallish, felt, dark blue or purple, and for 4 thick white silk shirts, turned open at the neck.

To H.B.
BASRAH, November 23rd, 1916.

As a fact I am not writing from Basrah but from somewhere on the Shatt al Arab below Qurnah after what seems to Me, looking back on it, to have been an immense journe Y but I'll begin at the beginning. I left Basrah on a Saturday night the I.G.C. motored me down to what we call the terminus station. I found the night train making itself ready, with a small guard's van hitched onto it for me. This I furnished with a camp bed, a chair and the station master's lantern and off we started about 6 into the desert. If ever years hence I come back into this country and travel to Bagdad by the Basrah express, I shall remember, while I eat my luxurious meal in the dining car, how first I travelled along the line in a guard's van and dined on tinned tongue, tinned butter and tinned pears by the light of the station master's lantern. What happened after that I don't know, for I went to bed and except for an occasional vague consciousness of halts in a wide desert dim with starlight, I didn't take note of anything in particular till the dawn crept in at my windowless window and I woke to find my van standing outside rail head camp in the middle of Arabia, so to speak. All this country was Sadun headquarters, the desert home of the ruling family in Southern Mesopotamia who came up from Mecca in the 14th century and are now immensely multiplied, the great aristocracy of the Iraq. Here they come in spring with their camel herds, for they are not only powerful landowners along the rivers, but also real Bedu, nomads of the open wilderness, a wide, flat, sandy land, good desert from the point of view of the camel breeder, for it grows much thorny scrub and plentiful tufts of coarse grass, eaten down now almost to the toot, an unbroken circle of horizon except where to the north it was intercepted by the palms of the river bank, ghostly through the mirage though they were only a few miles away. The eye doesn't travel far over a level waste.

At 8 o'clock there rolled in General Brooking's motor car and a motor lorry and we bumped over the grass tufts and over the sun split mud of what had been flood water in the spring, to Khamiseyeh, where we have had troops ever since Ibn Rashid came filibustering round last summer. For Kharniseyeh is one of the markets of Central Arabia and he who holds these holds the tribes, as Ibn Rashid found to his cost and perhaps has related by now in Hayil. A mud built, dirty little place is Khamiseyeh, watered by a small and evil looking canal from the Euphrates which runs into the town up to the walled square where the caravans lodge when they come up from Jebel Shamman. I drove straight into our camp, picked up General Tidswell, who is in command, and made him take me round the town. And there we met the Sheikh of Khamiseyeh, who is a friend of mine and on his pressing invitation went to his house and drank a cup of tea. He had a guest, Sheikh Hamud of the Dhafir, one of our friendly Beduin, and we sat for a while listening to the latest desert news, which I translated for the General. I hadn't met Hamud before, though he was one of the Sheikhs of whom I had heard much talk when I was riding up from Hail. And so on, over the desert, some 25 miles to Nasariyeh, putting up gazelle and sand grouse as we went. I never thought to watch them from a motor.

To F.B.
BASRAH, December 9, 1916.

The winter isn't really very nice here. One is usually sneezing, when not coughing, and one wishes one had a nice warm comfortable place to sit in. To think that I was once clean and tidy! However, these are things of the past. I've been busy with a long memorandum about the whole of our central Arabian relations, which I've just finished. It will now go to all the High and Mighty in every part. One can't do much more than sit and record if one is of my sex, devil take it; one can get the things recorded in the right way and that means, I hope, that unconsciously people will judge events as you think they ought to be judged. But it's small change for doing things, very small change I feel at times.

To H.B.
BASRAH, December 15, 1916.

* * * *Do you know I was thinking yesterday what I would pick out as the happiest things I've done in all my life, and I came to the conclusion that I should choose the old Italian journeys with you, those long ago journeys which were so delicious. . . . except only in that very big thing, complete love and confidence in my family I've had that always and can't lose it. And you are the pivot of it. But for that I don't care much one way or the other what happens, except that sometimes I should very much like to see you. But I'm quite content here, interested by the work and very conscious that I couldn't anywhere be doing things that would interest me so much.

The world continues to look autumnal scarcely wintry yet—in spite of the eternal green of the palms. There is a yellow mimosa in flower, fluffy, sweet smelling balls, a very heavenly little tree, albeit thorny. Yes, there's always plenty of small change, isn't there!

To F.B.
BASRAH, December, 1916.

The cold weather is just as uncomfortable here as the hot, or nearly as uncomfortable. The houses are so unsuitable for winter. We live in semidarkness, since all the windows are screened from the summer light and in perpetual cold in rooms that all open on to a court or a verandah. My working room at the Political Office is nice—dark, of course, but I have a little oil stove in it which keeps it warm. Still I feel I've almost forgotten what it is to be really comfortable—not that it matters much.

This is the 4th Xmas I've spent in foreign parts—Arabia, Boulogne, Cairo, Qalat Salih. The last is where I expect to be on Xmas Day and I'm truly thankful to escape any attempt at feasts here.

To H.B.
AMARAH, January 1, 1917.

I will begin the New Year before breakfast by writing to you and sending to you and all my dear family all the best of good wishes.

I must tell you I felt dreadfully depressed on Xmas Day thinking of other Xmas Days when we were together and used to be so absurdly happy a long time ago. I hope Maurice has been with you this year. However, I'm a monster of ingratitude to complain, for I have had a very interesting ten days and enjoyed them. Mr. Philby (Acting Reserve Commission) and I left Basrah on his launch on the 22nd, got up to Qurnah in the evening and spent the night with the A.P.o. We were off early next day and went up river to Qulat Sabib—it was a delicious warm day and the river was delightful. I don't know why it should be as attractive as it is. The elements of the scene are extremely simple but the combination still makes a wonderfully attractive result. Yet there's really nothing—flat, farstretching plain coming down to the river's edge, thorn covered, water covered in the flood in the lower reaches, a little wheat and millet stubble in the base fields, an occasional village of reed built houses and the beautiful river craft, majestic on noble sails or skimming on clumsy paddles. The river bends and winds, curves back on itself almost and you have the curious apparition of a fleet of white sails rising out of the thorny waste, now on one side of you, now the other. And by these you mark where your cruise must be, where the river divides wilderness from wilderness. We passed Ezra's Tomb and its clump of palms and got out to look at it. There's a very ancient tradition which is probably true, that the Prophet is buried here, but the aftual shrine is new. . . .

Two of these days we spent in riding out over the great farms on either side of the river. These rides brought us into a Mesopotamia which was quite new to me. Behind the high land by the river, the thorny scrub and the millet fields, lies the rich rice country watered by the canals from the Tigris. And here the land is densely populated, village after reedbuilt village standing on the canal banks, and everywhere the evidences of the great harvest in mounds of straw and garnered fields and grain laden boats panting up the canals. The farms we rode over were not very large as farms go here; the outer edge of the largest, that is to say, the point where the land sloping down from the Tigris runs into the huge marsh, was some 12 miles from the river; but the sheikh pays 11,000 a year in rent to the Govt. from whom he leases the ground. The calculation is nominally on the basis of half the profits, but in reality it is about onethird and the produce of the farm is about 33,000 pounds a year—a respectable output. . . . I spend my time in seeing local people and getting lots of information about tribes and families which had baffled me in Basrah, a satisfaftory occupation.

To F.B.
BASRAH, January 13th, 1917.

I came back to find the most delightful pile of letters. . . . if you have no time to die, as Maurice says, I wonder you have time to write me such splendid long letters! You really must not do it when you feel dreadfully run. Still, I won't deny that I do enjoy havin news from you both.

I feel so much ashamed of having bothered you about clothes, etc., especially as all the trouble you've taken has been fruitless, as far as I'm concerned, for nothing has arrived! But I still hope the things may be in time for next winter, when I shall doubtless be glad of them. I don't want any books on Persia, thank you, and as I never seem to have time to read anything, even books on Mesopotamia are unnecessary. I have written straight to Batsford at various times for essentials, and perhaps some day they will come. The failure in winter clothes makes me anxious for the summer, and I've thought of a plan which will spare you trouble. I shall write long and full directions (next mail) to the Ladies' Shirt Co., telling them exactly what I want in cotton gowns. But since the shop might perhaps have ceased to exist (one never knows) I shall send the letter under cover to you and, if they have by chance died out, the letter can be given to Harvey & Nichols as it stands. It's clear the only plan is to send things by post in small parcels, as you did last spring. One absolutely can't be without masses of summer things in this climate, as one needs a clean gown almost daily, and the constant washing destroys everything. So I'll be beforehand with my orders, and perhaps Moll, if she is in London, would just step into the shop and see that they are carrying out my requirements reasonably.

I'm going to move into a tiny suite of two rooms, which Sir Percy has been such a dear to allot to me in the Political Office. It will be much more convenient. What it's like plunging through winter mud to my work!—it's just as bad in the summer being far away, because one can't go backwards and forwards in the middle of the day without acute discomfort. I have two servants of my own, so I shall be selfcontained. I'm busy furnishing now, no easy matter, but I have a tower of strength in the angelic I.G.C., who produces everything with a wave of his sword, so to speak, the moment I ask for it. There really never was anybody so kind, and I don't know what I should do without him. He is so cheerful and competent. He is deeply interested in the development of the country. And we truly are doing something behind the battlefields. I have capital material in the local reports sent up to the head office, and I've just drawn up a little memorandum about administrative progress, which I think ought to give satisfaction to the High and Mighty at home. (Happy to tell you that I hear my utterances receive a truly preposterous attention in London.) just at this moment, this is the only theatre of the war where things look rather bright.

The only thing that keeps one going is to have lots of work. At times I feel as if I wasn't worth my keep here, and then at other times I think I'm doing a certain amount of good, but fundamentally, I am sure it is no good bothering as to whether one is or isn't useful, and the only plan is to apply oneself steadfastly to what lies before one and ask no questions. And at least there's plenty before me here. I like it, too, in spite of occasional depressions, generally caused by the sense of not knowing enough and of general inefficiency.

I hope you think I'm right to stay. I don't much enjoy the prospect of another summer in Basrah. There are still some pleasant months before us; it doesn't begin to be hot till May.

I must go to bed, for I'm going to try my new pony at dawn tomorrow.

To F.B.
BASRAH, january 20th, 1917.

A box has just arrived from Marte, through T. Cook & Sons it ought to have contained a black satin gown, but it has been opened (probably in Bombay, it was sent by Cook to his agents in Bombay) and the gown has been abstracted. Isn't it infuriating? All that was left was a small cardboard box inside, containing the little black satin coat Marte sent with the gown, some net, and a gold flower. These, by reason of their being in the small box, the thief couldn't get out, for he only opened a part of the nailed down lid, and made a small hole in the interior cardboard lining, through which he pulled the gown. I hope Marte insured it so that Cook will have to pay but that thought does not console me much at this moment! Marte had better repeat the gown as quickly as possible and send it in a small box by post. That is the only way of getting things. If it can't possibly go by post it must go through the military forwarding officer, but it takes 6 months Will you tell Marte.

To F.B.
BASRAH, january 26th, 1917.

In case my letter of last week didn't reach you, I send an abstract of my directions to the Shirt Co., which it contained. I feel, however, pessimistic as to receiving anything, and I expect I shall have to take to Arab dress next summer. I wrote to you a very doleful letter last week happy to tell you that I'm better physically but I'm suffering from a severe attack of softening of the brain, which I don't know how to master. It makes all work horribly difficult, as well as valueless when done. I feel so useless that I wonder they don't turn me out, perhaps ultimately they will. But what I should do next I can't imagine. Beyond struggling with this devil I've done nothing for the last week, except ride occasionally in the morning. I don't wonder the Arabs are sick of us—I am too. And oh, how weary we all are of the war! Are we going to be beaten do you think, at the end of everything, or praftically beaten? I suppose it would mean abandoning this country and that practically means backing out of Asia. Meantime would you be so very kind as to send me a new Swan Fountain pen, large size and broad nibbed. I've broken the sheath of mine. But if you could teach it to write interesting things before it sets out I should be all the more grateful. This one won't.

To H.B.
BAsRAH, February 2nd, 1917.

The news this week is overshadowed by Lord Cromer's death. I've turned to him so many times this last year for advice and help. He and Sir Alfred [Lyall] were the two wise counsellors to whom I never went in vain; now they're both gone and I can't replace them.

I'm getting over the attack of softening of the brain of which I told you, at least getting over it a little. I ride pretty regularly in the mornings, going out soon after dawn. I get back to the office about 9 o'clock in better heart, and above all in a better temper. War is very trying to that vital organ, isn't it. I've been doing some interesting bits of work with Sir Percy which is always enjoyable. Today there strolled in a whole band of sheikhs from the Euphrates to present their respects to him, and incidentally they always call on me.

I've been sorting out all the material which I gathered when I was up the Tigris, and I have written a good deal about it, confidential and unconfidential, but not as well as it might have been done, I'm sorry to say. However, I feel I've begun to see what the people are like in those parts. My acquaintance with tribes and with Ottoman conditions is a great help, but there's an immense amount to learn. You'll see a piece of mine in the papers about Ibn Saud. I gather the India O. are going to publish it. No, after all I don't suppose you will for they usually publish those things in papers which no one reads, which seems to me rather a waste of energy on all sides, and I wish I could have a free hand with Geoffrey Robinson who wouldn't need to be asked twice about some of them. If he would batter at the doors of Govt. offices he might get them to change their mysterious ways. It's not the setting forth that's of value, but the stuff is so new—a new bit of construction work in the midst of the waste of war.

I must make another attempt to get shoes. I'll write to Yapp again. Otherwise I shall presently go barefoot. Isn't it a tragedy about my black satin gown. Of course it's just the very gown most wanted.

To H.B.
BASRAH, February 16th, 1917.

It was the finger of Providence that led me to get into my new abode, for we have had five days of rain and Basrah is a unique spectacle. It is almost impossible to go out. I put on a riding skirt and a pair of india rubber top boots—which I had fortunately procured from India—and stagger through the swamp for half-an-hour after tea and it's all one can do. Yesterday the sun shone, and the I.O.C. and I managed to get down to the desert in a motor and walked along the top of some mounds on the edge of the palm gardens, which so much encouraged me that I jumped up at sunrise today hoping to be able to ride. But no sooner was I donned than down came the rain again, through the mud roof of my room too and there was nothing for it but to change sadly into ordinary clothes—and write to you. We haven't had anything like our proper allowance of rain this winter, so we shall probably get it all now in unmanageable quantities. They don't seem to have had it on the Tigris front, and so far operations continue but very slowly. I doubt whether much more will happen there and we shall probably spend this summer besieging the Turks in Kut. I hope they'll like it I feel sure we shan't. But it will be better this year than last owing to the fact that the mud deters even those who desire favours—with the result that I've got through a lot of work and blocked out an article on administration which I've long had in my mind. I hope it will see the light somewhere. All the tribal and other material on which I've been busy for a year has now reached the point of publication for official circulation, and I'm beginning to reap a harvest of proofs from India. When once it's printed and put on record I shall feel that the first goal is attained. It's not history, but it will furnish an exact account of the country as we found it. In and out of all other work it has been, and is still, a constant thread which gives me increasing satisfaction as I get a better grasp of it. On the whole it's the work I've liked best here.

Presently I shall have to ask you to send me a nice wig. I haven't got enough hair left to pin a hat to. I don't know what happens to one's hair in this climate. It just evaporates. A momentous event took place this week—the clothes Sylvia [Henley] bought for me arrived, hat and gown and everything. I feel it to be nothing short of miraculous and rejoice accordingly.

I'm so luxuriously comfortable in my mud rooms.

To F.B.
BASRAH, February 17th, 1917.
... The box and the umbrella have come too ! Isn't it great. I am so thankful for shoes, skirts, umbrella (we are in the middle of rain) silk coat and everything. If only that rogue hadn't stolen my black gown I should be well supplied till the hot weather comes.

You have taken such a lot of trouble-thank you so very much.

To H.B.
BASRAH, March 2, 1917.
I had a grand post at the beginning of the week with 2 letters from you (Jan. 11th and 18th) and 3 from Mother. I really was starved for letters from home and consequently fattened on them. . . . We really have got the Turks shifted this time, how far shifted we don't yet know. If they make a stand before Bagdad I suppose we shan't go on; in any case, I don't know that we shall go on—the line of communication is immensely long. But no matter; what we have already accomplished will make a difference and we may expect developments in other

directions. Congratulatory effusions are coming in from Basrah—I wonder what the real thought is at the bottom of most of them. But up country the people who have come in to us will be content, for they will feel greater security; and the people who haven't come in will have grave doubts as to whether they " backed the right horse "—they're having them already. The Turks thought the crossing of the Tigris in the face of opposition a sheer impossibility. We have that from the prisoners. Let's hope, in consequence, that they are not so well prepared for the achievement as they should be—indeed their headlong flight seems to indicate as much. My own belief is that they won't be able to hold Bagdad for long if we are close up.

Work has been slack for the last few days, at which times I get rather bored, but I've taken to reading Arabic history every morning, with one of our native secretaries, and at the worst I can always put in as much time as I like, and profitably, on Arabic, till things begin again. Today I've been asked to write a brief outline of recent Arabian history for the Intelligence Department (the sort of thing I really enjoy doing), so I've turned to that. The amount I've written during the last year is appalling. Some of it is botched together out of reports, some spun out of my own mind and former knowledge, and some an attempt to fix the far corners of the new world we are discovering now, and some dry as dust tribal analyses, dull, but perhaps more useful than most things. It comes to a great volume of material, of one kind and another, and I know I have learnt much if I haven't helped others to learn. But it's sometimes exasperating to be obliged to sit in an office when I long to be out in the desert, seeing the places I hear of, and finding out about them for myself. At the end of the war, there's one favour I'm going to ask of the Authorities and that is that they will give me facilities, so far as they can, to cross Southern Arabia. I would like to do one bit of real Arabian exploration, or attempt. But I shall come home first to see you and get theodolites and things. Dearest, I shan't come back this summer. Anyway, we are all begged not to travel more than we can help under present conditions. If I feel the summer too long I may go up to some hill place in India for a week or two, but it wouldn't amuse me at all.

To H.B.
BASRAH, March 10th, 1917.

We are now hourly awaiting the news of our entrance into Bagdad. I had a letter from Sir Percy today, from the Front, full of exultation and confidence. I do hope I may be called up there before very long. It's a wonderful thing to be at the top of the war after all these months of marking time, and say what you will, it's the first big success of the war, and I think it is going to have varied and remarkable consequences.

We shall, I trust, make it a great centre of Arab civilisation, a prosperity; that will be my job partly, I hope, and I never lose sight of it.

I had one foot in the grave for five days with a shocking cold in the head—it's now better, and I'm riding again before breakfast. . . . I never saw anything so beautiful as the kingfishers—flocks of them whistling through the palm groves, two kinds, a big and a little blue kind, and I rather think a third brown, but I have not been able quite to spot him yet.

I have been seeing something of a very charming General Lubbock, Mr. Percy's brother.

To H.B.

BASRAH, March 17th, 1917.

Since last I wrote the goal has been reached; we have been a week in Bagdad. I've had no news actually from Bagdad, but I hope I shall get letters this week. I need not tell you how much I long to hear exactly what it is all like. Just 3 years ago I was arriving there from Arabia—3 lifetimes they seem as I look back on them. I went to tea last week with the Matron in Chief, the notable Miss Jones, whom I like, and afterwards she took me to see the wounded Turkish prisoners. I stammered into Turkish, which I haven't spoken for 7 years, and they were even only too delighted to hear even a few words of Turkish spoken. There they were, the round faced Anatolian peasants I could have laughed and wept to see them—from Konia, from Angora, from Cxsarxa, even from C'ple, and we talked of their houses and what far country they lay in. Most of them were well content to be done with war for ever.

I long to go up to Bagdad, but it is no good bothering yet. Everyone is too busy and there is plenty of time, but I should like to have seen the first moments. Also there's very little work here now. I've finished all the outstanding things with a great effort this week so as to have the road clear when the moment comes. And now I'm wearily doing rather dull office jobs and receiving the countless people who come in with congratulations and petitions. The congratulations are not more than skin deep I fancy.

To F.B.

BASRAH, March 30th, 1917.

I'm sitting with my hands in front of me, practically, and shall remain in that attitude till I go up to Bagdad. It is the first time I have been idle since the war began. However, it is not my desire, and Heaven knows that marking time is far worse than working. Of course it's too late now for gray tweeds nor have they come! but I shall be truly thankful for tussore, and above all for cotton gowns. Heaven waft them on their way! All I've got now is one thin woollen gown—made, if you can call it making—in Egypt, which is very dirty from much wear. One can get nothing cleaned, made or even mended here. The temp. is already 80 so that the blue clothes Sylvia sent me are too thick to wear any longer. Happy to tell you I'm now extremely well, partly the rest, perhaps, and partly the exemplary habit of riding before breakfast. I feel ready to take on any amount of new work and am longing for it.

In spite of the drawbacks of Mesop. summers I do feel the people who are working at home are shouldering much the heaviest part of the business. I would far rather be in the East among surroundings which are a perpetual interest to me, places and people which have no sharp edge of memory. But here again I didn't choose, did I? The best one can do is to do what one's told, for as long as one is told to do it. It has not been easy, in many ways. I think I have got over most of the difficulties and the growing cordiality of my colleagues is a source of unmixed satisfaction.

To H.B.
BASRAH, March 30th, 1917.
[Before this letter arrived we had a telegram from Gertrude saying "address Bagdad," and knew that her ardent wish to go there had been gratified.]

Until they let me go up to Bagdad, I have nothing to do. I have telegraphed to my chief asking if I may come up to him and await his reply. I read Arabic, do various odd jobs in the office and see people and that's all. The centre of gravity has shifted up river and my job with it. This last week has been made very pleasant by having Sir Arthur Lawley here.

To H.B.
SHEIKH SAAD, April 10, 1917.
I think I might get a letter posted to you from here. It's the fifth day we have been on the way, and we have another four days before us—a long journey, but the river is full and the current strong. My companions are two nurses, two doctors and the ship's officer. And do you know one of the doctors is Brownlie of Middlesbrough! He is out here for a year. We have 600 troops on board, so closely packed on deck that one has to step over them to reach one's cabin, Indians almost all.

All day yesterday we ran through the wide, level lands of the Bani Lam, not much cultivation, but a great deal of grazing ground, and the tents drawn down to the river and surrounded by flocks. Horses too, the Bani Lam are noted horse breeders. In the afternoon the Persian hills loomed out of the haze, quite close to us really; the foothills are only 16 miles from the river, but partly hidden in heat mist and looking all the taller, for eyes unaccustomed to anything taller than a palm tree, for the veil through which you sought for their summits.

Printed in the United Kingdom by
Lightning Source UK Ltd., Milton Keynes
137132UK00001B/136/A